TILL
DOOMSDAY
IN THE
AFTERNOON

THE FOLKLORE OF A FAMILY
OF SCOTS TRAVELLERS,
THE STEWARTS OF BLAIRGOWRIE

D1600366

DEDICATION

Tae a' tinkers, kyards, gangrel-bodies, Romani gypsies, horners, hawkers, didekai, needies, potters, bucks and double-bucks, hedge-mumpers and the lave. Tae Traivellin' Folk throughout the mapamound.

TILL DOOMSDAY IN THE AFTERNOON

THE FOLKLORE OF A FAMILY OF SCOTS TRAVELLERS, THE STEWARTS OF BLAIRGOWRIE

Ewan MacColl *and* Peggy Seeger

MANCHESTER UNIVERSITY PRESS

Copyright © Ewan MacColl & Peggy Seeger 1986

Published by Manchester University Press
Oxford Road, Manchester M13 9PL, UK
and 51 Washington Street, Dover
New Hampshire 03820, USA

British Library cataloguing in publication data
MacColl, Ewan
   Till Doomsday in the Afternoon: the folklore of
   a family of Scots travellers, the Stewarts of
   Blairgowrie.
   1.   Folk-lore — Scotland
   I.   Title   II.   Seeger,   Peggy
   398'.09411   GR143
Library of Congress cataloging in publication data
   Applied for

ISBN 0 7190 1813 7 *cased only*

Printed and bound in Great Britain by
Biddles Ltd, Guildford and King's Lynn

CONTENTS

Illustrations
   Two plates appear between pages 8 and 9

ACKNOWLEDGMENTS

We are indebted to Clint Jencks, of New Mexico, who helped us to record material for this book in its early stages, and to Calum MacColl who assisted us in the final recording sessions. To Pattie Hutchison of Banff, who provided us with invaluable information on the history of the Stewart family, our sincere gratitude.

Our thanks are due also to Frank Harte of Dublin for his help in identifying some of the Irish songs in the Stewart repertory; to Norman Buchan, MP, for generously assisting us with a note on 'The Soor Mulk Cairt'; to Robert Thompson, of Huntingdon, for providing us with the *Madden Collection* references; to Hamish MacColl, for locating broadside versions in the library of the British Museum; to Iain MacGregor, Sheila's husband, and to Big Willy MacPhee and his wife Bella, for supplying additional information when it was needed.

FOREWORD

The organisation and scope of this book has undergone frequent changes since we first began working on it. Our original intention was to compile a collection of traditional songs and ballads from the repertoire of a family of Scots Travellers – the Stewarts of Blairgowrie. This modest objective didn't survive the first two or three months of field work. It was swept away on a flood of recorded anecdotes, jokes, riddles, bawdy rhymes and traditional tales.

As we transcribed the recordings, we began to envisage a different kind of book altogether, one which would present an accurate picture of a traditional culture operating inside the somewhat confined space of a family circle. Such a book should, we thought, include songs and ballads, folk tales, popular rhymes and riddles – the common stuff of folkloristic studies. It soon became apparent that these materials, fascinating though they are, did not add up to a complete picture; they needed the context of the family's particular way of handling words. Songs and stories possess a validity of their own but our understanding and appreciation of them is enhanced when we are able to examine the raw materials out of which they are fashioned. Those raw materials were abundantly present in our taped records of conversations, arguments and monologues; they were present in turns of phrase which could have been lifted straight out of a ballad, in usages which would have delighted a Dunbar or a Gavin Douglas, in potent metaphors and images like the one which gives this book its title.

Our original title 'The Stewarts of Blairgowrie' we abandoned somewhat reluctantly on the grounds that it was misleading. The Blairgowrie Stewart family is a large one and encompasses four generations; the greater part of the material featured in this collection has been selected from tape recordings made, for the most part, by Alec and Belle (progenitors of the present line) and their two married daughters Cathie Higgins and Sheila MacGregor.

Our first meeting with the Stewarts took place in Hatfield New Town, Hertfordshire, where the husbands of Cathie and Sheila were employed as building workers and where Alec and Belle, down from Scotland on a visit, were sharing an apartment with them. A mutual friend had given us their address and on New Years Eve, 1961, we set off to visit them bearing seasonal offerings. It was an abortive journey, as a severe snowstorm made the roads impassable. We returned home with unbroached Hogmanay fare in time to be our own first-footers. A week later, we tried again and this time we were successful.

That first meeting with the Stewarts was an exhilarating and memorable experience. It wasn't merely their warmth and friendliness which made the occasion unforgettable – it is the almost magical knack they have of making a stranger feel that he is returning to them after a long absence. There is no transitional stage in a relationship with them. One is accepted immediately into the family circle and, almost as quickly, into the wider circle of their many Traveller friends.

Our first impression was of a group of people joined together by immensely strong family ties, sharing common experiences, attitudes and possessing a dramatic sense which enabled them to transform the most trivial incident into an exciting event. Several years were to pass before we began to detect cracks in the family's apparent solidarity.

Of the individual members of the family, it was the personality of Belle which made the most immediate impact on us. A Traveller friend has described her as "a richt bonnie quaen", and she is surely that. He might have added that she is as intelligent as she is bonnie, that she is warm-hearted and generous, that she possesses a ripe, Rabelaisian sense of humour and that even at her most ribald she manages to maintain a marvellous sense of dignity. By comparison, her husband Alec gave the impression of being somewhat withdrawn and taciturn – but that was an image which disappeared upon further acquaintance. Alec's laconic utterances were a perfect foil for Belle's loquaciousness, and his highly-developed sense of the absurd, coupled with a deadpan delivery, provided an effective counterpoint to Belle's more direct style of humour.

Our first impression of Cathie was that she was wholly her father's daughter – the hint of scepticism, the taciturnity, even the inflections, were inherited from Alec. Later we got to know another side of her, the soft, sentimental side, Belle's bequest. The possession of such mutually hostile personality traits probably accounts for Cathie's occasionally abrasive manner.

Sheila takes after her mother; physically and vocally they are extremely alike. In manner, too, they share many of the same qualities though Sheila possesses little of her mother's ribaldry. What she does possess is a talent for organising and a willingness to accept the fact that some kind of organisation is necessary if the Travellers' way of life is to survive.

In the weeks following our first meeting with the family, we set up a regular recording schedule. Once or twice a week they would visit us, often accompanied by their children and grandchildren and sometimes by Traveller friends. After a leisurely meal, we would settle down to a two or three hour recording session. At the end of six weeks we had taped the major part of the family's repertoire of songs, stories and riddles. In addition, we had recorded some thirty hours of discussion ranging over a wide variety of subjects. In the course of the next two years we visited them in Blairgowrie on several occasions and recorded further material. In 1962–3, when we were engaged in the production of a BBC documentary dealing with English and Scots Travellers, the Stewarts' home virtually became our Scottish base of operations. It was largely due to them that we were welcomed into the homes and camps and caravans of scores of Scots Travellers.

Between 1968 and 1972 we succeeded in recording again most of the stories songs and ballads that we had first recorded in 1960. A comparison of the two sets of recordings shows that, as far as the songs are concerned, scarcely any melodic changes have occurred and the few textual changes are limited to an occasional word. Further recordings made between 1972 and 1979 produced similar results. Furthermore, during the entire period of our recording programme, a stretch of nineteen years, scarcely any new items have been added to the family repertoire of songs and ballads. From this it may be assumed that the Stewart family repertoire, and the individual items in it, had crystallised at some point before 1960.

As a family, the Stewarts are impressively articulate, and each one of them appears to derive intense pleasure from the act of talking. It isn't that they are garrulous or given to idle chatter; it is simply that they seem to regard conversation as a form of entertainment no less important than storytelling or singing songs.

Like most Scots Travellers, they are able to move from Doric to Scots-accented English with ease. They often did so at recording sessions when a stranger or foreigner was present. Their habit of using a Scots and an English pronunciation of the same word in the one sentence is less easily accounted for. *Awa'* and *away, ether* and *adder, twa* and *two, shouther* and *shoulder, aye* and *always* are some of the many twin words that the reader will encounter in the text of this work.

It was in Alec's speech that the English influence is most noticeable. He had spent several years in the army, and the army is a great leveller of dialects. The new recruit soon sloughs off any of the singularities which make him stand out from his fellows and, while a particular accent or regional intonation may survive indefinitely, the uprooted vocabulary quickly loses its more exotic blooms.

In Alec Stewart's case the small, everyday words had been most affected, words like *out, night, from, away*, etc., which were pronounced in a way that is more English than Scots. At the same time, Alec's speech was rich in old usages and interesting turns of phrase. A month is never merely March or June or September, but *March month, June month or September month*. The passage of time is referred to in the Elizabethan way: *Time wears on and time wears on*, or *the years roll on and the years roll on*. In their past tense, verbs such as walk, look, talk, catch become *walkit, lookit, talkit, catchit*. A man working in a wood is *a man workin' intae a wood*; a man from Spain is *a man oot o' Spain*; a deserted place is *a gouldritch place*. To be accompanied on part of a journey is to be *convoyed doon the road* and an enquiry about one's antecedents is phrased thus: *Whit folk do ye come aff o'*? On occasions when he felt that he was on the verge of committing an indiscretion, he would say: *Ye'll get me transported! Ye'll get me benished* (banished)! or *Ye'll get the heid aff my shouthers*!

Belle's conversation is larded with proverbial saws: *Auld love's soon kindled; the deil tak's care o' his ain; if you want to tell a lie, ye couldnae because if ye did the deil would help ye oot o't; nae coo, nae care; he's aye wise ahint the event; ye cannae tak' the breeks aff a hielan'man*. These are some of the sayings we have heard her use frequently.

Her vocabulary is rich in dialect words and phrases. She described a feeble-minded young woman as *an unricht cratur;* a family with a history of incest was *an adultrified faimily*; smoke from a woodfire is *stickreek*; unlucky things (or people) are *unsanctifit* (unsanctified); a lantern-jawed person is a *lantern-jack;* a song whose author is still alive is a *mak'-ye-up;* a thin branch of willow is a *willow-wand* and a cow or bull is a *cattle-beast*. On one occasion we were walking through Aberdeen with her when, on observing a prostitute, she exclaimed, "God bless me, there's that *shattery-jowls*!" The dictionary defines *gowl* as a hollow between hills, a defile between mountains. As used by Belle, the word has a Joycian ring to it.

The speech of the Stewart daughters is, oddly enough, frequently broader than that of either of their parents. Sheila, in particular, has a large stock of colourful dialect expressions. Of a person who laughs without cause, she said "We ca' that *lauchin' at a winnel-strae's waggin'*. Ye ken, a big lang grass straw stickin' oot o' the grund and the least puff o' wind blaws it back and forward. Well, we ca' that *a winnel-strae – a winnel-strae waggin'*." The seat of a chair which is either torn or broken is a *cuphole o' an airse*. Sheila's glosses of some of her more out-of-the-way expressions are extremely graphic: "I'm sittin' here and I'm whalkin' tae the wildest extent, richt tae the third knuckle o' my finger. That means I'm sittin' pickin' my nose to the third knuckle o' my finger." The analogy of extracting a whelk from a shell is a powerful, if not particularly pleasing, one. A sock, the foot of which is baked hard with sweat, is a *biscuit-fit*, while a *spune-fit* is a body that's wearin' shoes that's a' twisted and a' *skyowt*, a' doon i' the heel and doon in front and everything. A stupid person is a *lappert body* and if you're a' *buttered* it means your troosers is owre lang for ye and they're richt doon owre the heels o' your shoes. The word *spyeuchit* was interpreted thus by Sheila: "Noo, say you were awfu' drunk comin' doon the road. And we look it at you comin' and you slippit and fell. What we would say for that was '*Geh, dear, there's a man spyeuchit*!'" Almost all of Sheila's explanations have the same vivid quality; describing a *forrit belly*, she said "My faither's no' sae bad noo but O my God! he used to be the wildest *forrit belly* that ever you seen in your life. But he's been slimmin' this wee while, so that'll mebbe gie ye a hint what it is. A forrit belly is an awfu' big belly."

Contrary to our expectation, their knowledge of plants and birds was not particularly extensive and their names for them form one of the most meagre sections of their vocabulary. A stonechat is a *stanechaffer*, a curlew is an *Athol piper*, a lapwing is a *wheep*, a *whaup*, a *peasie* or a *goulli-pernicht*; a jackdaw is a *kyaa* or *kyaa-laddie;* a magpie is a *jaypyet*, an owl is a *hewlet* or *hoolet*; a sparrow is a *spuggie*, a wagtail is a *willy-wagtail* and a turkey is a *bubbly-jock*.

Their local names for plants were few in number. The wild rhubarb was *dishylaga*, the common bent was *benweed* or *coorkin* or *loch-corkin*; the earthnut was *the garnut or Lucy-Arnot*; the common alder was the *airn tree*. Domestic animals were generally referred to by their cant names, as were rodents and some creatures of the wild. Only the adder and the mole were referred to by their local names in our presence – the former was called the *ether* or *oak-snake*, and the latter was the *mowdie* or *mowdie-wark or mowdiewarp*.

The Stewarts' use of the lowland Scots Doric can give a sparkle and depth to the most humdrum topic. The relish with which they handle words and the skill with which they manipulate them to serve their needs has never failed to impress us. Time and time again we have heard a conversation explode in a brilliant display of verbal fireworks and seen a conversational topic abandoned in favour of a sudden stockpiling of synonyms around an old word.

Love of *the auld tongue* is an emotion which is by no means confined to the Travelling folk, but it is through the use of the Doric that Travellers assert their Scottishness and, consequently, their right to be treated as normal citizens of the country in which they live.

Travellers will aye exist to the end o' time, and you'll never get them to change their ways, and you'll never get rid o' Tinkers. They'll be there till doomsday in the afternoon.

(Belle Stewart)

INTRODUCTION

Belle Stewart bore her husband, Alec (who died in 1980), nine children, five of whom died in infancy. The remaining four – Andrew, John, Cathie and Sheila – have grown up, married and, in their turn, raised families. Indeed, the "bairns" are themselves grandparents. At the time of writing, Belle counted heads of children, husbands and wives and came up with twenty-five members. In addition to this there are twenty grandchildren and ten great-grandchildren, all of whom live in, or near to, the small Perthshire town of Blairgowrie.

Family background

Like most Travellers that we have met, both Alec and Belle have an extraordinary knowledge of family relationships, many of which are as complicated as those Celtic designs in which the central route is constantly disappearing amid innumerable interlacings. Their knowledge of family history is less impressive and rarely encompasses more than two genera- tions. For information about earlier times, one has to go to one of those old Travellers like Pattie Hutchison of Banff, who carries in his head the detailed histories of dozens of Traveller clans.

Big Jimmy Stewart was Alec's grandfather. Jimmy Stewart's mother was a Maggie Cameron, so Jimmy Stewart and his half-brother Donald Robertson should baith hae been Camerons. They were illegitimate bairns. Donald Robertson's faither was the Laird o' Struan. He faithered a bairn on Maggie aifter she left Dalkeith to come and work for him, and that bairn was Donald Robertson.

Well, aifter that happened he wanted her oot o' the way so he got her a job awa' up at Glenmuich or somewhere. Well, there wasnae much meat aboot the place at that time but she got a job wi' her bairn and then she fell in the faimily way to the fairmer at the place she was workin'. The bairn that she had to that fairmer was Big Jimmy Stewart, Alec's grandfaither.

Well, Maggie didnae ken much aboot beggin' and it wasnae easy for a lassie to get a steady job they days, particularly if she'd twa bairns. So it was a jobbie here and jobbie there until she mebbe met wi' a puckle o' tinkers and that's how she cam' to be awa' doon in Buchan.

Noo, Jimmy Stewart got up to be a man and he fell in love wi' a woman they ca'd Maria MacPhee and it was her that learned him to play the pipes. So Donald Robertson he lands awa' doon tae Buchan there and he had a big faimily and Jimmy

Stewart he had a big faimily tae and these faimilies is the same as is gaun round noo.

The idea of a woman teaching her husband to play the pipes is perfectly feasible, particularly when the woman bears the family name of MacPhee. The MacPhees are still regarded as the main clan of itinerant pipers. Maggie MacPhee of MacDuff told us that among the MacPhees it was the practice to teach each of the male children in the family the mastery of the great Highland bagpipe. If there were no male children then the lassies were "gi'en a chanter and learned hoo to play."

Big Jimmy Stewart appears to have been an eager and talented student. His prowess as a piper earned him a considerable reputation among Travelling folk and, according to Alec, was the direct cause of his death.

He was awa' up at a place ca'd Pitlochry and he'd buskit the toon, playin' the pipes. Well, he was walkin' hame frae the toon, a bit the worse for drink and there's twa-three Irishmen comin' alang the road. They'd been workin' in a quarry up by Fort William. Well, they stopped him in the road and one o' them says: "Can ye play the pipes?" He says, "Ay, I can play the pipes". "Gie us a tune then, play 'The Boyne Water'." "Oh," says my grandfaither, "I dinnae ken that tune." "Come on," they said, "you can play it. We've never met a Scotchman yet that cannae play 'The Boyne Water'." "Well", says my grandfaither, "I'll try it". And he played the tune and while he was playin', one o' them lifted up a big stane and hit him in the back o' the heid and killed him, battered him to death. When they found him, his pipes was lyin' at the roadside. But they never got the man that did it, they'd cleared oot. A' for playin' 'The Boyne Water'.

Both Alec and Belle were unable to supply us with pertinent facts concerning the lives of their respective grandparents. With both of them, knowledge was confined to a single spectacular incident like the one quoted above. Some time before his death, Big Jimmy Stewart taught his son, John – Alec's father – to play the pipes, thus initiating a family tradition. By all accounts John Stewart became a piper of more than average ability.

He was piper to Lord Dudley of Dunkeld. He'd gae doon in the mornin' and play roond the big hoose and he'd be back at nicht playin' roond the dinner table. In between he'd be up and doon the glens selling dishes. My faither had a big square caravan before I was born and he used to travel roond Aberfeldy, Blair Athol and doon the Speyside. Then he cam' doon tae Blairgowrie and started a lodgin' hoose. That's where I was born, in a lodgin' hoose in Tootie Street. After a time we left there and went to Pitlochry and stayed there aboot five or six years. Then we cam' back tae Blairgowrie and my faither and the rest o' us would be up the glens gatherin' scraps, rags, wool and sellin' dishes.

Belle, who knows to the exact minute the date and time of birth of each member of her family, has inherited the entire stock of facts, legends, anecodotes and omens connected with her husband's nativity.

Alec was born in a place ca'd Tootie Street, Alyth. Born in a lodgin' hoose. He was the first laddie after five lassies and, believe it or not, they put his name in the paper: "A son to John Stewart the piper". He was born on the sixth of February, nineteenth-hunder-and-four and because he was the first boy after a lot of girls he was ca'd 'Biddley', because biddle means brother.

John Stewart appears to have possessed a good deal of initiative and enterprise. In addition to his piping, hawking and scrap-gathering, he had some skill in the older crafts of basket-making, horning (fashioning horn spoons) and tinsmithing. He was also quick to take advantage of the early developments in cinematography and, for two or three years, toured Central Scotland and Northern Ireland with a travelling picture-show. Alec, his sister Bella and "a girl named Pritchard from Perth", used to sing, dance and play the pipes between pictures.

Alec was eight or nine years old when his father began teaching him the pipes. He was even younger when he first began to assimilate songs and stories from his mother's apparently inexhaustible repertoire. At some point in her life Alec's mother, Maria, changed her name from MacPhee to Campbell. Alec was unable to advance any reason for this change though both he and Belle pointed out that the adoption of new names was a common enough practice among Travellers. Often, apparently, it was an attempt to escape the obloquy attached to a particular name or to break a consistent run of bad luck. More frequently it was a ploy aimed at confusing military police in the hunt for army deserters.

Whatever the reason, it makes the task of finding one's way among real names, family names, assumed names, bynames, clan nicknames and pet names, a formidable one. It is made more formidable by the fact that few formal marital alliances were entered into and, consequently, written records are few and far between. Marriages between near-relatives is a further cause of confusion. Belle's reference to the convolutions of royal and aristocratic blood-lines is by no means far-fetched.

Lang ago, gaun away far back before my time, if ye married oot o the Travellers they wouldnae hae naethin' to dae wi' ye. Talk about the blue blood kind o' thing, and royalty! I'm gaun awa' back to my great-grandfather's time noo. My mither used to speak about it. You had to be blood-relatit. But no' too close. Anything past a second cousin was far too sib. Nooadays, ye see full cousins gettin' married, but that would hae been oot o' the question in they days. It would never have been heard of amang the Tinkers. They made oot that a child would be a weaklin' if it was too sib-bred.

Of course, there was never much actual marriage amang the Traveller folk lang ago, ye ken. I'm gaun awa' back a lot o' years, of course. If a woman's name was Johnston and her man's name was Burke they just stuck to their ain names. As for the bairns, well a man couldnae register a bairn if the parents werenae married, so nearly a' the bairns took their mithers' names. Tak' mysel', for instance: my name wasnae really MacGregor because my faither and mither were never married. If a' things were kent by their richt name I should be ca'd Greig or Graham, for that was my faither's name. My mither's name was Martha Stewart, for my mither never denied *her* name. My faither should hae been ca'd Greig, or Graham, but he took the name MacGregor. I dinnae ken what for.

The Grahams cam' frae Gartmore. They were definitely a clan people, but they werenae well-liked. Folks ca'd them "the lousy Grahams frae Gartmore – they butter their breid upside-doon". Times was very hard, you see, and though they had butter on their breid they turned it upside-doon to mak' the ither folk think it was dry breid they were eatin'. That's the legend as far as the Grahams are concerned.

When I was a wee lassie, I used to like sittin' wi' my granny and listenin' tae and auld tales o' this and that. And many's the nicht when she could afford a good wee dram, she'd sit crackin' wi' my uncle Henry – that was my faither's brither – and mebbe hae a wee bit argument and she would say, "Henry, ye're gettin' mair like your auld faither every day. Ye're gettin' mair like auld Jimmy Graham." So as I got up in years a wee bit, I would quiz my mither about it. "Why does my granny say that my grandfaither was auld Jimmy Graham when my name's MacGregor?" "Ach, Belle", she says, "that happened lang afore your time. Ye wouldnae understand." I've seen my brither Donald get my granny that drunk that she couldnae licht her pipe, yet she would never reveal why they changed their name. Definitely and truly, I would have liked somebody to have traced that back. A' that I ken o' my faither's folk is the place where my faither was born, and that was between Crieff and Comrie, near Monaverd, a wee campin' place whaur the Tinkers used to bide. They ca'd it "The Black Spoot".

As with Alec, Belle's knowledge of her grandfather is confined to the manner of his death. Her account of it is a splendid example of the storyteller's art.

A' this that I'm gaun tae tell ye happened afore I was born. My grandfaither and the four bairns o' the family that were able to work had been workin' at a fairm at Glenisla and wi' the money that they'd earned he bocht a yoke: a lovely pony-cairt. It was a real braw turnoot, cost six-pound-ten to build! Well, he had to come into Blair for some reason or other and he met up wi' some folk ca'd the Townsleys. And they had a dram thegither, for that was the usual thing when Travellers met. Well, Andra Townsley – he's deid noo and gone tae wherever God pleases – he was awfu' impressed wi' this new yoke and he was trying tae get a swap wi' my grandfaither. But he wasnae interested in swappin'. So the Townsleys were trying to get him drunk, ye see, in order to get the wee horse-and-trap aff him. So they're sittin' there just drinkin' and drinkin' until my grandfaither says, "I'm gaun tae Pitlochry".

Noo, ye can gang up the Parkhill Road, up by St Fink, and it tak's ye richt up the Glenshee way, oot tae the Mill o' Foyle and ye get onto the Pitlochry road by Kirkmichael. "So ye'll no' swap?" says auld Andra Townsley. "No", says my grandfaither, and he's awa' up the road tae Pitlochry wi' his twa laddies, Jimmy-Jack and Donald, and my granny and the bairns.

Well, the Townsleys were determined to hae the horse-and-cart, so they followed them. It was gettin' gloamin'-dark by the time they caught them up. They couldnae see my grandfaither, for he'd had a good few drinks and was sleepin' in the back o' the cairt. So my granny says, "Look, can ye no' leave us alane? He's lyin' drunk in the back o' the cairt". Well, what wi' the cursin' and shouting o' the Townsleys, he begins to get up in the dolours o' drink, and he manages to get oot o' the cairt. Oh, there's a hell o' a stir and carry-on noo.

Noo, in the cart, they had a bag for a' the different tools ye need for makin' tin. Well, one o' the Townsleys – we dinnae ken which it was to this day – took the hammer oot o' the tool-bag and hit my grandfaither on the back o' the heid wi' it, and he went doon, unconscious. Well, the Townsleys got feared when they saw a' the blood and they cleared oot.

However, my granny and the laddies got my grandfaither intae the cairt, and they
bandaged him up as best they could. The aulder Travellers didnae like doctors, but
aboot four days after, Oh God, his heid! He was fair aff his heid wi' pain and they
had to ca' a doctor then. Well, they took him tae the poorhouse in Perth and he died
there, exactly nine days fae the day he was hit. There was a trial and the hammer
was brocht in and measured against the wound in the back o' my grandfaither's
heid. It fitted right back intae the back o' the scalp where he was hit. They put it
doon tae a faimily quarrel.

It was murder, but they'd no proof against ony o' the Townsleys. They got off
scot-free. My grandfaither was only thirty-eight years auld when it happened. He
was killed a' owre the heids o' a horse-and-cairt. That's the true facts o' my
grandfaither's deith, and that's why we dinnae like the Townsleys and never will
like the Townsleys. "The Beetles", we ca' them.

Early days

Belle's account of her birth and early infancy has the same kind of dramatic
intensity. The time and place are described in the same meticulous way.
Conversations are reported verbatim, with the result that the listener gets
the impression that Belle was present in the dual role of infant and adult
observer.

I was born in a bow-tent at half-past-two on a Wednesday morning, on the
eighteenth of July, 1906. It was at a place ca'd Claypotts Farm, on the bank o' the
river Tay, no' far frae Dunkeld, and I was registered in the parish o'Caputh. My
faither was pearl-fishing at Tay, and he got a braw pearl that day. Mind ye, I was the
first lassie born to him, so he used aye to say to my mither: "Well, well, how could
one man be so lucky? I got twa pearls in one day."

However, that's a long time ago. That mornin' there wasnae a bite there and my
mither lay in her bed on the Wednesday, and she was up on Thursday dinner-time,
but there wasnae a bite in the camp. Well, my faither – God rest him – wouldnae ask
onything fae onybody, for though he was a man o' the Tinker class he couldnae hae
gone to the door o' a hoose and asked for a drink o' water. Never in his life did he
ever hawk or sell the goods that he made himsel'. No, he couldnae do it, he was
owre shy. He was a great man for workin' tae the fairmers, my faither, and he was
socht far and wide because he really was a great worker. But he preferred workin'
in the woods, ye ken, sneddin' trees – sawin' them doon. There were nane o' they
mechanical things in they days, they a' had to be done by hand.

But to get back to my tale. On the Friday night at aboot half-past-six, my mither
was at Braemar. She'd walkit fae Caputh, richt owre the Devil's Elbow and she was
at the back door of the hotel at Braemar. It was a wee bit early for the shooting
season, but there were plenty o' gentry there. My mither was lookin' for to get some
scraps o' food, ye ken, the left-overs o' the gentry's dinners. Well, she'd me in her
airms and I was only twa days auld, and when the cook cam' oot and saw me in my
mither's airms, she said "My God! Could I tak' that bairn intae the hotel and show it
to some o' the visitors?" So my mither said "Ay", and the cook's awa' wi' me into the
hotel. Well, anither servant lassie comes oot and says, "Would ye tak' somethin' to
eat?" "Well," says my mither, "if ye hae onything tae spare, would ye mind tyin' it up
in a bundle? I've anither twa wee laddies oot in' the road, and there's my man as
weel." Well, the lassie goes, and when she comes oot again she's got a' this meat
tied up in a table-cloth. It was some o' the lunches that the gentry had left when they
were oot on the hill shootin' or picknickin', ye ken. And when the cook brought me

back tae my mither – you can believe this or not – I had seiven-shillin's-and-sixpence! At that day, owre sixty year ago, seiven-and-sixpence was a fortune.

Noo, gaun back to my faither: he was a young man when he died. He was only thirty-four. I cannae say that him and my mither were married, for that wouldnae be true, but they were happy enough during the thirteen years o' their life thegither. There was nine o' a faimily o' us in the thirteen years.

On the day he died, he'd been oot gettin' some hay for his horse and some o' the hay fell owre his face while he was drivin' alang. A Tinkler that kent him gaed up to him and he says, "God bless me, there's something far wrang wi' MacGregor the day." So the man comes down wi' his van and he says tae my mither, "Look Martha, ye'll better come up and hae a look at Dan. There's somethin' far wrang wi' him, he's an awfu' bad colour." "Och", says my mither, "he's aye a bad colour. If he would bide aff the drink he wouldnae be sic a bad colour." "Ah", but he says, "I'm no' jokin', Martha, ye'll better come up and hae a look at him."

Well, my mither had been oot hawkin' the toon wi' me in her airms and when she gets tae the cairt there's a puckle folk gaithered roond. It was just opposite the doctor's hoose there, so they took my faither oot and carried him owre tae the doctor's. But the doctor wadnae hear a word o' him gettin' inside his surgery or his hoose there. Oh no! My faither was a Tinker and he had to go to the garage. So they took my faither and they stretched him oot on the stane floor o' the garage and the doctor sent a servant lassie intae the hoose for a drink o' milk. Noo, it was an awfu' cauld day. If he'd been taken intae a warm fire and gien a hot drink he'd mebbe hae revived. But here he was stretched oot on the cauld floor and the doctor says, "Och! This man's deid, I can dae naething for him." And my mither's stannin' there greetin' wi' me in her airms, and Donald and Andy was there tae . . .

Well, they put him tae the mortuary here and they said, "Hoo are ye gaun to pay for his coffin and the funeral expenses and a'?" And my mither, she says, "I havenae a penny. I've naethin'." Well, they were plantin' trees at that time at Lintrethan, mebbe six or eight miles frae here. So my mither and my uncle and my twa brithers got a job at a half-a-croon a week plantin' trees. And they had to bide up there and plant these trees till they earned the three pounds to pay for the funeral expenses. And that was the end o' my faither. He was just Tinker Donald MacGregor and that was the end o't.

After he died, it was gey hard on my mither, but she just had to carry on. She just hawked aboot. My brithers and my Uncle Henry MacGregor made baskets and they heather rangers – heather-scrubbers that ye clean pots and pans wi'. And they made heather besoms, brooms and brushes. At night they would mak' these things and she would hawk them during the day. She aye took my brither Andy wi' her when she went hawkin' up the glens. My ither brither, Donald, took mair after my faither. He was a keen worker but no' much o' a hand at hawkin'.

Well, that kind o' work would go on until the neep-thinnin' [turnip-thinning] come on, and that was in June month. In July, the berries [raspberry harvest] started, and whenever the berries was finished my mither would get a hoose in Blairgowrie at a place ca'd "The Croft". That's where the police station is noo, an auld, auld building it was at that time. That's whaur I learned to walk. And fae that day to this we've aye had a hoose in Blairgowrie that we've ca'd oor ain, ye ken.

Childhood

It is to this period of her life that Belle refers most frequently. Her memories of it affect her deeply and as she talks her use of the Doric becomes more pronounced.

I've kent my mither get up in the mornin' – I'd mebbe be aboot three years auld, but there's things that stand oot in a bairn's memory – and she would pack a basket fu' wi' bits o' odds-and-ends. And she'd tak' that basket on her back and she'd put me on the tap o't, and she'd walk tae the Bridge o' Cally. Noo, that's aboot six mile fae Blair if ye gang direct. But if ye're gaun aff the road tae fairm-hooses up an auld road here and an auld road there, it'll be mair like ten miles. And she'd come richt doon that side again. That's aboot twenty mile a day hawkin', wi' me on her back.

I'll gie ye an instance o' the way we was brocht up. I've seen me at the door o' a hoose wi' my mither – God rest her! – and mebbe I've been gey hungry, but still my mither would say, "Noo, if the manishie offers ye pennam, dinnae bing it, 'cause the hantle'll think I'm no' bingin' ye habben." That meant, 'If the fairmer's wife offers ye food, refuse it. Say that ye're no' hungry, because they'll be thinkin' I'm starvin' you.' Ay, and mony' s the time I could hae done wi' it.

Anither thing! There would be times when my mither would be hawkin' – it was mair beggin', for she seldom had onything tae hawk – and ye'd see a bairn's ba' or a wee doll or a wee barra lyin' awa' oot fae the hoose, ye ken. And I've seen me mony a time – ay, and Andy tae – sneakin' ahint my mither, trailin' ahint her. And I would mebbe lift a ba' and shove it under my jaiket. We never thocht it ony hairm tae tak' this toy. But she'd say, "Whaur did ye get that?" And we had to tell her. Well, if it was a mile back up the road to that hoose, my mither would walk right back and make us put they things doon whaur we got them. So you see, we never had very many toys.

I've seen my brither Donald – God rest him – makin' whistles oot o' a bit o' stick and that. Or I've seen him mak' me a wooden doll, a poor kind o' doll, but it pleased me. Or my mither would get a puckle auld rags, cloots as we ca'd them, and we'd hae a clooty-doll. That was aboot the best toys I had lang ago. Then of course, in the winter-time there was sledgin'. Andy was a great boy for sledgin', but he could never get the runners tae mak' the thing go. So it was aye a pair o' auld skates. Andy would tie or nail these auld skates on to a board and, by God, it would go! But we had to dae they things for oorsel's. Even when Christmas cam' roond there was nae gaun intae a shop and buyin' toys.

Almost all of her reminiscences are connected with work or places of work. Her grandfather dies while bringing a load of hay for the horse. She is born while her father is pearl-fishing. Toys are associated with hawking, and she is weaned – at the age of six! – during the berry-picking.

Amang the Tinkler folk lang ago, God Almichty, some o' the bairns would souk their mither's breist till they were four-or-five-year-auld. I can mind when I was aboot six-year-auld sayin', "Mammy, please let me see its nose ..." That's whit I ca'd the nipple, ye ken. I mind fine we were pickin' berries doon the braes and my mither was sick o' the sicht o' me, and I'd make her sit doon in a drill and say, "Gie me a wee souk noo, Mammy." And, of course, she would dae onything to please me, me bein' the only lassie. But she got kind o' sick o' me makin' her sit doon sae often.

Well, there was an auld buck man ca'd Bundle Willy, and he'd a great big stick and this bundle that he never took aff his back. It was Bundle Willy that spent [weaned] me aff my mither. This day when we were at the berries she gaed to him and telt him aboot me tormentin' her. Well, auld Bundle Willy cam' up the road tae me. I think I can see him yet. He battered on the ground wi' that stick and he battered. "If ever I see a bairn or a lassie in this field askin' for a pappie," he says, "I'll kill them stone-deid wi' my stick!" Well, I run tae my mither and I never looked at a pappie aifter that.

With the introduction of the Compulsory Education Act, Travellers were presented with a problem for which, as yet, no completely satisfactory solution has been found. For the family forced, by various legislative decrees and ordinancies, to be almost continuously on the move, the possibility of obtaining a formal education is, to say the least, remote. Even for those families like the MacGregors, who are fortunate enough to have a permanent dwelling-place, the difficulties are enormous.

We got little education, for we aye travelled in the summer. At the beginning of April we'd be awa' fae school and we wouldnae be back until October. My mither was aye feared, aye thinkin' tae hersel', "If I wander the country wi' they bairns, they'll mebbe be taken aff me." Ye see, if ye neglected your bairns in they days, they just cam' and took them and put them awa' tae a hame. But in the summertime we did travel, and I'd be awa' up the Speyside and awa' up Glenisla and doon at Brechin at a place ca'd Justinhaugh, four-and-three-quarter mile north of Forfar. That was the main living in the summertime for the menfolk. The women just did their hawkin'. When they were weel-aff, they would buy whit they ca'd "stock" to put in their baskets, instead o' waitin' for the men tae mak' scrubbers, besoms and the like. And if the lady ye were tryin' tae sell tae didnae hae ony money, you'd mebbe get some milk or eggs in exchange for the things oot o' the basket. Well, that kept the men at the pearl-fishin' and they'd mebbe get twa-three pounds for a pearl.

The concept of "the teenage generation" seems to be one that is foreign to Travellers. The overall impression that one gets from listening to the many hours of recorded interviews and discussion with members of the Stewart family is that there is no period of transition between childhood and adulthood. The average working-class youth who leaves school to work in a factory, mine or shop may abandon the pursuits of childhood and the circle of childhood friends but, nevertheless, he will continue to spend most of his leisure time with members of his age-group and his pursuits are those of that age-group. This does not appear to be the case with Travellers. For them, the family is the important social unit, and its activities embrace each member of the family, irrespective of age.

Among Travellers, the parent–child relationship is a particularly close one and, as far as we have been able to judge, it appears to be unaffected by the passage of time. Jimmy Higgins, Cathie Stewart's husband, obviously finds it perfectly natural that he should continue to feel responsible for his children's welfare, even though they have reached the age when they are capable of looking after themselves.

You see, if my son were sent to Siam or Egypt or onything, she – my wife – wouldn't rest till she had me aside him. She thinks I can mebbe look after him, though probably the boy could look after himsel' better than I could. But still, there's that love for the faimily! She thinks that the heid o' the family should be there. She'd say, "Well, young Alec's oot in Siam. Ye'd better do your best to gang oot there and see if he's all right."

Above Reproduced by courtesy of the Imperial War Museum.
Below Sheila MacGregor with her children at the berryfields in 1971. Photograph by Margaret Rosenbaum.

Alec Stewart with his son John, his grandson John and his father John in 1949.

Married life

While in many respects the parent–child relationship among Travellers is admirable, it can create difficulties when a son or a daughter attempts to set up a new family relationship by marrying. At such a time, the young couple may find themselves torn between loyalty to the parent family-group and the need to set up a new family-group in which they themselves play the leading role. Alec and Belle's early married life may be less than typical but it is not, by any means, unique.

We were married on the seventeenth of August, 1925, at a place ca'd Ballymoney, in Ireland. I worried my mither sair because she never wanted me to marry a Traveller and she never wanted me to marry Alec, because I was brocht up in a hoose and she didnae want me to wander.

Anyway, after twa-three months I got fed-up wi' Ireland and I cam' hame tae my mither. Well, I'd be aboot twa weeks back when Alec cam' owre fae Ireland wantin' me tae gang back wi' him. Well, my mither and Alec didnae get on at a', and I wasnae keen on the travellin' life, so Alec left and went awa' back to Ireland, to his faither and mither, and I stayed wi' my mither.

So Alec went away and oor first bairn, John, was born on the ninth of April, 1926. And Alec never saw him till he was five months auld. After that I went back wi' Alec to Ireland, leavin' John wi' my mither. She wouldnae pairt wi' him. She said, "I'm no' haein' the bairn livin' the life you've lived." Naturally, that caused a lot o' strife atween Alec and me. He wanted the bairn – after all, John was his first son. But my mither wanted the bairn tae. So it was a fight between the twa o' them as to wha was to hae the bairn. Well, my mither kept him, reared him up.

Every time I fell pregnant I had to come back to my mither. Five bairns I had and Alec was stayin' wi' me for just the twa o' them, Cathie and Sheila. Cathie was born on the second o' November, 1928, at Strabane in the county of Tyrone, Northern Ireland. And Sheila was born in Tanage Street, Blairgowrie, on the seventh of July, 1937. That's a' in the past, but it a' happened and Alec kens that it's the truth. Though I must admit it was maistly my fault because I just thocht mysel' that wee bit better than Alec and just didnae fancy wanderin' roond the country waitin' for Alec tae earn twa-three shillin's playin' the pipes and sendin' me oot hawkin', which was somethin' I'd never done wi' my mither. We just didnae get on and during the first ten years o' oor married life, Alec was maistly wi' his folks and I was wi' mine. It was just a come-and-a-go, a come-and-a-go.

During this period Belle, apparently, considered the possibility of setting up house on her own. Indeed, she rented and furnished a house in Blairgowrie for a weekly rent of half-a-crown. She didn't live in it, but it was *there*, a possible haven in an emergency. Equally important was that, as a householder, she was entitled to draw parish relief and was granted twenty shillings per week to support herself and her children. In order to supplement this modest income, Belle cycled every morning to Cupar-Grange where she was employed as a farm-worker for a wage of twenty-five shillings a week. On Alec's return from Ireland, the local authorities suspended the payment of relief on the grounds that caravan-dwellers were not entitled to receive municipal aid. Their appeal against this decision eventually came before the Court of Referees, where Belle was asked whether she wished to be reconciled with her husband.

To be quite honest, I didnae. I was sick of all the runnin' aboot. But the nicht before the case cam' up in court, my mither says, "Look, Belle – ye'll hae your man when ye'll nae hae me. Forbye he's the faither o' your bairns. So for goodness sake, gie owre this daft carry-on of aye bein' separated. Get thegither and rear up your bairns respectable and decent and bide thegither."

It spite of these early troubles, the Stewart family is an extremely close-knit one. It is, as Alec's sister, Jeannie Thompson says, "a typical Travellers family".

Travellers' families are very close-knit. If one of us is in trouble we cannae get there quick enough. Whitever ye're daein', ye pit it doon and whether ye've got the money or not ye get tae wha'ever's seik or in trouble. Whether ye walk or thumb a lift or if ye've got a car, it's "Gie me five gallons o' petrol, I'll see ye when I come back, I'm in a hurry". If Alec here didnae hae ony money, I'd say, "Here's the half o' mine", and if I didnae hae ony food, Belle would just gie me the half o' hers, and that would be forgotten aboot. We never speak o't. It's no' like that wi' toon folk. If ony o' their folk are seik they dinnae send oot to tell ony one, they dinnae seem to bother. But if Alec there was seik, Belle would be aff to the phone like a shot to phone me and I'd phone some ither body. It's a kind o' jungle drummin' thing that gangs a' aroond . . . and this yin and that yin'd be comin' to see him and find oot if he needed onything.

Work

References to family crises, accounts of illness and marital discord crop up from time to time in the Stewart recordings but, for the most part, work forms the most consistent part of their discourse. Alec, in particular, used work references to pinpoint experiences, places and people he has known. Even his childhood reminiscences were confined almost exclusively to descriptions of various types of work. By the time he had reached school-leaving age he had acquired several traditional skills and was ready to take his place in the adult world.

When I left school I started to work as the tailsman in the sawmill. A tailsman tak's aff the slabs and measures pitwood for coal mines. Then he tak's them away and puts them in squares a' aroond the sawmill. The next job I was at was in a fairm, daein' odd jobs in a fairm. Then I was at peelin' trees, peelin' oak trees for their dye. You tak' off the bark and put it on racks to be dried. Then they pack them up in bunches and tak' them away to the dyeworks. After that I come doon tae Blairgowrie. I did odd jobs there: I hawkit, gathered scrap, rags, woollens, odd things and furniture. Then I went frae that to flax-pu'in'. That was doon in Fife and Dunkeld and roond aboot Glenshee and Glenisla. We were a' roond daein' that for about five or six year. Then I cut corn at harvest time, wi' a scythe. We got five pounds an acre for cuttin' corn. Sometimes there were four o' us, other times just mysel'. Earlier in the year I'd be beatin' for the gentry, beatin' grouse, hare and deer for them tae shoot at. After that it would be the flax and the corn. You see, every year there would be the same thing over and over.

I think cuttin' corn is just as bad as onything because you're aye pu'in' and your side gets kind o' sore. Pu'in' the flax was bad too. I've seen me pu'in' flax till my hands were red-raw. We done three squares a day – a square was twenty-two yards. Your hands got sore, 'specially if the flax is hard. The scurf gets into your hands. Sometimes you'd wear gloves, but maistly ye didnae. It was a great thing, though, the flax – there was good money in it.

I'll tell ye aboot cuttin' corn. I was up at Banff, no' the place north o' Aberdeen, but just above Blairgowrie. I come to the door o' the fairm and the fairmer he was sittin' there in a wheelchair, he was paralysed. Well, I telt him we wanted work. "Hoo mony men hae ye got?" he says. I says, "Just me and my brother." "That'll be all right", he says. "Awa' yet go up to the field and ye'll see the grieve up there cuttin' wi' the binder. He'll tell ye what to cut."

So I went up and saw the grieve, and I tells him that I don't like leavin' patches here and there in a field. "So," says I, "If you'll cut a track right through the middle o' the field, I'll cut one half and you can cut the other." So he cut a track richt doon the middle o' the field and we stooked it and tied it. Then I gaed hame and I got the wife and her aunty, Big Belle's Knuckles, and there was three lifters. Well, we worked a day and a half in that field and we finished it. A fourteen-acre field! Well, then – I gaed up to see the fairmer and he says: "Have ye come for a sub?" "No," I says, "I've come to get paid for the field." "What?" he says. "That's impossible." "I'm tellin' ye," I says, "we've finished it." "Then it cannae be richt cut." And he sent a cattleman up for the grieve. Well, the grieve cam' doon and the fairmer says, "Whit kind o' a job hae they done?" "It's a bloody good job," says the grieve. "And hoo much hae *you* done?" says the fairmer. And the grieve says, "We havenae got the half o't finished and *we've* got a binder!" Well, the fairmer paid us but he kept five pounds off us. He thocht we were makin' owre much money.

I've shawed neeps. I've seen me up the glen at a place they ca'd "The Bleatin'". I went there every year. I went up one mornin' and the fairmer says, "Are ye up for the neeps?" I said, "Ay". Well, we shawed a' day but that nicht it started tae snaw. It was snawin' like blazes and there was a hard frost. I says, "Belle, we havenae a ha' penny, so we'll hae to go up." So me and her we went up. We'd a wee Austin-Seven at the time, wi' wire-spoke wheels and a black cap on the radiator. We ca'd them "Corkies". Anyway, we went right up tae the fairm and away oot to the field. Belle was takin' the snaw aff the top o' the shaws o' the neeps and I was comin' behind her shawin' them. Well, the fairmer lookit oot o' his window and he says to his wife: "Look what's doon in the field, and it snawin'!" So he comes doon tae me and he says, "My God, Alec, whit are ye daein' up here in this kind o' weather? Can ye no' wait till it's faired up?" I says, "I must dae somethin' for a livin' – I havenae a ha'penny." He says, "Can ye no' get on the broo?" I says, "I havenae got ony stamps." "Well," he says, "you come up tae the hoose and I'll gie ye somethin' for your bother. And then get awa' hame. It's owre cauld." So I went up tae the hoose and he handed me a five-pound note. He says, "That'll keep ye gaun for twa-three days."

Then, of course, there's the berries, the raspberry harvest, that's in July. That's aye been the big thing for the Travelling folk here. And I've done my share at the berries. I once had twelve acres o' my ain berries – planted them, picked them and sold them. Aifter the berries hae been picked and the leaves hae fa'n aff, you've got the cuttin' o' the canes. Ye've tae tak' oot the auld canes and some o' the young ones that ye dinnae need. You leave aboot six or seven strong canes in each stool. This is done in November. It's better done in the hard frost because if the ground's soft you'll pu' the whole cane oot.

In the summertime we did the pearl-fishin', the fresh-water pearls that ye get fae mussels. I did a lot o' pearl-fishin', for years and years. Ye get a good price for pearls noo. Most of the pearl-fishin' we done was in Ireland. We fished the Moy and the Sonen Bar, the Swaddlin' Bar as they ca' it, and Castlefinn, Castlederg, and the Blackwater. And here at hame we fished the Tay, the Tochert, Glen Lyon, the Gairn, the Spey, the Don, the Dee, the Clova and the Esk. But there's hardly ony pearls left. But in they days . . .

You get an auld jug, an auld tin, a big thing and you cut the bottom out of it. And you get a piece of glass and mark it with a wee chuckie-stane and then cut it roond with wee pliers and put it in the bottom of the tin. And that's a glass bottom. Then you get a candle and you light the candle and you hold it upside down until the wax begins to drop and you put it right roond the bottom of the glass, and that holds it like a vice, and there's never any water comes through from the bottom. You put the wax on the inside and the outside.

Then you get a long nice straight branch and you open the bottom of it to make it look like a clothespeg, the thickest end of the stick. You put a wee wedge on it and then tie it with a string so the stick canna split up. And it's just like a big clothespeg. And you get this glass-bottomed jug and an auld bag and you tie this roond aboöt your shoulders wi' a bit of string or rope and ye'll go in wadin' to the river, just wi' your troosers or your bare feet or whatever way you like.

When you press this glass-bottomed jug on the top of the water you can see everything so distinctly, the least wee thing in the bottom of the water. You may have to walk oot a bit before you see any shells. Some places, you see, shells travels under the water, you can see the mark o' them on the sand at the bottom o' the burn. One place you may get a shell here and a shell there; other places you may get two or three dozen o' shells a' in the one place. So you take this long stick, put it doon, lift the shell and put it in the bag that's roond your shoulders.

You keep wadin' on and wadin' on, bended doon of course, and lookin' through the jug, and if you lift a crookit shell – one that's a' twisted, ye'll have a good look at that before you put it in the bag, because you've a good idea there's a pearl in that shell. You ca' that a "crook". 'I've got a crook the day!' Of course, there's anither way you know there's a pearl in a shell: on a certain side o' the shell there's a long run, a straight run up the outside. You could be lucky and get a nice white pearl. On the other hand, it could be a brown pearl, which is of no value whatever. The pearl must be white, or a nice pink, a salmon pink. Now you could get a black pearl, that would really be worth something to you. But they're very scarce . . .

Anither job we used to dae was catchin' birds. We'd tak' them tae Dundee and Perth and sell them there. We used to get three-and-sixpence a pair – a cock and a hen – for siskins. We used to catch them in the airn [alder] trees. Ye'll aye get siskins in airn trees. We used tae gang doon there and the siskins'd be there in squads. We'd get up early in the mornin' when the hard, keen frost was on the water, and you made holes in the ice and put your sticks across them, lime sticks. And when the birds come doon for a drink, they get stuck to the lime. And there was bullfinches, goldfinches, redpolls, and they foreign birds, waxwings. But ye dinnae get ony o' them in airn trees. Ye get them in the thistles.

Anither thing I've done plenty o' is buskin'. Ay, I've buskit! Thon time I was away fae Belle, that'd be four year afore Sheila was born, I buskit doon in the borders, in Dumfriesshire and doon in Carlisle, Silloth, Cockermouth, Keswick, Ambleside, Windermere, Grasmere, Longtown . . . a' owre the place. I travelled wi' the Morrisons and wi' Henry Marshall. We'd gang tae Appleby Fair and travel a' aroond. Henry Marshall was a wee man, a great jockey. Onybody that wanted a rider for a trottin' horse, they'd get wee Henry Marshall at Appleby Fair. The last time I saw him he was on a white horse, and it could go!

Nooadays, the fair is away intae a field, but in they days it was on the main road.

There'd be three or four miles o' horse caravans right up this main road and a' the caravans would hae their fires burnin' a' alang the road.

Auld Lizzie Marshall, that was Morrison's wife, it was her that fed me. I'd be awa' a' day buskin' wi' the pipes and when I cam' hame at nicht she would hae my supper ready. They'd a son ca'd Joe Morrison and he used tae gang oot hawkin' wi' a pony-and-trap. He sold rugs, wee tables and that kind o' thing. He had a brother wha was a *mush-feeker* – he sorted [repaired] umbrellas, sharpened knives and scissors and och! they were daein' well. When they cam' tae the fair they were a' thegither, but when the fair broke up some would go this road and some would go that road.

Whenever I was doon and oot I always cam' back tae my pipes. I still dae a bit o' buskin'. I gang up tae Glencoe, Fort William, Ullapool. I play at the hotel at Fort William regularly on a Saturday and Sunday. I get five pounds for the two nights. And a' week I play doon at Loch Lochie, right through the summer. Then at the back-end [autumn] I'm back liftin' the tatties. Ay, ye lift the tatties roond about September month and intae October and you dress the tatties in the spring. It can be hard work liftin' tatties.

Tree-peelin' was anither thing that was hard work. It was maistly larch and oak trees. The larch bark was used for makin' dyes and the oak for medicine. Sometimes you'd peel the bark at the back-end when the trees were losin' their sap. Ither times ye'd peel them in the spring when the sap's comin' intae the bark. You did it wi' a peeler – that's a broad knife, looks a bit like a curved bread-knife. The longer the handle it had, the better it was for the job. If it had a wee short handle ye were aye cuttin' your knuckles on the tree trunks.

In the nineteen-thirties I was gettin' sixpence a tree workin' for Hamilton MacDonald. I was aboot three weeks wi' him and baith my hands were naethin' but raw flesh, the blood was dreepin' oot o' them. So I took a handful o' salt and rubbed it intae the cuts then washed it awa' wi' clear water. After that my hands were as hard as onything.

Belle asserts with some pride that her mother was the champion larch-peeler of Scotland and was known far and wide for her skilful handling of the peeling-knife.

She peeled them for a penny a tree. It was aye the larch she peeled because you could mak' mair money at it. It was a tree that was easy peeled for there was plenty o' sap in it. Wi' a larch tree ye could tak' mebbe eight or ten feet o' bark aff wi' one swipe and ye wasnae lang finishin' a tree at that rate. But wi' the oak, you mebbe got a foot or a foot-and-a-half aff at a time. April was the main month for the larch- the season would mebbe last five or six weeks then the sap seemed to go back. When that happened they'd spade-peel them, but you'd only get wee bits aff here and there because the bark was teuch [tough]. After the trees were peeled they were used for telegraph poles.

Anither job we did in the cauld time o' the year was pickin' the burrs aff the trees, the larch cones and the fir. I've seen us gaun awa' past Loch Ordie, that would be aboot twelve or fourteen miles fae Blair. We used to gang wherever they was cuttin' trees. For the cones were maistly at the tap o' the trees and ye couldnae climb them. October month was the time for burrs and it was often gey cauld up in they hills whaur ye had tae gang for them. Fir-cones were the best for they were bigger than the larch and it didnae tak' sae mony tae mak' a bushel. Twa shillin' a bushel you got for them. I'd be aboot fifteen then but I mind pickin' the burrs.

There's anither job that I mind when I was a bairn, and I dinnae think it's been done this last fifty year. But it was one o' the jobs that my mither aye tried to get. It wasna big pay, but they were good at it, her and Donald and Andy and my uncle Jimmy. It was gatherin' clover-stanes. Ye ken the clover fields lang ago had a lot o' stanes in them, and they didnae hae a' they tractors that could crush a' they stones doon or onything. Well, they maintained that they didnae get a good crop o' clover if there were owre mony stanes. So they gaithered them and made them intae wee heaps in the field. Ye'd tie an apron roond ye, and ye had a wee bit o' yon thick paling-wire to prise they stanes oot o' the grund. They got sixpence an acre and the four o' them could mak' as much as ten bob a day between them. The way I mind that is that I was about four-year-auld and while they were gaitherin' the clover-stanes I used to look for peasie's [lapwing's] eggs, for April was the time the peasies laid their eggs.

Alec's told ye a' the nice jobs that onybody can dae but we used to live aff makin' scrubbers and heather besoms, Donald, Andy and my mither. Maist o' the poorer class o' tinklers did that, ye see! And maist o' the folk in the villages and toons would rather hae a heather-scrubber than the fancy stuff ye hae noo. For one thing, they made a better job o' cleaning a porridge-pan. So my mither would gang roond tae an ironmonger ca'd Adamson and mebbe get an order for twa-three gross o' scrubbers. My God, she was happy then! So awa' up the hill they'd gang – Donald and Andy and my uncle Jimmie wi' my mither – awa' up tae a place ca'd St Fink, above Rattray. And they'd be shakin' the snaw aff the tap o' the heather, for no' every kind o' heather'll mak' a scrubber, Oh no! You must get the bull-heather, as the Travellin' folk ca' it, but you'll ken it as bell-heather. And the reason you need bull-heather to mak' a scrubber is because it's langer on the stem.

And we made the baskets and creels. There was one particular basket that the Travelling women could sell better than a' ithers: they were used for gaitherin' eggs and we ca'd them them "curlies". It was an even-rimmed basket, ye ken, wi' an awfu' nice plaited lip roond the tap. A "plait-lip", we used to ca' it. Some folk made them just bare and naked, but that kind didnae gie the hannel [handle] the same support. But when ye made it wi' a lovely plaited mooth aboot the wee rim . . . well, the fairm women would a' go for that kind o' a basket.

The willow-creels and the sculls, noo. Ye had to peel the willow-wands. In the summer-time they'd peel in their ain sap and a' the bairns in the camp would be sittin' doon peelin' the bark aff the wands. But they wouldnae peel in the winter-time. Well, winter-time or no', folk still wanted a nice white creel. So ye boiled them. Ye kept a big auld iron pot for that. And when the winter-time came, we'd fill the pot fae tap tae bottom wi' they wands that wouldnae peel. Ye'd put them richt roond the pot, starting at the bottom, as ticht as they'd go, and ye'd put a ticht lid on the pot wi' a stane on the tap o't tae haud it doon. And ye'd put them on the fire, and boil the wands for mebbe a couple o' hours. Then ye'd tak' a clothes-peg and nip the wand wi' it and draw it doon the hale length o' the wand, and the bark would come aff just lovely. Now, those particular wands that was boiled, in less than three months' time, they would turn a lovely brown colour, just as if they'd been dipped in tan.

They was the unusual jobs that we done, which the real poorer classes of tinkers did. Alec could skip some o' these when he was younger because his faither could aye provide for him. But we used to gang miles and miles awa' oot intae the country, willin' tae dae *ony* kind o' work.

Moving on

The urge to move on comes over you. I get a good job and I've every intention of staying in the place, but as time passes it peters oot and I get that urge to move on again. When I was workin' on the overhead lines and a train passed, I'd get that feelin': Whaur's it gaun? I'd like to be on it. It's just that feelin'.

Jimmy Higgins is expressing a feeling which is by no means confined to Travellers. The worker on the assembly-line, the nine-to-five clerk standing in line on the escalator in the crowded subway, the coal-face worker going down for the day's shift in the man-riding cage, the suburban commuter and the housewife – all, at some time or another, experience the sudden urge to abandon the daily routine and find a new life in a new place. The difference between the Traveller and the factory worker, the clerk, the collier, the commuter and the housewife is that the Traveller surrenders to the urge. The decision to move is generally taken on the spur of the moment and apparently without preliminary planning. Belle says that Travellers never plan. "They're camped here the nicht and God knows whaur we'll gang the morn." Jeannie Thompson described a typical move for us.

Noo, my brither Alec'll mebbe say – "Will we go to Skye for twa-three days?" I say, "Yes". Well, he just tak's the car tae the garage and fills it fu' o' petrol, comes back, "Are ye ready, Belle? Are ye ready, Jeannie?" "Ay." Wor blankets are under wor airms and we put them in the van and mebbe tak' a bag to haud wor messages when we gang tae the shop. And Alec tak's his pipes, puts them in the back wi' wor kettle, wor pan, cups, saucers, plates, a couple o' forks and knives. Then we jimp in the van and whsht! We're off! No dilly-dally at a', simple as that. And we never plan anything, never. Never plan. We never say what time'll we go away or what time'll we come back. The man that made time made plenty o't. As Rabbie Burns said, "The best laid schemes o' mice and men gang aft agley." Forbye, when the sun's shinin', you think aboot the open road.

That emotive final phrase is one that crops up frequently in conversation with Travellers. It is a painful reminder of the things that many of us have forfeited and which, for Belle Stewart, add up to a desirable way of life.

There's naething beats the lovely heather and the moors and the birds whistlin' and the nice, wee clear burn. And ye're sittin' there and ye've nae coo nae care, as the Scotchman says.

Belle's daughter, Cathie, faced with the task of bringing up a family of young children, is less enamoured of the Travellers' way of life.

That's all right for the summer-time but it wouldnae do in winter. When the winter comes and the snaw's aboot three feet on the grund and your children's got to go to school and ye cannae get washin' done and ye cannae get food for them. I wouldnae say that was a life at a'. Doon wi' it! Get intae a hoose and mak a bit o' life for your family.
It's security I'm aifter. We either find work and nae hoose, or hoose and nae work. We stayed three weeks in a car doon in England: slept in it, made oor food in it. The kids slept in the back o' the car and Jimmy and I slept in the front. I had the steerin' wheel up against my chest for three weeks.

Harassment and discrimination

An increasing number of travellers share Cathie's feelings of desperation, for it is virtually impossible today for a Traveller to follow the traditional way of life without breaking a law or falling foul of one or another of the innumerable local ordinances. Let him pursue his occupation of collecting and sorting scrap and he violates the Litter Act. Let him pull his caravan into the side of the road and he is liable to the fined under the provisions of the Highways Act of 1959. In certain areas he is breaking a law if he lights a fire on common land. A Traveller who buys a piece of land is breaking the law if he attempts to occupy it without receiving planning permission, and the 1960 Caravan Sites and Control of Development Act has made freedom to camp a thing of the past. For most Travellers it is still true, as stated in the Ministry of Housing Report of 1967, that to be within the law they must be perpetually on the move. The experiences of Belle's son, John, are typical.

The minute ye put your caravan doon by the side o' the road the police are on top o' ye. "Move on, move on!" We were workin' doon at Hatfield New Town in England and we'd got the caravan drawn aside on a right-of-way. Well, the police came and said, "Ye've to shift. Move on." I said, "I havenae got any petrol." The next mornin' the council-men came wi' a tractor and tow-bar. "Hold on", I said, "I'll go as soon as I've earned the price o' a gallon o' petrol." The man who was drivin' the tractor got into his car and drove doon to the garage and brought back a gallon o' petrol. "Here", he said, "Compliments o' the council. Now MOVE!"

So we moved on. We pulled in at a layby near Hertford and we were there aboot a week when they were back again, hounding us. "Move on, we don't want you here, move on!" I says, "Where are we gaun to go?" "Go back where ye came from." I says, "I cannae get work up there. What are we gonna do there? There are folk doon here dyin' for us to come and work but we cannae get work because we cannae get leave to stay. So where are we gaun to go?" "We don't give a damn where you go", he says, "you've got to move on." I tell you, we're sick o' it. We're hounded the same as Hitler hounded the Jews.

Jimmy Higgins, Cathie's husband, also worked at Hatfield.

Down there in England it was summonses every morning, police waiting at the caravan door when we got back from work. "Here's a summons for ye." Every mornin'! What chance do we stand? We're just a couple o' Jocks. We dinnae stand an earthly. While they want you, you're OK, while you're of use to them. But the minute they're finished using you, you can do what you damn well like.

I've worked in this toon, Blairgowrie, as a labourer, as a bricklayer, as an electrical engineer, and they liked me as far as my work was concerned, but at the end o' the day, ye're still a Tink. There was one time we had to go and see the water inspector and he said, "If I had anything to do wi' youse people, I'd burn ye aff the face o' earth. I'd chase ye right oot o' the country." And that's one o' the heid yins o' the toon!

Alec Stewart developed a somewhat philosophical attitude to discrimination. After having spent a lifetime encountering it in all its forms, he tended to take it for granted.

I was born and bred in Blairgowrie and I'm still not welcome in the town. In fact, not long ago two or three of the council said, "We want the town rid o' these people. We want them out!"

There is no ambiguity in Jimmy Higgins' eloquent statement of the social dilemma facing himself and most other Travellers.

I'm a Traveller. There's nae man worth his salt would deny his birth, but when they call us up intae the army ... well, we're a' Jock Thomson's bairns then, we're a' alike when there's a war on. In the last war we fought for four rights, four freedoms: freedom o' speech, freedom o' religion, freedom frae want and freedom from fear. But we're still under this fear. We can't even go and camp anywhere. They're gradually pushing us oot. They're in the majority, we're in the minority. They say, if you can't fight them, join them. Well, we're doin' oor best to join them. But they'll no *let* us join them.

Education

The constant harrassment of the Travellers has made nonsense of the Compulsory Education Act of 1944 (amended in 1972) which stipulates that all children between the ages of five and sixteen years must regularly attend school. The Caravan Sites and Control of Development Act of 1960 prevents Travellers from camping on a site other than one provided by the proper authorities. Since only a handful of such sites are available, Travellers are driven to be constantly on the move, with the result that their children grow up uneducated.

There was about five hundred Travellers up on Coney Heath and there was only one or two o' them that could read and write. My wee girl used to gang in and teach them A-B-and-C. They didnae ken a *B* fae a bull's foot. How could they? They was gettin' moved here, there and everywhere. Three days here, three days there. Schools wouldnae take them in. "Why should we take youse in? Ye've only a week here. We cannae educate you in a week." And people are willin' to *pay* for a place to stay, dyin' to get their kids to school. They want to rear them up wi' education.

Alec and Belle Stewart and their children are among that tiny minority of Travellers who are literate. Their memories of school are not happy ones, for at school, too, they are the victims of discrimination and prejudice. Jimmy Higgins puts his finger on the cause of this.

Round here, if kids get intae trouble their folk say, "You're behavin' like a little Tinker." Or if they do something bad, it's "Oh, ye wee Tink!" It's born into them when they're kids, so how can they get out of it? The townspeople and country people are ingrainin' it into their kids with every word they say. Whenever a kid does something bad, the word 'Tink' always crops up. And when these kids go to school and there's a family known to be Tinkers, then it's "Tinkie, tinkie torn bags, your rags is no' your ain!" If you're a good fighter then you can curb it for a while. You've just got to battle your way out of it. If you're top dog, you can cool 'em for a while. But some o' the others, the wee lads wha may not be strong as you, they've got to endure a' this and then gang hame wi' a sad hairt.

His wife, Cathie, has similar memories:

The other children used to take the clothes off me and lock me in the toilets. We'd stand together in the playground and no-one would play with us. It wasn't because we were poorer, it was because we were Tinkers, that's all. My granny would sometimes come and see us after she'd done her day's hawkin'. And she'd be wearin' her shawl and sometimes, at the playtime, she'd gie us a piece o' breid or something, and the other children would stand and gie us dog's abuse. Some o' the teachers werenae sae bad, but there was one wha used tae tak' me oot before the class and ca' [abuse] me for everything because I couldnae pay for my school-books.

Belle's experience, at the same school some thirty years earlier, were much the same as her daughter's.

The worst I got was fae the schoolmistress's ain son: "Tinkie, tinkie, tinkie! Dinnae play wi' her, she's a Tinkie!" I would never fight back or speak for mysel'. I would just stand back. But Andy, he fought all the time. It didnae matter if they were big or wee, if they ca'd Andy a Tinkie they never got away wi' it.

They wouldnae sit beside me on the seat. "I'm no' gaun tae sit beside her, she's a Tinkie." The teachers got to be the same, they would put the bairns tae anither seat, and I would sit by mysel'.

I have a brither, and him and I baith went to the Blairgowrie High School. That brither o' mine was kept seven years, seven whole years, in one class. He was never moved, never put tae anither class. I could come hame and read bits oot o' the paper tae my mither, or I could write a wee letter tae my ither brither that was awa' in France at the war. And my brither had been three years in the school before me and he knew absolutely naethin'. Well, my mither went to the schoolmaster and asked why my brither wasnae even able to sign his ain name, and why it was that I, wha was very much younger and had less time at school, could read the paper. The schoolmaster got in touch wi' the teacher, and she says, "Och! I would never dream o' learnin' that laddie onything, he's the best message-laddie I have in the school." So he sat there and he got picturebooks to look at, and she sent him messages here, messages there, clean the blackboard, sweep the floor! And to this day he cannae sign his ain name. That was because he was a Tinker!

Many Travellers now talk about the need for change. Some talk about abandoning the old ways completely and integrating with the Gorgios. Others argue, convincingly, that integration of a small minority with a large majority means the eventual annihilation of the minority. Belle Stewart's views are unequivocal.

There have been Gypsies and Tinkers since the beginnin' o' time. And why should someone else come and knock us aboot and tell us what tae dae? We're God's people, and we hae wor ain way o' livin. We hae different ways – we're just junkmen at the moment, we collect stuff, we're a benefit tae the community in wor way – but I don't think someone wha sits in an office a' day, liftin' a pen (that's the heaviest weapon that they can lift) has the right tae dictate tae us about changin' wor ways. Can you ever see a real Traveller that was brocht up on the road ever fitting intae the ither way o' life? They might try but they'll aye fail, because the blood's there, the wandering notion's there. And why should we change oor way just tae be like toonspeople when we've been what we are a' wor days? If there wasnae this word *Tinker* at the back o't and the stigma that goes wi' it, we'd be happy to live as we are. But they're doon on us! We're rogues, blackguards, we're thieves, robbers, we're everything that's bad wi' the word *Tinker* at the back o't! If they could say the word *Tinker* and be friendly wi' it and say, "Och, that's just a matter o' speech, that's just a word". But it's what goes at the back o' this word. We don't like the kids havin' tae face up tae it. But I don't see why we should change just to please somebody else. And a' for the sake o' that one simple word, *Tinker*.

Travelling ways

Belle is essentially a kind person, with a live-and-let-live attitude to the world around her. Those who would do her injury she treats with an odd mixture of indignation and compassion. The more violent calumniators of the Travelling people and their ways are referred to as "poor souls" who are not quite right in the head and who are, therefore, to be pitied. The rest of us she views with a kind of amused tolerance and her comments on the behaviour of society at large are not without irony.

Look at how many people are campin' noo: tak'the gentry that comes for the shootin', they're no' stayin' in the hotels like in the auld days. Oh no! The biggest half o' the gentry these days is awa' up on the moors wi' their caravans. They're takin' mair tae the travellin' life than some o' the ordinary Travellers is! Thirty or forty years ago, you'd never see a camp on the roadside. But noo there's gentry every place you pu' up. They're even awa' in the furthest pairt o' the moor, "drummin' up" as we ca' it: makin' their tea at the roadside. Real toffs are daein' it!

Anither thing: ye see the way they tie their heidsquares nooadays, wi' the wee bit doon the back? That's a real auld Tinker style. Ay, the gentry's takin' tae the Traveller ways noo, in dress, campin', drummin' up tea at the roadside, lightin' roadside fires and gettin' the smell o' smoke, the stick-reek a' roond them. There's everyday-folk gettin' that wanderin' lust as well as the ordinary tinker. Ay, the king'll come the cadger's road someday.

The very royalty wears a heidsquare the day and the lassies are a' wearin' these lang earrings and lang frocks and skirts doon tae their heels – apart frae them that has the minis. Noo, ye gang awa' back and that was just the real Traveller's way o't wi' dress. Tak' a' they ponchos and stoles that are a' the go noo: that poncho is just the way the auld Traveller women wore their shawls.

Could I tell ye something aboot the richt way to carry a bairn on your back? Well, ye've mebbe seen they new-fashioned things that you can get for carryin' a bairn. It sits there wi' its wee legs hingin' oot. Well, the auld-fashioned way o' the Travellin' women was tae carry the bairns on their backs. They had tae for the sake o' haein' their airms free to carry their baskets and dae their hawkin'. Well, they would tak' their plaid and tie it roond their waist, and back a' hingin' doon, three-cornered. Noo, while the back bit was hangin' doon, they'd mebbe get a wee bag or just a clout rowed roond hay or strae [straw]. And that'd be put at the mither's back tae mak' a saft seat for the bairn. Then ye'd get the rest o' the shawl richt up owre your shouthers. Noo, that puckle rags or strae for the bairn tae sit on was ca'd a *sunk*. And when you'd ta'en the shawl a' up roond ye, the bairn was quite comfortable, for it was closed in a' roond.

Tae mak' the thing secure you'd fasten the shawl wi' a skivver. That wasnae a safety-pin, but a big, lang kind o' preen. The men used tae mak' them oot o' tin sometimes. Some o' them were real fancy, in the shape o' a wee sword or something, like a hat-pin but langer. They had to be fairly strong for they'd tae haud the bairn so that it wouldnae slip. It was never ca'd a pin but always a skivver. Some o' them were gey braw. If ye were a weel-aff Travelling woman ye'd be prood o' your skivver and want tae show it aff. Mebbe your man would hae an auld siller watch, an auld silver lever, ye ken, and mebbe if it wasnae workin' right he'd smash it up and mak' ye a silver skivver oot o' the cover o't. Well, then, ye were somethin' tae look at, wi' your nice silver skivver!

Travellers will often speak bitterly about the different attitudes shown by the authorities and the public to tourist campers and to Travellers. A common criticism levelled at the latter is that they tend to leave a mess where they have camped. Belle's description of the old Travellers' camping habits is interesting.

If Travellers were bidin' beside a fairm they would go tae the fairmer and ask him for a bunch o' strae, and there were no' many fairmers would refuse that. Of course, that made quite a comfortable bed in a wee bow-tent and mony's the braw bairn was born on a bed o' strae.

If it was winter-time they might stay there mebbe a month or twa, for there was big storms o' snaw in they days, and they couldnae just move on, ye ken. So after twa-three weeks, they'd mebbe need anither puckle strae because the first lot was gettin' kind o' broken up wi' them lyin' on it. So when the snaw cleared aff, and this is the God's truth I'm tellin' ye, they would stand there aifter they'd pu'd doon their tent and they'd pick tae the last straw and carry that straw awa' alang the main road wi' them and set fire to it.

And if mebbe they bade awa', miles and miles fae a fairm, and they couldnae get ony strae they would look for a sheltered place in a wood, and if it was the good weather they could aye cut the brackens and hae a good bed o' them. Noo, that might be just for a nicht or twa, for in the good weather they moved as much as they could; but when they were leavin' that camp they wouldnae burn they brackens where they had cut them because that was generally in a woodland. They would pack that brackens in a bag and the wee Tinkler bairns, the wee tots, would carry that bag o' bracken on their backs until they cam' to what we ca' an *aipple-pit*. That was where the auld-fashioned stone-breakers used to break the road metal. And they would stand there and burn they brackens so that they wouldnae cause nae dirt nor onything.

Them that had a horse – this is the honest truth I'm tellin' ye – ye ken if a horse is tied up (and they aye tied them up to stop them strayin' intae a field o' corn or damagin' a fairmer's neeps or that) well, aifter a week or ten days there'd be a fair puckle dung there. Well, do you know this? They'd dig a hole and they'd bury it rather than leave it there to be exposed.

Of course, there was nae tin-foods i' they days, so there was nae tin cans to be disposed of. But I'll tell ye what there micht hae been: there micht hae been tin-clippin's where they'd been makin' a' their tin basins and their jugs and their pails and their flagons and a' the rest o't. And that they would throw awa' amang the lang grass o' a ditch. So I cannae see the idea o' folk talkin' noo about the back generations o' Tinkers makin' a mess, for that was somethin' they didna dae. They were owre *shan* to the *pleuch theekin'* them. That means they were owre feared o' the policeman gettin' them. They were that frightened, ye see. They were aye sayin', "O *shan, shan* the *plook'll theek* us. Dinnae *grib* that *shanness*." It means, 'get that stuff cleaned up oot o' there. The polis'll follow us wherever we're gaun and we'll no' get no place tae bide.' Ay, the polis were a gey feared class o' folk.

In they days, even the ordinary workin'-class folk didnae mix in wi' the Tinkers. There was nane o' these young Tinker lads and lasses gettin' a' dressed up and gaun awa' tae a dance, which is somethin' they can dae the day. For there's some o' they Tinklers the day can dress a damn sicht better than the folk we ca' the *shan hantle* or the *been hantle* – which means bad folk or good folk.

There was nane o' that then. At nicht they would a' gaither roond the camp fire and that's where they would exchange their stories, their healings and their superstitions and a' the rest o't.

I'm no' sayin' they didnae hae their wee bit fling and their girlfriends awa' in the woods, but no' wi' the ordinary public, for they bade far awa' fae toons and places. But even if they hadnae, the ordinary folk would never hae danced wi' a Tinkler laddie or lassie. It would hae been oot o' the question! So if ye think about it, the Travellers were a hairmless class o' folk though they could fecht amang themselves and some o' them were gey coorse, and some o' them could drink. Oh, ay! And maist o' them smoked fae a very early age, but it wasnae fags in they days, it was a' pipes. Even the bairns smoked pipes lang ago.

Nane o' them ever went tae a school. They were never taught onything but what their faimilies telt them, their faithers and mithers and grannies and grandfaithers and a' that. It was a quiet, hairmless sort o' a life – compared wi' noo, I mean.

Sometimes a Tinkler faimily'd draw intae a camp, and mebbe they'd meet anither faimily that they hadnae seen for a couple o' months. Well, they aye gied each ither something. The men would mebbe exchange pocket-knives or watches. The women would exchange earrings or a ring aff their finger and sometimes they would exchange tea-cans. You see, they never had a teapot or a kettle really, just a can. A buck would ca' it a drum, but a Tinkler ca'd it a tea-can, never a pailie or a drum, but a tea-can.

Noo, I'll tell ye the way that ye'd mak' tea if you were a Tinkler. First ye'd put this can on the fire and ye biled it fu' o' water and then you'd mebbe put a quarter o' tea in it and mebbe a whole pound o' sugar and a pint o' milk. It was nearly aye tin jugs they drank oot o' 'cause they made the tin jugs theirsel'.

Noo, the big can was on – it held about five or six pints and it was on this *snottem* – a buck ca's the big stick that you hang your kettle on a *jockey* but we'd ca' it a *snottem*. When you were a weel-aff Tinkler you could afford an iron one, but maist folk just had a branch wi' a crook in it, ye ken, and that was stuck in the grund and the can hung on it.

Well, when the can was nearly biled but no' bilin', you'd shovel in this quarter o' tea and it bubbled and it bubbled and it bubbled and then in went the pint o' milk. They couldnae measure a pint o' milk exactly, but they just poured in the milk till the brew was nice and thick, and then everybody just pu'd oot their can and got a jug o' tea. It took ye aboot a fortnicht tae get your lips open wi' a' the sugar in the tea! Wi' bein' strang the tea used tae leave a lot o' tannin inside the jugs – we ca'd it yellow kale – and we'd get that aff at the burnside wi' a sod o' earth. That's the way you'd clean your pans. It made them pure clean and white, ye ken.

Names

Scots Travellers have an elaborate system of nicknames, or bynames as they are called in Scotland. They fall into three main categories: (a) nicknames given to a group of families which share the same surname; (b) nicknames used in place of an individual's Christian name; (c) pet-names given to children by their parents.

Family nicknames are generally based on inherited physical family traits or features. If the feature is one which is commonly associated with a particular species or animal, then that animal gives its name to the family. Alec Stewart, commenting on his ability to give family names to Travellers he was meeting for the first time, said:

You come tae recognise certain features as belongin' tae certain families: the shape o' their eyebrows, their nose, the shape o' their face. A broad face wi' cheekbones stickin' oot, that's a Johnson or a Williamson. The Whites is a mair delicate sort o' person, very small narrow face and a pointed nose. And there's the MacKenzies , the *Rabbit-faced MacKenzies* we ca' them, because they're narrow-jawed and their cheekbones stick oot and they've big buck-stickin'-oot teeth.

The Wilsons are kent as the *Needleheids* because they're awfu' sharp-featured. The MacMillans are the *White Mice*, 'cause they're a' white-heidit when they're young, nearly blin' white [albino].

The Whites are the *Squirrels*, but they're sometimes ca'd the *Wheedleties*, the *Wheedlety-Whites*. The MacPhees are the *Spotties*. The Townsleys are the *Beetles* and the Kelbys are the *Reid Herrin's*. The Douglasses are known as the *Goats*. The Stewarts are the *Brochans*, the porridge-eaters, they liked their parritch made the nicht before so that they'd aye be sure there was something to eat in the mornin'. The Robertsons, the Hutchisons and the Higgins are a' *Brochans*, though the Higginses are sometimes ca'd the *Slavvery Higgins*, because they're aye dreepin' at the mooth. There's anither branch o' the Stewarts ca'd the *Tearrlachs* (Charleses). Then there's the Drummonds o' Inverness that we ca' the *Drummond Castles*.

Belle's additions to the list of names includes her own family name and a gloss which is typical of her racy style of delivery.

The MacGregors are ca'd the *Frosties*; they're cauldrife folk and some say they're a' stone-mad and they had to put frost on their heid tae cool their brain. Noo, the MacCallums, they hae a gey rauch [rough] nickname: they're ca'd the *Skittery MacCallums* because they aye shite their troosers when they get drunk.

Then there's a hantle o' folk, different families that we ca' *Screeves*. They're a' ca'd *Screeves*. They think they're better than the rest o' the tinker folk and we're supposed to be the rubbish so we just ca' them *Screeves*. I dinnae ken what the meanin' is, they're just a class on their own.

The bynames given to individuals are rarely known to the individuals concerned. They are often derisory and frequently refer to a humorous incident or a personal foible.

There were many Donalds, many Willies, many Johns, many Andras, and they a' got bynames so that ye'd ken wha they were. Noo, Martha MacGregor's man, big fat Alec, had dozens o' nicknames. They ca'd him *The Ogre* and *Haversack*. And the tail o' his shirt aye hung oot, so they ca'd him *Half o' Sark*. He used tae ride a bike wi'oot brakes or bell, and he aye ca'd oot: "Haud oot o' my road, lasses! Haud oot o' my road!", so that was anither byname he got, *Haud Oot o' My Road, Lasses*.

There was a woman and she never got ony other name but *Clink-ma-heels*, because when she walked her toe went forward and her heels come oot some way and clinked thegither. There was anither woman and a' her hair fell oot and she wore one o' them caps, an angora thing and it was green. And they ca'd her *The Wavy Green Hair*.

There's a Townsley boy in Blairgowrie and they ca' him *Meet the Wife*. He was late in gettin' married and a wife was a novel idea tae him, so whenever he met onybody, bairns and a', he would say "Meet the wife." Then there's *Pipe Empty*. They ca' him that because he's aye short o' a smoke. Whenever he tak's his pipe oot, he says, "Oh, my pipe's empty, will ye gie us the lend o' a bit o' tobacco?"

Auld Davy Stewart never got onything else but *Shootin' Hill Davy*, because he used tae bide in a place ca'd The Shootin' Greens, above Banchory. When Alec's aunty, the' one they ca'd Meric [Morag?] lost her first man, she got anither, auld Louis Hutchison, and he was ca'd *The Yellow Fish*. He sold hard fish, dried cod, and it was yellow. He gaed a' roond the country sellin' this fish, and that's hoo they ca'd him *The Yellow Fish*. There was anither man that they ca'd *The Golden Kipper*. He went roond wi' a wee horse-and-float, sellin' kippers. In the hot weather, after twa-three days, they would mebbe dry up, so he pished on them to keep them moist. He was a Watt. Willie Stewart [Alec's cousin] was ca'd *Padded Hooves* and his brither, Andra, aye got *Big Belle's Knuckles*.

At all levels of society, parents are given to adopting pet-names for their children. Occasionally, but not often, the pet-names outlast childhood. With the Travellers they last a lifetime and are used by everyone who is even remotely connected with the family.

Lang ago, the auld Travellin' people, they didnae like calling their children after anybody else. It had to be *in* the family, like my mither was ca'd Martha so Andy's lassie had to be Martha. My aunt that died when I was very young was ca'd Isabella. Well, I was ca'd after my aunt. Though really, we would never ca' a person after someone that was deid. When that person died, the name died wi' him. If a bairn was to be ca'd Donald, it would have to be after a *livin'* relative and never after a deid yin.

Here's anither thing: folk christen a bairn and they never ca' the bairn by the name they're christened wi'. Alec's cousin, Donald Higgins, they ca' him Billy, and Hughie they ca' Norman. When my brother Donald was a wee laddie they ca'd him Minnie and my brother Andy was ca'd Goldie because he had the maist lovely golden, glitterin' hair, it shone like glitterin' gold.

I had a sister ca'd Catherine, but she never got anything but Peasie. Another one was ca'd Annie and she was born intae Alyth at the top o' Tootie Street, so they ca'd her Tootie for a byname. And there was Mary that was ca'd Noonie, and there was Agnes that was ca'd Bunny, after John Bunny the fat man in the fillums lang ago.

And there was one o' them that had a laddie ca'd Alec and his byname was Buchten. And look at my brither Andra! A' his bairns has different names frae the ones they were christened wi'. There's a lassie, Brenda, that they ca' Bummelbee. And there's David that's ca'd Shepherd Boy. Raymond is ca'd Polla, Andra is Sunnyman, Guy is Alec and there's Katherine and she's ca'd Pawpee.

And there's Lassie-bairn and Laddie-bairn. They were identical twins, but that wasnae the reason for gi'in' them these nicknames. The right reason was this: they'd an auld pram and the twa bairns lay in it when their folks were pickin' the berries, and mebbe one o' them would start greetin'. And one o' the lassies would rin roond and say, "Mammy, wha's greetin' this time?" "Oh," they'd say, "it's laddie-bairn this time." So they'd lift Laddie-bairn, or whichever was greetin', oot o' the pram. They're baith married noo wi' their ain families, but they still get Lassie-bairn and Laddie-bairn.

Health, Hygiene and remedies

Disease and ill-health were also part of the "carefree life" of the Traveller. Inadequate hygiene, poor diet and constant exposure to the weather made them vulnerable to infection, stomach complaints and respiratory disorders. In the days before the creation of the National Health Service, the treatment and care of the sick among Travellers, and to some extent among the working-class population generally, was the preserve of older women in the community who practiced a rule-of-thumb medicine.

If ye were a woman gaun tae hae a bairn, there was nae doctors or nurses tae help ye. There was naebody but the ither women, and if there was a granny aboot the camp, well, she was the one wha's advice ye took. There would be complications in some cases, but ye just had tae struggle through your wee bit labour just as if ye were workin' in the fields. Ye just had tae fecht it oot.

As for hospital . . . Oh my God! They wouldnae go intae a hospital at a'. Oh no! That was somethin' they wouldnae dae. They'd rather go intae a jail than intae a hospital. So some o' them had gey hard times. And there was nae electricity, nae hot water and a' the rest o't. Just whatever you boil up in a wee pot or kettle or a pan. And ye'd mebbe hae a wee bit candle, if you were lucky. But they things happen at queer times and it wasnae aye easy gettin' tae a shop for a wee candle, so God knows how some o' these bairns survived. Mind you, them that did survive were hardy.

In hospitals nooadays, I'm led tae believe (it's a while since I had onything like that wrang wi' me!) they dinnae like ye tae bide lang in your bed after ye've had a bairn. So that's something that they hae in common wi' the auld Tinker folk.

Let me tell ye about my grandmither. She was oot hawkin' this day below Meigle Newtile, and she'd twa young lassies wi' her. Well, they're makin' their way back tae the camp when she says tae them, "You lassies just gang richt on tae the camp and put on the kettle, and I'll be just ahint ye. I'm gaun up the auld road tae this fairmhoose here, I'll no' be minutes ahint ye."

Noo, little did these lassies ken what was happenin' tae my granny. Well, she gaed up the auld road right enough, but she never got the length o' the fairm. She'd been in labour for three days, and how she got owre the dyke I don't know, but she did, and on the ither side o' that dyke my uncle Henry was born. Well, did they get a surprise when she landed at the camp wi' that wee laddie in her oxter! Somethin' she didnae hae when she went awa' in the mornin'! She didnae even go to bed until the usual time that nicht, and that was that. And my granny lived till she was eighty-nine years of age. So you see, good guidin' and lookin' aifter yersel' doesnae aye keep ye tae a ripe auld age.

Ye ken, the Traiveller menfolk was never allowed near camp when a bairn was bein' born. They had tae be oot o' the road nae matter whit was happenin'. They dursnae be near at hand when a woman was tae be confined; and a man dursnae sleep in the same tent as his wife for mair than a month aifter the confinement. And anither thing: a woman that had had a bairn dursnae put her hand tae mak' a bit o' meat or cook onything for her man till that bairn was mair than a month auld. They thocht that wasnae richt, that wasnae clean. They said it wasnae richt for a woman tae hannel [handle] a young wean AND mak' meat. That was their tradition and it still goes on in places the day.

Many of the remedies listed below were shared by country folk in general and, up until the late 1930s, by many urban working-class people.

Noo, there's a' kinna [kind of] complaints and ailments that a wee bairn can get, particularly in the winter when it's lyin' in a wee bow-tent. Well, the Tinkler folk had their ain cures and remedies. There was a' kinds o' cures and remedies for the ailments that bairns get. Heat was the first thing you tried. Ye tried to mak' heat, for heat was a cure for everything. The modern way is to hae pills for everything, though they might be curin' one thing and upsettin' anither. So hot poultices and hot compresses was favourite remedies. They didnae tak' much in the way o' medicine, just whisky, mebbe, or a hot drink.

If a woman that'd just had a bairn couldnae mak' enough milk they'd gie her a good drink o' whisky wi' oatmeal in it. Oatmeal drinks'll mak' ye flow wi' milk. So ony fairm wife would just fill a kettle and mak' the gruel and ye'd drink that and, by God, the bairn got plenty tae drink then!

When a bairn was scauded [chapped] between the legs, you used tae put a bit o' flannel intae the fire and burn it and rub it doon till ye got it intae a pooder and then ye'd rub it intae the bairn. That kep' it fae gettin' skinned.

For a bairn that was teethin', ye'd gang oot and find a jinifer [juniper] bush and cut the bark aff it into the white wood, like. And ye'd gie it tae the bairn tae bite on. There was supposed to be somethin' in the jinifer that cut the teeth the quicker.

They used to gie bairns sufferin' fae measles a good stiff drink o' whisky to drive the measles oot. Gie them a real stiff toddy before they go to bed and the next mornin' they'll a' be oot.

For chicken-pox, wash the skin in water wi' bakin' soda in it, and then put powder, talcum-powder or even flour-meal on the spots to keep them dry.

For mumps, ye'd just rub them wi' butter or grease or fat o' ony kind tae keep them warm.

For a croupy cough, tak' 'a bit o' butter and roll it roond in sugar and mak' the child swallow it, or melt doon some fat and gie it the child to drink. Or cut a piece of bacon skin and leave a wee bit o' the fat on it. Make a hold in it and thread some string through it, then tie it roond the child's neck or roond the waist. Leave it on till the bairn is quite clear o' its brochitis or its cauld.

If a bairn took the whooping-cough and that bairn was on the breist, it cleared up much quicker than if it was on the bottle. Where folk had a donkey, they would tak' a bairn wi' whooping-cough and pass it under the donkey's stomach three times. It was said tae be a complete cure. Or if the road was bein' rolled wi' tar, they'd tak' the bairn and make it stand above the fumes o' the tar. That would cure the whooping-cough.

For pneumonia, we used poultices, oatmeal, or linseed wi' a wee touch o' mustard in it. Or you'd just gang oot tae the neep-fields, the turnip-fields, and you'd tak' a swede (it had to be swede, no' the yella neeps). And you'd boil that and then chap it up and mak' a poultice o' it and put it on their chest, back and front. That worked just like a miracle as regards breakin' the phlegm so they could spit it up.

For pleurisy, use a poultice o' dry salt, salt burnt in a shovel. In a poultice there's aye dampness and pleurisy is a thing that disnae dae wi' dampness. But burnt salt is absolutely dry.

Maist o' young infants get stopped-up noses at some time or ither and sometimes their wee e'en are sticky in the mornin'. Well, the simple cure was to milk the mither's breist intae the baby's nostrils and intae its e'en. That was a perfect cure. Mebbe the eyes took a couple or three days to clear up, but it was still gettin' its mither's milk intae it twa-three times a day. I've seen this tried oot on one o' the better-class folk and it worked there, tae.

For toothache, tak' a wee leaf o' tobacco and roll it wee and pack it in the hole in the tooth; or ye could tak' a mouthfu' o' your ain water [urine] and haud it in your mouth.

For earache put a couple o' draps o' whisky in the ear or pour a wee drap o' perfume on a bit of cotton wool and hold it in your ear. But the quickest cure is tae chaw a bit o' strong tobacco and pit the spittle in your ear. That's an instant cure.

For the colic, a drink wi' whisky and honey in it is hard to beat. Whisky was used to cure constipation as weel. Here's what ye had to do: you'd take one o' they lang sticks o' barley-sugar and break it up in a tea-towel. Then ye put it in a pan and bile it until it melts doon. Put as much honey as you want in it and then in goes the whisky. Ye put that in a bottle and gie it tae the kids onytime they need it.

Diarrhoea. We used to gie the bairns biled milk and port wine (that's if ye could get it). Ye'd mak' a poker red-hot in the fire and stick it in amang the port. Ye'd gie them the milk tae drink first so that it would settle, and then ye'd gie them the port. Anither thing was saps, ordinary loaf-bread seeped and biled in water. Ye pour the water aff, put milk in it and gie them that for a couple o' days wi' no ither food o' ony kind.

Noo, here's a cure for indigestion that's gaun back tae the auld folks. At the end o' a bush o' broom ye'll get wee young shoots and if ye chaw them it'll cure heartburn or indigestion.

For a sore throat, just pish on an auld stockin' and row it roond your neck.

For dandruff, rub paraffin intae the scalp.

For an abcess in the mouth, tak' salt and hot water and hold it in the mouth.

For a festering whitlow or a boil, mak' a poultice o' soap and sugar. Melt the soap and squeeze the sugar intae it. It'll draw the inflammation oot and burst it.

Noo, here's something my mither telt me. She was a young lassie, sixteen-year-auld or thereaboot, and she cut her hand when she was at the larch-peelin'. Well, it festered intae what she ca'd a whittle [a whitlow]. They were camped mebbe five or six-hundred yards frae a spring-well. They shifted that camp richt beside the spring and my mither lay for three days and three nights wi' her hand in the spring water and she cured that whittle-beelin'. Aboot a week after they were doon tae Kirriemuir and she went tae the doctor and telt him what had happened. "My goodness," he says, "ye've certainly killed the poison. Ye've made a better job o' it than I could have done."

Here's anither thing. They used to pierce ears for earrings wi' a cork and a big needle. They's hold the cork against the lobe o' the ear to keep it stiff and then they'd push the needle right through. And they'd pu' a cotton thread through the hole and tie a knot in it, just as if you were sewin' a piece o' cloth. Well, naturally, the hole festered, so here's what ye'd dae. When ye wakened in the mornin' ye'd tak' the first spittle o' the day on your finger and ye'd rub it on the hole and, och, it was quite healed in a few days.

For a headache, soak a cloth in vinegar and put it on your forehead.

For a hangover, drink salt water to make ye vomit.

For wasp and nettle stings, rub the skin with a docken [dock] leaf.

Put the milk o' dandelions on warts and they will disappear.

For a weak bladder, drink a glass o' gin wi' naethin' added tae it.

"Hospital" and "poorhouse" are words which, at one time, struck fear into the hearts of the Travelling People. Times have changed. The poorhouses are no more and Travellers enter hospitals with no greater reluctance than any other section of the public. Their fear of contagion, however, their horror of infectious diseases, remains obsessive. It is a phobia shared by many Scots highlanders, for whom the nineteenth-century epidemics of cholera and exanthematic typhus are as much part of the collective memory as The Clearances.

The jaundice – the bloody fyuchs [flux], the auld folk ca'd it – well, if onybody in a faimily had the jaundice, there's no' a soul would come near them or bide wi' them, for they'd be terrified o' bein' smit wi' the jaundice. It was the same wi' consumption. There was nae cure for it in they days. If onybody had it, ye avoided them; even if it was your ain faimily ye wouldnae gang near them.

Oor John's wife had TB – consumption – and there wasnae a soul would gang near her. Even her ain dochter wouldnae gang in the hoose. Everything was taken oot o' the house: furniture, carpets, no' a paper was left there. The place was bare, just the bed she was lyin' in was left, wi' a wee table to haud her cup and her spittoon. The doctor would come and stand ootside the winda and the district nurse would come and stand there tae, but they wouldnae come in. And I said tae the nurse, "Why dae ye no' come in?" "Oh, my goodness", said she, "Mrs Stewart, ye wouldnae like me tae carry infection tae some o' my ither patients!" And I says, "Whit happens tae me and MY faimily? Well," I said, "thank God I dinnae believe in that infection at a'. It'll nae touch me." And it didnae.

Superstitions, omens and taboos

To say that Travellers are more superstitious than other groups in our society is to argue from insufficient evidence. One can say, however, that a significant number of once widely-held beliefs are still current among Travelling people.

As for ghosts, I dinnae believe in them, for I've never seen them, and I've never seen ony o' the wee people. I've been in Ireland where there's supposed to be a lot o' them, but I've never had the good luck to meet one. I hae my superstitions in my ain way, but as regards ghosts and unearthly things like that, I cannae believe in them for I've never seen them, and I'm a hard person tae convince. But superstitions, yes, I DO firmly believe in them. And I believe in warnin's before death.

Noo, I've aye had the gift o' the gab. I babble awa' a lot o' nonsense the whiles. But an awfu' lot o' that nonsense comes true and actually happens. And after a thing has happened, Cathie or Sheila'll say tae me, "Ye were richt enough, mither", or Alec'll say, "Ye were richt, Belle". But they dinnae believe me at the actual time.

Noo, I'll tell ye a strange thing that happened tae me in Ireland. Cathie was exactly three months old and and me and Alec was livin' in a caravan about eight miles frae Londonderry. Noo, Alec was a man that would never let a horse stand ootside if it hadnae something to eat. Well, it was about January, just after the New Year, and it was bitter, bitter cauld.

Well, we was sittin' there, me and Alec, haein' a cup o' tea, and Alec says to me, "Belle, I dinnae ken where I'm gaun to get some hay for the horse." "Well", says I, "I'm no' gaun awa' wi' ye lookin' for hay 'cause it's owre cauld tae tak' the bairn oot." So we were just sittin' talkin' there, and comin' doon this lane was a man wi' a dog. Alec stopped him and says, "Excuse me, is it far frae here tae the first fairm?" "O", he says, "it's just roond the corner. That's where I live."

"Ye wouldnae be able tae oblige me wi' a wee bundle o' hay for my horse? I've got it tied up and there's nae grass." "Oh sure, yes", he says. Noo, he was standin' at the door o' the caravan where Alec's pipe-box was lying and he says, "Do ye play the pipes?" Alec says, "Ay." "Well", he says, "bring them wi' ye when ye come and gie me a tune." So after Alec got his wee drap o' tea he set aff for the fairm.

The bairn was sittin' on my knee and what wi' the heat o' the fire, it fell asleep. Well, I set aboot tidyin' the place and I put Cathie on the bed and covered her richt up wi' a blanket, rowed really close up tae her face.

I turned aroond, and I cannae remember what I was daein' but somethin' drew my attention to the bed. As I looked back I saw the blankets bein' lifted aff Cathie and neatly folded richt doon tae her feet! And they stayed that way for Oh, a couple or three seconds. I couldnae tak' my eyes aff them. All of a sudden, the blankets went right back again in exactly the same way as I'd had them on the bairn before.

Well noo, I began tae tak' fright and I ran oot o' the caravan and doon the road. As luck would hae it when I got tae the turn o' the road I met Alec comin'. Of course, I telt him what had happened, but he just laughed at me and said, "It's the wind." "There's nae wind," I said, "there's no' even one blade o' grass blowin', man." But he kind of put me aff.

Well, I didnae sleep much that night, I can tell ye. The next mornin' we got up and we went tae Londonderry. Alec's folk were staying in some place ca'd the Bogside, a sort of poor part o' Derry wi' a big green in the middle o't. A' the Travellers were there. There must hae been eight or nine bow-caravans, a' horse-drawn.

Well, Alec's mither must hae seen us comin' for she cam' runnin' oot o' her caravan and she says, "Oh my God, Belle, it's the God's blessin' ye're here," she says. "The polis has been here twice lookin' for ye." "For ME?" I says. "I've been only once in Derry in my life. What do they want me for?" "I dinnae ken", she says, "they wouldnae tell me. But ye'll better get doon tae the police station as quickly as possible."

So we left the bairn wi' the auld woman and Alec and I went doon. When we got tae the police station the sergeant says, "We had a police message fae Scotland this mornin' to say that your cousin, Donald MacGregor, died last night at a quarter past seven."

That was exactly the minute on Alec's watch when he come up the road and the blankets was bein' lifted aff the bairn. Noo, I put that doon as a warnin'.

Belle is not the only Stewart to observe strange happenings. Cathie tells the following story.

Near Lochinver we'd a caravan – a 1959 Bluebird – and little Sheila was tooken tae hospital with suspected TB in the kneebone of her knee. She was about five days in hospital and I didnae eat, I didnae drink, I didnae sleep, I didnae onything. In fact, I pined away aboot her. On the second day, I went to the hospital and I saw the professor and he said that she definitely had TB in the kneebone of her knee. But they couldn't find anything in the bloodstreams of her blood. So the third night – I'm not religious, by no means I'm not – but I prayed so much in my bed in the small caravan just beside the kirkyard that there was a blue light come into my caravan, and when I got out that door I saw our Saviour. He was dressed in pure white and he had a peakit beard and he had starin' eyes, and he had his two hands held up and a white gown on him. He put his hand on me and I got frightened.

Dreams are regarded as serious indications of future events. Their dramatis personae are, almost always, harbingers of ill-fortune.

To dream aboot a boat is a sure sign o' death. And bagpipes! I hate tae dream aboot bagpipes, for it means either serious trouble in your ain faimily or word o' a deith o' someone connected. And if you dream o' the dead, something is definitely gaun tae happen tae the livin'. Tae dream aboot a postman or a polisman or onyone in uniform means ye're gaun tae hear bad news o' some kind. And tae dream o' a bull or a coo in a field is a sure sign o' a doctor or the polis.

It is believed that certain names can exert malign influence. The names of certain families are considered powerful and malignant until midday, after which they lose their potency.

Noo, it's about twenty-past-three in the afternoon that I'm recordin' this, but I would never dream o' mentionin' these names before twelve o'clock. I would never dream o't! There's the name KELLY, which was my brither Andy's wife's name – Kelly, Mary Kelly. I wouldnae tak' a good five-pound note to mention that name first thing in the mornin'. Oh god, that's a terrible name tae mention in the mornin'! In fact, if I even meet her on the road before twelve o'clock in the mornin', I says, "Oho! Somethin'll happen afore the nicht." And as sure as God's in heaven, it does!

And then there's MacPhee – and that was my granny's name – but honest to God, I'd gang aff my heid if ye mentioned it before dinner-time. I'll gie ye an instance. Yesterday when you were here, Alec thoughtlessly mentioned the name MacPhee. Well, you wasn't half-an-hour oot o' this hoose when me and him was haein' a' hell to pay. We argued, we bargued, until he cleared oot, went awa' for a couple o' mile in his car. I didnae think he'd be back for you at a' last nicht. And it was a' through the mention o' that name.

Anither unsanctifit name is MACALLISTER. You see, we go awa' back in these things. If there's an awfu' tragedy and you hear o't through a period of years in a certain faimily, you try tae avoid that faimily if possible. We ca' it "unsanctifit", and it means 'extremely unlucky beyond words'. Many's the time my brither Donald has said tae me when he was lyin' no' weel in bed: "Belle, Belle," he says, "if I just had listened tae my auld mither when she telt me tae hae naethin' tae dae wi' the MacMillans . . . I micht hae been a stronger, hardier man the day. The bad luck has followed them."

There are also a number of names for animals on which there is a taboo; with them, however, bad luck can be side-stepped by using a substitute name.

We never use the word "owl". We always say a *broad-faced chicken*.

It's unlucky to say "pike". We ca' it a *snapper*.

"Pig" is an unlucky word. We aye say *gruffie*, or *gruchie*. That's cant word for pig.

Never use the word "rat". Ca' it a *leuchie*, or a *lang-tail*.

If ye're gaun fishin', never mention the word "eel". Ca' it a *coiler*.

It's very bad luck to use the word "monkey". Ca' it a *swinger*. Monkey – that's a terrible thing to say.

"Snakes" are no' tae be mentioned in the mornin'. If you want tae talk about them, ye say *wrigglers*.

If a hare crosses your path at night, whether ye're walkin' or drivin' in a car, that's a very ill omen, that!

Bantam cocks are the unluckiest, unsanctifit things.

If you hear the first cuckoo and ye hae nae food in your stomach, that's very unlucky. Always hae a bit o' breid under your pilla and put it in your mouth quick before the cuckoo ca's. That way the cuckoo cannae hairm ye.

If ye see the first foal or the first lamb o' the season and its backside's towards ye, then ye're gaun tae hae bad luck. But if it's facin' ye, then your luck will be good. But we never gie things a chance tae gie us bad luck, for the simple reason that whenever we see them we quickly say, "God bless this" or "God bless that".

It's unlucky to see the new moon through a window.

Never look at the new moon unless you've money in your pocket or ye'll hae nane till the next new moon.

If you gang oot and see the new moon, never come in and tell ither folk in the hoose that ye saw it. They maun see it for themselves and they must say, "God bless what I see and God bless us all till the next new moon."

If ye gang oot bare-headed on a Christmas mornin', ye'll hae bad luck till next Christmas.

Dinnae sing when you're makin' a bed and dinnae sing *in* bed. It'll bring bad luck afore the day's oot.

Never look at a funeral through a window.

If ye were expectin' a bairn and a funeral passed by, then ye'd tae haud your apron owre your face, walk three steps after the hearse and then turn awa'. Otherwise your bairn might be born deficient o' sense.

If the soles o' your feet's itchy, you're definitely gaun tae gang on strange ground.

Early one morning we called on the Stewarts after not having seen them for almost a year. We had given them no warning of our visit. Belle opened the door and, to our surprise said, "I was expecting ye. I had the sleeps in my richt eye last night." She explained:

If my right eye is itchy, like on the tap o' the eyebrow and I rub it, that means somebody's comin'. If it's the left one, then somebody's gaun awa'. Last nicht my right eyebrow was awfu' itchy and I says tae Alec, "There's somebody comin' tae the hoose." I kent it wasnae just somebody fae nearby. Well, we ca' that *the sleeps*. It rins in faimilies. A' wor generation had that. My mither was the same.

The music

Our first recording session with the Stewarts was memorable. The flat where they were living at the time was full of people. There was Alec and Belle, Sheila and her children, Cathie and Jimmie and their children. As soon as recording was mentioned, Belle began to sing, even before the microphone was out. She was not yet accustomed to the routine set up by visiting collectors. She was not yet able to stem the flow of song and story so that a tape might be changed, nor could she remember unerringly – as she now can – where to begin again when the new tape was operative. She did not attempt to hush the roar of background conversation, sounds of tea brewing, or the babble of children. Singing was part of normal family activity.

To play an instrument, tell a story or sing a song is not considered extraordinary among Travellers. A contribution is expected from all who participate in a social occasion.

Alec's mother used to play the jew's harp ... played the mouth organ. The wee Echoes, they ca'd them.

... I was always wantin' one o' the laddies to be a piper, but none o' them could blow their nose, let alone pipes.

... and Alec went on to tell how one of his grandsons began to learn the pipes. Any instrument, the fiddle, the "Hohner box", and so on, had its place – or non-place – even the tin whistle: we thought it was a buck's instrument. It wasnae for Tinks to play that. In the name o' God, wha would play THAT? It's a buck's thing.

It was all very informal, but a musical encounter was worth remembering and recounting. In his youth, Alec had had a chance meeting with an Irish fiddler in Fermoy in the Free State at the top of the Moy River. He recounts the event in the same manner in which he would tell a story.

What do *you* do? He says, "I play the fiddle ... I'll be gaun to town tomorrow." "Well", I says, "you go in the mornin', I'll go in the afternoon. We don't want to clash against each other." He says, "That's all right, but ye've never seen my fiddle." And he went and took his fiddle out, and ye know what it was made o'? A cigar-box! It was a tin cigar-box, and it was helluva nice, awfu' nice.

Belle can remember where she learned each tune, story and song.

There's an awfu' lot o' this among the Tinker folk sayin', "Oh, I got this song fae my faither, I got that song fae my mither, handed doon at my faither's knee," and a' that. Well, they were handed doon to me all right, but my father died when I was seven-month-old and my mither couldnae sing not a word o' a song. I heard her diddle a wee bit o' a tune or canntaireachd, but no' a song. But my father: he really was THE singer in the auld days, ye ken, and I got the maist o' my sangs fae my brither, Donald, because he was fourteen when my father died. And at fourteen a Tinker laddie isnae a bairn ... at tryin' to mak' his livin', tryin' to help his auld folk. So he had a gey lot to dae to help my mither in they auld days. And me bein' the bairn, I was aye with Donald and he was really faither and brither to me and all. And I just sat there and I was able to be taught a song and I learned them aff him.

Not only will Belle recall the source of a song –

I got that one aff ane o' Davy Douglas' lassies. They're no' an awfu' nice faimily. They wadnae gie ye a song if they thought ye were listenin''

but she can tell you how her *father* learned some of his songs. He was "a great singer and a great man just for a dram" and was working at a farm in Glenisla. A ploughman at the same farm was known to have 'The Road and the Miles to Dundee' and 'Queen Amang the Heather', but he stubbornly refused to sing these songs in company.

So, noo, to find oot the richt words of the songs, my faither sat for a hale week every nicht at the door o' that bothy till he learned every word o' they twa sangs. If he had coaxed that plooman ootside-in, upside-doon, during the day he would not sing. But here, he sung tae hissel' at nicht in the bothy. So my faither sat ootside and he never kent that my faither learnt they twa songs off him. God knows where that plooman is the day.

The changing scene

Twenty years ago the songs and stories were a normal feature of the Stewarts' social life. Today they seem to underline the family's separateness. Belle recalls those earlier days somewhat sadly:

There was so much singin', apart from when you collecting people came. Every weekend that God sent, Donald or Andy would have a dram. But they wadnae go to the pub for it – they would carry it into the hoose and hae a ceilidh. And we used to sing first at Donald's hoose, then at Andy's hoose.

Times have indeed changed and the Stewarts' shared role of singers and storytellers has changed too. It seems to us that the songs and ballads which formerly helped the family to maintain its 'Traveller' identity are now being used, almost exclusively, to entertain the visiting folklorist, journalist and television crew.

In mid-1975, an interesting discussion developed between Belle and Rena (Belle's adopted daughter, now just over thirty years of age). For years, during the early recording sessions, Rena sat quietly in the background, shy and retiring almost to the point where her presence was not felt at all. She is more forthcoming now and is under the impression that she cannot sing – but she knows all the songs, the stories, the tunes, the cant. Her knowledge of the Travelling way of life is extensive. In one breath she will say that she does not feel she is a Traveller, but in the next breath she will confess

Oh, I'm a Traveller in the way I was brought up. I like the fact that I know cant and that I can go and mix with the Traveller people.

She laments the fact that Alec stopped storytelling at home when the grandchildren entered teenage (around 1965, when the Stewarts became personalities in the British folk revival) and she can recall an epic series of stories which Alec made up for her, the saga of 'Mecky and Sparra'. Even now, she listens to ghost stories with the same absorption as other Travellers.

I definitely *do* believe them, eighty per cent, and the other twenty per cent is saying, "No, that couldnae be true ... he wadnae do *that* ...!"

So Rena, with a foot in both camps, tends to be very objective when it comes to observing and commenting upon the changes that have taken place in the family life over the last fifteen years.

Rena: I remember me and you and my father and Sheila sittin' in the hoose and my father would get the chanter oot and Sheila and I would guess the different pipe tunes he was playin', and then my father would start off with a story. I cannae remember havin' drink there, but there was singin' and storytellin' ...
Belle: But you see, everybody's heard the stories and I think they get tired o' hearin' the same stories all over again.
Rena: But everybody's changed in that respect.
Belle: I don't know ... I still would like, any time anyone comes visitin', I would like a singsong. Like at Aberdeen ... they would have songs I still don't know and I've aye got my wee recorder and I'd be cheeky enough just to record them ...

Rena: Recorders have a lot to do with it, recordin' people, 'cause then it's not
spontaneous and they'll always got to think. You know, if they say, "Oh, I'll just
get a song down on tape", then *you* say, "Oh – what'll I sing then? What kind o'
song would you like?". Whereas if they weren't switching on that machine,
you'd just sing a song.

Belle: Oh ay, but Sheila's doon at her hoose noo, and Cathie's awa' at her hoose
and we're just here on our own, and I think it would be a daft thing for me to
start shoutin' and singin' in the hoose just for Rena and Alec and the bairns. I
mean, I wouldnae have nobody to appreciate what I was doin' or that.

Rena: You're supposed to appreciate it yourself, not just for an audience.

Sheila, in the course of another recording session in August 1979, was just
as emphatic:

We didnae learn the songs to entertain other people. We never ever sung them to
an audience, we never sung them to anybody else – it was just in the family or other
family that came in. We didn't learn them for any gain or anything. We learned them
because we loved them – to bring them to ourselves. Even going about doing the
housework, my mother sings all day.

One cannot avoid the suspicion that the editors of this book, and
folklorists, collectors and journalists in general, are – to some extent at any
rate – responsible for the alienation of individual Travellers from their
communities. We have entered into the orbit of their family groups,
bringing with us concepts, values and attitudes which have forced them to
regard themselves in a new light. They have discovered that their songs and
stories are held in high esteem by scholars and that, occasionally, even the
mass entertainment industry is prepared to view them as viable commodi-
ties.

As a result, the family singers and storytellers have been transformed
into "entertainers"; they have been encouraged to go out into the folk-
clubs, the concert halls, the festivals. Faced with audiences so different
from the small family circle, they have attempted to cope by creating
stereotyped formats of presentation, borrowed from the music hall, the
cinema and television.

The development of what might be called "the performance syndrome"
is merely is a sympton of the process of alienation in the Stewart family:
alienation of the family from the travelling community and alienation of
individuals in the family from one another. It would be strange if, in the
course of the last twenty years, no changes had occurred in the Stewarts'
world. Apart from the fact that they live in a society in which the 'unofficial
culture' is under continuous pressure, there have been the usual births,
deaths, separations, leave-takings, marriages, etc., events which are common in many families. The children of Cathie and Sheila have grown up
and started families of their own, have developed their own allegiances.
Instead of one family, the members of which are bound together with

strong family ties, we now have three or more family groups connected to each other by the flimsiest of ties.

At our earlier recording sessions, Sheila and Cathie would turn up for an evening of singing and sociability even when they lived ten to twelve miles away. When we visited them in 1975 – and the two girls lived only half a mile away – they were hardly in Belle's house at all. Belle confessed that when they *did* come, the evening was spent in conversation rather than in music and entertainment, unless there were visitors present.

> ... but the family relations are breakin' up. For all that they're in the town beside me and we can go and see each other in a matter o' minutes wi' the car ... there's no' this closeness in the hoose at nights like we used to have.

She returned to the same theme during a recording session in 1979:

> I don't have any of my generation to get together with now. I don't have my people that used to get together at nights. At the moment, Sheila's here but Cathie's got her ain faimily and her ain hoose. She cannae neglect them and say "Oh, I'm awa' to my mither's, we're gaun to hae this get thegither." Her faimily's a' in different places, they're a' on their own noo. But you see, when I was younger, we were a' just a' roond about this wee corner o' Rattray here. It was just a matter or saying, "Oh, well, we're all gaun to auld Mattie MacGregor's hoose," (that was my mither's name) and they would a' come to my mither's hoose and that's the way it would happen. But noo ... it's a' changed.
>
> A' they auld stories and the riddles and the songs, the auld tales o' lang ago ... it would be very, very hard for me to expect the younger folk, even them that are no' just bairns, to accept the things that I had. Because I was a bairn, that was my life, our life, listening to they auld things. But there are so many other things to draw the young people's attention nowadays. Even Cathie and Sheila, though they likes that sort of thing, there are some wee times that they kind of look sideways on it. They're no' so deeply involved as we were ...

Over the years, the Stewarts have travelled less and less. Up until 1975, Alec was still doing a regular summer busking stint in Glencoe and the Perthshire Highlands, but a severe illness put a stop to that. For years, the annual raspberry harvest, once the main event in the Travellers' calendar, made it possible for them to keep abreast of the news, to know who had married who, who had born children and who had died. It furnished them with the opportunity to renew old friendships and to make new ones. Nowadays, however, fewer and fewer Travellers are "going to the berries". Their place has been taken by working-class families who are brought by the truckload from Dundee every morning and taken back again each night. For the farmer, this is eminently convenient; he is freed from the necessity of providing accommodation for Travellers' caravans. For the Stewarts, it means that an important link has been severed.

Television too has had a profound effect on the Travellers' traditional culture. Maybe John Stewart, Alec's brother, is correct in saying that "the old storytelling was better than the telly", but it could scarcely have been as clamorous or as persistent. It took a lot more concentration and effort to sit down and tell a story than to turn a knob or push a button. And how can the solitary voice describing the tragic career of 'Tifty's Annie' in twenty or thirty stanzas compete with four or five young men and women pounding out a two-beats-to-the-bar frenzy of thwarted desire? Belle is of the opinion that the television will be the angel of death as far as the old ways are concerned.

Just look at the damned thing! I've nae time for it at all. But you see other people and they're glued to it ... they're fanatic. They cannae be bothered wi' naething else. "Oh, my favourite programme's on!" Or, "When's it on? Switch it on." They'll sit and they'll peel tatties and they're lookin' at it, they cannae get away from it. They'll be doing something in the house, cleaning the house and they've still got their e'en fixed on it. And their mind's awa' wanderin' a' the time.

Sheila is equally pessimistic:

I think it's because o' television that the cant and things like it are goin' to die oot wi' the bairns, because they're no' takin' the same interest that we did. When me and Cathie were younger we didnae hae television.

It cannot be denied that the Stewarts' contact with the Gorgio world has resulted in their becoming entertainers, personalities and public performers, and has accelerated the process of their alienation from the Traveller community. At the same time, it has alerted them to the danger of their imminent destruction as a cultural and social unit. It is one thing, however, to be aware of a situation and another to actually do something to change the course of events. Twenty years ago, the Stewarts saw themselves as Travellers, as members of a community of outcasts. Time has changed their view of themselves: from being members of a community they have become observers – sympathetic, but detached observers. The "us" and "them" of early Stewart conversations referred to Travellers on the one hand and Gorgios on the other. That is no longer the case. The "us" and "them" now seem to indicate the distance that lies between the Stewarts and other members of the Travelling community.

The following remarks, recorded by Belle in October, 1979, illustrate the change in perspective:

We never changed. It didnae matter how poor the people were, the Tinker class o' folk, I still go and see them and love meeting them, and I like talking about their auld ways. I cannae help if they're livin' in tents. I mean, that's their way of life, isn't it? I'm in a hoose, but I've never changed my ways. I've had to change, like, in meeting you folks and a' that sort o' thing – that has definitely changed, because if I hadnae been a Tinker I'd never have met people like you. We've got something to offer that the ordinary public doesn't have.

The statement made by Sheila at the same session is even more revealing:

Just a few weeks ago, I got this hoose in Hunter's crescent in Perth. Now, in Hunter's Crescent there's an awfu' lot o' Travelling folk. Well, I went and moved in there and

I was walking doon the street one day – I was going to the shops – and this man
came up to me and he knew I was a Traveller. He knew who I was, but to approach
me the way he would have done years ago, well, it just wasnae on. It was altogether
different. Instead of coming up to me and saying, "Hello, are you one of the
Stewarts?" (ye ken the way they used to, not long ago), he came up very humble,
"Excuse me, ma'am, but I would like to ask you a question. Now, please don't be
angry with me, I'll no' hurt your feelings for what I'm goin' to say, but are you one of
the Stewarts from Blair?" I mean, to me, to my point of view, they tread a wee bit
warily until they see us smiling and then they let themselves relax ... they're
treading warily until they see our reaction to them. They seem to think that because
o' the wee bit position we're in, that we're gaun to be a bit uppish, which we'll never
be. Because I couldnae do that wi' Travelling folk.

Acceptance in the Gorgio world of the folk club and the concert stage
has undoubtedly conferred on the Stewarts a degree of respectability
denied to their Traveller friends. It has also, in some small measure, added
to their material well-being. Unfortunately, Gorgio attitudes are just as
easily assimilated as Gorgio know-how. How strange to encounter that
hoary, middle-class "coal-in-the-bath" myth in the mouths of Travellers:

There was a crowd of folks called Whites and they got a house down at Montrose
and they'd never been in a house before. They was always in a wee bow-tent. Then
they got this lovely house. They went inside, they got a piece of red hot iron and
they bored holes in the floorboards. And they put up their bow-tent in the middle of
the living room. Then they lit a fire in the middle of the floor and burned the bloody
house down. And there were the ones in Perth. They went and got a lovely new
sideboard off the welfare. And they went and made it into a ferret box!

We have recorded identical versions of these stories in many different
areas of Britain. The erectors of the indoor tent have, at various times,
been described as New Forest Gypsies, Dorset Gypsies, Irish Tinkers,
Kent Gypsies and, to add a pinch of foreign flavouring, Roumanian
Gypsies visiting Brough Hill Horse Fair. The ferret in the sideboard is an
equally widespread tale. It is occasionally a chest of drawers, a wardrobe or
an upright piano which houses the ferret. Sometimes instead of a ferret it is
a rabbit, a hare, a fox, an otter or a fox-terrier bitch with a litter of pups.
Of course, it isn't only Travellers who behave so curiously. The same tale is
told of West Indians, Irishmen and Pakistanis. Indeed, the most colourful
variant of the tale to come to our ears concerns a Pakistani family who
gutted a piano supplied by the welfare in order to house a pet cobra!
    The "them" and "us" mentality is fertile in the production of such tales;
those two small words used in conjunction and with the right inflexion can
open the door to every kind of prejudice and every variety of intolerance.
The Travelling people have their faults like the rest of us, but racist
attitudes have so far not been numbered amongst them. After all, racism is
not only a set of attitudes and behaviour which sets one group in society
against another – it is a way of thinking that can set members within a

group against each other. It would be a great pity if Travellers were to fall victim to this pernicious disease at this late stage.

Whatever the future may hold, there is no doubt that the weakening of the family structure, the performance syndrome and the coming of television have combined to undermine the conditions which ensure that a folk culture is delivered safely into the hands of the next generation.

THE CANT

One of the definitions of the cant given in the *Shorter Oxford English Dictionary* (1st edition) is "the secret or peculiar language or jargon of a class, sect or subject". The Stewarts define it as "the tongue used by Travellers for private conversation when they don't want any strangers to understand what they are saying".

We showed the Stewarts a copy of *The Gulls' Horn Book*, Thomas Dekker's Baedeker of Elizabethan low-life. They experienced little difficulty in reading and understanding the canting songs printed therein. The vocabulary of cant is drawn from a wide variety of sources. In addition to hundreds of words borrowed from the artificially created thieves' jargon, there are archaic Gaelic words and phrases, debased Latin and French words, words borrowed from Romani, Arabic and half-a-dozen other languages and dialects. The Stewarts were insistent in pointing out that the vocabulary and pronunciation of cant shows considerable variation from district to district, and even from family to family.

There is little agreement among scholars when it comes to explaining the origins of cant. The one thing upon which they are all agreed is that it is of considerable antiquity. We asked Belle how she thought the cant came about and she replied that "it was something that was added to the English". But when we asked what the cant meant to her, she said,

I'd never want to drop the cant. Never! I've passed it on to all my family. Cathie and Sheila and Rena know it, so does John and Andy and they've passed it on to their bairns. Mind ye, there's a gey lot o' snobbish Travellers. Och, I've met them mysel', especially at the berry-time. There's some o' them livin' aroond here and when you talk the cant, it's "Oh my goodness, what're ye talkin like that for? Ye surely dinnae speak like that tae your bairns, do ye?"

Of course, they're above this type o' thing. They think it's an awfu' low thing to talk cant. "Oh *shan a shan*, there's *hantle ja-in'* wi' your man and they'll *jan* ye're a *nakkin*." And that means, "Oh goodness, ye shouldnae speak like that! People'll know you're a Tink." I often say to them, "Who's ashamed o' bein' a Tink?" Why should they be? Mind, the ones I'm talkin' aboot are the real rinnin'-aboot gey rauch [rough] straggly yins, bidin' still in the tents yet. They say, "Terrible, the hantle jan who we are." That means, "The people'll know who we are, you should never speak like that."

And I say, "My dear, d'ye ever stop to think that you can choose your friends but not your parents? And if your father and mother and all your back generation had to

live with it and lived well with it and was respected, why the hell should you no'
keep it up?" I'm not the least bit ashamed o' bein' a Travelling person. Definitely not.
And nane o' my faimily's ashamed!

Prior to our association with the Travellers, we regarded the cant as a
dying mode of communication, as a few stock phrases generally used
to impress or confuse Gorgios. Our friendship with the Stewarts has
dispelled this impression completely. There is a large (if limited) vocabu-
larly in the cant, and it is used at home as well as among strangers. Belle
will sit at the lunch table and chat away in both English and the cant. "Pass
the *smout*." Or, "Sheila, look at the *been looer chaets* in Peggy's *clewishes*"
(look at Peggy's pretty earrings).

In compiling the following vocabulary, we did not conduct extensive
research down all the avenues of Stewart memory. On occasion we would
ask the name of an object, or "How do you say this in the cant?" We would
always ask for a translation of a conversation if it were incomprehensible,
and we kept lists of words on envelopes, chip-bags and scraps of paper.
Finally, we sat down with Alec, Belle, Jimmy Higgins and Rena, and read
right through the glossary given in McCormick's *The Tinkler Gypsies*. For
each English word we requested an immediate translation. Many of the
words they gave were in Gaelic, Romani, Doric, as well as the cant, but
they usually made an attempt to identify the linguistic origin of a non-cant
word. They could also identify the approximate geographical territory
covered by a cant word. "In Aberdeenshire, you say *jigger* for door, in
Perthshire its *belliment*", says Belle. "No, *billament*", says Alec.

Glancing quickly over the list will reveal that the bulk of the words are
basic nouns, adjectives and verbs, with a very small sprinkling of adverbs.
It would seem that Belle's definition of cant as "something added to
English" is quite precise. The cant does not have a grammar of its own,
but is dependent upon the usage and structure of English. Nor are there
many gradations in the naming of related objects. The name for a group of
objects will often apply to any member of that group. For instance, fish – or
any particular kind of fish – are *flattrin*. Should you wish to specify herring,
trout, plaice, you would have to revert to English. A goat, a sheep, a lamb,
are all *meggat*. Body, stomach – and sausages! – are all covered by the one
word, *moricans*.

Because of this limited vocabulary, one word may have to carry an
enormous variety of meanings. *Been* can mean good, fine, sunshiny, rich,
gentle, large, aristocratic, holy – or indeed, anything positive or desirable.
Consequently, a *been cowl* may mean God, the King, a member of the
local gentry or just a kind man. *Chaet* is, in Belle's own words, "a
multitude of things" and is usually qualified or accompanied by an
adjective. But, the adjectives being what they are, a *been chaet* may be
anything from a good television programme to a win on the pools.

We have noted that many cant words and phrases are often reinforced by accompanying gestures or significant looks. The hearer needs to see, or be shown, what the speaker is referring to. Certain words seem to be applicable to visually similar objects. *Yaik*, for instance, meaning the numeral *one*, may also mean similar shaped items like key, wand, whip. *Faizim* also denotes a shape and is applied equally to grass, wire, hair, thread. *Filsh* is wood in a long, thin shape, and may refer to a walking stick, a small tree, a piece of firewood, a stake. *Toorie* expresses sharpness, usually in a long thin piece of manufactured metal – a knife, a sword, a pin – although it may also mean a thorn.

The need for mutual – preferably visual – understanding during a conversation may be on several levels. An item may be given a different word if its functions or position changes. A scarf is a *napyen* when it is on the neck as a neckerchief, but it is a *scroof* when placed on the head as a covering, or hat. Conversely, one word may suffice to refer to several different items, the choice of which is indicated by the speaker. When we had assembled the vocabulary, we were surprised that so many everyday objects were not represented at all. For instance, we had cant words for *feet, fingers, neck, head, eyes, ears, mouth*, but

There's no words I know for just toes, elbows, knees, buttocks, stomach or arms. The whole body is called *moricans*. If I said to you, "That *manishie* has *shan moricans*," I would mean that she has a sore stomach. Stomach is the real word for *moricans*, but it covers the whole body. Now, if I saw a woman with very bad varicose veins in her legs, I would say, "That *mort* has *shan moricans*," meaning that the part of the body was her legs, but that they were *shan*. You would *see* what I mean.

We then asked Belle if Travellers ever felt the need of more words in the cant.

Oh yes, but in the cant you can always make up as you go along. Now, that's a *broskin elements* up there [pointing skyward]. And over there is a *whuddin chaet*.

"Sky carriage" and "talking thing" are logical descriptions of an airplane and a television – thus two new names are made up out of older, commonly used cant words. The word *chaet* is frequently used in conjunction with an adjective describing its function or quality. *Glimmer chaets* are anything to do with a fire, from fire-tools like tongs, poker and fire-irons to fuel in general. A church bell, literally translated, as "a good preacher's thing", and a *been looer chaet* (with all the possible definitions of the three basic words) could be almost any precious or worthwhile item. Often a composite phrase will be used where a single word already exists. Ring has been given to us as *granyie, femmel-granyie* ("finger ring") and "the *been looer chaet* on the *cowl's femmel*" (the good, gold thing on the man's finger). This method of instant description is reminiscent of the communicatory efforts of bilingual children, or of the mock Indians in American

Westerns, who will often use words from one language with the grammar of another. Perhaps it is easier to combine many familiar words into a general phrase and accompany it with a look or gesture than it is to remember the one precise word for that object.

Because of this instant approach to language, it is no wonder that, for instance, at one session a group of four Stewarts translated *policeman* into *ploop, plook, pleuch, hornie, musker, feekie* and *shan cowl*. They later added *gavmush* ("a Romani word") to the collection.

The Stewarts' love for the cant is intense. It expresses their uniqueness as Travellers and helps them feel secure and proud as a community within a community. Whether cant is a "language" is debatable. It has accreted – and still continues to accrete – words from Doric, Gaelic, Romani, English and contemporary pseudo-scientific speech. Each family in its travels adds phrases picked up from surrounding communities and from the mass media. Each individual, from our experience with the Stewarts, adds their own mak'-ye-up words and onomatopoeic creations, which may then enter the larger pre-existing vocabulary.

The cant is an active language. It seems designed to communicate action on a very basic level, not to communicate ideas. There are very few words for values, for concepts, for emotional states. When the Stewarts' conversation enters the realms of philosophy, religion, personal experiences, or dealings with Gorgio officialdom, the cant is rarely used. But when it turns up on an everyday level, it can definitely impress – and confuse – a Gorgio.

Cathie: We've to bing avree to the vavver vile because Jimmy is feekin' vavver gribben. It's gonnae tak' us twenty reejes tae feek tae t'ither vile. And twenty reej back doon again.

We've got to go to the other town because Jimmy is looking for different work. It's going to cost us twenty pounds to get to the other town. And twenty pounds back down again.

Belle: But there's nae gribben up there at a'. Ye'll just be stallin' wi' his naismort or stallin' wi' your sproul – but still, wi' a' the kinchens your sproul has . . .

But there's no work up there at all. Ye'll just be stayin' with his mother or with your sister (brother). But still, with all the children your sister has . . .

Cathie: But it'll be a holiday tae us, onyway.

Belle: Oh syet, syet. I jan.

Oh yes, yes. I know.

Sheila: Well, we've a place to stall in this vile and if we could feek hantle in th'ither vile we could feek a kain – a barrie kain.

Well, we've a place to stay in this town, and if we could find people in the other town we could get a house, a nice house.

Cathie: But I was tellin' my naismort today that she could dae that here, that she could get the cowls tae bing us lav . . . to gie us lav . . .

But I was tellin' my mother today that she could do that here, that she could get the people to give us names, . . . to get names . . .

Belle: I jan that, but ye couldnae do   I know that, but you couldn't do that
         that withoot the hantle mangin' . . .   without people asking . . .
Cathie: But the hantle manged ay!   But the people said yes!
Belle: Ay, they grib at the darkment   Yes, they say that tonight, but they didn't
         but they didnae mang that the   say that the other night.
         vavver darkment.
Cathie: Ay, but he's mangin' it *noo*,   Yes, he's saying it *now*, and when you
         and when ye bing in the mornin' tae   go in the morning to the man's house
         the hantle's kain and mang them   and tell them that you got the fellow
         that ye feekit the cowl doon here   down here to give his name [as a
         tae bing his lav . . .   reference] . . .
(murmurs of assent)
Sheila: So where are youse gonnae   So where are you going to work then?
         grib then?
Belle: I dinna jan. We'll stall here for   I don't know. We'll stay here for two or
         twa-three davieses yet. There's nae   three days yet. There's no use going
         use o' bingin' avree for I cannae   away, for I can't leave the child to sleep
         slum the kinchen her nagin.   by herself.
Cathie: What dae ye think, naiskel?   What do you think, father?
Alec: Well, we'll have to do
         something.
Belle: Well, we cannae stall the way   Well, we can't stay as we are, can we?
         we're gribbin', can we?
Cathie: Could ye no' play the stiumers,   Couldn't you play the pipes, father?
         naiskel?
Belle: Ay, could ye no' bing tae the   Yes, couldn't you go to the towns and
         viles and play your stiumers?   play the pipes?
Alec: I couldnae dae that.
Belle: Oh syet. Why could ye no' grib   Oh yes. Why couldn't you do that?
         that?
Alec: The hantle'd bing me avree. The   The people would take me away. The
         quod.   jail.
Belle: Oh no no, ye could easy grib   Oh no, you could easy get some money
         some looer onyway. Grib some   anyway, get something wouldn't you?
         chaet, wouldn't it?
Alec: My plastie's a bit thin . . .   My plaid is a bit thin . . .
Belle: No, the ploops'd never mang ye   No, the police would never arrest you
         for that. You could easy stiumer.   for that. You could pipe easily. You've
         Ye've gribber'd afore that, man,   done that before, man, and the police
         and the ploops didn't . . .   didn't . . .
Sheila: Ye could mang the hantle and   You could ask them and maybe they'd
         they'd mebbe let ye grib.   let you work.
Belle: You're just getting shy.
Alec: I'll bing the mornin'.   I'll go in the morning.
Belle: You'll bing the morgen?   You'll go tomorrow?
Alec: Ay.
Belle: Barrie, barrie. Beenship.   Good, good. Good.

In assembling the following vocabulary, we have not attempted an
etymological analysis, but have been satisfied to set down merely the
Stewart usage.

Spelling

For the sake of uniformity and purposes of comparison, we have used – for the most part – the same spellings as those employed by McCormick. In a number of cases, the Stewart's given word departed so radically from any interpretation of the McCormick spelling that we spelled the word as logically as we could.

Stress

Primary stress is indicated by a single dot; secondary stress by two dots, thus: bēn păt·rĭnz chāt:. Occasionally, dipthongs occur at mid-syllable, almost creating two syllables out of one – but not quite. We have marked this phenomenon with a small dropped apostrophe underneath the pertinent syllable: mū·tyē may thus be also pronounced mū‚ĭt.yē.

Composite phrases

Where such phrases occur that are made up of other single words to be found elsewhere in the vocabulary, we have merely given a literal English translation instead of duplicating the pronunciation guide.

The vowels

ā   as in ale, break
â   as in there, heir
ă   as in fad
ä   as in ah, bother (see note to ŭ)

ē   as in me, leave, machine
ĕ   as in fend, feather, bury
ę̆   as in weird, hear

ī   as in mice, sleight, guy
ĭ   as in still, guild

ō   as in old, foam
ô   as in order, law
ŏ   as in odd (see note to ŭ)
oi   as in boil, toy
ŏŏ   as in foot, would
ou   as in cow, flower

ū   as in mood, blue
yū   as in beauty, feud
û   as in stern, absurd

ŭ   as in up, dub (*Note*: this sound when not stressed is often
     indistinguishable from ä and ŏ. Travellers will often pronounce this
     vowel with slight differences depending on the surrounding
     consonants.)

The consonants

dʒ   as the sound represented by *j* and *dg* in judge
g   as the sound of *g* in go
gz   as the sound of *x* in exist
hw   as the sound of *wh* in where
ks   as the sound of *x* in six
kw   as the sound of *qu* in queen
ŋ   as the sound of *ng* in ring
ŋg   as the sound of *ng* in finger
r   indicates the soft *r*, as in run
R   indicates the "Scots *r*" a hard consonant produced by fluttering the
     tongue once on the roof of the mouth just behind the teeth. It is as
     if one were saying *ŭdr* as one syllable, but barely pronouncing the
     d. The Stewarts use this hard *r* in much of their speech and it has
     the effect of adding an extra syllable to a word. *Flattrin* becomes
     flatterin, loor becomes *looer*, etc.
TH   as the sound of *th* in tithe
th   as the sound of *th* in thin
χ   as the sound of *ch* in the German ach or the Scots och.

Note: a number of the consonants are borderline cases and are soft or
hard depending on the speed of the speaker, or sometimes depending upon
the nature of the surrounding words. Under varying conditions, the
following changes may take place:
ch may be pronounced *sh* (*kinchens, kinshens*)
d   may be pronounced *dʒ* (*dougal, jougal*)
f   may be pronounced *v* (*holovers, holofers*)
k   may be pronounced *χ*
b   may be pronounced *p*
ch may be pronounced *ty*
Only where this interchangeability is consistent have we given alternative
pronunciations.

Pronunciation in general

Often it is difficult to notate the exact prununication of internal vowels
when the speaker is going at full speed. Vowels often disappear completely
in a rush of consonants, especially in a composite phrase, so that *whuddin
chaet* may become virtually *whdn chaet*, or *moudment* they become

moudmnt. Pronouncing the given consonants quickly in succession will give the correct pronunciation.

The vocabulary

afraid *trash (Aberdeenshire)* trăsh
airplane *broskin elements* (sky carriage)
anything *okri* ôk·rē
apples *han chaets* hăn·chāts
    crunchers kʀŭn·ûrz
apron *fordrum* fôr·dʀŭm
ask *mang* mäŋ
ass *oozel* ū·zl
avenue (of trees, bushes) *remydem* rĕ mī·dm
away *avree* ŭ vʀē·

baby *peekie* pē·kē
bacon *gruffie's karnish* (pig's meat)
bad *shan* shän
badness *shanness* shän·ĕs
bag *blasswug* blăs·wŭg
bagpiper *stiumera cowl* styū·mr̩ŭ koul:
bagpipes *stiumers* styū·mûrz
baker *pennam cowl* (bread man)
bakery *pennam kain* (bread place)
    pennam chova (bread shop)
barn *granzie* grăn·zē
    grennam kain (grain place)
barrow *hurlie* hŭr·lē
basket *ruskie* rŭs·kē
beautiful *barrie* bä·ʀē
    beenship bēn·shĭp
bedclothes *kip fechles* kĭp fē·χlz
beef *karnish* kär·hĭsh
beer *ringel* rĭŋ·l
beggar *sprachin gadgie* spräχ·ĭn gä·dʒē
bell *been patteran's chaet* (good minister's thing)
bent (the plant) *lochkulkin* lŏχ:kŭl·kĭn (lŏχ:kôr·kĭn)
bindweed *fyochins* fyô·χŭnz
bit (little) *cant* kănt
  (a little beer) *a cant peeve* a kănt pĕv
black man *shan cowl* shän koul
blankets *coories* koo·ʀēz (kū·ʀēz)
blind *shan winklers* (bad eyes) (the man has s.w.)

blood   *been yerrim* (good milk)
boat   *beerie*   bē·Rē
body   *moricans*   mô·rĭ knz
bog   *gulyen*   gŭl·yĭn
boiling (as of a kettle)   *wammelin*   wă·mŭ lĭn (wä·mŭ lĭn)
bone   *rulyen*   rŭl·yĭn
bonnet   *scroof*   sкRūf
           kaidie   kā·dē
boots   *strods*   strŭdz (strôdz)
bottle   *ruble*   rū·bl
bowl   *brockler*   brŭk·lûr
bow-tent   *gailee*   gā·lē
boy   *geddie*   gě·dē
bread   *pennam*   pā·nŭm (pě·nŭm)
break (v.)   *mar*   mär (mäR)
brooch   (*see* jewellery)
broken   *marred*   märt
broth   *shach*   shäχ
brother   *sproul*   sproul
bull   *routler*   rout·lûr
burning   (*see* boiling)
burnt   *wammelt*   wă·mŭlt
butcher   *karnish gadgie* (meat man)
butcher's shop   *karnish chova* (meat shop)
butter   *smout*   smout

calf   *young routler* (young bull)
camp   *wattle*   wä·tl
can (container)   *pinkie*   pĭŋ·kē
candle   *deeklie*   dē·klē
car, cart   *broskin*   brôs·kĭn
carriage, coach (horse-drawn)   *purstigie*   pŭR stē·dʒē
cat   *meowin' chaet* (meowing thing)
     meowchaet myou·chēt
chair   *stallin chaet* (sitting thing)
chapel   *whuddin keir* (talking place)
cheat (n.)   *shan cowl* (bad man)
cheese   *kaizum*   kā·zŭm (kā·zĭm)
chemise   (*see* shirt)
child(ren)   *kinchen*(s)   kĭn·shĭn(z) (kĭn·chĭnz)
choke   (*see* kill)
church   (*see* chapel)
cigarettes   *pan chaets*   păn·chēts
cloak   *tippet*   tĭp·pĭt

clock *clocker* clô·kûr
clogs (*see* boots)
clothes *toggerie* tŭg·ʀē
clout, hit (*see* break)
coal *yag* yäg
coat *tog* tŭg
cockroach *boag* bō·ăg
constable *ploop* plūg
         hornie hôʀ·nē
         musker mŭs·kûr
         pleuch plyūχ
         shan cowl (bad man)
corn *grennam* grĕ·nŭm
cup and saucer (*see* dish)
curlew *gulipernicht* gū·lĭ pûr nĕχt:
curse *sallachan* sĕ·lŭ χĭn (să·lŭ χĭn)

day *davies* dā·vēz
daylight *lightment* līt·mŭnt
daughter *sproul* (also *kinchen*) sproul (kĭn·shĭn)
death *moudment* moud·mnt
deserter *nash* năsh
       kliestie bung avree (soldier come away)
devil *ruffie* rŭ·fē
dirty *ajeer* ŭ dʒēṟ·
      akakkie ŭ kä·kē
dish *mahzie* mä·zē
dizziness *meegrin* mē·gʀĭn
dog *buffert* bŭ·fūʀt
     yaffin yă·fĭn
     dougal dū·gl (dʒyū·gl)
dog (pure breed) *been yaffin* (good dog)
    (mongrel) *shan yaffin* (bad dog)
donkey (*see* ass)
door *belliment* bĕl·ĭ mnt (bĭl·ŭ mnt)
drink *peeve* pēv
drunken *peevie* pē·vē
duck *quacker* kwă·kûr

ears *clewishes* klū·ĭ shĭz
earth *lennum* lĕ·nŭm
eat *ha* hä
eel *coiler* koi·lûʀ
eggs *yarras* yä·ʀŭz

eight   *och*   ôχ
eyes   *winklers*   wĭŋ·klûrz

face   *chackers*   chă·kûrz
farm   *grennam kain* (grain house)
father   *naiskel*   nā·skl
feet   *tramplers*   trăm·plûrz
field   *a cant of lennum* (a bit of earth)
fight (v.)   (*see* break)
fine   (*see* good)
finger   *femmel*   fĕ·ml
finger-ring   *femmel granyie*   fĕ·ml grăn:yē
fire   *glimmer*   glĭ·mûr
firewood   *kashties*   kăsh·tēz
                     filshes   fĭl·shĭz
fish   *flattrin*   flă·tRĭn
flour   *pennam chaetrie* (bread things)
folk   *hantle*   hăn·tl
food   *habben*   hä·bn
fool (n.)   *cull*   kŭl
forest   *baysh*   bāsh
fortune-telling   *drukkin*   dRū·kĭn (dRŭ·kĭn)
                             drukkerin   dRū·kRĭn
frock   *hinger*   hĭŋ·ûr
frog   *lowpin chaet* (jumping thing)   lou·pĭn chāt:

garden   (*see* earth)
get   *feek*   fēk
gentle   *beenship*   bēn·shĭp
gentlewoman   *been mort* (good woman)
girl   *dillie*   dĭ·lē
             goorie   gū·Rē
give   *grib*   gRĭb
Glasgow   *a been vile* (a large town)
go   *ja*   dʒä
        nash   năsh
        bing   bĭŋ
go away   *bing avree*   bĭŋ: ŭ vRē·
go in   *bing anee*   bĭŋ: ŭ nē·
go on   *bing anay*   bĭŋ: ŭ nā·
goat   (*see* sheep)
gold   *looer*   lŭ·r (lū·ûR)
God   *been cowl* (good man)

good (ness) *been* bēn
                  beenship (ness) bēn·shĭp (nĕs)
granary (*see* barn)
grand *barrie* bä·rē
great (*see* grand)
grandfather *gran-naiskel* grăn·nā: skl
grandmother *gran-naismort* grăn·nās: môRt
grass *faizim* fā·zŭm (fā·zĭm)

half-crown *yowp* youp
hand *femmel* fĕ·ml
          famm făm
handbasin *femmel brucklie* fĕ·ml bRŭk·lē
handkerchief *nab chaet* (nose thing)
ha'penny *make* māk
hare *makken* mä·kĭn
hay (*see* grass)
head *test* tĕst (tĕs)
hear (*see* listen)
hedge *ticknie baysh* (small wood)
hen *gaunie* gä·nē
horn *meggis chaet* (sheep thing) mĕ·gĭs chāt
horse *gry* grī (gRī)
          prod prôd (pRôd)
horsedealer *gry-gribber* (horse worker)
                  gry-gadgie (horse man)
                  gry-nakkin (horse tinker)
hose, hosiery *holovers* hô·lĭ fûrz (hô·lĭ vûrz)
hot (*see* boiling, burnt)
house *kain* kān
          keir kẹr (kēR)

in *anee* ŭ nē·
Irish (the people) *bulyarrans* bool yä·Rn
                          boonyuchers būn·yŭχ ûrz
itchy *yuckie* yô·χē

jewellery (*see* gold)
              chaetrie (things)
              been looer chaetrie (good gold things)
jug (*see* dish)

kale *shach* shäχ

kettle   *kekavie*   kŭ kä·vē (kûr kä·vē)
    (*see* pot, for cooking)
kettle props, tripod   *chittie*(s)   chĭ·tēz
key   *yaik*   yāk
    cowie   kou·ē
kill(ed)   *moud*(it)   moud (mou·dĭt)
kilt   *coorin*   kū·ʀĭn
kindest   *barriest*   bä·rē ĕst
king   *been cowl* (good man)
kiss (n.)   *mookie*   moo·kē
  to be kissed   *to be mookied*
  to give a kiss   *to bing a mookie*
knife   *cutler* ("a buck's word")   kŭt·lûr
    choorie   chū·ʀē (tū·ʀē)
knocker   *belliment chaet* (door thing)
know   *jan*   dʒän

lady   (*see* woman)
lamb   (*see* sheep)
large   *barrie*   bä·ʀē
    (*see* good)
lice   *paries*   pä·ʀēz
licence (pedlar's)   *slang*   släŋ
light   *deeklie*   dēk·lē
listen   *soonie*   sū·nē
lizard   *mankeeper*   măn·kē pûr
lodgings   *skipper*   skĭ·pûʀ
look, look at   *pyre*   pī·ûʀ

mad   *raj*   rädʒ
madman   *raja gadgie* (mad man)   rä·dʒa gä·dʒē
magistrate   *shan ploop* (bad constable)
magpie   *jaypyot*   dʒä pī·ût
man   *cowl* (Perthshire)   koul
    gadgie (Aberdeenshire)   gä·dʒē
    bodyach   bôd·yäχ
marry   *akum*   ä·km
  married   *akumt*   ä·kmt
  getting married   *feekin akumt*   fē·kĭn ä·kmt
match   *blinkum*   blĭŋ·kŭm
    deeklie   dē·klē
meal   *bla*   blä
meat   *karnish*   käʀ·nĭsh
metal   (old)   *casties* ("ayĕ, castirons")   kăs·tēz

midget, small man *pech* pĕχ
mild (*see* good)
milk *yerrim* yĕ·ʀm
  sour milk *shan yerrim* (bad milk)
minister *patteran* pä·tʀĭn
monkey *swinger* ("O, that's a horrible thing to say!") swĭŋ·ûr
moonlight night *been darkment* (good night)
morning *morgen* môr·gn (môʀ·gĕn)
mother *naismort* näs·môʀt
mouth *mun* mŭn
move on *nash avree* (go away)
myself *my nagin* mī nä·gĭn

name (n.) *lav* läv
  (to name someone, to *bing someone their lav*)
neck *scrabben* skrä·bn
neckerchief (*see* scarf)
needle *bavver chaet* (sewing thing)
night *darkmans* därk·mnz
no *ruffert* rŭ·fûʀt
nose *nab* năb
nothing *nix* nĭks
      nitchles nĭch·lz

one *yaik* yāk
other *vavver* väv·ûr
ourselves *wor nagins* wôr nä·gnz

pail *pinkie* pĭŋ·kē
pay *pacer* pä·sûr
pease *groats* grōts
peats *glimmer chaets* (fire things)
penis *carrie* kä·ʀē
penny *wun* wŭn
people, folk *hantle* hăn·tl
petticoat *mort's toggerie* (woman's clothes)
pig *gruffie* grŭ·fē (grŭ·χē)
pin (ornamental) *skivver* skĭ·vûʀ
pin (small) *prinkler* prĭŋ·klûr
pipe (for smoking) *stiumer* styū·mûr
piper (*see* bagpiper)
pistol *marrin chaet* (fighting thing)
pitcher *chappin can* chă·pĭn kăn
place (*see* house)

plaid *plastie* plăs·tē
plantation (*see* woods)
plough *lennum chaet* (earth thing)
    gry's chaet (horse's thing)
pocket *poris* pô·rĭs
policeman feekie (*see* constable) fē·kē
poorhouse *parrin kain* pä·ʀĭn kän:
porage *paplers* păp·lûrz
pot (cooking, quart-pot) *blackie* blă·kē
potatoes *neds* nĕdz
    mutteramingoes ("a gypsy word") mŭ:tûr ŭ mĭŋg· ōz
    bulrumpies bŭl ʀŭm·pēz
pound note *reej* rēdʒ
preacher *naiskel* (father) nā·skl
prison *staurdie* stär·dē
    quod kwäd
prostitute *loodnie* lūd·nē
pub *peevin kain* (drinking house)

rabbit *muitie* mū·chē (mū·tyē, mū, ĭt·yē)
radio *whuddin chaet* (talking thing)
rags *fechles* fē·χlz
rat *lyeuchie* lyū·χē
red *ruadh* rū·ôd
rhubarb *shelaga* shĕ·lŭ gŭ
  wild rhubarb *dishie laga* dĭ·shē lä·gŭ
rich man *been looer cowl* (good gold man)
ring *granyie* grăn·yē
road *lig* lĭg
rock *cadyuch* käd·yŭχ
rosin *rozet* rŏ·zĕt

sausages *moricans* mô·rĭ knz
sabbath *been davies* (good day)
salt *salliment* sĕ·lĭ mnt
scarf *napyen* nāp·yĕn
    scroof skʀŭf (skʀūf)
sea *panie* pô·nē (pä·nē)
    (*see* water)
see *deek* dēk
self *nagin* nā·gĭn
sell *wanner* wä·nûr
servant maid *dill* dĭl
sew *bavver* bä·vûr

shawl (*see* plaid)
sheep *meggat* mĕ·gĕt (mĕ·gĭt)
shells (for making of jewellery) *sheepy-mez* shē·pē mĕz
                        mydyeuchs mī·dyŭχz
shilling *hog* hôg
        juss dʒoos
  two shillings *deuce* dyūs
shirt *kirmush* kûr·mŏŏsh (krĕ·mŏŏsh)
shoes (*see* boots)
shoemaker *strod cowl* (boot man)
shop *chova* chō·vŭ (chō·vûr)
shut *grib* grĭb (gʀĭb)
silver (*see* gold)
sister *sproul* sproul
sit *stall* stĕl
sixpence *sy* sī
          syce sīs
sky *elements* ĕl·ī mnts
sleep *slum* slŭm
  go to sleep *bing to slum*
small *ticknie* tĭk·nē
  smallest possible item *freedyeuch* frēd·yŭχ
soap *sapler* săp·lûʀ
soldier *kliestie* klē·stē
soup *shach* shäχ
  soup vegetables *shach chaetrie* (soup things)
son *chavvie* chŏ·vē
      geddie gĕ·dē
sparrow *spuggie* spŭ·gē
speak *mang* mäŋ
spectacles *prospecs* prŏ·spĕks
          winkler chaets (eye things)
spoon *tillum* tĭ·lŭm
stay (*see* sit)
steal (ing) *chor(in)* chôr (chôʀ·ĭn)
         kly klī
stick and staff *filsh and castie* fĭlsh and căs·tē
sticks *casties* căs·tēz
stockings (*see* hose)
stomach *moricans* mô·rī knz
stone (weight) *clach* kläχ
stop (*see* sit)
straw *strammel* stʀă·ml
stupid *moich* moiχ

sugar *sweetnie* swēt·nē
sword (*see* knife)

talking *whuddin* hwŭdn
tea *weed* wēd
     slab (Aberdeenshire) släb
teapot *weed mahzie* (tea dish)
teeth *crunchers* kRŭn·chûRz (krŭn·chûrz)
telephone *whuddin chaet* (talking thing)
television *whuddin chaet* (talking thing)
thigh *lisk* lĭsk (lŭsk)
thing, things *chaet, chaetrie* chāt (chēt); chā·tRē
three *thrums* thRŭmz
tobacco *fluffan* flŭfn (flŭf·ŭn)
tongue *mangen* mäŋ·ĕn
  hold your tongue *stall your mangen*
tongs *glimmer chaets* (fire things)
town *vile* vīl
          gaave gäv
train *rattler* răt·lûr
Traveller (well-off) *screeve* skrēv (skRēv)
Traveller (ordinary) *nakkin* nä·kĭn
                    kyards (Buchan usage) kyärds
                    gangerel bodies (Aberdeenshire) găŋ·ŭr ĕl bŭ:dēz
tree (*see* stick)
trouble (*see* badness)
trousers *brickets* bRĭ·kĭts
          calshes kăl·shĭz
turnip *sneep* snyĕp
two *juce* dʒūs (dʒūz)
twopence *juce wuns* dʒūz wŭnz

umbrella *mush* mŭsh
umbrella mender *mush feeker* mŭsh·fä:kûr
uncle (father's brother) *naiskel's sproul* nä·sklz sproul
  (mother's brother) *naismort's sproul* näs·môrts sproul

vagina *blut* blŭt
          juravil dʒûr·ŭ vl
vegetables for soup *chaetrie for bingin' anee shach* (things for putting into
  soup)
village *ticknie vile* (small town)

watch (*see* clock)

water   *monteclear*   môn·tĭ klḙr
       panie (Jimmy Higgins says that this is Hindustani)   pä·nā
wheelbarrow   (*see* barrow)
whisky   *peeve*   pēv
window   *widdera*   wĭ·dŭ rŭ
woman   *racklie* (Romani)   rä·klē
      manishie (slang)   mă·nĭ shē
      mort (the cant)   môʀt
  old woman   *cailleach*   kăl·yăχ (koul·yăχ)
work   *grib*   gʀĭb (grĭb)
write   *screeve*   skʀēv (skʀēv)

yes   *syet*   sĭ·ĕt

THE FOLKTALES

Introduction

The storyteller's art is highly regarded in Scots Traveller communities and a surprisingly large number of traditional tales are still current there. Over the last twenty years or so we have interviewed many Travellers, several of whom have had extensive repertoires of stories of various types. All of them, without exception, have been able to tell at least one or two tales. This is not to say that all Travellers regard themselves as storytellers any more than all those who can sing a song or two would describe themselves as singers. It is not uncommon for a Traveller to begin a session by saying, "I'm no' a singer but I ken one or two songs". We have had the experience of recording some thirty songs and ballads from a man who, at the end of the recording session, said, "Of course, I'm no' the singer o' the faimily, I'm the storyteller". In the Stewart family, it was Alec who was The Storyteller, though the other members of the family can also tell stories and tell them well.

Sheila sees the stories as belonging to two distinct categories:

There's a children's section, stories like 'Appley and Orangey', something to attract the children and prepare them for the bigger stories. A wee bairn wouldnae understand tales like 'The Fiery Balls'. That was too educational for a wee bairn, so they started them off wi' a tale like 'Appley and Orangey'. You've got to capture a bairn's imagination wi' things like that and then when they get older you tell them bigger stories.

In the Stewart family, the children's tale category is divided into two parts: standard folktales and improvised stories. Belle says that Alec made up most of the tales he told his children "and they were nearly all in cant". In the course of a discussion of the storyteller's art, which took place in August 1979, Belle observed:

When Alec's telling a story, or Big Willie MacPhee, you'll look at them and you'll weigh them up and they're enjoying it thoroughly themselves. They're not only telling it for the rest of the company, to entertain them, but you can see by their attitude, by the look on their faces, that they're enjoying it themselves. They're entertaining *themselves*, amusing *themselves*, as well as telling it to the company. They put their whole heart into it and that's the thing that tickles me. Sometimes

you'll have heard the story dozens of times before and there'll be bits left out of it
and different bits added but it'll still be very amusing and entertaining. And Alec or
Willie or whoever's telling it will be living the story.

John Stewart, Alec's brother, was away in Canada during the time we
were first recording the family. We met him for the first time in 1979 and he
recorded the following passage:

When we were travelling, way back in camping times, you know, my father would
make a big fire, the tent would go up and we'd be sent for straw to make a big straw
bed in the tent. Everything was comfortable enough, even though it was camping.
And we always had plenty of grub in the pot. Well, we'd a' get to bed wi' a candle or
mebbe a hurricane lamp and we, the bairns, would a' start girnin' and shoutin' to my
faither or my mither to tell us a story. And we'd lie wi' the candle burnin' in the tent
and mebbe the wind'd be wheein', y'know, or the rain patterin', or mebbe a distant
thunder roll.

Someone'd be tellin' a story, and you know this? It was better than the telly! It was
that ... there you were, cooerin' right down in this lovely big straw bed, warm
and mebbe fighting each other to see who would be getting the blankets; and my
faither or mither telled a story. And sometimes you'd get two camps, two bow-
tents, you know, joined at the centre by a bivvy. Y'know, a tent on each side wi' a
fire in the middle. The people in the other tent would mebbe be strangers or
mebbe you'd ken them, it didnae matter ... your folks would tell a story and then
someone in the other tent would tell one and you'd be lyin' there listenin'. It was
great!

Among Scots Travellers, the two most popular story types are those
which deal with ghostly encounters and the ones commonly known as
Burkers – tales inspired by the exploits of Burke and Hare, the two
notorious body-snatchers who plied their trade in Edinburgh between 1827
and 1829. 'Granny in a Bag' and 'Bogle Brig' both belong in the *Burker*
category. On the whole, the *Burker* tales show little of the inventiveness
that characterises so many of the older tales; their plots are depressingly
hackneyed and their characters are as stereotyped as the interchangeable
cops and robbers of television drama. Storytellers generally preface
Burkers by stating: "This is a true story", or "This actually happened", and
then proceed to underline the non-fictional nature of the narrative by tying
it in with an incident involving a member – or members – of the
storyteller's family.

The creation of a credible world, or a world in which the incredible can
be made to appear credible is, of course, central to the storyteller's art. A
good storyteller can transform even the most threadbare Burker tale into a
fascinating narrative; conversely, an indifferent storyteller can bury the
most fascinating tale under a mass of trivial detail. We have heard, for
instance, 'The Black Bull of Norrowa' told at inordinate length (54
minutes) and in such a way that the main line of the story was lost in a
morass of superfluous information.

Oddly enough, the most fluent speakers are often the poorest storytellers;

loquacity is generally the cause of their undoing. Their habit of dotting every *i* and crossing every *t* while providing parenthetical commentaries on the action destroys the natural rhythm of a tale and inhibits the listener's imagination. The skilful storyteller uses words with the same familiarity and the same care that a cabinet-maker handles his saw and his chisels. His art lies in creating the right balance between fantasy and reality, between the extraordinary and the prosaic, between the mass and the detail.

Maria Campbell, Alec Stewart's mother, appears to have possessed more than her share of the special skills that are needed to make a good teller of tales. Her repertoire was, by all accounts, enormous and among older Travellers there are those who still talk about her "uncanny way wi' an auld tale". All her children have been inspired by her example. Alec, in particular, was a storyteller of compelling power and, fortunately, both Cathie and Sheila have inherited some of his skill.

List of folktales

1	The Bumbee and the Pishmol	19	The Leprechauns
2	The Fiery Balls	20	The Miller and his Daughter
3	The Cripple in the Churchyard	21	The Headless Man
4	Jack and the Puddock	22	The Beech-hedge Wager
5	Silver and Gold	23	How Muckle Hour got its
6	The Vinegar Bottle		Name
7	Appley and Orangey	24	Granny in a Bag
8	The Laddie that Became a Lass	25	Bogle Brig
9	The Three Wishes	26	The Ugly Man
10	The Scabby Heid	27	The Deer Child
11	The Ghost in the Chapel	28	The Dead Cheroot
12	The Auld Man's Wake	29	The Strange Bird
13	The Ghost Wife	30	The Ghostly Gatepost
14	The Devil Lover	31	Granny's Still
15	The Duke of Roxburgh's Soul	32	The Beggarman and the
16	The Auld Couple's Son		Minister
17	Sheep's Turlies	33	The Wrestler
18	The King of the Liars	34	The Woman on the Scales
		35	OOT!

In relating texts to international tale types, we have followed the system set down in the Aarne-Thompson *Type Index*. Motif-numbers are from Stith Thompson's *Motif-Index*.

1 THE BUMBEE AND THE PISHMOL
(*Cathie Higgins*)

Onc't upon a time this was a wee bumbee, and she bade away in this wood intae a tree. This bumbee had a big faimily. She had aboot ten or twelve o' a faimily, and they were a' young. So she was busy cleanin' awa' at her hoose, her and the bairns, and they're cleanin' awa', and the mother says, "Well", says she, "bairns, I'll hae to go awa' to the toon", she says, "to get twa or three messages." She was kind o' low on the rations.

So the mither dresses hersel' up and puts her coat on and her wee shawl and her hat and her twa wee baskets on her airm, and off she goes. But before she goes away, she says, "Noo listen, bairns: mind and look aifter the hoose. Keep the fire on and the kettle boiling and dinnae answer the door, nae matter wha comes to the door."

So away she goes, and she's fleein' awa' till she comes to the toon. And of course after she'd got her messages and twa or three odds and ends, she'd to get the bairns a' different kinds o' sweeties. So she's makin' her way hame noo and oh my God, the clouds gets awfae dark, and the rain begins to pour doon and thunder and lightin'.

"Well", says she, "I dinnae ken hoo I'm gaun tae get hame the nicht because", she says, "it's gaun to be an awfae nicht." So she comes on and she tears on, and she had tae walk. And her twa-three messages is gettin' kind o' weet. Until she comes up and she says, "I think I'll gan to the king o' the pishmols. Surely to God", says she, "he'll let me in for the night wi' a' this rain fa'in'."

So up she goes to the door and she knocks at the door, and out comes a wee pishmol wi' its wee white apron and its white hat. It was a servant.

"I wonder", says she, "wad ye gang to the king o' the pishmols and ask him if he wad let me in for shelter till I dry my wings and my bits o' claes till I get hame to my bairns?"

"Oh well", says she, "I'll have to go and ask the master himself." So away goes the wee pishmol. But when she goes to the king, the king says, "Na na! Tell the bumbee to haud awa' hame, she's get nae nicht's shelter in here."

So out the servant goes, she says, "I'm very sorry, madam", she says, "but the king of the pishmols won't allow you in."

"Very well", says she, "some time or other he'll need a nicht's shelter fae me and we'll see whit we'll dae then." So on the road goes the wee bumbee, and she trods on and she trods on. Oh, that's well onto the mornin' afore she lands hame, because her wings was that wet that she couldnae flee. So when she comes in, the bairns is a' upside doon and the place is in an uproar.

"What happened to ye, mither, in the name o' God whit kept ye till this time o' morn afore ye got hame?"

"Well", says she, "my wings were soakin' wet and I couldnae get hame,
I couldnae flee."

"What did ye get me, mammy? What did ye get me?" And there's the
way they're carryin' on, till she issued oot the sweeties that she'd bocht
them. So they pit on their tea, on their dinner, whatever they're gaun tae
hae, and they ate their wee bite o' meat onyway.

So the time come on for the shootin' noo, and a' the gentry was a'
shootin' through the wood, and oh, they're havin' a great carry-on. So the
king o' the pishmols he's oot and he's doin his best, shootin' awa' intae the
wood for the hens and the cocks and other kinds o' things they shoot, and
the pheasant and the rabbits and the hares.

So out come an awfae nicht o' thunder and lightnin' – it just fair poured
doon. So the king o' the pishmols says, "I know what we'll do", he says,
"we'll go to the bumbee", he says. "*She* won't refuse me a night's shelter."
So up he goes to the bumbee's hoose and he chaps at the door and oh my
God, it was a night not fit for man or beast.

So out comes the wee bumbee. He says, "I wonder", he says, "Mistress
Bumbee, will you let me have a night's shelter here?" he says. "It's a
terrible night", he says, "not fit for man or beast."

"Ay", says she, "King, do you mind the nicht", says she, "that I was
awa' to the toon and I asked *you* for a nicht's shelter? And what did you
tell me?"

"Oh", he says, "surely to God you'll let bygones be bygones!"

"Na, na!" says she. "Nae fear! You tak' this," says she, "and think
yourself lucky you're gettin' aff wi' that." And she threw the pot of boilin'
kale that was on the fire aboot his heid.

And he was burnt alive, and that's the end o' my story.

Type: similar to 280A (The ant and the lazy cricket).
Motifs: Q. 2 (*King and unkind*); B. 857 (*Revenge taken for injury by one animal on
another*).

2   THE FIERY BALLS
(*Alec Stewart*)

This is a story about a fisherman and his auld wife. They stayed not far
from the shore and they never had nae family. So one day the auld man
was out on the sea and he was fishin' away and fishin' away and he heard a
baby cryin'. And he's lookin' all round him tae see where the baby was
cryin'. And he lookit just round the back of the stern of the boat and there
was a basket and he got his oar and he pulled in the basket. And this was a
baby was in the basket.

So he took the baby out and lookit at it and it was a wee boy. He lookit all round about him to see if there was a big ship there or any kind o' a boat at all.

"I don't know where that baby come from", he says, so he waited for a while to see if onybody would come and claim the baby. Then he oared his boat right in tae the shore and he says, "Wife, ye're aye cryin' for a bairn, aye speakin' about a baby tae me. Well", he says, "I've got one now. Have a look at this one."

So he put the basket down on the floor and the baby's startin' tae cry. So the auld wife she made a dive at the basket and took the bairn oot, and she says, "Where did ye get this baby?"

He says, "I got it in that basket, floatin' in the sea."

And she says, "Were there no boats round about?"

He says, "No, no – no boats. I made sure o' that."

So they kept the baby for months and months and months and then it happened to be years and years, till the baby was about fourteen year auld, a wee boy. One day he was doon tae the shore sortin' the nets and he lookit out to sea and he saw this big ship. And there was a captain on the deck o' this ship and he was throwin' these seven fiery balls up in the air. They were a' on fire, and he was throwin' them up and throwin' them up and throwin' them up.

And the young boy said tae the auld man, "Look at that man! What's he doin' wi' they seven fiery balls? I wish to God", he says, "*I* could do that."

And the auld man lookit oot and he says, "My God, he's good, he's very good."

So they sat doon and they're mendin' the nets when they saw a wee boat gettin' lowered tae the sea and it cam' oarin' in. In it was the captain and two sailors.

"Well, man, you're sortin' your nets."

"Ay", the auld man says, "I am that."

"That's a nice boy ye've got there."

"Oh ay", he says.

Noo, the auld man thought the captain had come tae claim the boy, but no, he didn't. He just says, "Could I have that boy for a year? And", he says, "I'll make him one of the cleverest boys in the warld. I'll make him that he can do anything then."

"Oh", says the auld man, "I cannae tell ye that, ye'll have tae come up and see the auld wife and see whit she says."

So they went up tae the hoose and the auld man said tae his wife, "This captain here wants the boy for a year. He says he'll make him the cleverest boy in the warld."

"Well", she says, "If ye promise to bring him back within the year I'll let him go."

"Oh", the captain says, "I'll hae him back all right." So the young boy he's got his clothes packed up and he's away in this ship now, away in the ship.

So time passed till the year come up and the auld man was doon on the shore lookin' oot to see if the ship had come in. And while he was stannin' there and lookin', he seen the ship come in and the wee boy was on the top o' the deck and he was throwin' the seven fiery balls up. And he's throwin' them up and throwin' them up. Then he stoppit and he stannit and he's wavin' tae his father at the shore. So they come in tae the shore and the captain says, "Well, what do you think of your boy now?"

"My God", he says, "He's doin' it just as good as you now wi' the seven fiery balls."

"Oh ay", he says, "but I can make him cleverer than that. If ye gie him tae me anither year I'll guarantee he'll be twice better than he is."

"Oh, ye'll have tae see the auld wife", the auld man says. "Ye'll hae tae go up and see the auld wife, for if I was tae gie ye my word the noo to take him away, I wad just be killed by her."

So they went up and they asked the auld woman would he get the wee boy for anither year. And the auld woman says, "Well, he was away a year already and I missed him."

"Oh", but the captain says, "I'll guarantee he'll be back in a year's time."

"Well, well", she says, "take him away, but be sure and come back, mind."

So the young boy, he went away wi' the captain. And a year passed, and eichteen month passed and the boy didnae come back. So the auld wife she got a besom and she's layin' intae the auld man. "Ye'd better go and find the boy at once. Either that", she says, "or *you* go away and never come back."

So the auld man, he got a bannock bakit and he's away lookin' for the young boy, now. And he's comin' on this road and comin' on this road till he went for about fifty or sixty mile and he come tae this wee hoose at the roadside and he rappit at the door. And wha come oot but a man.

"Ah", he says, "I was expectin' ye. I heard word ye was comin'," he says. "They tell me you're lookin' for your boy."

"How d'ye know that?"

"Ah", he says, "birds tell me a' these things. Ye'll better come in and get something tae eat first." So he went in and he got his food and the man says, "There's your bed, ye can lie there till morn. I'll tell ye a' aboot it in the morn."

So the auld man, he went tae his bed.

The next mornin' when he got up, the man says tae him, "Now, ye go on for another hunder mile and ye'll come tae anither wee hoose at the roadside, and that", he says, "is a' that I can tell ye."

"That's a' ye can tell me?"

"Yes", he says, "you carry on till ye come to the next hoose."

So he went on and on and on and on till he come tae this hoose. And he rappit at the door. The door opened and here's anither auld man. And he says, "Aye, c'wa' in. My brither sent me ward ye was comin'. Come awa' in, and get somethin' t' eat." So he gaed in and he got his food and the auld man says tae him, "Noo, ye can get tae your bed and I'll tell ye in the morn where ye can find your son."

In the mornin, when he'd had his breakfast, he says, "Can ye tell me where my son is now?"

"No", says the man o' the hoose, "I can't tell you. I got ward in the middle o' the night that ye'll hae to go on for anither hunder mile."

So he's marchin' on this road and marchin' on this road till he come tae a wee hoose again and he rappit at the door and anither auld man come oot.

"Come away in", he says. "I was expectin' you. I got word ye was comin'." So the auld man is intae the hoose and he got his tea and whitever he's gettin' t' eat. And the man says tae him, "There's your bed, I'll tell ye in the mornin' where your son is."

The auld man says, "I hope you won't be the same as your ither brithers, for they told me naething at all."

"Och", says the man, "I'll tell ye in the mornin'."

So he got up in the mornin' and he got his breakfast. "Now", says the man, "I'll tell ye. Ye go on aboot ten or twelve mile alang this road. It's a sea captain ye're lookin' for?"

And the auld man says, "Yes, it's a sea captain."

"Your son's there", he says, "and they're looking for a groom to look after the horses in the stables. Just gang up tae the door and ring the bell and ask for that job and ye'll get it."

"Oh", but he says, "where's my son?"

"Ye'll find him", says the man, "when ye go there and get the job."

So he come tae this big hoose and he rung the bell. And the butler come oot and he says, "Well, what do *you* want?"

"I'm lookin' for a boy", he says, "my son. I lost him over twa year ago. Are there any strange men or boys roond aboot here?"

"Well", says the man, "I hear tell that there's three or four strange men workin' up at the big hoose. If ye go up there, ye might hear ward o' him."

So he marched away up tae this big hoose and he rappit at the door, and wha come oot but a butler. And the butler asked him what he wanted.

He says, "I'm lookin' for a young chap. Fair-haired, blue eyes, and he's aboot five-foot-five or six. Have ye seen him?"

"I don't know", the butler says, "but I'll go and ask the gentleman." So he went away, and while he was gone, the wee boy come roond the corner and he says, "Oh dad, is that you?"

And the auld man says, "Ay."

And the boy says, "We'd better run and try and get away." So the two of them ran doon the road and they sent the butler after them but he couldnae catch them. At last the boy says, "Faither, I learned a lot while I was wi' that gentleman. I can turn mysel' intae onything, onything at a'," he says. "But before we can go home, we'll hae to get some money."

"All right, laddie, if ye can dae it."

"Oh", he says, "I can dae it a' right. When we come to this toon, there's gaun to be a mairket. I'll turn mysel' intae a horse," he says, "intae a stallion. You walk me through the town and offer to sell me to the first buyer, but he'll try and get the helter. But you tak' the helter aff me", he says. "Then I'll be able to come back tae ye."

The auld man says, "All right."

So they come to the toon and the laddie turns hissel' intae a stallion and he's prancin' up and doon in the mairket. And a man comes across and he says, "Are ye sellin' the stallion?"

"Yes, I'll sell the stallion. I'll sell ye the stallion at a big price, but I can't let ye hae the helter, I cannae gie ye the helter."

"All right", says the man, "tak' the helter aff him."

So the man's away wi' the stallion, leaving the helter in the auld man's hand. He was just aboot half-a-mile oot o' the toon when the laddie jumpit oot and he says, "All right, faither. You done well there. Now the next time", he says, "I'll turn mysel' intae a greyhoond, and you'll do the same that ye done wi' the horse. Just take the collar aff my neck."

The auld man says, "All right."

So they come intae a toon and the laddie turns hissel' intae a greyhoond and oh, he was a nice dog. Jist a beauty o' a dog. And a fairmer comes up tae the auld man and he says, "What'r ye wantin' for the greyhoond dog?"

The auld man asked a price for it, nearly twa-three hunder pound.

"All right", says the fairmer, "I'll tak' him."

"Ye cannae get the collar on his neck", says the auld man. "I cannae gie ye the collar."

"Well, just gie me the loan o' it, so that I can see him rin up and doon the road here." So he got the loan o' the collar and he's away and he never come back. So the auld man is just as bad as ever he was. He had to go and look for his son again. So he's back tae the big hoose and on the way there he met an auld man and he said, "Did ye get your son?"

"Yes", he says, "I got him but I lost him again."

"Aha, laddie. I kent ye wad loss him again", he says. "They're fly up in that big hoose, and I ken he's there because I feed them every day."

"Feed them every day, whit d'ye mean?" says the auld man.

"I mean that the gentleman's turned him intae an auld horse, your son, and he's intae the stable, and I doot ye'll ever get him oot."

"My God", he says, "how's that?"

"Just you go up and see", he said. "Ye'll find him in the end stall, the farthest wee stall."

So he's marchin' doon the road and doon the road till he come tae the big hoose and he rings the bell, and the butler come oot. "I hear you're lookin' for a groom", he says, "to look after the horses."

The butler says, "Yes, but the gentleman is away on the hill today. But we're lookin' for a groom." And he says, "Ye see that wee hoose doon there?"

The auld man says, "Yes."

"Well", he says, "that's where ye'll be stayin'." And he says, "Twice a day ye must feed the horses and gie them a drink. They got water this mornin' but tonight ye'll hae tae gie them anither drink, a bucket apiece."

So the auld man went doon to the hoose and he made some tea and he sits there waitin'. Aboot five o'clock he went down to feed the horses. So he fed the first horse and he fed the second horse. There were six horses in the stable, and he fed them a' but one, the one in the end stall.

Then he went in, and the horse said, "Ah, faither, I knew ye wad come for me. I'm tied here", he says, "and I cannae get away. This helter's roond my neck but once I hae it aff I can get away ony time. But", he says, "I cannae get the helter aff my heid." And he says, "Ye're supposed to gie me one bucket o' water."

And the auld man says, "Yes".

"Well", he says, "tomorrow mornin' when ye come tae feed me, tak' me oot tae the river", he says, "and gie me a drink."

"But", the auld man says, "I'm no' supposed to tak' ye doon tae the river."

"It doesn't matter, faither", says the horse. "It's the only way I can get away. The gentleman'll be on the hill and a' the gamekeepers'll be on the hill. So that'll be oor chance when we're at river."

The next mornin' he got up and went oot to feed the horses, and he seen all the gentlemen gaun away tae the hill and the gamekeepers away tae the hill, and the beaters. So he went intae the stable and he fed a' the horses but the last one. And when he went intae the last stall, the horse says, "Now, faither – tak' me oot. They're a' away at the hill and they can't see ye. But", he says, "once ye take the helter aff my heid a' the bells o' this big castle'll ring and they'll make back."

"A' right", the auld man says. "But what'll I do then?"

"You run", says the horse. "Get away on the road as fast as you can. They'll no' bother *you*", he says, "it's *me* they'll be after."

So the auld man lowsed the horse and he took it down to the river. "Now", says the horse, "tak' aff the helter fae my heid." So he took the helter aff the horse's heid and the horse dived right intae the middle o' the river and turned intae a saumon. And it's swimmin' away up the river. And the bells start to ring in the castle and they're ringin' and ringin' and the horses was gallopin' doon wi' gentleman and the gamekeepers. And the auld man started to run up the road. And he's rinnin' and rinnin' till he got aboot ten or twel' mile on the road.

And that comes back noo tae the young lad. He was swimmin' up this river as a saumon and the gentleman come tae the water-edge and he dived intae the water and he turned intae an otter. Well, he's swimmin' after this saumon and the saumon says, "Well, if I keep mysel' intae a saumon they'll catch me, for the otter's faster than the saumon. I think", he says, "I'll turn mysel' intae a hawk."

So he turns hissel' intae a hawk and he's away intae the air, flyin'. And when the gentleman seen that, he turned hissel' intae an eagle and he's after the hawk. So they were passin' owre a great big castle and the hawk lookit doon and he seen this chiminey. And the eagle was just gaun tae catch the hawk when he dived right doon intae the chiminey, and he turned intae a ring on a girl's finger, lyin' in the bed. And the lassie cried, "Oh, what's that?"

"Don't be alarmed", the ring said, "It's me", he says, "I'm Jeck. I was caught by this wild gentleman at the castle doon the road aboot forty-fifty mile fae here and they're after me. But", he says, "don't you tell onybody you've got the ring, not even your faither or your mither there. And in the mornin'", he says, "when ye get up, the bell'll ring at the front door and there'll be two men lookin' for a job."

"What will I tell them?" she says.

He says, "I'll let ye know when they come."

So next mornin', she got up and the bells started tae ring. The butler went oot and he come back and he told the auld gentleman, the king, "There 's two men at the door", he says. "They're builders and they're lookin' for a job."

"Oh", says the king, "I'm lookin' for builders to build me anither castle. This castle's too wee for me," he says.

"Well", the butler says, "Will I ask them in?"

"Ay, ask them in." When they come, he says, "So you're lookin' for a job?"

They says, "Ay."

"Well", he says, "I'm lookin' for somebody for to build a castle for me. How long would it tak' ye tae build one?"

"It'll tak' us one night", says one o' the men.

"What!" says the king, "Just one night?"

"Ay, I'll build one o' the finest castles in the warld in one night's time."

And the king says, "That'll surely cost a lot of money."

"It'll cost ye naethin' at all", says the man, "but the ring that's on your lass's finger there."

So the king lookit roond and he says tae the lassie, "Have you got a ring on your finger?"

And the girl says, "Yes, there it is."

"Well, will ye gie it tae these twa men for building a castle tae me?"

"Yes", she says, "I will. But before I gie them the ring they must build a great big bonfire. And", she says, "I want two bags o' barley scattered roond the bonfire."

"Oh", but the man says, "we'll dae that."

So these two men they started awa' to build this castle now, and a' the folk in the castle went tae their beds. The next mornin', the king got up and he lookit oot the window and he seen this great big castle three times as big as the one he was stayin' in and it was a' diamonds. And it was goin' round and round and round on the hill. "Goodness gracious", says the king. "That's a great castle."

And the builder says, "Yes, that's a great castle. And now", he says, "what about my ring?"

"Oh", says the king, "wait a minute. We must celebrate this castle wi' a bonfire."

So they built this great big bonfire and they got three or four bags o' barley and they scattered it roond the bonfire. "Now", the lassie says, "you want this ring."

And the gentleman, the builder, says, "Yes."

"Well", she says, "before ye get it, there's the ring!" and she cast it, she throwed it intae the centre o' the fire. So the builders turned theirsel' intae water and they drownded the fire oot. When the ring seen that, he turned hissel' intae a barley amongst a' the rest o' the barley. So these two builders they turned theirsel' intae twa cocks and they start tae peck the barley up, peckin' and peckin' and peckin' the barley. And Jeck he turned hissel' intae a fox and he snappit the heids clean aff the cocks, and that's the last o' my story.

Type 325.
Motifs: S. 301 (*Children abandoned, exposed*); S. 331 (*Exposure of child in boat, floating chest*); R. 131.4 (*Fisher rescues abandoned child*); D. 1711 (*Magician*); S. 212 (*Child sold to magician*); D. 1711.0.1 (*Magician's apprentice*); D. 1721 (*Magic power from magician*); H. 1385 (*Quest for lost son*); D. 100 (*Transformation: man to animal*); H. 62.1 (*Recognition of person transformed to animal*); D. 612 (*Protean sale: man sells youth in successive transformations*); K. 252 (*Selling oneself and escaping*); C. 837 (*Tabu: losing bridle in selling man transformed to horse*); D. 722 (*Disenchantment by taking off bridle*); D. 671 (*Transformation flight*); D. 615.2 (*Transformation contest between master and pupil*); D. 610 (*Repeated transformations*); D. 641.1 (*Lover as bird visits mistress*); H. 1104 (*Task: building castle in one night*); L. 142.2 (*Pupil surpasses magician*).

3 THE CRIPPLE IN THE CHURCHYARD
(*Alec Stewart*)

This story that I'm gaun tae tell ye noo is aboot a tailor. He was a cripple a' the days o' his life and any time he wanted tae go tae the bar in the public hoose, they had tae tak' him in a barra. Either a barra or a invalid-chair, or maybe a cart and horse. So one night, they took him tae the bar and they were a' sittin' talkin' aboot various things, aboot haunted places and ghosts and things like that.

And this man says, "Well, John" – they ca'd the tailor John – "would you sit in the graveyaird? They say it's haunted doon there."

"I would", the cripple says. "I would sit the whole night, right up to aboot four or five o'clock in the mornin'."

"Well", says the man, "if you sit in the graveyaird up tae two or three in the mornin' I'll gie ye five pound and the makin's o' a new suit."

Well, John thought about it. "All right", he says, "you take me down in the cart and horse and I'll sit the whole night in the graveyaird."

So time wore on till it come tae aboot eleven o'clock. They yokit up the horse and gied him a bottle o' whisky wi' him, then doon tae the graveyaird. And John says, "Ye better gie me a pair o' stockin's tae mend tae pass the time."

"Oh", they say, "ye'll get that." So he got a pair o' stockin's tae mend and they took him right down tae the gate o' the graveyaird and they carried him in. And they put him on top o' a tumstone – ye ken whit a tumstone is? And he's settin' there warkin' away at his hose.

So time wore on till it come aboot half-past-twelve, and he lookit a' roond aboot him. He lookit up and he lookit doon and he lookit in the grund, and he seen the earth come up oot o' a grave. Earth was bein' thrown up and thrown up oot o' the grave. "My God", he says, "what's that?"

The first thing that come oot o' the grave was a hand and a voice says, "Ye see that, John? There's nor flesh nor blood on it."

John says, "Ay, I see it. But I'll finish this in the meantime." And he's aye sewin' away tae his stockin's, see?

So the thing howkit up more sand and more sand and more sand, till the arm come up and the voice says, "Ye see that, John? Wi'oot flesh nor blood on it."

He says, "Yes", he says, "I see that. But I'll sew this in the meantime."

So the thing come up tae the shouthers, and the voice says, "Ye see my face and my shouthers, wi'oot flesh nor blood?"

He says, "Yes, I see it, but I'll keep sewin' in the meantime."

So it come right up tae his knees. "D' ye see me noo?" the voice says, "wi'oot flesh nor blood?"

"Yes", he says, "but I'll finish this in the meantime."

At this, the skeleton rises right up tae its feet and the voice says, "D' ye see me noo, John? I'm a big man without flesh nor blood".

"Yes", says John, "I see ye without flesh nor blood but I'll finish this in the meantime."

And the skeleton says, "All right, John. Here goes!" And he made a wind at him wi' his hand, and wee John – he was an invalid y' see – he just throwed hissel' sideways owre this tumstone and the skeleton's hand come right on top o' the tumstone, and the mark o' that skeleton's hand's on that tumstone yet. Many's the time I've measured my hand in the place the skeleton's hand was. This was away up in the north o' Scotland. Och, I was only a wee boy when I was at the place. My faither was there and he measured *his* hand tae, but the skeleton's hand was twice as big as his.

So John ran oot fae the graveyaird. Him that was a cripple a' the days o' his life, he ran oot o' the graveyaird, and he throwed hisself intae his wife's hoose. "My God", says the wifie, "what's wrang?"

"Oh", he says, "I got a fright in the graveyaird. I'll never forget it."

"Nae wunner", she says, "just look at ye noo", she says. "Ye can run and walk and ye hae been a cripple a' the days o' your life. How did ye manage that?"

"Oh", he says, "I forgot. I didnae ken I'd got my faculties back. Noo I can rin, I can walk, I can dae onything."

And that's the last o' my story.

Type 326A.
Motifs: H. 1416 (*Fear test: spending night by grave*); E. 261.2.1 (*Coffin bursts. Dead arises and pursues attendant*); E. 200 (*Malevolent return from dead*); E. 250 (*Bloodthirsty revenant*); V. 113.1 (*Cripple at shrine frightened and runs away without crutches. Variant*).

4   JACK AND THE PUDDOCK
(*Alec Stewart*)

Once upon a time there was a king and he stayed in a castle away up in the north, somewhere in the Hebrides, and he had three sons. He was gettin' an auld man and one day he said to the sons, "I'm gettin' auld and I dinnae ken which o' you tae leave the castle to. The best thing I can do wi' ye is tae put youse away on a trip and them that brings me back the best gold ring'll get the castle."

So the day come roond and the king says, "Which ways will ye go?"

Jeck says, "We'll hae tae pick oor road oorsel's."

But the eldest brither says, "I ken whit tae dae. We'll get three feathers and we'll throw them in the air, and whichever direction the three feathers will go, we'll gang that direction." So in the mornin' they got three feathers and they threw them up in the air. The auldest brither's feather went away by the north. And the next brither, he cast his up in the air and it was away tae the south.

And Jeck says, "Well, you got north and south, mine s'll be east or west." So he threw his feather up and it went richt tae the back o the castle, richt doon by his feet. "Oh my goodness", he says, "there's no direction at a' that way. It's richt doon through the earth."

Well, they got seven days for tae find this gold ring and on the sixth day Jeck was sittin' in the hoose. "Ye'd better go", the faither says, "and try tae get something. Ye've tae follow your feather anyway."

"But", Jeck says, "where have I tae go? It went richt tae the back o' the castle, doon intae the earth."

"Well", the king says, "ye've tae gang there onyway and see where your feather is."

So Jeck gaed roond tae the back o' the castle, and the feather was lyin' on the tap o' a great big flagstone. Jack lifted up the feather and he walkit away when there's a voice came frae below the big stone: "Hey, Jeck!" it says, "are ye no' gaun tae try and get that ring?"

Jeck lookit roond and he's lookin' a roond aboot to see whaur the voice come fae. Then he gaed doon on his knees and he lowsed the top o' the big stane, and he heard a mutterin' comin' fae below. "There must be a tunnel or something below this stane", he says. So he got doon on his knees and he lifted the great big flagstane and there's steps gaun doon intae a dungeon. He walkit doon the steps and doon the steps till he cam' doon tae the bottom, and he lookit in the middle o' the flair and he saw a great big stane wi' a frog sittin' on the tap o' it. Jeck lookit roond and he says, "Is there naebody here?"

"Ay, Jeck. I'm here."

"Wha's speakin'?"

"Me, Jeck."

"Oh", he says, "it's the frog! Can ye speak?"

"Oh, ay", says the frog, "I can speak. How is it ye no' cam' here lang ago?"

"I didnae think there was ony use lookin' whaur my feather went", Jeck says.

"Your brithers'll be comin' back the nicht", the frog said, "and they'll hae some guid rings. But nevermind aboot that", he says, "sit doon, Jeck, and we'll hae somethin' tae eat." So he got a wee napkin and he throwed it on the flair.

"We'll no' get much puttin' on that napkin", says Jeck.

But the frog he ris' up on his hind-end and he gien his elbow a hit against a big drum, like a bell, and there's five or six frogs come hoppin' in carryin' a' these dishes, and they put them doon on the tap o' this wee napkin and the wee napkin started to grow and grow and grow and grow. And it rose up higher and higher until it got to be a great big table.

"My God", Jeck says, "that's wonderful, that."

"Sit doon and get somethin' tae eat", the frog says, "and we'll hae a dance after." So Jeck sat down and oh, he got a' kind o' meat ye could imagine: hens and ducks and roast chicken and everything. And drink! as

much drink as ye could tak' . . . So Jeck's sittin' there, and they've finished
wi' their meal and the frog says, "Noo, Jeck, we'll gae intae the next
room."

And Jeck says, "Is there anither room?"

"Oh yes", says the frog. "There are a hunder rooms in this place. D' ye
ken where we get a' that drink, Jeck?" he says. "It's a' frae your ain
faither's larder. There's as mony rooms here as your faither's got up there,
and we've got yin extra doon in this dungeon."

So Jeck he went awa' ben tae this ballroom. And they're a' dancin'
there, hundreds o' people dancin'. And Jeck he's dancin' tae, dancin' awa'
wi' a wee frog intae this ballroom.

"Noo, Jeck", the frog says, "ye'd better haud awa' hame noo because
there's one o' your brithers that's hame a'ready."

"Oh", says Jeck, "which one's that?"

"It's no' the eldest one", said the frog. "It's the next one, and he's got a
lovely ring."

"Well", Jeck says, "he'll beat me, for I've nae ring at a'."

"Oh but your ring's waitin' on ye, Jeck", the frog says. "When ye gang
tae the bottom o' the stair just you lift the box that's lyin' intae the stane
and ye'll get your ring. Tak' the box wi' ye."

So Jeck come tae the steps gaun up noo and he lookit in this big stane
and there's the wee box sittin', a wee black box and he lifted it up and he
put it in his pocket and he gaed awa' up hame. And the frog cried aifter
him, "Jeck, when ye get tae the top, pu' the stane across!"

"I'll dae that!" says Jeck, and he pull't the big stane across and he's awa'
up tae the hoose.

"Well", his faither says, "did ye get onything, Jeck?"

"Ay", he says, "I got something. I've got a box here, but it'll hae tae
wait till I see my brithers' rings first." Well, the eldest brither come in then
and they a' had something tae eat and drink.

Then the king says tae the eldest yin, "Let me see yours". And he took
out a diamond ring. "Oh", says the king, "that's a good ring. Put it doon
there and we'll hae your mither in tae judge them." Then the next son took
his ring oot and put it doon, and it was a' gold wi' diamonds set in it. "Noo,
Jeck", the king says, "you put your ring doon."

So Jeck he put his hand in his pocket and he pull't this box oot and he
opened the lid and put it doon. Oh, they just had tae haud their eyes awa',
they couldnae look at it for the diamonds and platinum and gold. "Oh
Jeck", says the king, "ye've won the day. Yours is the best ring!"

But the auldest brither says, "Na na, it's no' fair! That's only one task",
he says. "We'll hae tae hae anither task." And he says tae Jeck, "Whaur
did ye get that ring, Jeck?"

"I'm no' gaun tae tell ye", says Jeck. "Whaur did ye get yours?"

"Oh, I got mine awa' in the north."

"Oh", says Jeck, "I got mine awa' in the sooth."

"Well", the king says, "are ye agreeable, Jeck, for anither task?"

"Onything ye like", Jeck says, "as lang's I please youse, faither."

"Well", the king says, "the next thing is a table-cover. Whaever brings the nicest table-cover'll get the castle."

"Ye're best tae mak' it three tasks, faither", Jeck says, "because my auldest brither'll no' be pleased if I win the second."

"Well, three tasks it'll be", says the king. "Three tasks and no more." So they a' gang up tae the top o' the castle, up in the turret, and they threw their feathers intae the air again. But Jeck's aye went tae the back o' the castle. It wadnae gae further than the back o' the castle. The two brithers got on their horses and they're awa' lookin' for their table-covers. But Jeck waited and waited until the third day, then he said, "I'll gang roond and see what the puddock says".

So he gaed roond tae the back o' the castle and his feather's lyin' on the top o' the big stane. And he lifted the feather and he put it in his pocket. And he pull't the stane awa' and he's doon the steps and tae the bottom where the puddock's waitin'.

"Aye, Jeck, we're waitin' on ye", the puddock says. "We heard a' that went on, ye ken. It wasnae fair, Jeck, haein' three tasks. The first task was your faither's promise."

"Och", Jeck says, "it doesnae matter."

And the frog says, "A' richt, Jeck, let's hae somethin' tae eat", and they're settin' doon and they're eatin' awa'. "Noo, Jeck", he says, "we'll gae intae the ither room and we'll hae anither bit dance." So they gaed ben the room and here's a wee puddock sittin' on tap o' the big chair and playin' these Irish pipes, and anither one's playin' the fiddle, and the drum is beatin' and by God the wee puddocks are a' hoppin' aboot the flair.

Jeck says, "By God, there's no' much o' them tae see but by God when they get on the flair they can dance!" So he gets up on the flair and he's dancin' aroond wi' this frog, a nice wee yella puddock. So time wore on and time wore on till it come on to near six o'clock at nicht and Jeck says, "I'll hae tae gang noo."

"Ay, Jeck", the auld frog says. "It's six o'clock. Now you just lift your parcel when you're gaun up the stair, and mind and close the door when ye get tae the tap. Pu' the big stane across."

"Och", Jeck says, "I'll dae that." So he's awa' up and he pull't this big stane across the hole, and he's awa' roond the front door o' the castle and he's in. And his twa brithers is in, and they had a' their table-covers spread oot on the floor, and oh, what braw table-cloths! They're a' sewn wi' gold, the nicest table-covers ever ye saw.

"Noo, Jeck", says the king, "there's the twa table-covers. And noo let's see yours." So Jeck spread his table-cover oot and oh, my goodness, it was the best table-cloth ye ever seen in your life. You've never seen a table cover like that.

And the queen she says, "I'll hae Jeck's. I'll tak' Jeck's."

"Well", the king says, "that's twa, Jeck. But ye've anither tae dae yet. The next one", he says, "is tae bring back a wife. Him that gets the bonniest wife and the cleverest wife gets the castle."

So Jeck's awa' the next mornin' and it's up wi' his feather intae the air. And he thocht tae himself, "My God, I'll never get a woman doon there. And I cannae tak' a yella puddock up tae my faither. It'll never dae." But he threw the feather onyway and it went richt doon tae the back o' the castle on top o' this big stane. So he's gane doon and he's sittin' on the tap o' the stane and he says, "I might as well gae doon for I'll get a feed onyway, and a drink."

So he gien hisself a shake and he's pull't the stane awa' and he's doon the stair again to whaur the frog's sittin'. "Ah, Jeck, your last task's fa'en."

"Ay", Jeck says, "and it's a bad yin this time, Mister Frog. It's a bad yin this time. It has tae be a woman this time, a wife."

"Och, never heed that, man Jeck," the frog says, "we'll soon get a woman tae ye."

"Ay", Jeck says, "yin o' they yella puddocks. But they'll never tak' a frog for a woman."

"Never you mind, Jeck", the puddock says. "We'll soon sort that oot." So they had their dinner and something tae drink and then they're ben the room dancin' again. It was the frog he had tae tak' wi' him that he was dancin' wi', roond and roond the floor.

And Jeck says, "Ye're a frog and I been dancin' these three nights wi' ye."

"Ay, I'm a frog, and I'm the one that has tae gang wi' ye tae the castle. I'm tae be your wife."

"Never", Jeck says.

"Oh ay", she says. And she'd big auld splay-feet, ye know, webbit feet, and she was dancin' roond and roond this hoose.

Jeck says, "If I brocht ye hame fae here, and took ye tae my faither, my faither'd thraw ye oot, and my mither wadnae tak' a frog", he says. "No' for a dochter-in-law. Never in the warld o' God." But he's up wi' the wee frog sittin' on his airm and gaun up the stair noo.

"Mind the door, Jeck!" says the auld puddock. "And when ye gang intae your hoose mind and put the wee frog doon on the flagstane richt at the front o' your door."

"Oh," Jeck says, "I'll dae that. I'm no' carryin' that thing in onyway, ye can be sure o' that." So he pull't the stane owre the door and he sets aff carryin' this wee puddock. And when he got tae his door, the door o' the castle, he thrawed it doon on tap o' the stane and up jumps a bonnie princess. She was just like Peggy there, bonnie as onything, wi' a curl on her heid and silver shoes and lang robes a' doon.

"Noo, Jeck", she says, "we'll gang in and see whit your brithers have got." So they marched intae the hoose and a' the folk and stannin' there

and gapin' at them as they come through the door. And they're a' shoutin'
"Ye won, Jeck!" "Jeck's the winner!" "Ye've won, ye've won, it's no' use
lookin' at the ither yins at a'!"

And they're there yet. And the last time I was there I got a drink o'
whisky and a cigarette. And that's the last o' my story.

Type 402.
Motifs: H. 1210.1 (*Quest assigned by father*); H. 1306 (*Quest for the finest of linen*);
D. 1472.1.7 (*Magic table supplies food and drink. Variant*); B. 493 (*Helpful frog*);
H. 1301.1 (*Quest for the most beautiful bride*); D. 735.1 (*Beauty and the beast.
Disenchantment of animal being kissed by woman. Variant*); H. 1242 (*Youngest
brother alone succeeds on quest*).

5 SILVER AND GOLD
(Sheila MacGregor)

Onc't upon a time this was a miller, and he'd two beautiful daughters. One
o' them was named Silver and the other one's name was Gold. And one o'
them had the beautifullest tresses that ever ye saw: they were pure gold.
The other one's was pure silver. This miller would never let Silver or Gold
take the hats off their head. He always made them wear their hair *under*
the hat – it was a sort of a mutch, never let them take the mutches off.

Well, they had a brother – he wasn't their real brother, rather a step-
brother, and he was a sort of a simple boy, y'know. He worked for this
miller but he didn't get much money and he slept up in the old attic in a
garret and just got a meal here, there and everywhere, y'know.

So this day, the simple boy said to his father, he says, "Father – next
week is the great fair of this town. May I be allowed to take Silver and
Gold in the buggy to the fair?"

So his father says, "No no no", he says, "you know perfectly well I never
let Silver and Gold out of my sight."

So he says, "Oh please, father, I'll work and work and work. I'll go
errands to the shop and errands for the fairmers and I'll get money", he
says, "that'll help me take Silver and Gold to the fair."

So his father says, "Well, if you can rake up the money, I'll give ye
permission to take them. But", he says, "if ye've no money you'll not be
allowed to take them." So he goes out and he works the whole week, day
and night, day and night, till he gets one silver piece and one gold piece.

So the night before the fair he was away along a walk with his dog, a wee
puppy it was, a walk away along the fields. So he's sittin' on this sort of a
stile and he hears this beautiful, beautiful voice singing, you know like an
echo, w—a—y in the distance.

So he goes towards this voice and it's a little brook, and it's a sort of a hauntin' melody, right through the brook, right up to the end of the cliffs. So he follows this brook, and it leads on for miles and miles, but he still follows it. And he comes to the end of the brook – it just goes into a huge cave.

And there's an old man sittin'. And he's got gray hair right down and a great huge long beard. And he's sittin' and the tears is streamin' down his face and he's got his two hands on his head and he's settin' singin' "My Silver and Gold, My Silver and Gold." And he's cryin' till his heart's breakin', for his silver and gold.

This simple boy says, "Oh, my goodness, it's a shame", he says, "that man's cryin' for silver and gold. Now back in my attic", he says, "I've got a silver piece and a gold piece. We don't *really* want to go to the fair tomorrow", he says. "I'll take the silver piece and the gold piece up to the auld man. It'll maybe make him happy, stop him crying."

So he rushes back to his mill and goes up to the attic and under his bed-tick, y'know, there's the silver piece and the gold piece. He runs back to the old man and he throws it on his lap, and the old man grabs it from him and throws it into the brook. The silver piece and the gold piece gets lost forever, away down the brook. And the man's *still* settin' and he's cryin' for his silver and gold.

So the next day was the fair but they couldn't get to the fair because he'd lost his silver and lost his gold. However, time wore on and time wore on until he couldn't keep back from this brook. He had to always go and sit and watch this old man.

So one night he said to Silver and Gold, he says, "I'll take ye up tonight and let ye see the auld man." So Silver and Gold gets all prepared and ready, and he says, "Och, that's awfae-lookin' things on your heids", he says. "Tak' they mutches aff. You'll no' need them now because your faither'll no' see you." So they tak' the mutches aff their heid and they throw them awa'.

So aff they go and they're followin' this wee stream up to the cavern and they come up b'where the auld man's still sittin' and he's roarin' and greetin'. Whenever he sees the two lassies, he makes a dive out at them.

"My Silver, my Gold, my Silver, my Gold!" Oh, and he's rejoicin' like anything, y'know. He says. "That miller down at that mill", he says, "I had two small babies years and years ago. One of them was Silver and the other was Gold and", he says, "that miller stole my two babies from me. He vowed that I would never ever get them back. But", he says, "now that I *have* got ye back he will *never* get ye." So the two of them went back to their father and the simple boy went back to the mill. He married. I can't remember whether it was Silver or Gold, but he married one of them and they lived happy ever after.

Motifs: D. 1275 (*Magic song*); H. 75 (*Identification by hair*).

6 THE VINEGAR BOTTLE
(*Sheila MacGregor*)

The moral tae this story is aboot greed. Onc't upon a time there was an
owld man and an owld woman and they lived into a vinegar bottle. They
had nae hoose and nae nothin', just lived in a vinegar bottle. So, och, this
man was aye sittin' aboot and sittin' aboot and she couldnae get the place
cleaned because they were sae cramped for room and everything. She
could do nothing. She was always complainin' aboot this vinegar bottle and
she had her auld man died. She was just layin' intae him – dyin' for a
hoose.

So this day she gets really angry wi' him. She puts him ootside. So he's
away through the wood and he's roarin', and he doesnae ken whit tae dae.
So he sets doon on this stane. And he hears this voice, y'see. So he looks
roond and ahint this wee stane sees this wee freedyeuch o' a man; no' the
size o' a freedyeuch. And he's sittin' ahint this wee stane.

So the wee man says, "My God Almichty, what's wrang wi' ye, man?"

"O, my dear", he says, "it's that wife o' mine", he says, "I'm puttin' oot
o' my mind", he says, "aboot the hoose we bide in."

"God bless me", he says, "it must be an awfae hoose."

"Well", he says, "we live in a vinegar bottle."

"O, ay", he says, "that's terrible man. Ye must have an awfae life o't."

"Ay", he says, "terrible."

"Well", says the wee man, "you go hame and never heed", he says,
"you just gang hame."

So he gangs awa' hame and when he lands to the place where the vinegar
bottle was in, was the beautifullest mansion you ever clapped your eyes on.
And his wife's into this mansion. And she's doin' it all up and cleanin'
everything. So in he goes and she's fair proud now, she's got this mansion.
And she's layin' his supper and everything's goin' smashing – for two or
three days, till she gets into the way o' this mansion, y'see.

"This is too big for me," says she "I could dae wi' a servant to help
me." And she's gaun on to him aboot this servant and he's mowdit wi'
her.

So away he goes again and he says, "Well, maybe if I go back to thon
wee stane I'll see thon wee man again and he'll help me." So he sits doon at
this wee stane and the wee man comes to him and he tells him.

"Och", he says, "never mind – you go back," he says, "and everything'll
be a' richt."

So when he goes back, doesn't his wife have the wildest sicht o' servants
that you ever seen in your life? And they're a' goin' to *his* needs and doin'
her needs, y'see. So the wife's settin' back and, man dear, she's enjoyin'
hersel'.

So – everything comes oot a' richt, but ach, the wife's gettin sick. "Na na", she says, "I dinnae like this place at a'", she says, "I want it redecorated. Completely redecorated." Y'see?

"Oh, my God", he says, "woman, you're never pleased", he says. "If it's no' one thing, it's the next." So, however, he gans oot again and he sees the wee man.

And the wee man says, "My God, that must be an awfae woman you have. She's never pleased wi' nothin' I give ye. Na, I dinnae ken what we're gaun tae dae wi' her. So, however, never mind", he says. "You go awa' back hame and everything'll be quite all right. You just go back hame."

So he goes away back hame, and whenever he comes to the spot where the big mansion was, the wife's back intae the vinegar bottle. And that's what she got for her greed.

Type 555 (Variant).
Motifs: N. 821 (*Help from little man*); F. 341 (*Fairies give fulfilment of wishes*); Q. 338 (*Immoderate request punished*); L. 420 (*Overweening ambition punished*); J. 514 (*One should not be too greedy*).

7 APPLEY AND ORANGEY
(Cathie Higgins)

Noo, sit doon bairns, and I'll tell ye a story. Onc't upon a time there was this woman and a man and they bade awa' in a wee village. Well, the wife dee'd and the man married anither woman. And this woman had a wee lassie, and her name was Orangey. And the man had a wee lassie by his first marriage, and her name was Appley.

Noo, his second wife didnae like wee Appley. She couldnae stick her. She was always findin' fault wi' her, and wee Appley was never daein' onything richt.

One day, she says, "Come in here, wee Appley, and gang for a message tae me. Go up tae the milk-dairy and get me some milk."

And Appley says, "Mammy, please – let me tak' your bonnie jug."

"No no", says she, "you're no' tak'in' my jug because I like that jug. If ye tak' my jug and break it, I'll cut the heid aff ye." But the wee lassie tormented her mammy that much that she gied her the jug and she says, "All right, tak' it. But mind, if ye break it your heid's aff."

So away the wee lassie goes, up tae the milk-dairy and gets the milk. But comin' hame she starts to fol-de-rol on the road and to skip and play, and she broke the jug and spilt the milk. So she started to roar and greet in the middle o' the road. A lady was passin', and she says, "Whit's wrang wi' you, my dear? Whit are ye greetin' for?"

"Well", says wee Appley, "I broke my mither's jug and if I gae hame withoot it my days is numbered."

"Wait", says the lady, "and I'll gae up tae the shop and get ye one like it."

"It must be the same kind o' a jug, because it's a special one."

So the woman goes up tae this wee shop and she tries tae get the same kind o' a jug. Well it wasnae the same, but it was something similar. So the bairn was hame wi' the milk noo tae the mither. But when she gangs intae the hoose, her mither started tae carry on.

"Run, Orangey", she says, "and bring me the axe, till I tak' this lass's heid aff." So Orangey, she gangs oot and tak's in the axe, and the mither puts wee Appley's heid on a lump o' wuid and cuts the heid clean aff her. Then she says, "I've no meat for your faither's dinner the nicht, so what I'll hae tae dae is put Appley intae the pot and mak' soup o' her." So she cuts the wee cratur o' a lassie up, puts her intae the pot and boils her.

Noo, whenever the faither comes in for his tea he aye asks whaur his favourite bairn is, wee Appley. "Oh", says his wife, "she's ootside playin' somewhere. I dinnae ken whaur she is. She'll be in in a wee while. Sit doon, man, and hae your dinner."

So he sits doon and he's puttin' the soup intae him, and did he no' come across the wee bairn's finger and the wee ring that he'd gien her for her birthday. The man nearly went aff his heid. He went clean entirely moich, as the sayin' is. "Whit happened?" he says. "Whit did ye dae wi' my bairn?"

"Well", says she, "I put her for milk tae the dairy and she broke my milk-jug on the road, and I just cut her up and put her in the pot and made soup o' her."

"Whit did ye dae wi' my bairn's bones?"

"Well", says she, "I put them atween twa marble stones."

So time wore on and time wore on, till it come that twa year passed by, and there was an awfae bonnie wee doo – a dove as some folk ca's it. And it used tae flee roond aboot the mither's hoose. Well, it flee'd tae the toon this day and it cam' tae a big watch shop, ye ken, a jeweller's what sells watches and rings. It come intae the man in the shop and it says:

> My mammy kilt me,
> My daddy ate me,
> My sister Jeannie pickit my banes,
> And put me atween twa marble stanes,
> And I growed in a bonnie wee doo, doo.

And then she says tae the man in the shop, "If ye gie me a bonnie watch oot o' your windae, a man's watch, I'll sing that wee sang tae ye." And she sung it:

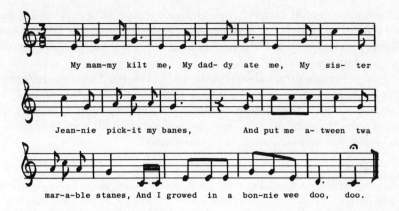

My mam-my kilt me, My dad-dy ate me, My sis-ter

Jean-nie pick-it my banes, And put me a-tween twa

mar-a-ble stanes, And I growed in a bon-nie wee doo, doo.

The man was surprised to hear a bird singin', so he gied it the watch and awa' the bird flees. Well, next it comes tae this big toy-shop. There were a' sorts o' things for wee lasses, some lovely dolls and big prams. And the doo says, "If ye gie me yin o' your biggest dolls in the shop, I'll sing ye a wee sang." So the wee doo sang:

> My mammy kilt me,
> My daddy ate me,
> My sister Jeannie pickit my banes,
> And put me atween twa marable stanes,
> And I growed in a bonnie wee doo, doo.

The woman in the shop was dumfoondert. So she gaed and pickit the biggest doll and gien it tae the dove. Hoo she took it oot o' the shop I dinnae ken, but she took it. Well, noo this wee doo goes tae an ironmonger's and asks the man there tae gie it the biggest aix he's got in the shop. And then she sings the wee sang:

> My mammy kilt me,
> My daddy ate me,
> My sister Jeannie pickit my banes,
> And put me atween twa marable stanes,
> And I growed in a bonnie wee doo, doo.

So the man gied the doo the aix and it's awa'. It gangs richt back tae the hoose where it was born and brocht up. And then tae the tap o' the chimney-pot, it roars doon, "Are ye there, faither?"

The man was dumbfoondert, and he said, "Wha's that that's speakin'?"

"It's your wee Appley. Come and look up the chimney, faither, till ye see whit I hae for ye."

At that day, it was auld-fashioned fireplaces that ye could stand intae. So the man keeks up the chimney and here's the wee doo, and it thraws doon the watch tae the faither. Oh, the man was dumbfoondert.

And noo, the doo says, "Is wee Orangey there, faither? Send her here and tell her tae haud her twa airms oot. I've got a prize for her." So wee Orangey come roond and she held oot her airms and the wee doo thrawed the big doll doon.

"Noo, I hannae forgot aboot my mither", says she. "Send my mither tae me. Tell her tae come and put her heid up the chimney till I speak tae her." The auld woman come rinnin' ben and put her heid up the chimney and wee Appley flung the aix doon and cut the heid clean aff her. Then the wee doo flew awa' and that's the last o' my story.

Type 720.
Motifs: S. 31 (*Cruel stepmother*); V. 63 (*Bones of dismembered person assembled and buried*); G. 61 (*Relative's flesh eaten unwittingly*); H. 94 (*Identification by ring*); E. 607.1 (*Bones of dead collected and buried. Return in another form directly from grave*); E. 613.0.1 (*Reincarnation of murdered child as bird*); B. 211.9 (*Speaking bird*); Q. 412 (*Punishment: millstone dropped on guilty person. Variant*); B. 131.1 (*Bird reveals murder*); N. 271 (*Murder will out*).

8   THE LADDIE THAT BECAME A LASS
(Belle Stewart)

Once upon a time there was a young laddie and he'd be mebbe nineteen or twenty year auld. He'd been oot wi' his lass when it come on an awfae, awfae thunder and lightnin', and awfae storm ye ken. He couldnae bide lang wi' his lass that nicht so he left her early to hurry awa' hame.

On his way hame he'd to pass yin o' they auld-fashioned country places whaur a' the plooman and lasses gaither tae dance, ootside the village. Well, there was a dance on that nicht and as he was passin' the place he heard the music and the heuchin' and he says tae himsel', "I'm gaun in here onyway," for he was soaked tae the skin. "At least," he says, "I'll mebbe get something tae eat and drink."

Well, when he went tae the door, they werenae gaun tae let him in because it was some kind o' a special dance and ye had tae have a ticket. The man at the door says tae him, "Na na", he says, "ye cannae get in the nicht." So he mentioned a fairmer's name and he could see the fairmer frae the door whaur he was standin'. "You just mention my name tae *him*", he says, "and I ken fine I'll get in."

So the man gaes and brings back a coupla fairmers tae the door and they say, "Och ay, come awa' in." Well, they telt him that they were just in the middle o' Tasks [Forfeits].

"If ye gie me a glass o' whisky", he says, "I'll tak' on ony damn task ye like, for I'm shiverin' tae the hairt wi' cauld."

Well, the fairmer that he kent says, "I'll gie ye mair than a glass o' whisky. Noo, here's the task: doon at the waterside there's an auld boat lyin' thonder. It's been lyin' there a lang time, but there's a water-lifter in it, one o' they things wi' a lang hannel like a ladle, that'll help ye tae lift the water oot. Noo", he says, "we'll gie ye ten minutes tae bail a' the water oot o' the boat and ten minutes tae fill it fu' again. That's twenty minutes a'thegither. If you bail the water oot, fill it fu' again and get back here in twenty minutes, ye'll get a good feed and a dram."

"Och", the laddie says tae hissel'. "That's gaun tae be an easy job that. So they gien him this water-lifter and he's awa', whistlin' doon tae the boat and feelin' fine after his dram. When he comes to the auld boat he starts bailin' oot the water and bailin' oot the water. "What the hell", he says, "I think I'd dae better if I got *in* the boat." So he sits on the spar across the end, ye ken, and he's bailin' the water and bailin' the water. But little does he ken that the boat's movin' – it's gettin' awa' oot intae the water.

So, he's well oot noo and it becomes awfae foggy and misty. So he put his hand in his pocket and he teukit a match and struck it. "God Almichty", he says, "I'm oot in the water! Hoo in the name o' God did that happen? I'm no' oarin', so it must be the wind blawin' me oot. By God", he says, "I'd better get busy wi' this ladle or I'll be drooned," he says.

By this time, though, there was nae water comin' intae the boat. It was perfectly dry, a lovely dry boat. "I cannae see the land at this time o' nicht", he says, "so I'll just hae tae sit here whaur I am until daylicht comes. I think I'll hae a smoke o' my pipe."

So he put his hand – as he thocht – intae his troosers pocket tae get his pipe and t'bacca. But, by God Almichty, there was nae troosers there. He'd on the loveliest frock on him, just a lovely dancin' dress. It was beautiful. "What the hell's wrang here?" he says tae hissel', and he was lookin' a' roond the boat for his troosers. "There's somethin' wrang wi' me, I doot," he says. So he puts his hands up his skirts and here's hair hangin' doon. "God Almichty!" he says, "is that me? It must be me. There's nae ither body in the boat wi' me."

But he was a curious kind o' a lad – as a' Scotch ploomen are, ye ken – and he felt further up tae see if there was onything wrang wi' him. And when he put his hand richt up whaur he had the business tae put it, he was a woman. He'd changed entirely tae a woman. Even his voice when he spoke tae hissel' i' the boat was lovely and clear, different a'thegither.

"Well", he says, "I think I'm the same boy, but there's something far wrang here. But ach", he says, "there's naethin' I can dae aboot it." So he shut his e'en and kind o' dovered awa' tae sleep. By the time he opened his e'en it was lovely bricht daylight and the sun was shinin'. The boat was richt intae the shore.

"This is no' the place that I got on the boat", he says tae himsel'. He's still a woman, he's got a' these bonnie claes and he feels like a woman noo, feels just like a woman every way. But he was awfae hungry. Oh, most terrible hungry and cauld, shiverin' wi' cauld. He'd nae coat, y' see, just this lovely dancin' dress.

Well, she stepped oot o' the boat – we'll hae tae ca' him *her* noo – she steppit oot o' the boat and she's walkin' doon the shore and doon the shore, and she saw a wee dog rinnin' alang the beach. There was naebody wi' it, but it ran barkin' in front o' her and she folla'd it. She went up this lang avenue through rhododendron bushes and a' that sort o' thing, and she cam' tae a beautiful big hoose.

"Well, thank God", she says, "there's somebody in this place onyway." So she went to the door and she knockit at it and she knocked two or three times and then the door was opened by a lovely young gentleman.

"Good gracious", he says. "Where did you come fae?"

She says, "My boat's just up the beach a bit. I was just walkin' around and I met your dog, so I folla'd it."

He says, "You're cauld."

"Yes", says she. "I'm terrible cauld. I'm freezin'."

"Well", he says, "I cannae offer ye nothing very nice because I live alone here. I've no servants of any kind, but however I'll gie ye something hot. Would ye like a drink of spirits or some tea or something t'eat?"

"Oh", she said, "I'd rather have something t' eat." So he fixed her up a meal of some kind and she's quite comfortable noo, and she fell asleep in this big chair. How long she slept she didnae ken but she wakened up a' amazed to see such a lovely hoose and such beautiful furniture. The young gentleman had been sitting at a table across from her and he noticed she was a' startled when she wakened up.

She says, "I'll hae tae get awa' back. I'll gae and see if my boat's a' richt."

"I'll walk alang wi' ye", he says. Well, they walked and walked and walked until they were exhausted. They covered miles and miles o' that beach but there was nae boat. "Are ye sure", he says, "ye cam' in a boat?"

"Oh yes", she says, "I cam' in a boat."

"Strange – I've been here for years", he says, "and I've never kent o' a boat tae come tae this side o' the water."

So noo that the boat was gone, she stayed in the hoose wi' him. However, the time rolls on, the time rolls on, and they became very attached to each other. They couldnae get married because there was naebody on that island but themselves. Nae priest, nae minister, nae nobody. So they just married theirsel' in their ain law and she had three o' a faimily tae him, twa boys and a girl.

So time wore on, but she aye had this notion that a boat was comin' tae the island. She couldnae get it oot o' her heid, and she come tae be very depressed and no' weel. And her man was gettin' worried aboot her for she was losin' weight.

Hooever, the youngest laddie – he was just seven year auld – was oot playin' ae day, and he must have been awa' a couple or three hours. They got alarmed noo, and they set oot tae look for him, a' gaun different directions. When the mither finally got the bairn he's sittin' in a boat, the same boat that she'd been in and it was lyin' half fu' o' water. Everything came back, just as it had been, and she said tae the bairn, "Look, son, run ye hame and tell daddy that it's a' richt and I'll be hame in a wee while. Run hame noo, at once."

So the bairn ran awa' back hame tae tell his faither, and she got intae the boat. The same auld bailin' ladle was lyin' in the bottom o' the boat, so she started bailin' oot the water and bailin' oot the water. And the same thing happened as before; a thick fog began tae fa' and she discovered that she was oot on the water. After a while it became pitch-black. She couldnae see onything.

So now she's beginnin', she thocht, tae become a man again. The same notion's runnin' in her mind. She put her hand doon and she felt the corduroy troosers that he'd been wearin' when he went intae the boat. He got oot his pipe, his t'bacca, his matches, and he had a smoke. Then he put his hand doon again intae his privates and ay, he was definitely a man. So he just sat there and smoked his pipe and he forgot that he'd been a woman.

And then it come broad daylight and he's back on the shore. When he got oot o' the boat, the dance is still gaun on and he says tae hissel', "I wonder if I've made it in time?"

So he went back intae the dance-hall and the chap at the door says, "My God, you were a while. You been twenty-two minutes awa'. Ye had ten minutes tae bail the water oot and ten tae fill it fu' again. Ye've been twa minutes owre your time. Hooever", he says, "you'll still get your dram and something t' eat."

So he gaed back intae the ha' and he got his dram and went hame. And that's the end o' my story.

Motifs: D. 10 (*Transformation to person of different sex*); D. 12 (*Transformation of man to woman*); D. 11 (*Transformation of woman to man*).

9 THE THREE WISHES
(Cathie Higgins)

D'ye ken the yin aboot Jeck and the three wishes? This is a short yin ...

Well, y'see, onc't upon a time this is a mother and a son and they bade awa' on this hill. And they hadn't a bite aboot the hoose, not a sup of no kind. And all they possessed was one wee coo.

So Jeck he's settin' and his mither says, "For God's sake", says she,

"Jeck, arise and gie yoursel' a shake", she says, "and gang to the fair wi'
this wee coo."

"But mither dear", he says, "what will I get for that coo?"

"Well", says she, "at least we'll get something to eat." She says, "My
inside's rumblin' for somethin' to eat."

So wee Jeck gies himself a wash and puts his muffler roond his neck and
goes ootside to the byre and tak's his wee coo. And it's the thinnest coo
that ever ye clapped your e'en on. There's not a bite nor a pick on it.

So he's trudgin' on this road and on this road and he stops a wee minute.
And he stops on the side o' this road, and he's stannin' and he's fair
sweatin' because the heat was roastin'. And oot jumps a wee man.

"God bless me!" says Jeck, "what are you?"

"Well", says he, "I seen you comin' alang the road wi' that coo and by
the look o' it", he says, "it could do wi' a good diet o' meat."

"Ay", says Jeck, "and so could I because I'm starvin', man."

"Well, Jeck, I'll tell ye what I'll dae", he says. "I'll grant ye three wishes
for that coo."

"Oh", he says, "ye cannae be serious."

"Ay", he says, "I'm serious a' richt. I'll grant ye three wishes."

"Oh well", says Jeck, "you can have the coo willingly if ye gie me three
wishes."

So Jeck he's braggin' noo, he gets these three wishes and he's hame tae
his mither like a shot. "Well", says his mither, "what did ye get?"

"Well", he says, "mither, I didnae get money, I didnae get meat – but I
got three wishes."

"Oh, for God's sake, Jeck, dinnae mak' a fool o' me", says she. "I'm
stairvin' and the way you torment me, it's puttin' me silly."

"Look", he says, "mither, I got three wishes, put your coat on", he says,
"and I'll gan tae the mairket."

So she pits on her coat. She says, "I dinnae ken whit kind o' a silly laddie
I hae at all, but I cannae mak' heid nor tail o' him. But I suppose I'll hae to
follow him." So she gets on her wee bit coat, her basket on her airm, and
she's awa' to the market wi' Jeck. So they come to this market and they're
lookin' through all these beautiful stalls. There's everything in it – the very
chickens is roastin' and everything.

But she comes to this still where there's a ladle hangin', for soup. "Oh,
God bless me", says she, "I could do wi' that ladle."

"What in the name o' God are ye going to dae wi' a ladle?" says Jeck.

"I wish I had that ladle", – and as sure as God made me, she had the
ladle in her hand.

Jeck says, "That's one wish you wished, mither, and you got it. You
mind you've only two." And he says, "What in the name o' Christ you're
gaun to dae wi' a ladle I don't know", he says, "I wish to Christ it was stuck
up your airse!"

Up the ladle goes! Oh my God, she's goin' roond the mairket like a mad hare, wi' this ladle stuck in her back-end, y'see. She says, "For God's sake, Jeck", she says, "dae something to help me! What am I going to do wi' this ladle?" she says. "Take it frae me for God's sake!"

"Well", he says, "I wish to Christ the ladle was stuck *oot* your airse!"

So he got the ladle back in his hand and they finished up back hame in the hoose. And if ye dinnae believe me you can haud up to the hoose if ye like.

Type 750A.
Motifs: D. 1761.0.2 (*Limited number of wishes granted*); J. 2071 (*Three foolish wishes*); J. 2075 (*The transferred wish*).

10 THE SCABBY HEID
(Belle Stewart)

Once upon a time there was an auld blacksmith and his wife and son. They were livin' in this wee country place awa' up in Aberdeenshire somewhere and he wasnae daein' an awfae lot o' trade because he wasnae an awfae guid blacksmith.

But this day onyway he's oot wi' his son at the forge and the auld woman she's peelin' tatties for the dinner. And he looked and he sees this gentleman come ridin' alang on a horse.

"Good mornin', smith", he says.

"Good mornin', sir", the auld man says.

"Could ye shoe my horse?"

"Oh well", he says, "I'll try". It was an awfae done auld horse, just an auld, auld nag. So the blacksmith's makin' the shoes and the gentleman says to the laddie, "I wonder could I get a lend o' your big hammer?"

"Oh ay", says the laddie. "It's lyin' here in the corner. I'll get it for ye." And he lifts the hammer and gies it tae the gentleman. So while the auld man's makin' the shoes for the horse the gentleman puts the auld horse across the anvil and he's batterin' it with this hammer and he's batterin' it wi' this hammer. And he batters till he batters the auld horse flat. But oot o' the auld horse springs the loveliest young steed that ever ye saw, just aboot three or four year auld it is, and oh, it was prancin', a beautiful young steed.

The auld smith he turned roond and he says, "My God, that horse is no' needin' shod. He's got four new sheen on't, man."

"Ay, I ken that", says the gentleman, "and I thank ye for the lend o' your hammer. And here, laddie", he says, "tak' this ring. Just wish on it, whiles, and it'll tak' ye oot o' a lot o' difficulties." So the laddie tak's the ring and thanks the gentleman, and the gentleman rides aff on this lovely young steed.

Well, the auld blacksmith has an auld, auld horse, owre twenty or thirty year auld, doon in the bog. He looked at the lad, and he says, "Man, I think we'll try that wi' the auld horse. Whit d' ye think?" So the laddie's awa' doon tae the bog for the auld horse and they get it on the anvil and the auld man batters it and batters it. But the puir auld thing just dees.

"Oh, God Almichty", he says, "if the wife kens I've kilt the horse I'll get my heid in my hands." He says, "We'll need tae wait till nicht, then we'll gang doon tae the bog and bury it." So they waited till dark nicht and awa' they went doon tae the bog, him and the laddie, and they buried the auld horse.

A year and a day fae that time, the same thing happens. The gentleman comes ridin' alang and on the horse in front of him this time he has an auld, auld woman. She must have been a hunder-year-auld. She'd teeth all the way roond the back o' her heid and a big Roman nose. She was the ugliest woman ever ye seen. So the gentleman rides up and he says, "Will ye shoe my horse for me, smith?"

"Oh ay, sir.", the auld man says, "I'll try." The gentleman lifts the auld woman doon and gies the smith his horse tae shoe.

And he says tae the laddie, "Is that hammer o' yours handy, son?"

"Ay", he says, "it aye lies in the corner there."

So the gentleman lifts the auld woman on to the anvil and tak's the hammer. Oh my God, he's batterin' and batterin' till he batters her flat. Well, oot o' the auld woman rises the loveliest young woman ever ye saw. Oh, she was bonnie!

The auld man and the laddie's been lookin' and the gentleman gies him the money noo for shoein' the horse. He lifts the lady on aside o' him and he's awa'. Just at that minute, the auld wife comes oot and she's throwin' some water oot o' the doorway. And the auld smith says, "I wonder if I wad try that wi' the auld wife?" So awa' he gaes and gets his ain auld wife, and mak's some excuse or other for her tae come owre tae the smiddy.

And the laddie and the auld man are haudin' her doon tae the anvil and then the smith's batterin' her and batterin' her wi' this hammer. Oh, the puir auld soul – she's kilt. She's died. Oh, God bless me noo, the auld man's near off his heid. "I've kilt my auld wife! Whit am I gaun tae dae?"

"Well", says the laddie, "it was *you* thocht o' it, faither. *I* never thocht on killin' my mither!"

"Och, well", the smith says, "there's naethin' we can dae noo but tak' her doon and bury her aside the auld horse". So they tak' the auld woman doon and bury her aside the auld horse in the bog. And they went tae their bed that nicht and oh, the auld man's hairt-broken, thinkin' o' the auld woman lyin' deid. For as auld as she was, ye ken, she could aye dae a guid turn aboot the hoose. The auld man just couldnae sleep. He just walkit aboot a' the nicht.

The next mornin', when they went owre and looked at the anvil, oh, it fair got on their nerves. And the hammer, the smith thrawed it awa' in the corner, a'thegither oot o' their sicht.

Well, the auld man couldnae rest, and he says tae his son, "I think, laddie, we'll gang awa' for a while. I cannae bear the look o' the place." So they're awa', and they're marchin' on and they're marchin' on. They had awfae little money in the first place because they were gey poor, and noo what little money they had run oot and they're starvin' wi' hunger. They come intae this big toon, and there was an awfae roarin' and carryin' on – aebody was roarin' and shoutin' terrible.

So the laddie gaed owre tae a man and said, "What's tae dae?"

"Oh my God", the man says, "the king's took an awfae disease, a terrible disease, and naebody can cure him. We've had doctors, specialists, everybody fae hunders o' miles roond and they cannae cure him."

"God bless me", said the laddie. "What's tae dae wi' him?"

"Oh, it's some kin' o' a disease in his heid and his face, and he's gaun wrang in the mind wi' pain and the itch."

Well, noo the laddie minds on the ring that the gentleman gied him. And he says, "Man, onybody that could cure him", he says, "they'd surely get a gey lot o' money." And he turns tae his faither and he says, "Faither, they say there's something wrang wi' the king, and onybody that'll cure him'll get a pack o' money."

"God bless me, laddie", the smith said, "I wish *I* could cure him."

"I think I'll go and hae a try at it, faither."

"Laddie, for God's sake, ye never was awa' fae the smiddy in your life. Hoo could *you* cure onybody?"

"Well, it'll no' dae ony hairm tae see him onyway, father." So the laddie gangs up tae the hoose wi' his faither behind him, and he rings the bell. A man comes oot and he says, "What d' *you* want?"

"I've come tae cure the king." Well, the man started tae laugh at him.

"*You* cure the king? Have ye ony idea hoo mony folks been here tryin' tae cure the king? Na, na, laddie", he says, "I doot ye'd better gang aff."

"There'll be nae hairm seein' him", the laddie says.

"Well, I suppose no'. Ye'll best be tae come in." And the laddie and his faither gaed in and oh, this king's gaun aff his heid wi' the itch. Ye couldnae see him, his face was a' broken oot, it's a' festered and the discharge roond his eyes is terrible. The laddie looked at him, but of course he couldnae speak he was in such agony and pain. There were nurses and folk a' roond aboot him, ye ken, and the laddie says, "Could naebody cure him?"

The queen says, "Naebody can cure my man."

"Well", the laddie says, "I'll hae a go at curing him. Get me a large tub of wine, one large tub of wine, the best wine in the palace. And a tub of milk", he says, "and as many buckets o' saft soap as ye can get, and a hard, hard scrubbin' brush."

Well, all this was got. The wine, the milk, and a' the rest o' 't. A' the things he needed. And then the laddie says, "Hae ye a sharp knife?" And they brocht him a big gully knife, and he cut the heid aff the king.

Oh, the queen she's in an awfae state, and she's rinnin' and roarin', "Oh, he's killed him a'thegither! He's killed him a'thegither!" But hooever, the laddie tak's the heid and puts it intae this big vat o' wine and he's scrubbin' and he's scrubbin' the scabby heid intae this barrel o' wine. And oh, the roars o' the king's heid! It's screamin' and roarin'. So aifter he scrubs it and scrubs it in the wine he tak's it oot and puts it intae the tub o' boilin' water, and the heid's now intae the tub o' boilin' water and he's scrubbin' and scrubbin' and scrubbin' wi' the saft soap and scrubbin' brush. And the scabby heid's screamin' "Murder, murder!"

But after the laddie's finished wi' the boilin' water and the wine, he dips the heid intae the cool, cauld milk, and the heid turns the loveliest young man ye ever saw. No' a mark on his face of no kind, nor on his heid. So the laddie gangs back wi' the heid noo and he puts it on the body.

Oh, the king, he's rejoicin', and everybody else is rejoicin', and they hae a huge feast. They cannae dae enough for the laddie. But this king had nae dochter tae marry, so he asked the laddie what he would tak'.

"Well", he says, "there's me and my faither, and money'll dae us fine. We're really sair needin' money." So the king gets a big big bag o' gold filled up for the laddie and he gives it tae him.

So the laddie and his faither are awa' doon in the toon noo, and the first thing they dae is go and get a good meal. They were starvin' o' hunger. The faither was aye an awfae drunkard. Oh man, he was fond o' the bottle, and he says tae the laddie, "I'm your faither", he says, "and ye're far owre young tae keep a' that money. Ye'll better gie it tae me."

"Faither", the laddie says, "ye ken whit ye'll dae wi' the money. Ye'll drink it."

"That's nae business o' yours", the auld man says, "and you're owre young tae tell me whit tae dae." So the argument got up and the laddie got angry and he threw the bag o' money tae his faither and walked awa'. So, naturally, the faither *did* go and get drunk, but the laddie he's marchin' on and marchin' on and he's no' worryin' aboot his faither at a'.

Well, weeks and weeks passed, and he hasnae seen his faither. But noo, the money's a' spent and the faither hasnae a ha'penny left, and he walks on and on until he comes tae anither toon. And the same thing is gaun on this time, but noo it's no' a king, it's a prince, and he has just a disease o' his mooth and lip. His tongue and his lip has some awfae disease. He couldnae eat, he couldnae drink, and he couldnae swallae.

Well, the faither hears o' this and he says tae himsel', "Well, if my laddie could cure a king, there's naethin' tae keep me fae curin' a prince. Onyway", he says, "I'm needin' the money." So he gangs up tae the hoose and intae the place whaur a' the folk are gaithered and he looks at the prince. And mindin' what the laddie had done, he asks for the barrels o' wine and water and milk, and that sort o' thing. Then he ca's for a sharp knife and they gie it tae him, and he cuts the heid aff this prince, and puts it intae the barrel o' wine.

Well, he's scrubbin' and scrubbin' and scrubbin' and the prince is in torture, screamin' "Murder!". He tak's the heid oot o' the wine and puts it intae the barrel o' hot boilin' water, and noo he's got the scrubbin' brush and the saft soap, but it's haein' nae effect. And the heid's screamin' and screamin' and screamin', so he tak's it oot and puts it intae the barrel o' milk. But no, it'll nae do – the auld man noo is in an awfae fix. A terrible fix. He's tryin' his best to get the prince's heid back on but it winnae stick.

Noo, tae get back tae the laddie. He come tae this toon and *he* was needin' money tae. He heard aboot the prince and little knowing that his faither was already in the hoose, he gangs up again tae try and cure the man. And when he gaes in, wha is there but his faither, intae this wee room, trying tae get the prince's heid on. He cannae get the heid on and the mooth and the tongue are still sair.

Well, the laddie lookit at his faither and he felt sorry for him, for he kent that he would be beheaded, ye ken, if he didnae cure the prince. "Well, well", the laddie say, "ye dinnae deserve it, faither. But aifter all, ye *are* my faither and I'll ... ach, get oot o' my road!" he says.

So the laddie tak's the heid and he does the three things again wi' it – intae the wine, intae the boilin' water and intae the milk. Makes a lovely job o' the prince. Of course, he had this ring, y'see, and ye can dae onything wi that kind o' a ring.

So he puts the prince's heid back on and he's great. Man, the prince is ten years younger, and the laddie gets anither bag o' money. And he's come oot noo and his faither's ahint him, lookin' no' weel at a'. He looks auld, auld and haggard-lookin'. And the laddie felt sorry for his faither and he says, "Faither: if I hadnae have come there, whaur were ye?"

"Ay", he says, "son: I ken. I ken I did wrang, but my God", he says, "I'll never get the thocht o' what I did tae your mither oot o' my heid. And the auld horse."

"Ach", the laddie says, "I think the best thing we could dae, faither, is gae back hame."

Noo, they'd been awa' for twa-three years, and they're comin' back hame noo, and they're just maybe a quarter-mile fae the hoose. They come owre a brae and doon in the holla is their wee hoose and the blacksmith shop. So they're walkin' on and they're baith tired, deid tired. And they're aye dreadin' comin' tae the hoose, ye ken, for they grieved for the auld woman and the horse.

Then the laddie looked up and he says, "Faither – do you see whit I
see?"

"Whit, son?"

"Look – there's the auld horse doon in the bog."

"A-help me God", the smith says, "it *is*, son. God bless me! That's
queer – I could swear to God I kilt that horse on the anvil."

And they walkit on anither wee bit and here's the auld woman, the
laddie's mither, thrawin' some water oot at the door, just the same's she
was when they took her and put her on the anvil.

And she looked at them: "In the name o' God", says she, "what kept
ye? You're tea's cauld. Ye've been an awfae lang time awa' the day." And
that's the end o' my story.

Type 753.
Motifs: D. 810 (*Magic object a gift*); D. 817 (*Magic object received from grateful
person*); J. 2411.2 (*Imitation of miraculous horseshoeing unsuccessful*); J. 2411.1
(*Imitation of magic rejuvenation unsuccessful*); D. 1662 (*Magic object works by
being stroked*); D. 2161 (*Magic healing power*); D. 1500 (*Magic object controls
disease*); D. 1865.1 (*Beautification by decapitation and replacement of head*); D.
1865.2 (*Beautification by boiling and resuscitation*); J. 2412 (*Foolish imitation of
healing*).

11   THE GHOST IN THE CHAPEL
(*Alec Stewart*)

I'll tell ye anither story. My faither had a fairm one time at a place called
Tullymet. Was ye ever in Tullymet? It was thirty-five acres o' a fairm. I was
a sma' laddie at the time and I had tae dae aboot three-four miles tae
school. My faither had twa sons-in-law. One was a plooman and the ither
was a shepherd.

Well, at the back o' the fairm was a chapel. It wasnae a church, it was a
chapel, and an awfae nice wee chapel. But it was never finished. The folk
that was building the chapel some way failed and there wasnae enough o'
population o' Catholics. So they shifted oot o' it and they left this chapel.

One Sunday, aboot ten o'clock, we went up there. There was five or six
of us, a' lads and lasses. The chapel was empty. There was a big pulpit
there and rows o' seats, just a big bare gouldritch place. So we a' went in,
and a man ca'd Tammy Stewart, a cousin o' mine, says, "We'll hae a
concert in here."

So we a' sat doon and he went up tae the pulpit and he was singin' that
song 'The Troosers That Hing at the Back o' the Door'. Then my sister
went up and she sung a song. And a' the rest o' us sung a song and some o'
them said poetries. Afterwards we went awa' hame for wor dinner and the
five or six laddies that were there for that day had tae gae hame.

So they sat up till aboot eleven o'clock at night tellin' stories intae the fairm. Then somebody said, "I think we'll hae tae go now." So they went oot and we was convoyin' them a bit doon the road, when all of a sudden we heard wor ain voices comin' fae the chapel. Twelve o'clock at nicht, and Tammy was singin' 'The Troosers That Hing at the Back o' the Door'. And we *a'* heard it and stood listenin'. My faither and mither cam' oot too and they heard it tae. Oor voices in the chapel and us stannin' in the road listenin' tae it.

The next day my mither went up tae the shop for messages and the woman in the shop says, "That was an awfae noise in the chapel last nicht. Wha was it?"

My mither says, "I dinnae ken." She didnae like to tell the woman aboot us bein' in the chapel through the day.

"Well", says the woman, "it went on the hale nicht." And that's the truth. It lasted the whole nicht. The same thing over and over again, and they laddies, they didnae gae hame that nicht. They stayed wi' us. They didnae gae hame till daylicht cam' in.

Motif: E. 586 (*Dead returns soon after burial*).

12 THE AULD MAN'S WAKE
(*Alec Stewart*)

I was stayin' in Ireland one time, and in Ireland when you can play the pipes 'n' that there's always crowds comes at night to hear ye playin'. So this night there were hardly anybody come and there was a man and I says to him, "Where is all the fellas the night?"

"Oh", he says, "they're a' away to a wake." (You know what a wake is?) "Are ye gaun up tae 't?"

"Oh", I says, "I don't mind."

So we went up to the wake and they were a' smokin' round the table, you know, smokes, and tellin' jokes and singin' songs and that. So we sat there. It was an old man that had died. So I said, "What was wrong wi' him?"

"Och, – natural causes. He just died. If ye like", he says, "I'll take ye tae the funeral tomorrow."

I was doin' nothin' anyway. "All right", I says, "I'll go to the funeral wi' ye." So we went tae a place ca'd St Johnson, that's awa' up from Londonderry, and the auld man was buried.

"Are ye gaun in for a pint o' stout?"

And I said, "I don't mind."

So we went in and we had a pint of stout. And we had anither pint o' stout. And we had anither pint o' stout. And I was never used wi' the drink, I was nae very auld at the time. He says, "Would ye like to come round to my house?" he says. "They may have a singsong there."

I says, "I don't mind."

We went right round where his house was and they were a' singin'; there was dancin' and singin'. So I stayed, oh aboot one o'clock in the mornin'. He says, "I'll convoy ye doon a bit o' the road."

I says, "All right."

So I had to go right round, ye see, and my place was over here and he was away, about three mile the other side o' that again. And I had to come past this auld man's house, where the wake was. However, I thocht nothin' about it. So I was comin' down the road – he left me then – and I'm comin' whistlin' doon the road and I was aboot fae here, say, to your car oot here. It was a moon – moonlight. It was clear as anything. And I lookit – there were nobody in the house, the auld man's house, but I saw him stannin' at the gate, the auld man that'd died. He was stannin' at the gate, and he had two sticks and he was stannin' lookin' up the road right at this gate.

So I come down a bit and down a bit and down a bit and I says, "It *must* be him. It *is* him." So I didnae know what to do, whether to go back or rin forward; I didn't know *what* to do. I rin across the fields but I couldnae get across the fields because there was a big ditch at that side. So I just went down a bit and down a bit and I looked right intae his face. And it was the auld man right enough, 'cause I saw his corpse in the hoose.

And I just put awa' doon my eyes and I just went right on the road. And I told two or three people after that the same story but och, they just laughed at me.

But it was true.

Motif: E. 586 (*Dead returns soon after burial*).

13 THE GHOST WIFE
(*Alec Stewart*)

Here's a story that was telt tae me by an auld, auld man. His name was Docherty and he cam' fae a place ca'd Letterkenny in Ireland. He says:

I was stayin' above Letterkenny there, and next door tae me was a blacksmith. He had a young wife, a nice-lookin' bit o' stuff, but he had no children. So time rolled past, and she was gaun tae hae a wean. But afore she had this waen, she died.

Oh, the man was in an awfae state. I couldnae get him settled. I went in every night. I was at the wake and I tried tae get him settled, but it was no use.

Well, he come for me and I went tae the funeral. He yoked the auld pony and the jauntin' car, and we gaed tae the funeral. So we buried the woman, and we're back in the jauntin' car and he was drivin'. I was aye tryin' tae speak tae him, but och, his hairt wasnae in drivin' and he was aye thinkin' aboot his wife.

When we was comin' hame, I lookit in front o' me, and I seen a woman comin' alang the road. She'd a shawl aboot her and a basket on her airm as if she was gaun tae the shop. I says, "Michael – look whit's comin'". He lookit up.

"My God", he says, "pull up, pull up!" And he pull't the horse up, for this was his ain wife comin' alang the road. The woman stoppit. He says, "Whaur are ye gaun?"

She says, "I'm gaun tae the shop."

"Gaun tae the shop?" he says.

She says, "Ay."

He says, "We'll turn back and tak' ye there."

"No no", she says, "youse go on and hae the kettle boilin'. I'll be back within the hour." And she marched on. We drove on and I says, "It cannae be, it cannae be! It's impossible. We buried her the day."

"Well", he says, ye saw her for yoursel'. It's no' like I'm tellin' ye a story. Ye see'd her yoursel'."

I says, "That's right, I did see her."

And Michael says, "We'll hae tae wait till she comes back. We'll know then." So we went tae the hoose and we sat doon. And waited and waited while the kettle's boilin'. Well, the gate bangs and in she comes. Her man's sittin' there lookin' at her and lookin' at her. Then he gaed across and he felt her airms. "You're richt enough", he says.

"Whit's wrang wi' ye?" she says. Well, he was feart tae tell her. "I dinnae ken whit's wrang wi' ye', man", she says, "I dinnae ken whit's wrang wi' ye at a'. Ye're lookin' awfae queer, and so's Docherty there. Ye're lookin' awfae queer."

Well, her man says, "Docherty, I'll hae tae tell her." And he says, "We buried ye the day."

"Ach, awa'!" she says. "Hoo could ye bury me and me here?" So while she was makin' the tea, her man rins oot richt doon tae the priest and the priest come up and he lookit at her.

"Get the pony yokit, Michael", he says. "Get the pony yokit."

"Whit for, father?" he says.

"Never you mind. Get the pony yokit."

"Are ye no' wanting the tea?" she says.

"I'll get my tea when I come back", Michael says. So they yokit the pony and they went richt back tae the graveyard and the men was just new-finished happin' the grave.

The priest says tae the gravediggers: "Dig that grave up." So they dug the grave and they opened the coffin, and what was in the coffin? A birch besom. They opened the coffin and a birch besom was in it. The woman lived for twenty year after that, and that's a fact.

Motifs: E. 322 (*Dead wife's friendly return*); E. 586 (*Dead returns soon after burial*).

14 THE DEVIL LOVER
(*Alec Stewart*)

Well, once upon a time there was a girl and she bade in a wee hoose wi' her faither and mother. She was going to a dance this night and she went away at aboot half past seven. And when she landed at the dance she danced the maist o' the night wi' one man. "Can I see ye home?"

"Yes", she said, "ye can see me home."

So, come aboot eleven o'clock, they put on their coats and they marched awa' hame. They'd a good three mile to go back tae her hoose. When they got there, they kissed and said goodbye.

"Will I meet you the morn's nicht?"

"Yes", she said.

There was no dance the next night, but she went down the road and she met him and he walkit her home again. Once again they kissed and separated. And then the third night come.

On this nicht, when they come back tae the gate they stood and talked a long time. And then they started tae kiss. Well, she dropped her handkerchief and when she bent tae lift it she lookit and she saw one o' his feet was a cow's foot. A cloven fit, we ca' it. And she says tae hersel', "Oh, this is terrible." But she never said nothing tae him. She just walkit in. And she told her faither when she went in.

He says, "Oh well, say nothing the nicht. We'll see aboot it in the mornin'." The next mornin' her faither said, "Just you go and see him the nicht as though naethin' has happened."

So that night she saw him at the same place again and they walkit hame. "Last night", he says, "you promised to marry me in a year's time."

"Did I?" she says.

"Yes", he says, "you promised tae marry me."

So they parted again and she telt her faither. "Oh", he says, "that's terrible. Ye didnae dae that!"

"Oh yes", she says, "I did. I promised to marry him in a year's time."

So her faither says, "We'll hae tae go and see the priest." They were Catholics, y' see. So they went doon tae the priest and they telt the priest a' aboot it.

The priest says, "When has she tae marry him?"

"In a year's time."

"When was this?"

"Oh, last nicht."

"Oh well, I'll mark it in", he says. "And when a year time's up you come down tae me, and I'll speak tae him."

So time rolled past till the year was up and the night come when she's tae meet him and she went away doon tae the chapel and she telt the priest that the man had not arrived yet.

"Oh, he'll come", says the priest. "You just come in here." So when she come in there, there was a circle of fire. There was a stone floor in the chapel and he'd made a circle of fire with peats right across. "Now", he says, "I'll lift you in here, into the circle of fire." So he lifted her into the circle of fire. "Now, I'll stand beside you", and he went into the circle of fire, too. And he's stannin' there and he's prayin' intae this Bible.

And then a chap comes at the door, but they never paid ony attention tae it. And anither chap comes, louder, at the door. But they never paid ony attention tae it. And the third chap comes and the man says, "I come for my wife."

"Well", the priest says, "if ye've come for your wife, come in and marry her."

"I can't come in", says the man.

"Well", the priest says, "I'll give ye your wife when you gie your hand in my hand."

"I can't!" the man says, and he started chappin' and kickin' at the door. But the priest wouldnae pay ony attention tae him. He just kept prayin' on and prayin' on and prayin' on. And the man at the door turnt intae a fiery ball. It was the Devil. He went right away frae the door and he took half o' the chapel wi' him. And that's the last o' my story.

Type 810.

Motifs: S. 211 (*Child sold (promised) to devil or ogre. Variant*); D. 1381.11 (*Magic circle protects from devil*); K 218.1 (*Devil cheated by having priest draw a sacred circle about the intended victim*).

15 THE DUKE OF ROXBURGH'S SOUL
(*Alec Stewart*)

This was in the 1914 war, and it was a man ca'd Archie MacKay o' Dunkeld. He stayed in Tarbert, but he's dead now. Died aboot four-five month ago. In 1916, he come over tae see my faither and he says tae him, "Have ye seen what's in the paper the day, John?"

My father says, "No".

"There's a story in the paper", he says, "and I've read it right through."

"What was it aboot?" says my faither.

"Aboot a ship come over from America. They're a' dinin' and haein' a dance or a ba' or somethin' in the ship. It was aboot twelve o'clock at nicht, a bonnie nicht. The moon was shinin', and they're a' oot on the deck. All on a sudden, they lookit up in the sky and they saw a chariot come across and twa horses tae it. Just flyin' through the sky. And the captain was there and he gied a roar tae the man that was drivin' the chariot: 'Where art thou gaun?' And the man pu'd up the pair o' horses and stoppit, and he says, 'I'm gaun for the Duke o' Roxburgh's soul.' And he keppit on.

"The next nicht at aboot the same time they lookit up and they seen this thing come by again, the twa horses and the chariot. And the captain roared up tae him: 'Did ye succeed?' And he pu'd up and he says, 'No, dammit! With youse prayin' and the folk in England and Scotland prayin', I never succeeded.' And he drove on."

That was in the paper!

Motif: K. 218 (*Devil cheated by religious or magic means*).

16 THE AULD COUPLE'S SON
(Belle Stewart)

This is aboot an auld fisherman and his wife. He wasnae always auld but frae the time I kent the story he was an auld man. Well, they bade in this wee village and I dinnae think there would be ony mair than fifty or sixty inhabitants in it. It was a kind o' wee island, y'see, and if they wanted onything such as claes or things like that they'd aye tae go by boat across the water tae the big toon. But oh, they were a real happy crowd on this wee island, and if ye needed onything ye didnae hae it's 'come tae me and I'll gie it tae ye and I dae the same wi' you'. There was nae selfishness, naethin' like that. Whatever I had was yours. And what's yours was mine.

They made their livin' entirely by fishin'. They fished a' day and nicht, whatever time they wanted to go and the boats cam' owre and collected their fish and took them back wi' them. Oh, they were gettin' on fine, prosperin' grand. But this auld man and woman they never had ony faimily. That was the one worry that they aye had. They were awfae fond o' bairns but they were never blessed wi' ony.

So the time were on and I dinnae ken whit happened, whether it was a storm o' the sea or whether it was a dry spell, but it got to be that they were gettin' very few fish. And time wore on intae weeks and intae months, till they were gettin' nae fish at a'. Absolutely nane at a'. Nane. And soon there was naethin' left in the shops. The groceries was a' bocht up. They were in starvation, the hale island.

As for the auld man and his wife, they'd used up a' the tatties that they'd growed for theirsel' and there was naethin' left. Them that was able left the island and went away and tried to get wark ither places. But the aulder ones wadnae leave the island. It was their hame, for they were born and bred in it and they said 'If we dee, we'll a' dee thegither. We'll just bide whaur we are.'

The auld man got fair sick o' gaun tae the water and he says, "There's nae use me gaun, wife", and she says, "Ye never know. God micht change oor luck. So awa' ye gang doon and see."

Well, the day come when the auld man says, "This is my last try."

And she says, "You'll be lucky if I'm livin' when ye get back, for I'm that weak I cannae stand on my feet."

"Well", he says, "we're baith far gone. I dinnae ken hoo I'm gaun tae get doon the length o' the water."

"Well, I'll tell ye whit tae dae", she says, "Ye tak' that rope and tie it across that beam and put the chair under it. And", says she, "If ye're no' back by seven o'clock the nicht I'll be hanged. I'd rather end my days quick", she says, "than dee gradually fae starvation, for I ken I'm deein'."

So the auld man's awa' doon tae the water and he threw in his net. But when he pu'd it in, it was empty. Well, he was fair weak and his airms was that tired that he sat doon on the bank. So he's sittin' there hingin' his heid and he thocht he heard footsteps comin' towards him, and he lookit up and here's a gentleman comin'. A tall gentleman wi' a big hat, a lang coat and a walkin' stick, a very well-dressed gentleman. He come up and he says, "Good evening, my man."

The auld fisherman looked up at him and he says, "Oh, good evening, sir."

"What are ye daein'?" says the gentleman. "You look very tired."

"Ay", he says, "I'm tired." And he telt him a' his worries aboot there bein' nae fish and hoo everybody in the village was deein'.

"Dear me", the gentleman says, "can things be as bad as a' that?"

"Oh, yes sir", says the auld man, "they're as bad as a' that."

"Hae ye tried your nets today?" the gentleman asked.

"Oh ay", he says, "my net's lyin' there. I'm just after pu'in' it oot but there's naethin'."

"Och", the gentleman says, "I wadnae despair. Try again. Throw your net intae the water again."

"Tae tell the God's truth, man", said the auld man, "I hannae the strength tae lift the net."

"Come on", the gentleman says, "try it onyway, just once mair and see whit happens."

So he lifted his net and he threw it intae the water and it wasn't minutes until he seen the movement, ye ken, like the splashin' and a' that in the water. "God bless me", he says, "what's that?"

The gentleman said, "Draw your net noo."

Well, he doesnae ken whaur the strength come fae, but he managed tae pu' the net and it was just swellin' wi' fish. It couldnae hae held anither yin. So this gentleman gies him a wee hand tae help pu' it in. And what wi' the excitement the fisherman forgot all aboot his auld wife and aboot the time. "Oh, God bless me!" he said, "I wonder what time is it?"

And the gentleman says, "Well, it'll be aboot five minutes tae seven."

Well, he'd a good bit to walk hame tae the hoose and he's thinkin' whit his auld wife said aboot no' bein' hame at seven o'clock. So he began tae run, left the fish as they were and run hame tae the auld woman tae tell her aboot them. The place was a' in darkness and awfae still when he got there. "Oh", he says, "she's deid, she's hanged."

But when he gaed in, he found her asleep hingin' owre the table. So he wakened her up and he telt her a' aboot the fish. "Come on doon, come on doon till ye see it!" he says. "My net's fair fu' o' fish."

"Oh, God forgi'e ye!" she says.

"I'm tellin ye!" he says. "Come on, come on!"

And the poor auld soul, though she wasnae able to trail the one foot after the other, he's trailin' her doon tae the water to see the net fu' o' fish. The man was still stannin' there when they got there, but they didnae pay ony attention tae him. But when they kinna come tae themselves owre the excitement, the man says, "Now empty these out and throw your net in again."

"Oh", but the auld man says, "I cannae dae that. A' the folk in the toon's stairvin'. I'll hae tae gang and gie them some o' they fish."

"Oh, d'ye mean to share them?" the gentleman says.

"Oh, ay", says the auld man. "I'll hae tae share them, 'cause if *they* had them they'd share them wi' *me*."

"Well", says the gentleman, "there's one thing ye'll hae tae dae. Ye'll hae tae gut every one o' these fish afore ye gie them tae your friends."

"Oh dear me", the auld man says. "It would tak' me a week tae gut a' they fish. I'll just gang tae the village and tell them tae come doon wi' their creels and fill them."

"*You gut the fish*", the gentleman says. "I'm tellin' you, richt noo where they are. And ye can send the auld woman up to tell them tae bring their creels. But tell them no' tae come for an hour. And by that time ye'll hae them a' gutted."

"Oh dear me", he says, "I wadnae gut a' that in a week nevermind in an hour." Well, the first fish he guttit, there wasnae guts in it at a'. It was pearls and rubies and a' the maist precious stones that was intae it. And the auld man couldnae believe it, but when he'd gone roond a' the fish, every one o' them was the same and he just had a heap o' precious stanes a' roond, ye ken.

"Noo", the gentleman says, "you cover them up. Don't let onybody see them, and you tell your folk noo to come and fill their creels."

Well, the folk were a' bewildered when they saw them gutted. "Och", says the auld man, "I just done that for to save ye the bother. I kent ye'd a' be hungry, so just gae hame and cook them noo withoot the bother o' guttin' them.''

So they're awa' hame and their creels is a' fu' o' fish.

"Noo", the gentleman says tae him, "ye're a very rich man, ye know. Or ye will be when ye sell a' these precious stanes. But first ye must mak' me a promise."

"Oh well", the auld man says, "if it's humanly possible at a' and in my pooer, I'll promise ye onything."

"Well", he says, "I want ye to gie me your first-born son."

"God bless me!" says the auld man tae hissel'. "That man's mad. My auld wife's near eichty-four." Of course, he wad never let on tae the gentleman the age o' his wife, because he thocht it was a good promise because it wad never happen. So he says tae the gentleman, "Och, weel, I think I can promise *that* a' richt."

"I'll want your wife's word on it as well. So awa' ye get up tae the hoose and bring her doon."

So the auld man telt his auld wife when he went back tae the hoose. He says, "This man's stone mad doon here. He wants ye tae gie him wor first-born son. But woman", he says, "you're eichty-four and I'm eichty-six. Whaur in the name o' god will we ever hae a bairn noo?"

"Ah", says she, "he's mad a' richt, but I'm no' carin'. I'll promise onything. It's a' the same tae me, for I ken I'll never hae a bairn at this stage."

So the auld woman's awa' doon tae the gentleman. "That's an awfae queer request", says she, "that you're askin' o' me, sir."

"Oh", but he says, "I'll need to get something in return for what I've done for ye, and I want that bairn, your first-born son when he's exactly twenty years of age."

"Oh", says she to hersel', "I'll be deid lang afore that."

So they're awa' hame noo and naturally when they selt a' these precious stones and that, they bocht a lovely big new hoose and though they never got nae mair precious stanes intae the fish, he couldnae gang tae the river but he was gettin' his nets fu' afore they were richt intae the water. They prospered terrible, got awfae rich, awfae weel-aff.

Well, the time wore on and they forgot a' aboot the gentleman, and they'd been maybe a year in the hoose when the auld woman turned no' weel, and she says, "God bless me, I'm no' weel at a'. I kent fine", says she, "wi' livin' too fast a life at wor age, and daein' too mony things in a short space o' time – I kent I wadnae live lang." But she's no' weel and she's no' weel, and the auld men gettin' kinna worried aboot her noo. And she says, "There's nae use gettin' a doctor tae me at my age, for I'm done. I'm finished. I'm deein'."

"Oh", says he, "it'll dae nae hairm onyway, for we can weel afford to pay a doctor noo, ye ken."

Well, the doctor cam' fae the mainland and aifter he examined the auld woman, Oh God bless me, it was terrible! She was gaun tae hae a bairn. She was pregnant, y'see. Well, she near went aff her heid and so did the auld man. But the hale o' the village was rejoicin'. The word spread a' owre and there were folk fae far and near come tae see this auld woman of eichty-five who was gaun to hae a bairn.

Oh God this is terrible! How could this ever happen? Hooever, it wore on until she turned no' weel tae hae her bairn. And she'd nae bother i' the world. She'd her bairn wi' nae bother. She wasnae a couple o' hours at it. Oh, they're that happy! They're beyond theirsel's wi' happiness. They forgot aboot their age, they forgot aboot everything. And the presents is pourin' in tae the bairn and tae the auld woman and she was only one day in her bed till she was up and aboot feelin' just like a young woman. That was their happiness complete.

So, tae my story noo. And tae mak' a lang story short. When the laddie was aboot ten year auld he had an awfae notion tae be a minister. It wasnae his faither's idea, for he didnae want a minister in the hoose. "No", he says, "I'd rather ye was a doctor. I'd sooner hae a doctor than a minister in the hoose."

But, unknown tae the faither, the laddie's mither bocht him a Bible and he aye went up tae his ain wee room and preached tae hissel', and kept gaun wi' this Bible unknown tae his faither.

So it come on till he was aboot eichteen, and he's awa' tae the college, as his faither thocht tae be a doctor – but he didnae tak' a wee bit o' medical schoolin'. It was aye a minister he'd set his mind on. So the time come on and the time come on till it was to be just a week afore his twentieth birthday. Well, there's a great carry-on, ye see, aboot this birthday. A' the village gaithered and they a' had presents and everything for him. Oh, they'd a grand do. And there was an awfae carry-on i' the hoose and the auld man, his faither, says, "Och, I'm awa' oot for a breath o' fresh air."

He tak's a walk doon by the side o' the river and who does he meet but this same gentleman, after twenty year! "Well, well", the gentleman says, "I'm very pleased to know that ye mindit that I wad be here the day."

The auld man had nae mind o' him at a' till he'd seen him comin'. "Well", said the gentleman, "I kept my side o' the bargain. You're a rich man and you've a lovely son, and I ken that he's very well educated. He's a doctor, is he no'? But I'm afraid", he says, "this is the very day ye'll hae tae part wi' him, for this is the day ye promised him tae me."

Noo, the auld man's aboot aff his heid, for he'd forgot a' aboot this. "Oh", he says, "I could never tell my wife."

"Oh", the gentleman says, "ye'll *hae* tae tell your wife."

So the auld man plucked up courage and he went tae the auld wife hissel' and he said, "Somethin' awfae terrible's happened. D' ye no' mind we gien thon man wor faithfu' promise that we wad gie him wor first-born son when he was twenty years of age? Well, I've just been doon the water and he's there waitin' on him."

"Oh, God bless me", says she, "I forgot a' aboot that." And she's near hysterical. "Hoo can we tell the laddie?"

"Well", the auld man says, "He'll hae tae be telt."

So they cracked atween their twa sel's for a while and finally they telt the laddie. "Oh", he says, "ye've never telt me that afore. That's an awfae-like thing, mither. But ach, he'll no' be wantin' me for lang. Maybe I'll just be awa' for a wee while. There's naethin' tae hinder me. At least", he says, "I'll go see the man onyway."

"Ah", says she, "ye'll hae tae dae mair than see him. Ye'll hae tae bide wi' him."

"Och, well", says the laddie, "I'm a grawn man noo. I'll no' be feared tae bide wi' onybody, and I can aye come back."

So, he's packin' up his pajamas and shirts and things tae tak' wi' him, and he gets doon the stair and he's ready tae leave when he says, "Oh mither, I forgot something. Wad ye haud my case for a minute? Could I please take yon wee foldin' table that ye gien me when I was a bairn?"

"Oh, dear son, ay", she says. "Onything that's in the hoose is yours if ye want it."

So he gaed up the stair and he got his wee folding table and his most precious Bible and then he's doon the stair again. Then he says, "Ye'll come doon tae the side o' the water wi' me, mither."

And she says, "Well, I'd raither no', son."

"Och, ay", he says, "it'll no' dae ye ony hairm tae see me in the boat. My faither'll row me across."

So, they come doon tae the water and they seen the gentleman standing there and the auld man says tae him, "This is my son."

"Ay", the gentleman says, "I ken that. And he's a far handsomer man than I thocht he'd be. Of course", he says tae the laddie, "ye'll ken ye've tae come and bide wi' me."

"Ay", says the laddie, "I ken that. And seein' that I'm gaun awa' tae leave my faither and mither for a while, could I just have one wee request?"

"Oh ay, by all means", says the gentleman. "Whatever ye want."

So the laddie says tae his faither, "Gie me up my table, faither." And he opened oot the wee table and took oot the Bible and began tae pray. At this, the gentleman went awa' in a flash o' fire. He was never seen, sawn, or heard tell of. So he must have Auld Nick hissel'.

And the laddie went back hame wi' his faither and mither and he lives there tae this day, as far as *I* ken.

Type 811A.

Motifs: G. 303.3.1.2 (*The devil as a well-dressed gentleman*); S. 223 (*Childless couple promise child to the devil if they may have one*); G. 303.10.7 (*Devil gives luck with fishing and hunting*); K. 218.2 (*Devil cheated of his victim by boy having a Bible under his arm*).

17 SHEEP'S TURLIES
(*Cathie Higgins*)

This is a man and a woman and the man's name was Johnny and the wife's name was Maggie. So they're awa' up in Argyllshire somewhere and they're looking for some kinna wark. But they'd no' way o' conveyance that would tak' them ony place. Just a wee barra they had, and a wee bow-tent.

So they're trudgin' on and the wind and the rain's fair scuddin' doon the roads. And he says to her, "We'll hae to get somewhere, Maggie, for the nicht because we're gaun tae be drenched if we dinnae get someplace."

So they come on and they come on and they looked awa' up on the moor and they seen a fairm. "Well", he says, "I'm gaun up here to see can I get in somewhere for the nicht." So up they goes to the fairm. They chapped at the door and this man come oot, he was aboot six-foot.

"Well, my good man", he says, "Whit can I do for you?"

"Well", he says, "sir, I've only come to ask ye to gie me a nicht's shelter or maybe ye can gie me some wark."

"You wark, man? By the look o' ye it's a good diet o' meat you're needin'."

"Ay", he says, "I could dae wi' somethin' tae eat, 'cause my belly's rummelin'. Me and the wife's fair deid for somethin' tae eat and some-wheres to sleep."

The fairmer says, "Hae ye a camp?"

"Well", he says, "I've a bit o' a thing whit I camp in."

"Well", he says, "go way doon yonder tae the bottom o' the glen and put your tent up there. Try tae find a dry bit and then come back up", he says, "and the wife'll gie ye something tae eat."

So doon he goes. "No' a bad man", he says to Maggie, "a darlin' man." Doon they go and put their tent up and they get their bits o' blankets thegither.

"I'm no' gaun back up there, John", says Maggie. "It's dark. Ye'd better gang yoursel'", she says, "for I dinnae like the look o' thon man."

So up he goes to the hoose and he chappit at the door and the woman comes oot. She says, "I thocht it was the woman that was comin'."

He says, "She's awfae feart o' the dark, mistress – she'll no' come up." So she mak's up a wee parcel for him and he gangs back tae the camp and they ate whatever was in the parcel. Then they go to their bed and they're lyin' there when something pu'd at the tent, ye ken.

John says, "Wha's that?"

"It's me, the fairmer", says the man. "I want ye to get up at five in the mornin'. I've a puckle neeps for ye tae shaw."

"A' richt, sir", says Johnny, "but I micht sleep in, ye ken, for I'm no' used to risin' early in the mornin; it's aye aboot dinner-time when we rise."

"Well", the fairmer says, "it's five the morn, man."

So they're lyin' doon and Maggie says, "Ye'll never dae it, Johnny. I've never seen ye rise at five in my life", she says. "That'll be the day when I see ye rise oot the tent at five in the mornin'."

"Well", he says, "we'll hae to try it somehow."

"We'll listen for the cocks crawin'", says she. "That's how we'll get up." They'd nae watches nor onything!

Hooever, they made it onyway. He gets up the next mornin', tak's a wee bit o' breid and he's awa' back up to the fairm. "Hae ye ever shawed neeps afore?" says the fairmer.

"Oh, ay", he says. "I've shawed reeps, but I've shawed them in my ain time."

"Ah", the fairmer says, "ye'll shaw them in *my* time the day." And he tak's him oot intae this big field o' neeps. "Noo, get stuck intae them!" he says.

So Johnny's shawin' awa' and shawin' awa' and he's aye waitin' for Maggie, but she never turns up. So it comes aboot five o'clock and he's just aboot droppin', hadnae a bite the hale day. So he goes back up to the fairmer and he says, "Am I no' entitled to my day's pay?"

The fairmer says, "Hae ye shawed a good puckle?"

"Oh ay, I shawed a guid puckle neeps." So the fairmer handed him twa-three shillin's onyway.

"Now", he says, "I've a job for ye the morn. It's diggin' a drain."

He says, "Death's on my body now, I'll never dae it."

So of course the fairmer cries him at five o'clock the next morn again and he's puttin' him oot tae this drain, and he gies him a shovel. "Now", he says, "that's whaur ye've tae dig and the grund's as hard as stane."

Johnny says, "I'll never dae it! I hannae the pooer tae lift the shovel, nevermind tae dig the drain." The shovel's that big for him, for he's just a wee cratur o' a man.

So he's diggin' awa' and he's cuttin' awa' tae try and get this drain done, but na na – he sits doon and wipes his bree and he says, "This is gaun tae kill me. I'm in anither warld", he says, "if I hae tae dig this drain." So he's sittin' doon and he'd a wee bit o' a fag in his pocket and he's lichtin' it. And he says, "I dinnae ken what I'm tae dae. God, but if I was deid this is murder!"

But he's sittin' doon there onyway, pickin' awa' at the grass when a wee thing crawls oot o' the bushes tae him. And this is a wee fairy. "God bless my soul!" he says, "Whit's that?"

"I'm a man. What dae ye think I am?" the fairy said to him.

"Well, you're the wee-est man ever I seen", he says. "Ye're no' the size o' a bumbee."

"Nevermind," he says, "I could tackle your job onyway, Johnny. Whit the hell are ye daein' sittin' there when ye should be gaun on wi' your wark?"

"I hannae the pooer to lift the shovel, man, nevermind dig that drain", he says. "That grund's like iron."

"Well well, Johnny", he says, "I'll tell ye whit tae dae: ye gang doon to thon well, doon at the side o' your tent-door. Lift thon flagstone and clean oot thon well and I'll dig your drain for ye."

"O God bless me! Dinnae mak' a fool o' me!" he says. "I ken I'm no' wyss", he says, "but *you* tae dig that drain, man, you're no' sensible."

"I'll dig your drain", he says, "and you do *my* job."

"Oh well", he says, "there's nae hairm in't," and doon he goes tae the well. But it's just as bad cleanin' the well as diggin' the drain – but he comes up at last and the drain's lovely and dug. Oh, beautiful lovely soil, all dug oot o' this drain! "Upon my soul", he says, "the wee man can dae it!"

So he gangs doon tae the fairm and he says, "I'm finished."

"Get oot, man!" the fairmer said. "You're no' half-an-hour up there."

"Well", he says, "I finished it."

"I'm comin' up tae see", says the fairmer. So he come up. "My God", he says, "you've made a marvellous job. It'd tak' ten men a month tae dae that."

"Ah", he says, "but I'm Johnny, y'see!" And he claps his breist.

Then the fairmer says, "I've anither job for ye. I want ye to clear oot the byre. It's in a hell o' a mess."

"Oh, dear God", he says, "it was bad enough clearin' your drains – but when it comes tae a smell, I'm finished."

"Well", he says, "ye'll hae tae tackle it onyway."

So Johnny goes intae the byre and he's cleanin' awa' at this dirt and oh, it's murder. It's years since it was cleaned. Then he's sittin' doon smokin' a fag and he says, "God bless me, it's gettin' fae grund tae cow-dirt and I'm seik wi' it."

Oot comes this wee fairy again and he says, "You stuck again, Johnny?"

"Ay", he says, "faith, I'm stuck again."

"Ye're an awfae man", says the wee fairy. "Is there naethin' ye can dae?"

"No", he says, "there's very little, there's very little I can dae. I cannae dae much but shaw twa-three neeps, or lift twa-three tatties."

"Well", says the wee man, "I'll tell ye whit I'll dae. You dae this job for me and I'll gie ye something that'll help ye a' the days o' your life."

"Oh God bless me", he says, "it's bad enough clearin' places, but if I get this warld, I'll dae it."

"Well, there's a cave doon there", he says, "and it's fu' o' sheep's dirt. I want ye tae tak' a puckle o' that sheep's dirt and eat it."

"Oh God bless me", he says, "it's bad enough clearin' places, but if I get that intae my mooth", he says, "that'll be finishin' me all thegither."

"You dae it, Johnny", he says, "and I'll pay ye."

So doon he goes intae this cave and as sure a God the sheep's dirt's lyin' there, a' wee turlies, ye ken. So he lifts three-four o' these turlies. "Well", he says, "I wished I was deid afore, but I'll dee after I put this into me. If I dee noo, it's better noo than never." So he eats the turlies. "They're no' bad", he says. "They taste like Licorice Allsorts." So he cleans his mooth and he's back up to the place where the wee man's cleanin' the byre.

"Well, Johnny, did ye dae it?" he says.

"Ay, I done it", he says, "and, man they're no' bad."

So then the wee man says, "I'm gaun tae gie ye something and for the peril of your life don't let anybody touch them. Dinnae even let your wife put her hands near them."

"God bless me", Johnny says. "It must be something awfae funny when my wife cannae put her hands on them. What is it?"

"It's a set o' pipes", the wee man said. "But they're that sma' ye could put them in your nostrils. They're just wee, wee seedy things, ye ken, and ye'll hae tae watch and no' loss them."

"Oh", says he, "I'll no' loss them." And he puts them in his pocket. So awa' hame he gangs and he's intae his tent and he gets his drap o' meat and he's intae his bed. But this nicht he dreams the hale nicht, and he has the tent nearly torn doon. Well, his wife's batterin' at him.

"Whit in the name o' God", says she, "is wrang wi' ye? Waken up, man!"

"Whit's wrang wi' ye, Maggie?"

She says, "Ye've got the tent torn doon on tap o' me. Whit are ye dreamin' aboot?"

"Ach", says he, "silly things. Never heed. Lie doon." So she lies doon again.

The next nicht, there's to be a ball at the fairm. The dochter's engaged and she's to hae a ball. So the fairmer's wife says, "Why no' ask Johnny up tae the ball? It'd be a richt guid laugh, onyway."

"Oh, good God, ye couldnae tak' thon up to the ball. God, we'd be shown up." But the woman gangs doon and she invites Johnny onyway, and asks Maggie to come up.

"No' me", Maggie says. "I've nae claes tae put on to nae ball. I couldnae gang, the mess I'm in."

But Johnny gangs oot and he tak's a wee puckle grass, cleans his boots, tak's a taste o' water and rubs it owre his hair, and he's aff tae the ball.

So of course it comes tae the time that someone has tae dae an act, or a sang, or a dance, or something. And somebody shouts, "Get Johnny to gie us a sang!"

"Oh, mercy me", Johnny says, "I cannae sing." But they say that he has tae dae something, and then he min't aboot the pipes, y'see. And he tak's oot this wee set o' pipes and of course they a' start laughin' at him, made a real fool o'm.

"Och", the fairmer said, "I thocht ye were daft, but ye're mad tae try and play on them."

Johnny says, "Well, I'll try it onyway." So he puts the pipes on his shouther and he starts to play and it was the sweetest music ever ye heard. Oh, the folk were a' aboot him then as he played the eightsome reels, the sword dance, 'Strip the Willow', and a' the rest o' it.

Hooever, Johnny's gettin' drunk noo and he's carryin' on the warst ye ever seen in your life. He's drinkin' everything he can lay his hands on, black tea and everything. Anything that come tae his hand, he drunk it. And everybody's askin' him for a go of his pipes, ye see, but he says, "Oh, no no no – they never leave my possession. They're mine." But mind, he was gettin' that drunk he didnae ken what he did and somebody took the pipes fae him.

Well, whaever took them, they disappeared, and he's forgot a' aboot them noo and he's awa' hame. By the time he came tae the tent he's stottin' drunk, and Maggie started intae him. "Ah", says she, "I thocht there was somethin' goin' on up there. You're gaun wi' the dochter o' the hoose. There's nae man'll come hame in that state", she says, "and laugh and carry on the way ye're daein' if there wasnae somethin' gaun on." So of course they have a row and she sleeps oot at the door o' the tent, and he sleeps in the tent.

In the nicht, he starts the same carry-on as before, roarin' and carryin' on and he near pu's the tent doon. So Maggie wakens up and says, "In the name o' God, Johnny, what's wrang wi' ye?"

"Oh, Maggie", he says, "I had the awfae-est dream the nicht that ever I had in my life. I dreamt I was in a tunnel and I was followin' this thing", he says, "and it was like a licht and I followed it that far that I landed at the bottom o' the drain in amang the sheeps turlies and suddently", he says, "the turlies werenae turlies at a', they were real diamonds, and there's somethin' telling me to tak' these diamonds and anither thing tellin' me no' to touch them."

"Well", she says, "I don't know what it was, but ye've got me puttin' mad and it's nae wonder I'm grey-heided wi' the way ye're carryin' on."

The next mornin' he gangs back up tae the fairm and the fairmer says, "Well, Johnny, ye've been a guid while wi' me, aboot a month onyway. And", he says, "ye've been a wonderfully guid worker."

"That's richt", Johnny says, "I've been a hale month wi' ye and no' a penny hae I got yet but one day's pay tae keep me the hale month. It's just been bits o' things I been gettin' fae the woman o' the hoose", he says. "But ye'll hae tae gie me some money noo."

"Ay", the fairmer says, "your money's tae come and ye'll get it a' richt, but", he says, "ye've anither twa-three days tae dae yet and I'll pay ye a' thegither."

"Thank God", says Johnny, "I'm gaun tae get something."

So dinnertime come aboot twelve o'clock and he's finished noo whit he was daein' and he's settin' at this wee burnside. Oot comes the wee fairy man tae him and he says, "Well, Johnny, your time'll soon be up here."

"Ay", says he, "and I'm gaun tae miss ye for ye've been a guid freind tae me", he says. "Ye've helped me oot o' my difficulties and ye've passed the time tae me."

"Hoo is it", says the wee man, "ye hae nae money? Aifter all, ye've nae faimily and ye bide in that wee tent."

"Man", says Johnny, "I dinnae hae the sense o' it tae keep money. When I get it, I drink it. I dinnae hae the sense tae fight for 't. I hae nae sense o' money."

"Oh, well", the wee man says, "I suppose that's your life." So they say cheerio and awa' hame he goes tae Maggie. That night they're lyin' quiet in their bed, no' a soond. All o' a sudden, Johnny jumps up in the bed.

"Did ye hear that, Maggie?"

"Not me", she said. "I didnae hear nothing."

"Ay", he says, "there's an awfae rummelt at the back o' the tent."

"Ah", says she, "lie doon, ye're startin' that dreamin' again aboot sheeps turlies. I'm seik wi' ye!" she says. "Since I come tae this camp there's been nothin' but sheeps turlies and drainpipes. I'm seik o' it! Lie doon, and gie me a nicht's sleep, for God's sake."

So he lay doon again.

"Noo", she says, "for God's sake sleep this time or I'll hit ye a whaup on the broo, and I'll mak' ye sleep mysel'."

"God bless me", he says, "ye're a wild woman, Maggie. Ye'll no' gie me peace."

"It's you'll no' gie *me* peace", she says. "Ye've haunted me nicht and day since I cam' tae this camp." So they lay doon again.

Aboot two in the mornin, he wakens her again. "Na na", says she, "I'll hae tae gang awa' ootside, for that man's mad."

"Maggie", he says, "I dreamt I put my hand aneath my heid and there was gold in it."

"Ach, for God's sake", says she, "lie doon, man! Ye're nae wyce."

So he lies back again. "I dinnae ken whit kind o' a body I am," he says, "I must be gaun mad. The fairmer's put me silly atween neeps but, for the rest o' it, I'm puttin' mysel' silly."

Hooever, when he got up in the mornin', he said, "Maggie, I think there's somethin' under my pillow." She put her hand aneath his heid, and what do ye think she took oot?

It was sheeps turlies.

Motifs: H. 1129.3 (*Task: cleaning enormous cistern in one day. Variant*); F. 346 (*Fairy helps mortal with labour*); N. 821 (*Help from little man*); D. 1224 (*Magic (musical) pipe*); C. 181.1 (*Tabu: woman not to touch husband's magic drum. Variant*); C. 423 (*Tabu: revealing the marvelous*).

18 THE KING OF THE LIARS
(Alec Stewart)

Once upon a time there was an auld man and woman and they stayed in a
wee hoose. They had a son and he sat in the ashes a' the days o' his life. He
sat in the ashes and his mither was aye checkin' him and chasin' him away
tae get the floor swept and get the ashes oot o' the grate. But na na – he
wadnae rise, he would just midge a bit and then gang back the same place
again. He wad hardly wash his face and his mither 'times had tae go and
wash his hands.

So one day his mither says, "Jeck, are ye gaun tae set there a' the days o'
your life and never gang tae try and wark or get a shillin' tae yoursel'? Or
even gae oot tae a dance or hae a walk through the town?"

"Na na", he says, "I cannae dae that. I was never oot in my life. I'd be
feared tae gang oot."

"Well", she says, "if ye dinnae gae oot there'll be something happen tae
ye. There'll be a trouble come on the top o' ye."

"Well", he says, "I cannae help it."

One day his faither come in and he catched him by the cuff o' the neck
and he throwed him oot, oot on his fours, oot intae the yaird. So Jeck's
sittin' there and he says, "What'll I dae?" They lockit the door and he
couldnae get in. "Ach", he says, "I'll gang awa' for a coupla-three days
and see if I can get onything." So he gaed back tae the door and he rappit
on it and his mither come oot and she says, "Now, Jeck, ye'd better keep
oot because your faither's in and he's tak'in' his dinner. If ye come intae
the hoose he'll kill ye."

Jeck says, "I'm no' carin'. I'm gaun awa' for twa-three days, mither, and
I'd like ye tae bake me a bannock or a scone tae keep me gaun on the
road."

"Oh", she says, "I'll dae that."

So Jeck he got his bannock or his scone and he put it in his pocket, and
noo he's awa' doon the road. And he's walkin' on the road and walkin' on
the road and aifter twa-three hunder mile he comes tae a great big gate at
the roadside, and he sat doon. He lookit up and he see'd a big bill on this
gate, but he couldnae read. And he said tae hissel', "If I kent what was on
that bill I'd maybe get a job here." He waited till a man come by in a cairt
and horse and he says tae the man, "Hey, can ye read?"

"Ay", the man says, "I can read a wee bit."

"What's it say on that bill there?"

"Oh", he says, "it says that ony man that can mak' the king a liar'll get
the king's dochter tae marry."

"Tae mak' the king a liar? What dae ye mean?"

"Oh", he says, "tae tell a story maybe and mak' the king say 'Ye're a
liar!' and ye'll get the dochter tae marry."

"Och, well", he says, and he sat there and he thocht and he thocht for aboot an hour. "Will I try it?" he says. "I think I will." So he's marchin' awa' up this drive, aboot a mile-and-a-half tae get tae the door o' the hoose. So he rappit at the door and wha should come oot but a butler.

"Well?" he says. "What dae you want?"

And Jeck was a' raggit and torn, ye ken, nae bonnet on his heid, his hair stannin' on the ends like he'd had a fright wi' a ghost or something. "I come tae see the king", he says, "tae see if I can get that dochter o' his."

"Och, man", the butler says, "there was a hunder o' them last week tryin' tae get her, but they could never mak' the king a liar."

So Jeck says, "Will ye tak' me in, then, and let me see the king?"

The butler says, "A' richt. Just ye come awa' in. But before ye start, ye must tak' somethin' tae eat." So Jeck got somethin' tae eat and somethin' tae drink and he went in tae the king.

And the king says, "What's *your* name?"

"Oh", he says, "they ca' me Jeck."

"Well, Jeck, what d' ye want?"

"I come tae tell ye a story, king", he says.

"Whit story is that?" the king says.

"Oh, let me start", Jeck says.

"Afore ye start", said the king, "we'll gang intae the library, intae a wee room by oorselves. I gie everybody a chance." So the king took Jeck intae this wee room and they're baith sittin' at the fire. "Noo, Jeck, start awa'", the king says, "and if ye mak' me ca' ye a liar, ye'll get my dochter richt enough, for I cannae keep her back fae ye."

"Well", Jeck says. "Doon in the wee hoose that I belang tae we keppit an awfae lot o' bees. Boxes o' bees. Och, they were great boxes. I used to get five or six tons o' honey aff them."

"My God", says the king. "They must hae been awfae big boxes, Jeck."

"No", Jeck says. "They were just wee boxes. D' ye mean tae mak' me a liar?"

"Oh, no", the king says. "I'll no' mak' ye a liar."

"Well", Jeck says, "one mornin' I come oot and b' God I seen one o' my bees and he's strippit tae the waist and he's fechtin' the king o' the bees oot o' Spain. The twa o' them is fechtin' like onything and b' God", he says, "the bee that's come fae Spain is gettin' the better o' *my* bee. So I run across and I catched him roond the waist and I gied him twa kicks in the backside and I put him awa' back intae his ain country. Just wi' the one kick."

"My God, Jeck! Ye must hae gien him an awfae kick!"

"Ay", says Jeck. "I gien him a kick richt enough. Noo", says Jeck, "I've got five brithers. And my biggest brither he's aboot seventeen foot tall."

"My God", says the king, "he must be an awfae size o' a fella."

"Ay. He's a big man. D' ye mean tae mak' me a liar?"

"Oh no, no", the king says. "I'll no mak' ye a liar."

"My middle-size brither, he's aboot fifteen feet."

"Ay?" says the king.

"Ay. And my next brither, he's aboot twelve feet. Then it gangs richt doon tae the wee-est yin and he's only aboot half-an-inch."

"My God", the king says. "He must be a wee man."

"Ay. He is, that. We was oot huntin' one day and we'd a' the dogs wi' us and we'd a Labrador who was oot in front o' my wee-est brither. He was rinnin' ahint this dog and he fell intae his paw-print in the snaw and, by God, he couldnae get oot. He was lost for three days."

"My God", the king says. "He must hae been awfae wee when the couldnae get oot o' a print amang snaw."

"D' ye mean tae mak' me a liar?"

"Oh no", says the king. "I'll no' mak' you a liar."

"I was gaun oot huntin' mysel' one day and me and my biggest brither, him that's seventeen feet tall, started arguin' intae a wuid. He was tryin' tae shoot a grouse or something, but he couldnae get it and I started arguin' that I could shoot better than him. And he catched me and he gied me a thraw and it took me four months tae land. I landed on the moon."

"My God, he must have been a strong man", said the king.

"Ye mean tae mak' me a lair?"

"Oh no, I'll no mak' you a liar."

"Well, it was a new moon that I landed on. It was curlit, and I was sittin' on the edge o' it, on the edge o' the moon."

"My God", the king said. "Did ye no' feel dizzy?"

"No", Jeck says. "I lookit at the back o' me and I saw a door. But I couldnae get roond tae the door to get rappin' at it. I was feared I'd fa' aff that moon. So I gied twa digs wi' my elbow and who should come oot but a man. 'What d' ye want?' he says. 'Let me in', I says, 'or I'll fa' aff o' this.' He says, 'Ye'll fa' aff richt enough because I'm gaun tae knock ye doon.' And he had a big hatchet and he gied three swipes and he knocket the point o' the moon awa', and I'm wi' that bit o' the moon.

"Well, I'm comin' tummelin' doon, tummelin' doon and tummelin' doon, and wha was gaun past but a drove o' swans that used tae bide doon near my faither's wee hoose, intae the dam. And they said, 'Here's Jeck comin', we'd better catch him or he'll be killed.' So they spread a' their wings oot like this and didn't I land on the tap o' their saft wings."

"My God, Jeck", the king says. "You were lucky."

"Ye mean tae mak' me a liar?" says Jeck.

"Oh no, Jeck", the king says. "I'll no' mak' ye a liar."

"Well, they keppit on like that until they come doon near the grund and they says, 'Oh we cannae carry you ony further, Jeck. We'll hae tae let ye go.' 'Oh', I says, 'dinnae let me go. I'll be kilt.' But the swans say, 'We're gettin' tired. Ye'll hae tae go.' So they just tummelt owre and they let me go, and my God Almichty, I landed intae a rock right up tae the neck."

"My God", says the king. "Did it no' kill ye, Jeck?"

Jeck says, "No, it didnae kill me. Ye mean tae mak' me a liar?"

"Oh no, I'll no mak' ye a liar", says the king.

"Well", Jeck says, "I was sittin' in the rock richt up tae the neck and I couldnae get movin'. I couldnae pu' myself oot o' the rock. I was tryin' my best tae get oot, but it was nae use. And then, I got my hand and my knife oot and I cut my heid aff. And I says tae my heid, 'Rin! Rin tae my biggest brither tae come and pu' me oot o' this rock.' And my heid says, 'Ay, I'll dae that, Jeck.' Well, I throwed my heid doon and it's rollin' awa', rowin' and rowin' and rowin' owre this field tae rin and tell my biggest brither tae come and pu' me oot."

"My God Almichty. That was awfae!" says the king.

"D' ye mak' me a liar?"

"Oh no, I'll no' mak' ye a liar."

Well, my heid was runnin' and by God when I lookit I seen a fox come oot o' the bush, oot o' a whin-bush, and it made a dive at my heid and I'm roarin', 'Run, heid! Run, heid! Run, heid! Run, heid!' and b' God, didn't the fox mak' after my heid. So I gien mysel' three twists and three twines and I jumpit oot o' this rock and I run owre tae the fox and I kickit and I kickit and I kickit and I kickit nine young foxes oot o' this fox and the youngest fox's shite was better than *you*, king!"

"You're a liar!" says the king. So Jeck got the dochter and half o' the castle, and they're livin' there to this day.

Types 852 and 1920C.
Motifs: H. 342.1 (*Suitor test: forcing princess to say "That is a lie." Variant*); X. 1041 (*Lie: the large man*); X. 1021 (*Lie: the large animal*); X. 921.0.1 (*The unlucky hunt*); X. 916 (*Lie: man carried through air by geese*); X. 905.1 (*Master brought to say "You lie"*).

19 THE LEPRECHAUNS
(Sheila MacGregor)

Onc't upon a time there was an owld man and he was a man that cut peats for six month o' the year and for the other six month he sold them at the market in the toon. So it come tae the time he was sellin' the peats and he went away tae this village and he sold them. So he's comin' hame wi' his donkey and all of a sudden it stopped and it wadnae go anither inch.

"My God Almichty", the owld man says. "That's a mighty funny way tae carry on." Then, all of a sudden, he jumps off the donkey and he sees this hole in the ground. "My God", he says, "but you're a clever mare tae stop here."

So he looks down intae this big hole and fae the tap doon intae it is awfae wee steps, terrible wee. And he says, "Well, I'll never get doon there wi' my boots on, so I'll tak' them off." So he tak's his boots off and climbs doon this hole. It's no' very deep, just doon twa-three foot, but there at the bottom there's the awfae-est amount o' gold nuggets ye ever clapped your eyes on.

"Man", he says, "this is braw! Christ, I'll be a rich man when I get this up tae my wee cottage, ye ken. I'll no' hae tae sell peats the rest o' the days o' my life." So he goes back up the steps again and gets the wee basket he has for the peats and then he crawls doon again.

When he fills this basket he says, "Man, man – I'll never get up the steps wi' the weicht o' these baskets. The only thing I can do is tae empty them and carry them up by hand." So he goes back up the steps again and leaves the baskets at the top. Then he starts carryin' up twa-three at a time, they're sae heavy. And whenever he lands at the top he starts fillin' his baskets.

He just gets them filled when the awfae-est lot o' these wee leprechauns and gnomes and fairies gaithers a' roond him and they're makin' dives and wallops at him. However, tae mak' a lang story short, they tell him that he was stealin' their gold and that's an awfae thing tae happen. Terrible, man, it was terrible, stealin' their gold.

The auld man was shudderin' wi' cauld. He was frozen. He'd nae boots on, y' see, and he was stairvin' wi' hunger, and it was gettin' kind o' dark. And this wee leprechaun sees him and says, "Man, this is an awfae cauld place here. We just come in on the boat last nicht fae wor place. We heard this was an awfae rich country. Folk in the aulden time used to bury treasures, ye ken, and we kent the right spot just tae come tae tae get this gold. Naebody in this land could get it but us. But this place is owre cauld. The place we come fae has an awfae amount o' trees and we can cut doon branches and mak' fires tae keep warm. But", he says, "this is a God-forsaken country. Ye cannae get warm at a'."

"Ah", the owld man says, "but that's where you're wrang. We can mak' oorselves warm enough, for though this country has nae trees we've got braw peats."

"Peats? We never heard o' them", the leprechaun says.

"Oh man", the owld man says, "they're braw. They're a sort o' twigs and moss and bog that coils thegither and we cut them oot in slabs and lay them on the grund at the side o' the road tae dry. And whenever they're dry we fire them", he says. And he says, "I've got a braw load o' peats back hame."

The leprechaun says, "Well, if you can steal fae us, we can steal fae you."

Noo, the day afore he went tae mairket tae sell his peats, he made a saddle for his donkey and the donkey wadnae move an inch unless it had this saddle tae haud the twa baskets. So the leprechauns got the donkey and twa-three o' them made the owld man sit down. And anither twa-three took the donkey and went back to his hoose tae steal the peats. When they come back wi' them the heid-man o' the leprechauns sat doon and started in blawin' and lichtin' the peats and they got a kinna smoulderin' red flame fae it, ye ken. So they're a' sittin', and oh man dear, it's a braw fire, ye ken.

So whit happens now but they're a' stairvin'. They're a' goin' mad wi' hunger. "Hae ye naethin' tae eat in this country?" the heid leprechaun says.

The auld man says, "Oh ay, and what wad I gie tae be back at my fire roastin' twa-three tatties under my cinders."

"Tatties?" the leprechaun says.

"Ay, tatties", says the owld man.

"Have ye got these things back in your cottage?"

"Yes", says the auld man. So they're awa', and they bring back half a bagfu', and the auld man shows them how tae roast them, and they're a' roastin' them at the fire and pluggin' intae them, eatin' them ye ken. And as each one fills himself fu', he's sittin' doon and fa'in' asleep at the fire.

But some o' them turn on yin o' the party and begin tae mak' a fool o' him because he's got big feet. They cannae suffer him because he's got big feet, and they're makin' a fool o' this wee leprechaun because his feet are the same size as the auld man's. Hooever, they're a' fa'in' asleep noo, wi' their bellies bein' fu' and a' fine and contentit and warm at the fire, they fa' asleep.

A' except this wee leprechaun wi' the big feet, they're pushin' him oot fae the fire. So the owld man says, "You come and sit aside me. Ye're as much entitled tae a heat as the rest o' them." So he tak's him beside him. And noo they're a' soond asleep, a' except the auld man. And he says tae himsel', "I wonder, man, if I couldnae get up and sneak awa' while they're a' sleepin'?" So he gets up and he's tiptoein' awa' past the fire. He looks back, and they're still soond sleepin'.

So he creeps on anither wee bit and he sees a' this gold lyin' there. "Now", he says, "I can either take the gold and be a rich man or tak' my donkey. I cannae tak' the twa o' them because the saddle that was on the donkey has been pu'ed aff and burnt i' the fire." The donkey, y' see, wouldn't move withoot his saddle.

So the owld man says, "Well, I'll just hae tae leave my auld donkey. I'll miss it, but ... och, I cannae help it. I'll tak' the gold." So he tak's yin o' his baskets and he half-fills it wi' gold. "I'll no' be too greedy", he says, "because it's an awfae distance tae my cottage and I'll never carry it that far."

So, he thraws the basket on his back and he's marchin' owre the moors. It's aboot twa mile tae his hoose, an awfae distance, but every step he's takin', man dear, the weight o' the basket's getting lighter and lighter and lighter. "My God", he says, "whit's happened here?" And he tak's the basket aff his shouther and thraws it doon on the grund. And there's nothing in it but straw.

"My God Almighty", he says, "is that no terrible? I micht hae kent! I'm a damn fool tae think that any human being could steal fairy gold, because fairy gold is strictly for fairies, no' for human bein's." So he's settin' doon and he's fair sickenin' 'cause he thocht he was gaun tae be a rich man. Well, he starts pu'in' this straw oot o' the basket and he's just sittin' there thinkin', lookin' doon, and this is him weavin' a saddle. He's startit weavin' a saddle. "Ach", he says, "I may as well." So he goes at it and it doesn't take him ten minutes tae make it because he's so used tae daein' it. He's made hunders o' them.

So he made the saddle for his donkey. "I wonder, noo", he says, "if they're still sleepin'. I'll go back for my auld donkey, 'cause withoot my donkey I can dae nothing. I cannae even get the peats selt." So he creeps back tae the fire and he looks a' roond aboot and they're still a' soond asleep. He goes owre tae the donkey, throws the saddle owre its back and he's tiptoein' awa' wi' it when a' o' a sudden he turns his heid and looks roond at the wee leprechaun whase e'en are open.

He gies a jump, because he's feart that the wee leprechaun'll tell the ithers. But the leprechaun winks tae him and the owld man pointed tae his feet and tells him, "Ye can have my boots." Ye see, the leprechaun had such big feet that the buits would hide them fae the rest o' them, and they'd no' mak' a fool o' him.

So the owld man went hame. He had his donkey and he still has it to this day, and that's the end o' my story.

Motifs: B. 462.1 (*Animal shows man treasure*); N. 512 (*Treasure in underground chamber*); F. 351 (*Theft of money from fairies*); N. 558 (*Raised treasure turns into charcoal or shavings*).

20   THE MILLER AND HIS DAUGHTER
(*Alec Stewart*)

Once upon a time there was a miller and his dochter and they stayed on the banks o' the Ayr. They had a mill and they took corn in and they made it into meal. One day the miller was walkin' up the banks o' the river Ayr and just aboot a field-breadth fae his hoose was the hoose that the laird used tae bide in.

Well, on this day, the laird come walkin' doon the river and he met the auld miller. "Ah, miller", he says, "I see you're takin' your walk."

"Oh yes", the miller says, "I'm takin' my walk."

"And where is your dochter the day?"

"Oh she's warkin' i' the mill."

And the laird says, "Is she no' thinkin' aboot gettin' married yet?"

"Oh no, not yet", he says. "She's all I've got, and I've naebody tae look aifter the mill but her."

"She's a very bonnie lassie", the laird says. "I wadnae mind tae marry her mysel'."

"Oh, I dinnae ken her mind", the miller says. Well, he knew that the lassie was carryin on wi' a shepherd that bade awa' in a hoose on the side o' the hill.

So time rolled on and he met the laird again, and the laird says, "I think I'll tak' that dochter o' yours for a wife."

"Na na", says the miller, "ye cannae dae that because she's carryin' on wi' the shepherd."

"Well", says the laird, "I dinnae ken but if you willnae gie me your dochter, I'll hae tae put ye oot o' your hoose."

"Oh", the miller says, "is that so?"

"I'll tell ye whit I'll do", the laird says, "I'll gie ye three guesses and if ye cannae answer the three guesses ye'll get oot and I'll tak' your dochter. But if ye *can* answer the three guesses ye can stay on in the mill withoot rent, and ye can keep your dochter."

"What is the three guesses?" said the miller.

"Well", the laird says, "the first thing ye've tae tell me is the weight o' the moon. And the second thing is ye must tell me, hoo many stars is in the heavens. And the next one ye must tell me what I'm thinkin' on."

"My my my", the miller says, "they's terrible three hard ones ye've given me."

"Well", the laird says, "ye maun find the answers. If ye cannae guess them I'll tak' the mill fae ye and your dochter as well."

So the auld miller he's awa' hame noo, thinkin' aboot these three guesses. A' his wark was fa'in' behind – the corn was lyin' there and he couldn't hardly do onything. His dochter asked him three-four times whit was wrang wi' him, but the auld miller said, "Och, I cannae tell ye. Ye couldnae help me onyway", he says.

Well, one day, she's awa' up tae the shepherd – that's the laddie she was carryin' on wi' – and she says tae him, "There's something wrang wi' my faither. He's fa'in' back wi' his wark."

"What can be wrang wi' him?" he said.

"I don't know", she says, "I don't know what's wrang wi' him."

So he says, "I'll come doon when I get my tea and I'll hae a talk wi' him." So the dochter gaed awa' back and she's sittin' waitin' on the shepherd. When he come in, he lookit a' roond aboot the mill and he seen a' the corn lyin' and he says, "Whit's wrang wi' ye, miller? Look at a' this corn lyin' here."

"I dinnae ken whit's wrang wi' me", the miller says. "I met the laird up the river and he gied me three things tae dae and I dinnae ken hoo tae get owre it."

"Whit things?"

"Well", he said, "the laird wants Annie for to be his wife."

"Oh", the shepherd says, "he cannae dae that."

"He's gien me three guesses", says the miller, "and if I cannae answer them he says he's gaun tae put me oot o' the mill and tak' Annie awa'."

The shepherd thocht a while and says, "Tell me the three guesses."

"Och", he says, "there's nae use me tellin' ye, for ye wad never ken them."

"Let me hear them onyway", the shepherd says. So the miller told him aboot the weight o' the moon, hoo many stars was in the heavens and what he was thinkin' of. "Och", the shepherd laddie says, "nevermind. Nevermind him at a'. Just get on wi' the wark", he says. "When hae ye tae meet the lairdie?"

"On Sunday night", the miller says, "when it's gettin' gloamin' dark."

"Well, come on and I'll help ye tae get this corn done." So the shepherd gied him a help and he got the corn grinded and he made the meal. Time rolled by till it come tae Sunday. The shepherd come doon tae the miller's hoose aboot an hour before he had tae meet the laird. "Miller", says the shepherd, "gie me a suit o' your auld claes and I'll gang as you."

The miller says, "Whit d' ye mean?"

"Well", says the shepherd, "I'll go in your place if ye gie me your claes." So he got the miller's auld claes on and he's march up this riverside wi' his hands behind his back. And he met the laird, wha was just comin' doon.

"Ah", says the laird. "Ye didnae forget, miller."

"Forget what?" he says.

"Ye didnae forget tae meet me the nicht and tae answer the three guesses."

"No", he says, "I didnae forget, but I've no' thocht much aboot them", he says. "What was the three guesses again?"

"Well", the laird says, "the first one ye must tell me the weight o' the moon."

"Oh that's easy told", he says. "The weight o' the moon's a ton-weight. There's four quarters in the moon and there's four quarters in a ton."

"That's so", the laird says, "but the next one'll catch ye. Ye cannae tell me hoo many stars is in the heavens."

"Och", he says, "that's easier done. There are twenty-four million, five-hundred-and-fifty-thousand. Ye can coont them yoursel' if ye dinnae believe me."

"My goodness!" says the laird, "ye catched me there. But you'll no' ken the next one."

"And what is that?" he says.

The laird says, "Ye'll nae ken what I'm thinkin' o'."

"Oh ay", he says. "Ye think ye're speakin' tae the auld miller, but you're speakin' tae the shepherd." So the miller got the mill, the dochter married the shepherd, and they're livin' there still. The last time I was past the hoose I got a cup o' tea and some breid, and that's the end o' my story.

Type 922.
Motifs: H. 512 (*Guessing with life as a wager. Variant*); K. 1961 (*Sham churchman. Variant*); H. 702.1 (*Riddle: how many stars in the heaven, etc*); H. 691.1.2 (*How much does the moon weigh, etc*); H. 524.1 (*What am I thinking?*).

21 THE HEADLESS MAN
(Belle Stewart)

Now, I would like to tell you something that really did happen to a family called Reid. I suppose if you were going far enough back, there would be some connection to myself, because my granny's own name was Reid. That's my father's mother, y'see.

Noo, there's a place not very far fae the Beech Hedges, a place that long ago the travelllin' people were allowed to camp as long as they liked. And it was called the Island of Kinclaven. It's just doon the bottom o' the hedges, you turn on the Stanley road there and you could camp there for, oh, months and months at a time.

So there'd be maybe eight or nine families a' campit there and it was just coming to the end o' June. I ken it was the summer-time anyway, and this is what happened.

They were a' campit there and it was this young lassie and just like the young lasses nowadays, they began their courtin' and their love carry-on just pretty early in they days tae, and that's going back a long time before I was born – and that's no' the day nor yesterday. This lassie, noo, she was only comin' up sixteen, and her man would be a laddie of aboot seventeen. Noo, the lassie's name was MacDonald and the laddie's name was Reid, as far as I was telt. And this lassie took no' weel to have her baby, and it was her first bairn.

Long ago, it was just the one old traveller woman, the mother-in-law or the granny who always attended to these cases. But this woman comes on, and the lassie takes no' weel, and she'd maybe be in labour two days, you ken. They didnae hurry these things. Their belief was 'Let God tak' his ain time'. That was what they aye said – nane o' your new-fangled drugs, hurryin' on your labour and a' the rest o' it. They believed in havin' God's time for that.

So, however, the lassie had been ill for about twa days. But the eldest woman who was there, she began to ken that there was something wrong, that they couldnae dae onything, and she says to the lassie's father, she says, "I think you'll hae to get a doctor", she says, "because, honestly, Mary's no' makin' much of it and she's gettin' awfae weak. She's that young, y'see."

Noo, a' these things happen at a queer time in the night and ... roond about half-past-ten they said to the laddie that was the faither o' the bairn, "I doot you'll hae to go to Blairgowrie", for where they were biding would be to Blairgowrie aboot five-and-a-half miles. He'd to go right up the Beech Hedges and then to Blair.

"I'll manage by myself fine", says the laddie. "I'll no' be needin' naebody wi' me. I'll manage mysel' fine", he said. "I'll no' tak' lang runnin' that road."

So he sets off, comin' away on, hurryin' as hard's he could, richt up till he come aboot the middle o' the Beech Hedges. And he hears, like, a foot at the back o' him. But in they days it was nothing for folk to walk ... there wasnae ony o' your buses and very few folk would even go a-bike at they days. So he took it to be some o' the ploomen fae some o' the fairms and he never took ony notice. But the feet's comin' nearer, but he never looked roond because he was hurryin' on.

By this time he was nearly at the top o' the Hedges, just where you come out on the clearing for the Blairgowrie road. And he just happened to look roond. And there was a man, he said ... the man would be six or seven feet. He turned roond and he looked at him. And ye ken it wasnae richt dark at that time, it was the gloamin' as we talk aboot it up here. And here this man didn't have a heid. No head on his body at all!

Course the laddie got kinda feared but och, he kept runnin' then and he put it doon tae his imagination, bein' all upset and excited, so he thocht nae mair aboot it. Right up he cam' to Blairgowrie. Now, the doctor at that time was a Doctor Loonen, dead many many many year ago, and he stayed in one o' the big hooses above the post office in Blairgowrie.

So the laddie come to the door and the doctor asked him whaur he was bidin' and a' that. They were used, you see, with the Traveller folk at that time, and especially a birth among the Tinkers was quite an occasion for a doctor; they liked to be at it, somehow, it was an unusual surrounding.

And old Doctor Loonen says, "Oh ay, laddie, but I'll no' be able to tak' ye wi' me, for I've only got my Sheltie. Awa' ye gae hame and tell whoever's with the lassie she's to leave everything until I come. I'll hurry as quick as I can."

So the laddie, he's noo awa' and hurrying alang the road as usual. And just as he was comin' towards the Beech Hedges he got a wee bit feared because he'd been runnin' the maist o' the way. But "Ach no", he said, "that wasnae a man withoot a heid that I saw. I just *thocht* I seen him." But with him runnin' so much and the warm summer evening, – it's wearing on noo, it'd be one o'clock noo – he's awfae dry.

So he hadnae gone many yairds on doon the hedge when he sees a horse-troch. "God bless me", he says, "I could dae wi' a drink o' cauld water." So he sat doon and he drank his heart's content o' that cauld spring water, and he felt quite refreshed.

He lookit back and nae sign o' the doctor comin' yet. "But", he says, "I neednae run this wee bit for I hannae ony mair than a mile noo to go. So I'll just walk." So he's walkin' on and walkin' on. But here he gets this foot at the back o' him again. This foot's at the back o' 'm. But he wouldn't look roond. But oh my, the sweat's just pourin' aff him. He's that feared and he wouldnae look roond.

When he come to the bottom o' the hedges where the clearin' was, he looked roond, and there as plain as daylight he saw that man. But the minute he come to that last end o' the hedge that man disappeared and was never seen again.

So he took to his heels and he ran, and he collapsed when he got to the camp. He was so tired he fell asleep before the doctor come. But when the doctor come, he didnae hae an awfae lot to dae until the lassie was a' right. And she'd a nice wee laddie, aboot five-six pund, no' a big laddie for she wasnae a big lassie hersel'. A lovely wee boy.

So when everything was a' by, the doctor asked for the laddie. So somebody said he was sleepin'. "Ah, but I'll hae tae see him." So they got the laddie up and they telt him that everything was all by and he'd a wee son. And the doctor put his hand in his pocket and pulled oot two half-croons and he gave them tae the laddie. He says, "I was gaun tae give them tae your wife for the bairn, but", he says, "I think you deserve them for you did a wonderful job." So he bid them a' good mornin', and away the doctor went.

Noo – they got kinda tired o' bidin' in that camp, for they'd been there for maybe three weeks or a month and they thought it would be about time they would go. The young couple were the first to get ready in the mornin'. Her bairn in her oxter and whatever wee bits o' things they had they packed them a' up and said they were gaun to Blairgowrie 'cause it was comin' on the berry-time.

So they're comin' on, and just before they come to the Hedges he started tellin' his wife aboot where the man left him, comin' up fae the bottom o' the Hedges. And of course, she's laughin' at him, sayin', "You're daft, that wasnae true, ye never seen onythin' there."

Aboot the middle o' the Hedge there's a fairm ca'd Bridge Fairm, and the lassie says "I could do wi' a drink o' tea."

"Ay, and so could I", said the laddie. "I'll tell you what. Just you go up to the water-troch. It's just up there on the left-hand side into the hedges. I'll gae doon tae the fairm here and get a drap milk. And mebbe I'll get a piece fae the plooman's wife or the fairmer's wife."

So the laddie he's away doon to the fairm now and was a good wee while, tellin' aboot his wife haein' the bairn, and he's comin' back and he's away lookin' for some sticks to light a fire. You could light a fire any time they days, or anywhere. So his wife, she cam' doon, she says, "Honestly Davy, there's no water-troch to be gotten and I cannae get nae water."

"Ach, for God's sake", he says, "gie me the kettle and I'll soon get the water." But he went up that hedge and he went doon that hedge and he crossed in through a gap in the hedge and he went up and doon the far side and if he'd been gone yet there was no such thing as a troch in the Beech Hedges.

"Ye're right enough", he says, "I cannae see nae troch o' water. Sit ye there and I'll go back to the fairm for a kettle o' water." Down he goes to the fairm for a kettle o' water and he says to the woman, "What happened to the water-troch in the Beech Hedges?"

She says, "What troch, laddie?" And he telt her aboot what happened. She says, "Are you *sure*, laddie?"

"O ay", he says, "I'm perfectly sure. I had a richt good drink o' it."

"What kind o' a man did you see?" she says. He telt her.

"Come wi' me", she says, "to the auld cattleman's hoose. He's retired years ago. He's a man near ninety. My family has tended this fairm for twa-hunder year and *I* never heard o' nae horse-troch in the Hedges."

Onyway, he telt the story to the cattleman and the auld man says, "Ah, gae wa' w' your haverin', man! There never was a troch there!"

So the laddie says, "Well, well, it was there that nicht."

"Na na, what kind o' man did ye see?" So he telt the auld cattleman. "Well, laddie", he says, "I'm no gaun tae say I *didnae* hear aboot the man I'm no' gaun tae say I *did*. But", he said, "that man didnae mean you no hairm, none whatever. In fact", he says, "I think that man was guiding you to safety. But for the water-troch, son – I think you must hae made that up."

Motifs: F. 511.0.1 (*Headless person*); F. 771.6 (*Disappearance of phantom house at dawn. Variant*).

22 THE BEECH-HEDGE WAGER
(*Belle Stewart*)

This auld tramp-man was intae a pub in Perth one night. I dinnae ken hoo lang ago it was, but it's lang, lang afore my time or your time. Well, he was down and out and he couldnae even get the price o' half-a-pint o' beer. So he's wanderin' intae this pub and pickin' up wee fag-ends, and just dyin' for a drink. There's a few toffs owre in the corner and they're drinkin' lovely, and the puir auld tramp-man he's fair lickin' his lips lookin' at them.

They were discussin' the Seven Wonders o' the World, and a' this sort o' thing, the places they'd been, the things they'd seen and a' the rest o' it.

And one of them was supposed to have a horse that naebody could beat at jumpin'. That horse couldnae be beat.

So this toff, he's braggin' aboot his horse, aboot what it could dae. There was never a dyke, a fence, a hedge nor a place but this horse could jump it. This auld tramp-man he's just strainin' his ears, listenin' tae what they're sayin', and he thocht tae himsel', "I'm damn sure *I* ken a hedge it'll no' jump."

So he gaes up tae the toffs and he says, "Excuse me, sir. I just overheard ye talkin' there. Ye've a grand horse, a grand jumper?"

"Yes, my good man", he says, "I have that." Well, they didnae want tae entertain the auld tramp-man in conversation at a'. But, hooever or not, they couldnae put him awa'.

"I'm a poor man", the auld tramp says, "but I'll bet ye a hunder poond I can tak' ye tae a hedge your horse'll no' jump." The toffs were interested tae hear this: a poor tramp man bettin' a hunder pound. So they took him on. But where was this hedge? How could they see it?

Well, the auld man says, "I'll tak' ye." And he took them tae the Beech Hedges which are awa' owre twa-hunder feet. The toff just looked at the auld man and he says, "There's your hundred pound". For, ye ken, it *was* a beech hedge.

And the auld tramp-man had mony a guid drink for mony a lang day.

23 HOW MUCKLE HOUR GOT ITS NAME
(Belle Stewart)

The Beech Hedges up in Perthshire are supposed to be one of the Seven Wonders. There's a fairm ca'd Brig Fairm no' very far fae the Beech Hedges, and the fairmer there was awfae sair needin' a bit o' harness oot o' Perth, aboot twelve mile awa'. So he says tae the plooman lad, "I'll hae tae get that bit harness. I cannae dae ony langer wi'oot it, so ye'll hae tae gae tae Perth for it. Noo mind", he says, "ye'll hae tae hurry up. Hoo lang d' ye think it'll tak' ye?"

The plooman lad says, "I should be back in aboot an hour."

"Well, awa' ye go, then." So he's aff and he didnae come back for three weeks. So when he cam' intae the fairmyard, the fairmer said, "By God, that's been a muckle hour!"

And that's how the village got the name o' Muckle Hour.

24 GRANNY IN A BAG
(Alec Stewart)

Well, my mother's mother – this is, well, I don't know how long this'd be ago, but it's a long time ago – they were travellin' on the road. And they came to a fairm. And they asked for lodgin's. Generally in Scotland they go to the fairm and they get lodgin's and they put them in the barn amongst straw or in aside the cattle or anything like that. Keeps them warm.

So, they went in and they askit lodgin's. And it was my mither's granny and her husband and a bairn or something, I don't know. But my mother told me this. They went into this barn and they're lyin' down near half sleepin', when they heard this machine come, and only one horse. So they pulled the machine right into the yard and they went to the fairm.

And the farmer come on out and he says, "Oh, you're landed".

And he says, "Have ye anything?"

"Yes", he says, "I've got somebody in the barn".

"What is it", he says, "man or woman?"

"A woman", he says, "and a man, too. What do you want the night?"

He says, "We'll take a woman the night."

So they went into the barn and they catched my mither's granny, and oh, they started fightin', y'know, but the man was knocked out. And they put the granny intae a bag. A ten-stone bag. A big bag, onyway. They put her intae a bag and they tied the mouth o' it.

So they carried her out. So the auld man o' the fairm, he didnae ken onything aboot this, y'know. It was his son that was daein' this, and he didn't ken onything aboot this, and he come oot and he says, "What's wrong? What's wrong?"

"Oh", he says, "nothing's wrong, father, nothing's wrong."

"What have you got in the bag?"

"Oh", he says, "nothing", he says, "but my pig we're puttin' awa'."

So the man says, "No no, put the bag doon."

So they ran wi' the bag to put it on the machine, but the man fired two shots across their heid with a double-barrelled gun. And they drappit the bag and they broke two ribs o' the woman, my mither's granny. They broke two ribs. And they went and told the police, but ach, the police couldnae dae nothing. No' in these days.

Type 955A* (Variant).
Motifs: K. 2294 (*The treacherous host*); R. 116 (*Rescue from robber's den*).

25   BOGLE BRIG
(*Alec Stewart*)

There's a place the ither side o' Perth there, they ca' it the Bogle Brig. I used tae go wi' my faither tae the sales, the horse sales, and one day we was comin' back and my faither says, "Watch this. You're a young laddie, so you watch this. If ye see onything in the road", he says, "don't talk to it, or don't speak."

So he chappit the horse on, y' see and we come right intae the middle o' the Brig. And there's five-six women stannin' there, right in the centre o' it, and it was ... it was like a tunnel. The Brig was like a tunnel. Dash near aboot four or five-hunder yards long.

And my faither says, "Them's no' women", he says. "That's men dressed up in women's claes for tae catch bodies tae sell them. They get five–six pound apiece for the bodies, y' see."

26 THE UGLY MAN
(Alec Stewart)

This is aboot mysel'. When I was in the Territorials I went tae a camp on the other side o' Edinburgh. We usually stay a fortnight but I only stayed a week. So when the week was up I telt the colonel, "I'll hae tae go home."

So I got my pay and I landed in Edinburgh, and I was lookin' in a shop windae for some kind o' a present to buy my mither, when who should pass but a girl. She was aboot eichteen. We walked past a couple o' yards and then she looked roond. "Hello", she says.

I says, "Hello."

"You're Sandy Stewart", she says.

"Ay. Who are you?"

"Oh", she says, "I'm your cousin Peggy. Where are ye gaun?"

"I've been at the Territorial camp but I have tae go back hame noo."

She says, "Are ye no' comin' for a cup o' tea afore ye gang awa'?"

"I don't mind", I says. "D' ye stay far frae here?"

"Och, no, just roond the corner there." And she says, "What time's your train?"

I says, "I get the quarter-tae-four train. It'll tak' me right intae Perth." So I went awa' up wi' her, intae a close, then anither close, up a stair, two stairs. She took me intae this hoose. "Where's your man?" I said.

"Oh", she says, "I'm no' married."

"Are ye warkin', then?"

"No", she says, "I'm no' warkin' at the present time. I was warkin' but I'm no warkin' noo." And she says, "I've plenty o' tea, though, and sugar, but I've no bread in the house."

"Oh", I says, "I'll gie ye money tae get bread." So I gave her a pound, and I says, "And get half-a-bottle when you're oot."

"I'll dae that", she says. "But before I go oot", she says, "you get into bed."

"Oh", I says, "it's too early to gang tae bed yet."

"We'll see when I come back." So she went awa' oot and she was a guid while awa'. I smoked near five fags afore she come back. When she come back, she says, "Hae ye the kettle on?"

I says, "Ay, I put the kettle on." So we had wor tea and we're sittin' talkin' and speakin' aboot this body and that and once or twice I asked her, "Whit folk d' ye come aff o'? How are you my cousin?" But she aye turned the conversation tae somethin' else. So time wore on till it come near time for me to catch the bus for my train.

"Ach", she says, "What d' ye need tae tak' a bus or a train for? Ye can lie wi' me a' nicht."

Well, I was young at the time and I didnae think nothin' aboot it, so I said, "Oh, that would be a' right. Whit aboot anither half-bottle afore we turn in? Here's anither pound. Get anither half-bottle."

"Ye get intae bed, noo", she says, "afore I come back." So I tak' a' my claes aff. When I'm intae a hoose like that I tak' everything aff. Shirt and everything. So I'm lyin' naked intae this bed, y' see, and it was one o' them fastened, locked-in beds, and the back o' the bed was a' wuid. So I'm lyin' there smokin' away and listenin' tae hear if she's comin'. But I heard a rappin' at the back o' the bed, and I lookit roond and I says, "Whit's that?"

Well, there was a door slid back on some kind o' wheels and there's a man wi' a beard awa' doon there, and he says, "Whit are ye daein' in my wife's bed?"

"Your *wife*?" I says.

He says, "Yes. In my *wife's* bed." He'd a knife in his hand and he made a dab at me wi' it. But I thrawn mysel' sideways oot o' the bed and I heard the knife hitch onto the blankets and the sheets. So I made ootside, naked, I'm gaun doon the stair, right oot into the middle o' the street roarin', "Murder! Murder! Murder!"

Twa-three folks stannin' there and they were sayin', "Whit's wrang wi' this mannie, whit's wrang wi' this mannie?" And the policeman come, and he says, "Whit's wrang, whit's wrang here?"

"There's gaun tae be murder up that stair", I says.

He says, "Up whit stair?"

I says, "Up this close here, there's a woman up there. She took me in and she said she was my cousin." And I telt him the story. And I says, "A man come oot o' the back o' the bed and he was gaun tae kill me wi' a knife."

"My God", he says. "Come on and show me."

Well, if I got Edinburgh tae mysel' I couldnae mak' oot the same place again. I went up one close, up anither close, up anither close, up stairs and doon stairs. It was aye the wrang place. The polisman thocht I was daft. He thocht I was daft, and I seen yin o' the folk puttin' his hand tae his heid as much as tae say, "He's aff his heid."

Well, he made a dab at me, but I run, right up this main street, up Princess Street. Right oot, and a' the polismen's whistlin' wi' their whistles and the folk's a' aifter me. Oh, they're comin' in thoosands and there's a hard, keen frost. Crisp, ye ken. The stars were shinin' and the moon was oot. Aroond corners, I went like a hare, till I come tae the end o' the toon. And I'm walkin' alang this road and I'm shiverin', perishin' wi' cauld.

"If only I could find some hoose", I says, "whaur I could get some kind o' a coat or something." And as well as the cauld, I was feared the folk would come and see me naked. So I gaed the back o' this hedge and I'm crawlin' on my hands and knees, and I lookit and seen the skyline, and there's a man and a girl sittin' at the tap o' a fence, on a gate. And he had his hand roond her. So I says tae mysel', "If I could get nearhand that man I might get his coat or something tae put roond me."

So I crawled up and I crawled up and I crawled up, and then I whistled. I stood up and I whistled and I waved my hand. And the man lookit roond and he seen me. And the woman lookit roond and *she* seen me. They seen me stannin' naked. Well, the lassie gied a roar, and she ran, and the man ran tae. And I'm aifter them. But it was nae use, I couldnae catch them. They ran doon a big field and awa' intae a wee hoose. I thocht, "I'll get them noo if they're intae this hoose." But aboot a dozen folk come oot o' this hoose and they lookit and then they a' ran awa', every one o' them. They a' ran awa' wi' fright and made for the mountains.

Well, I come doon tae the hoose and I rappit at the door. No answer. I went in, and the table's a' laid wi' every kind o' meat. So I sat doon and I took a good tightener o' grub. There was a bottle o' whisky there tae, and wine. So I took a bite o' this and a bite o' that, and a drink o' this and a drink o' that, and then I'm awa' through the hoose lookin' for claes.

I come tae a cupboard place and there I got a great big lang coat and a pair o' buits. I couldnae get nae stockin's, so I pull't the buits on my bare feet and I put the coat on. A hard hat was lyin' on a chair, so I put that on tae. Then I went tae the door to see could I see the folk, but there was naebody there.

So I travelled on till I cam' tae a place they ca' Queensferry. Well, I was comin' alang this road, ye see, and I heard *scrape scrape* at the back o' a hedge. It was in an avenue, and I lookit in this avenue and I seen a man rakin' the stanes wi' a rake. I says, "Hey!" I says.

He says, "Who's there?"

I says, "Me."

He says, "What d' ye want?"

"I've come tae see if ye've an auld coat or an auld suit o' claes", I says. "I'm naked, I'm mither-naked."

"Na na", he says, "I hannae got onything like that."

"Have ye no' got a coat?" I says.

He says, "I never wear a coat."

"Ach, tae hell wi' ye!" I says, "What are ye daein' at this time o' nicht rakin' stanes?"

"Well", he says, "I'm the ugliest man in the warld. I'm that ugly that I cannae come oot i' the day 'cause everybody's watchin' me. And they come rinnin' after me and lookin' at me."

"Ach", I says, "let me see you. Haud up the light till I see ye." He had yin o' they hurricane lamps, and he held it up and I lookit at his face. Oh, it was an awfae face he had, richt enough. "Och", I says (just to keep him quiet, ye see), "I've seen uglier faces than yours many's the time."

"Well, laddie", he says, "if you can find me a face uglier than mine I'll gie ye five pound and a suit o' claes."

"Just gie me a suit o' claes", I says, "and keep the five pund, and I'll get a face uglier than yours."

And he says, "Then bring me back the face."

"Ach, awa' tae hell!" I says, "I cannae be bothered wi' ye." So I gaed awa' doon the road till I cam' tae a hoose and there was a wake in this hoose, and I walkit through a' the rooms lookin' for claes. It was dark. Nae licht in ony o' the rooms, ye ken. But I felt a bed under my hands and I felt this person on the tap o' the bed, ye see, and I says, "God Almichty, there's somebody here." Then I thocht, "I'll gae up tae the tap o' the bed."

And as I move up fae the foot o' the bed, I'm liftin' the claes up like this, and I'm lookin' at a backside, and I says, "My God, my God Almichty, if I took that face back tae the auld man I'd get the five pounds and the suit o' claes." So I went doon tae the kitchen and I got a knife, then back up tae the bedroom, and I skin't this face that I saw beneath the blankets, I took the hale skin awa'. It was a woman.

Then I gaed back tae the man wi' the rake. "Are ye there?" I say.

"Ay", he says. "I'm just aboot packin' up and awa' hame."

Says I, "I've brocht ye an uglier face than yours."

"Na na", he says.

I says, "I'm tellin' you. Hoo aboot this?" And I threw it owre tae him.

And he lifted it up and he said, "My God, there's a funny face!" And he held it up in front o' his ain face, like, and his nose was oot o' the yin hole and his tongue was oot o' the ither. For instead o' the mooth gaun fae east tae west, it was gaun north tae sooth.

So I got the five pound and the suit o' claes and I went awa' hame.

Types 955B* and 963*.
Motif: K. 735.4 (*Capture in trap-bed*).

27 **THE DEER CHILD**
(*Belle Stewart*)

Here's a wee story aboot Loch Ordie. There's a place ca'd Rechep and another ca'd Ramore, two different places, and they say

> Bonnie Rechep and bonnie Ramore
> Are two bonnie places I'll never see more.

Loch Ordie was the place where we used to pick the larch-cones. Now, away back, there was a lady and gentleman and it happened at yin o' they shootin' things. My mither used tae tell this. Lots o' gentlemen used tae come tae the shootin' and a servant lassie had a bairn tae yin o' them. Her faither and mither wadnae tak' her back. She dursnae gae back hame, ye see.

So she had the bairn, and she managed tae hide it till it was aboot twamonth auld. But when the gentleman that she had the bairn tae come back the followin' year tae the shootin', he wadnae hae naethin' tae dae wi' her. So she used tae keep her bairn awa' far, far oot fae the big hoose, and she wad gae back and for'ard tae it.

Well, whether she had a wee hut or a place for the bairn tae bide in, I couldnae tell ye, but she gaed back and for'ard and gied it its breist, ye ken, and fed it till it got up. And the bairn grew till it was able tae rin aboot, and the lassie left that service and went awa'. She forgot a' aboot the bairn and just left it there.

That bairn rin wild through the wuid, and it was rared up wi' the deers. This went on for a lot o' years and the bairn rin aboot inthe forest wi' the beasts and a' that, and there was hair growed on it, for there was never nae claes on it, ye see.

Well, there was a shootin' party oot one day on the hill and they thought it was a queer-lookin' thing. They kent it wasnae a deer and it wasnae a beast. They managed tae catch it and they took it back, but it couldnae speak or onything. I didnae ken if it was ever traced, but the mither was never found and what happened tae that bairn I dinnae ken, but they did catch it, and it was ca'd Lady Arvorlich, for it was a lassie.

This was just something that come intae my heid noo when I spoke aboot Loch Ordie whaur we pu'd the cones. And that was where my mither telt us aboot this. Says she, "This is whaur the bairn suckit the deer and run aboot wi' the beasts o' the wuids." That's what my mither telt me.

Motifs: S. 301 (*Children abandoned, exposed*); S. 352 (*Animal abandoned child, etc.*); B. 531 (*Animals provide food for men*); B. 535 (*Animal nurses abandoned child*).

28 THE DEAD CHEROOT
(*Alec Stewart*)

My granny used to gang aboot the countryside selling' soft goods frae a pack. This happened when my mither was a wee girl aboot ten or eleven year auld. She was rinnin' in front of her mither and they had tae gang owre a stile and across this field. My mither found a wee parcel and she started t' open it and a dead cheroot was in it.

My granny says, "Put that doon, lassie. Whit are ye daein' wi' that?" So she thrawed it doon and they went on across the field.

When they lookit back, they saw the dead cheroot standin' straight up on the top o' the stile wavin' tae them tae come back. It was wavin' on them tae come back. That's a fact. The dead cheroot was stannin' on top o' the stile, wavin' on them tae come back.

29 THE STRANGE BIRD
(*Alec Stewart*)

I was in Ireland one time and there were four-five families o' us. Belle wasnae there at that time, just mysel'. We was pearl-fishin' at the time, five or six o' us, a' men. My brither was there.

Well, we was pu'd intae a great big green at the far side o' the road and on the other side was the railway, and beyond the railway again was the sea. Ahint us there were big high cliffs.

So, we come back at nicht fae the pearl-fishin' and we kindled a big fire and made wor tea. Then we got intae oor bivvies, wor tents ye ken, and I was readin' a book. I was an awfae man for readin' at nicht.

Well, aboot ten minutes tae twelve, I heard this rummelin'. I gae oot o' the tent and it come right whooooooh! right across the tap o' the tents. And it flew richt away across the railway. Right back tae the tap o' the cliffs again. Then it come doon again whooooosh! and then

chree-cham chre-cham   chree-cham chre-cham

it was just like the second part o' the 'Cock o' the North', and it kep' goin' like that till the cocks crew in the mornin'. And then it went away. I didnae ken what it was. It was a big bird, bigger than what an eagle would be. Swish! it come doon, richt doon on tap o' the tents.

The last time I was across in Ireland I said tae her (Belle), "We'll go roond that way and see the place whaur we heard the Chreecham-Chrecham Bird. That's what we ca' it." So we went that road, but I couldnae find oot the place again.

30 THE GHOSTLY GATEPOST
(*Alec Stewart*)

This happened tae my faither when he was a young laddie. He'd mebbe be fourteen or fifteen year auld and his brither was a wee bit aulder. They were a' camped, aboot ten or twelve faimilies o' them, ootside o' Pitlochry. It was on a Sunday, and my faither and his brither, aifter they'd got their dinner, said they were gaun awa' tae meet wi' some ither freinds o' theirs. So awa' they went – it was a bonnie day at the back-end o' the year.

Well, ye ken whit young laddies are when they a' get thegither. They stayed awa' till it was late and the aulder folk at the camp they were visitin' was advisin' them tae hurry and get awa' hame, for they'd a good bit tae go. So they set aff, and awa' they went.

And they're comin' alang, talkin' away, and though they were fourteen or fifteen year auld they were gettin' a wee bit feart. Hooever, they twa laddies are comin' alang whistlin' tae theirsel's and they got tae aboot five-six-hunder yards fae where they were stayin'. They could see the reek o' the fires o' the camp through a gap in the hedge.

Just then, they saw a man stannin'. So my faither's brither says, "Jock – ask that man the time. It must be bonnie and late." But the way he said it was, "Mang the cowl the clocker."

So my faither said, "What time is it, sir?" There was no answer. So they lookit towards him again. He was kind o' in the shade. "Could ye please tell me the time, sir?" There was no answer. Well, they'd heard the auld folk at the campfire talkin' and sayin', 'If ye ask a body twice, never ask him a third time if he doesnae answer ye.' And they got kind o' feart.

Noo, there was a cairn o' stanes lyin' there, so (laddies that they were) they up wi' these stanes and they're batterin' at this man and they're batterin' at this man, and aye rinnin' on doon the road a bit and aye throwin' back stanes. But the man never answered them. Well, they got the length o' the camp and the auld folk said, "My God, whit's a-dae wi' ye, laddies? Whit's wrang wi' yese? Whit's happened?"

My faither says, "There's a man up there and we asked him the time twice and he wadnae speak tae us."

And an auld man in the camp says, "I hope ye didnae ask him the third time, laddie."

"No, we did not", he says. "But I'll tell ye what we *did* do, we battered him wi' stanes."

"Oh, my God", an auld woman says. "Ye mebbe hurt the man."

"I'm no' carin'", my faither says. "He wadnae tell us the time onyway."

So an auld man says, "Whit kin' o' a man was he?"

"He was a tall tall man wi' a lum-hat, a black lum-hat and a white front richt doon. He stood there lookin' at us and he never answered us." Some of them wanted tae gang back, but ye ken whit the womenfolk are.

They said, "No no – that's no' richt. You're no' gaun back the nicht."

So the next mornin' they're a' packed up and movin' on, and the laddies are rinnin' in front o' them and they says, "This is where we saw the man." But when they went and lookit – well, an auld man gaed forrit, and he says, "Whit kind o' a man did ye say ye saw?"

"A tall man", my faither says, "wi' a black lum-hat and a black suit, but it had a white front."

You'll never believe it: it was a gatepost, all tarred black at the top, white in the middle, and then black doon again.

Type 1318.
Motif: J. 1782 (*Things thought to be ghosts*).

31 GRANNY'S STILL
(Belle Stewart)

Well, this is supposed to be really true. No doubt you been in Ireland and heard aboot how they make the whisky up in the Free State. But they dinnae call it whisky there, they call it *poteen*. Well, this auld woman and her auld man, now, they had a wee still way up in the back hills o' Donegal. And they used to come down every Friday, at least the auld woman did, wi' a cartload o' turf ... what we ca' peats in Scotland, but it's turf across there. And she aye come down *every* Friday wi' a wee donkey-load o' turf tae the toon.

Noo, the Civvy-Guards, what's the policemen over there, the Civvy-Guards they knew perfectly well that they were makin' the whisky, the poteen. But they coud never find it on them. But they knew for a fact that this auld woman was disposin' o' it some way in the toon. So these two young laddies, these Civvy-Guards now, they were gettin' curious. And they said, "Oh, we'll get it all right. We'll go and find it."

So, they knew the time that she was due to come intae the toon. And they're away to the end o' the toon now and they see the auld woman comin' doon wi' her donkey-load o' turf. And they stopped her, and they says, "It's very warm, mum."

"Yes it is, son", she says, "it *is* warm."

"He says, "Are ye for the town?"

"Oh, ay", she says, "I'm sure I go to the town every Friday with my turf."

And he says, "Are ye sure ye don't make a wee drop of the hard stuff, granny?"

"*Me*?" says she. "Oh no, son. I wouldn't know *how* to make it."

But there's one o' the laddies very very curious and he says, "What do ye carry in the cart?"

"Oh", she says, "ye see it. My turf, of course."

"Would there be ony harm in us dockin' it down, takin' it all down?"

"Well", says she, "that would be a damn foolish thing to do. I'd just have to load it all up again."

"Oh no", says the laddies, "we'll give ye a hand to load it up again."

But she wasnae very sweet on them doin' it. However, they took all the turf oot o' the cart and here on the bottom was two big jars o' poteen. That's where she'd hid it, y'see. Under the turf. So, right reason or none, *now* they were goin' to take her and lock her up with this turf, about this poteen under the turf.

And well, "God help us", says she, "now ye've fund oot that I have it", says she, "would ye not let me go down because it's the last Friday I'll ever be able to take it in. Would ye no' let me, for God's sake", says she, "go into the toon wi' this wee drop?"

"Well", he says, "on one condition: if ye tell me where the still is." Y'see?

"Oh well", she says, "if ye let me go to the toon anyway", she says. So off she goes to the toon and she disposes of her turf and she gets rid of her wee drop poteen. And she thought that the laddies would forget all aboot her comin' back oot o' the toon. But no no, the two of them was there waitin' for her, the two Civvy-Guards.

"Well", he says, "Granny – have ye got rid of your stuff?"

"Oh, ay", says she. "I got rid o' it."

"Well", he says, "keep a promise now. We kept our promise to you."

"All right", she says, "just you come hame wi' me", and hame they go and she louses oot the wee donkey and she goes into the hoose.

Noo, the laddies is waitin' to see whaur the still is. She went up and she threw hersel' on top o' her bed – and they auld-fashioned women away in Ireland, they never wear no knickers, nae pants no anything, jist the bare thing as it was. So she threw hersel' on her back on the bed and said, "Now laddies, there's the still, that's the still there", pointin' to her fanny. She says, "And if ye wait till my man comes hame he'll show ye the worm."

32 THE BEGGARMAN AND THE MINISTER
(*Alec Stewart*)

There's a beggarman gaun on his way tae the minister. And he met anither beggarman, and he says, "Dinnae go up there, for ye'll get naethin'. That man", he says, "wouldnae gie ye a cross o' a cuddy."

"Oh", says the first beggarman. "I'll try him onyway and see what I can do." So he went up and he rappit at the door and the minister came oot.

"Well", the minister said. "What do *you* want, my man?"

The beggarman says, "I come tae see if ye'll learn me the Lord's Prayer, your reverence."

The minister looked at him and says, "The Lord's Prayer?"

The beggarman says, "Yes".

"Come on in", the minister says, and he took him intae a room and he says, "Do ye know it at all?"

And the beggarman says, "No, no. I don't know it."

"Can ye no' even start it?" the minister says.

"No, I cannae even start it."

"Well", he says, "it begins like this: Our Father ..."

"Wait a minute", says the beggarman. "Was He *your* father?"

"Yes", he said, "He was my father."

"Well", he says, "me and you must be twa brithers."

The minister looked at him. "Well, if it comes to that, we *are* two brothers."

"Well", says the beggarman, "ye wadnae see your brither gaun wi' a pair o' buits like this, would ye?"

The minister says, "Oh, I must do something aboot that." So he gied him a line tae gae tae the cobbler's tae get a pair o' buits. He's awa' doon for the pair o' buits and then he's awa'. The minister come doon tae the cobbler's shop and he says, "Here, John, I never saw ye at church last Sunday."

"Oh no", he says. "I wasn't at church, I was too busy."

"Ye wasn't there the Sunday afore, either."

"I was busy that Sunday tae", the cobbler says.

"Well", says the minister, "D' ye mind the Lord's Prayer?"

"Yes", the cobbler says.

"Then let's hear a bit of it."

The cobbler says, "Our Father...."

"Wait a minute", the minister says, "Was He *your* father?"

"Yes", he says.

"And He was *my* father tae?"

The cobbler says, "Oh yes."

The minister says, "Thon tramp-man wha' got the boots from ye – was He *his* father tae?"

"Oh, yes", the cobbler says.

"Well, you pay one half and I'll pay the other."

Type 1833.
Motif: X. 434 (*The parson put out of countenance*).

33 THE WRESTLER
(*Alec Stewart*)

Once upon a time, when pigs was swine and monkeys chawed t'bacca, there was faimily stayed awa' in Caithness, and there was a laddie and they ca'd him Jeck. And he aye used tae sit awa' in the ashes o' the fire. He would never get oot o' it, and his mither couldnae get bakin' and she couldnae get cookin' and she couldnae get daein' naethin' at the fire. She aye used tae shove him awa' tae one side, but he aye crawled back tae the fire again.

So there was a market in a place ca'd Wick, if ye know the place. A great man used tae come there, a wrastler, and he used tae gae through the fair wi' a sash hingin' fae his waist, trailin' behind him. Ony man that wad lift the sash had tae wrastle him that day.

So time rolled on till it came tae Saturday, which was the mairket day, and Jeck asked his faither whaur he was gaun.

"I'm gaun tae Wick mairket, laddie."

"Can I get wi' ye?" says Jeck.

"Oh, laddie laddie dear, ye couldnae walk tae Wick." Well, Jeck started tae cry, though he was a big lump o' a man, a stout, stout man. But he was simple, and he started tae cry. His faither says, "Noo, listen, Jeck – if I tak' ye, ye'll hae tae stay beside me because if ye gang through the mairket wi' sae mony people", he says, "ye'd get lost."

So they went tae the mairket, walkin' through the fair and walkin' through the fair. And the laddie's aye beside his faither. So when they was walkin' through the fair, didn't this man come doon, the wrastler wi' his sash, and it was pink and yella and red, a' different colours, and it was trailin' on the grund.

So Jeck he run across and he lifted the sash and he says, "Here, man", he says, "tak' your sash – it's trailin' on the grund."

The wrastler clapped the boy on the shouther and he says. "You're the man that has tae fight me the day", he says.

Jeck just laughed and he run back tae his faither and his faither catched him and gied him a shake. "Why did ye dae that?" he says, "That man'll kill ye!"

"Well", Jeck says, "I cannae help it, faither, if he kills me or not. His sash was trailin' on the grund."

Time rolled on now and there's a big stage where the wrastler had to go and wrastle. Well, Jeck's faither gaed up tae him and he says, "My son is a simple laddie", he says.

"I ken that", the wrastler says, "I've got anither man tae fight. But I said that tae the laddie just tae frighten him."

So Jeck's at the side o' the stage and he's taen aff his coat and he's stannin' there. He jumpit intae the ring and his faither says, "Come on doon oot o' that, laddie", he says. "Whit're ye daein' up there?"

"I hae tae fecht the wrastler", says Jeck.

"Na na na, come doon, come doon!"

But Jeck says, "I'm gaun tae fecht the wrastler. I lifted his sash and I've got tae fecht him."

So Jeck's faither gaed up tae the wrastler and he says, "Listen. Just gie him twa or three tosses and he'll get fed up and come oot."

"A' right", the wrastler says. "I'll dae that." So Jeck went across tae him and the twa o' them's gaun roond aboot, tryin' tae get tae grips. And then Jeck catched the man and he had his airms intae his grip. He's holdin' him, and Jeck's faither says, "Throw him, son, throw him!"

"I'm feared tae throw him, faither, I'm feared tae throw him."

"Why are ye feared?" he says.

"I'll get the jail", Jeck says.

"Not at all", his faither says. "Throw him!" So Jeck just gied him a throw and the man was stone-deid. His ribs went right through his hairt and through his lungs. He squashed him tae atoms. Jeck got the prize-money and I suppose he's the champion yet, and that's the last o' my story.

34 THE WOMAN ON THE SCALES
(Belle Stewart)

There was this old fat woman, you know, and she come fae the country and she was goin' tae Glesca and she cam' into the station and she had a half-an-hour to wait on her train.

Well, she saw these machines at the station, you know, where you put the money in and she's walkin' doon the platform and she sees this one 'I can tell your weight'. She says, "I dinna believe it!"

However, she puts in the penny and the weight says, "You're fifteen stone. When you step off this machine you'll fart." She stepped off the machine, she give a hell of a fart. She says, "God, that's great! It *does* know."

So on she goes again, and it says now, "You're fifteen stone and you're gaun tae be raped when you walk off this machine." Off she gets, off the machine, and doon comes a man tearin' along the platform and he rapes her. Oh my God, she's so exhausted. She says, "That's great! That's good! I must try it again."

And she put another penny in. And the thing, this time it says, "You are fifteen stone, but with your fartin' and your effing aboot you've lost your train!"

35 OOT!
(Cathie Higgins)

Well, y'see, this was a man and a woman and they were very comfortable in this nice wee cottage. And this woman had aye a habit when her man came in to have his slippers ready for him and his easy chair and his cigarettes and a' the rest o' it.

So this nicht she had his slippers a' laid oot for him and his fags and a' the rest o' it a' laid oot for him. But he never come in.

"God 'lmichty me", she says, "whit's happened to that man o' mine?"

But, however, three month gaed on. Six month gaed on. Twenty year gaed on. Nae man.

So this nicht he came in, miraculous. Set doon in his chair. Put his bachies on. And she just come fillin' ben fae the kitchen.

And she says, "Whaur hae *you* been, then?"

"Oot."

RIDDLES

Introduction

The prophet Ezekiel was told by the Lord to "propound a riddle and speak an allegory to the house of Israel." Nebuchadnezzar made the prophet Daniel chief of his magicians because he possessed "an excellent spirit to interpret dreams and explain riddles". Samson, the Bible tells us, began his violent career among the Philistines by propounding the riddle of the dead lion and the honeycomb.

The Koran contains riddles, as does the Rig Veda, sacred book of the Brahmins, and in popular story, riddling has played an important part from very remote times.

Both the ancient Egyptians and the Greeks appear to have enjoyed riddling. Indeed, Aristotle in his *Rhetoric* puts the riddle on a par with metaphor; both of them, he says, can be used as instruments of instruction or as tools of deception. They were also used as a test, the non-fulfilment of which could earn the unfortunate examinee the death penalty. A correct answer, of course, could win valuable rewards. Sophocles has Oedipus win the kingdom of Thebes for providing the correct answer to the riddle set by the Sphinx.

In Britain, too, riddling has enjoyed a long and vigorous history. The three earliest surviving English collections of riddles are written in Latin and are said to be the work of Aldhelm, Bishop of Malmesbury (*c.* 640–709); of Tatwine, an Archbishop of Canterbury who died in 734; and of Eusebius, Abbot of Wearmouth (*c.* 680–747). The earliest surviving examples of Anglo-Saxon riddles are the ninety-six items which form the final entry in the *Exeter Book*, the "large Book in English verse about various subjects" bequeathed to the Cathedral library by Leofric, Bishop of Exeter at his death in 1072.

As one might expect of a collection made to be donated to a cathedral library, the riddles are, for the most part, lacking in the kind of sexual innuendo which characterises so many of the later riddle collections. Only seven of the riddles in the Exeter Book are of the *double entendre* type, a modest percentage if compared with the thirty-four bawdy pieces included in the collection of riddles made in Bohemia in 1365 by the Benedictine

monk known as Claretus. As a form, the riddle can, of course, accommo-
date all kinds of sexual metaphors, however bizarre or convoluted they
may be. It is a form which lends itself to oral transmission. Almost all of
the Stewart *double entendre* riddles are either variants or analogues of
riddles printed in sixteenth-century collections.

The earliest printed collection of English riddles is *Demaundes Joyous*
(1511) and throughout the sixteenth-century, collections of bawdy riddles
were printed in England, France and Italy in large numbers. By the end of
the century fashions in humour had undergone a significant change and
riddling began to be regarded as a pastime fit only for rustics.

It survived, of course, but in the mouths of children and today, in Gorgio
society, it is children who keep riddles and riddling alive. This is not the
case among Scots Travellers. As far as they are concerned, riddling is still
regarded as an adult form of entertainment. It is an unforgettable
experience to be present at a Stewart ceilidh and to hear the riddles flying
thick and fast from every corner of the room, riddles that were current in
Britain before the Normans came, others the raw material of which has
been culled from popular TV programmes. Some of them have spent their
entire existence in the mouths of the folk; others have the unmistakable
ring of the literary riddle. What they have in common is the knack of
throwing into comic relief the ambiguities of words.

1 Come a riddle, come a riddle, come a rot tot tot,
   A wee wee man in a red red coat;
   A staff in his hand and a stane in his throat,
   Come a riddle, come a riddle, come a rot tot tot.
       (*A cherry*)

2 A wee wee hoose a' fu' o' meat,
   Nae doors and windows,
   I cannae get in to eat.
       (*An egg*)

3 Double lockit, double sneckit,
   Cannae open till ye break it.
       (*An egg*)

4 The bull bull't it,
   The coo calfed it,
   It growed in a wuid,
   And the smith made it.
       (*A bellows*)

5　Whit's round as the moon,
　　As clear as crystal?
　　If ye cannae tell me that,
　　I'll shoot ye wi' my pistol.
　　　　(*A watch*)

6　Whit hings high, greets sair,
　　Has a heid but nae hair?
　　　　(*A bell*)

7　A lang man nakit,
　　Through the fields he straikit (streaked);
　　Keep in your cocks and hens,
　　For your dogs I dinnae care.
　　　　(*A worm*)

8　He's doon on his knees and he's at it,
　　Wi' a thing in his hand that'll fit it;
　　"Is it in?" says he.
　　"Ay", says she, "it's a richt ticht fit, and I like it!"
　　　　(*A shoe salesman fitting a woman with a shoe*)

9　Hairy oot, hairy in,
　　Lift your leg and shove it in.
　　　　(*A stocking*)

10　Oot o' his troosers he took it,
　　Between two legs he put it;
　　First through hair, then through skin,
　　And he pushed it gently in.
　　　　(*A gamekeeper gutting a rabbit*)

11　Between two hills I heard a roar,
　　I listened, I listened, I heard no more.
　　　　(*A man breaking wind*)

12　A blind man saw a hare,
　　A dumb man cried, "Where?"
　　A naked man without arms or legs lifted it
　　And put it in his coat pocket.
　　　　(*The height o' damn nonsense*)

13　As I cam' owre the Brig o' Doon, I met a man. I cut aff his heid,
　　I drank o' his blood and I left his body standing.
　　　　(*Drinking a bottle of wine*)

14 As I cam' owre London Bridge, I saw the dead carrying the living.
   (*A boatload of people*)

15 What is alive at both ends and dead in the middle?
   (*A ploughman with a pair of horse*)

16 What is the difference between yours and mines?
   (*Ewers is for holding water and mines is for producing coal*)

17 Whit is it a coo has four o' and a woman has two o'?
   (*Legs*)

18 What goes round the wood and round the wood and never touches the wood?
   (*The bark on the tree*)

19 What is it that everybody puts out of their mouth but wadnae tak' a fortune to put it back in?
   (*Spittle*)

20 What resembles a pig going through a fence?
   (*A penny, head on one side, tail on the other*)

21 I got it in the wuid, I come ootside the wuid to look for it. I went back in the wuid and I couldnae get it in the wuid.
   (*A thorn in the foot*)

22 Why is the Duke o' Edinburgh the poorest sportsman in the world?
   (*Because he cannae enter the Queen's premises without disturbing the hares*)

23 What did thought do?
   (*He planted a feather and thought it would grow a hen*)

24 If you let off wind and I let off wind, what football team would that represent?
   (*Ayr United*)

25 Wee MacGregor on the tap o' Rattray steeple: whit would that represent?
   (*A ride on tick*)

26 If it took a cut o' woo' tae mak' a jumper for wee MacGregor, whit would it tak' to mak' wee MacGregor?
   (*Two balls, a finger-length and a cut – of wool, of course!*)

27 There was two sisters. One o' them went to bed wearin' two nightdresses and the other didn't wear any at all. What were their names?

   (*Shy Anne and Raw Hide*)

28 What does a nightdress cover?

   (*Two milk dairies, a naval base and a hame for wee children*)

29 If the sun and moon cover the whole o' creation, whit does a lady's knickers cover?

   (*The hole o' temptation*)

30 Whit's the difference between a hare and a rabbit?

   (*You can pu' a hair oot o' your arse, but no' a rabbit*)

CHILDREN'S RHYMES AND CATCHES

Introduction

Of the twenty-five items included in this section, thirteen could properly be called "nursery pieces", that is, rhymes and catches used by adults to instruct and entertain very young children. Five items belong in the category of songs and chants associated with traditional games; three are typical examples of what one might describe as a rural children's repertory; only four are part of that enormous group of urban children's rhymes that are known throughout the English-speaking world.

Twelve items, then – if one excludes the thirteen nursery pieces – representing the rich world of the children's oral tradition! A meagre harvest, indeed. It can be argued, of course, that adults are a poor source of children's material, though this is not borne out by our experience. The three Stewart women who recorded this material for us have, from early childhood, been accustomed to learning songs, ballads and stories. Belle, in particular, has prodigious powers of recall.

Among Travellers, children are integrated into the close-knit family structure from the time they begin to walk. Their activities are the activities of the family and not of a special group based on school or neighbourhood. They accompany their parents on their travels, they learn to do simple jobs at a very early age, and they participate in every aspect of the family's social life. On each of the many occasions that we have attended Travellers' *ceilidhs*, there have been children present. Often these events have gone on until three or four o'clock in the morning. As the children drop off to sleep, they are covered with a blanket or a coat, but they are never sent off to bed. In this kind of situation, children assimilate the songs and traditions of the adults around them. Even in the school playground – a fertile breeding place for so much children's folklore – the children of Travellers are hedged around with the same kind of prejudice and intolerance that isolates Travellers as a whole from the rest of the community.

It is, perhaps, considerations such as these that account for the fact that children's songs form such a small section of the Travellers' total traditional repertoire.

1   *For a Child at the Breast*

> Belly to belly,
> Hand roond back,
> Raw flesh in the hole,
> Clap airse, clap.

2   *The Body Route*

Playing with an infant and touching the parts of the body mentioned in the rhyme. Both the places mentioned are in Perthshire.

> Roond abune fit,
> Up by Ballinluig,
> Roond by the Devil's Elbow,
> And into bellybutton bay.

3   *Fingers or Toes*

Cathie: My granny used to sit and play with our toes and she used to say:

> Broke the barn,
> Stealt the corn,
> Rin awa',
> Telt her,
> And peerie-weerie-winkie paid for them a'.

4   *Questions*

Belle: Tak' the wean in your oxter – maybe a bairn a year auld or so – and as you say the rhyme they'd a' be noddin' their heads, sayin', "Ay, ay, ay . . .".

> Are ye my wee lassie?
> Are ye my wee wean?
> Are ye my bonnie dog Swaddie?
> Are ye mine's the noo?
> Will ye be mine the morn?

Sheila had a somewhat different version:

> Noo, are ye gaun tae be my laddie?
> Hour and time,
> Nicht and day,
> Sleepin' or waukin'
> Hay time or hairvest,
> My dog Swaddie,
> Or late or early?

5 *Hand Clapping*

aπ[1]

O, clap-a clap- a   hand-ies Dad-dy com-in' hame

Tat-ties in his   pock-et   for a wee   wean.

O, clap-a clap-a handies,
Daddy comin' hame;
Tatties in his pocket
For a wee wean.

6 *To a Snail*

Snail, snail, pit oot your horn;
Whit kind o' a day will it be the morn?
It'll be a day for cuttin' corn,
Snail, snail pit oot your horn.

7 *Dandling Rhyme*

aI (ending on VI) or pAe

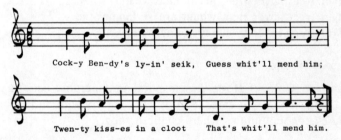

Cock-y Ben-dy's ly-in' seik, Guess whit'll mend him;

Twen-ty kiss-es in a cloot   That's whit'll mend him.

Cocky Bendy's lyin' seik
Guess whit'll mend him;
Twenty kisses in a cloot,
That's whit'll mend him.

8 *Good Luck Rhyme*

Sheila: When me and my mither gets a wee bairn that belongs tae a
Traiveller and the folk's no' there listenin' tae us, we tak' the wee bairn
in oor airms and we're throwin' it up in the air and up in the air and
we're singin':

aπ (ending on II)

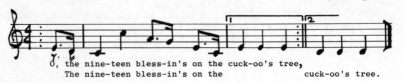

9 *Lullabye*

aI/Ly (ending on VI) or MAe/D

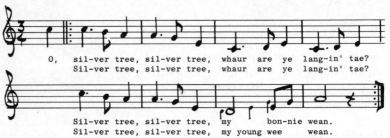

Silver tree, silver tree, whaur are ye langin' tae?
Silver tree, silver tree, my bonnie wean.
Silver tree, silver tree, whaur are ye langin' tae?
Silver tree, silver tree, my young wee wean.

10 *A Mak'-ye-up*

The tune of 'Colonel Bogy' has inspired innumerable sets of popular
verses. In the 1920s and early 1930s it led a vigorous life in the streets of
working-class communities where children sang:

aI

By 1938, a new version was being sung to a slightly altered melody, and its popularity was such that it was quoted in the columns of *The New Chronicle*, a popular newspaper of the time:

mI

Hit-ler   has on-ly got one ball.   Goër-ing's   are ver-y, ver-y   small,

Himm-ler   is some-what sim-i-lar,   But Doc-tor Go-balls has no balls at all.

Sheila says: I used to sing this tae Gregor when he was just a wean. It was only a mak'-ye-up.

Gregor has only got one ball,
The other is in the Albert Hall.
His mother – the bloody bugger –
She cut it off when he was small.

11   *Dandling Song*

The following fragment represents this popular nursery song in its most basic form. It has been reported frequently from Northumberland (where *mammy* or *minnie* is sometimes mentioned instead of *daddy*) and from Scotland (where the mother is rarely present in the song). Stokoe says that the song was written by William Watson of Newcastle around 1840, to an older air. Watson's verses, which include a stanza borrowed from 'The Keel Row' deal (for the most part) with the mother's life, her attitude to her husband (an amiable drinker) and her own attitude to drink. In its full form it does not appear to have become popular. None of the Scots versions contain Watson's stanzas. As in many children's songs and lullabies, the reward motif forms a substantial part of the text. Cathie Higgins' version is the first we have encountered in the cant.

aI/Ly

Grib to your naiskel, my beenship kinchen,
Grib to your naiskel till the beerie bings anee;
You'll feek a flattrin in a wee mahzie
If you'll grib to your naiskel till the beerie bings anee.

Trans: Dance to your daddy, my bonnie laddie,
Dance to your daddy till the boat comes in;
And you'll get a fishie in a wee dishie
If you dance to your daddy till the boat comes in.

12 *Spider Tale*

Incy bincy spider went up the water spout;
Down came the raindrops and washed the spider out.
Out came the sunshine and dried up all the rain,
So incy bincy spider went up the spout again.

13   *Nursing Rhyme*

This strange little piece is fairly widespread. The Opies report the following, "scribbled down by a child in the 19th-century":

> A girl in the army
> She longed for a baby
> She took her father's greyhound
> And laid it in the cradle.
> Lullabye, Baby Bow Wow
> Long legs hast thou,
> And wasn't it for thy cold snout
> I would kiss thee now, now.

A Swedish version (1842) shows remarkable similarities to the above example:

> The old woman wanted to rock the cradle
> But no child had she,
> So she took in her foal
> And laid it in her cradle.
> Lulla, lulla long-shanks mine
> Long legs have you,
> If you live till summer
> You shall be like your father.

Several Scots versions have been reported. One from Dumfriesshire begins "There was a farmer's dochter was keen to hae a baby, O". It is not unreasonable to suppose that the *dodder* – or *doctor* – in our version is a corruption of *dochter*. A version from the Huntly district begins: "There was a nice young lady was ill about a baby".

In each of these rhymes, the baby-substitute is a greyhound with a 'lang cauld snoot' or a 'hairy mou'. Cathie Higgins' version lacks the greyhound but is more frank in its terminology, though the final line of our fourth stanza (and its cant equivalent) is matched by one of the Opie lines:

> If it wasn't for your long nose,
> Tha'd have a drop of titty oh.

After singing a verse and refrain in cant, Cathie sang the song again in a rough translation.

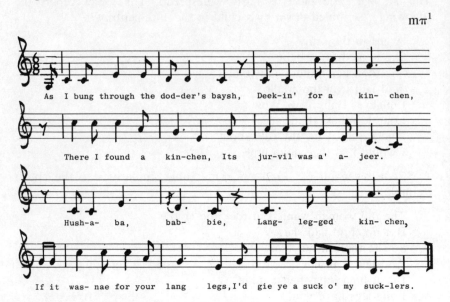

mπ¹

As I bung through the dod-der's baysh, Deek-in' for a kin- chen, There I found a kin-chen, Its jur-vil was a' a- jeer. Hush-a- ba, bab- bie, Lang- leg-ged kin- chen, If it was- nae for your lang legs, I'd gie ye a suck o' my suck-lers.

As I went through the doctor's woods
Lookin' for a peekie (baby),
There I found a peekie
Its airse was a' akakkie (dirty).

Hush-a-ba, babbie,
Lang-legged laddie,
If it wasnae for your long legs
I'd gie ye a suck o' my pappy.

14 *Counting-out Rhymes*

(*a*) One potato, two potato, three potato, four,
Five potato, six potato, seven potato, more,
YOU'RE OUT!

(*b*) Scotty Mallotty the king of the Jews,
Bought his mother a pair of shoes;
When the shoes began to wear
Scotty Mallotty began to swear;
When the swearing began to stop,
Scotty Mallotty bought a shop,
When the shop began to sell,
Scotty Mallotty bought a bell;
When the bell began to ring,
Scotty Mallotty began to sing:

Do re mi fa so la ti do. Do ti la so fa me ri do.

(*c*) Teddy on the railway pickin' up stones,
By came an engine and broke Teddy's bones;
"Ah", says Teddy, "that's nae fair."
"Well", says the engine-man, "ye shouldn't be there."

15 *Ring Games*

aI

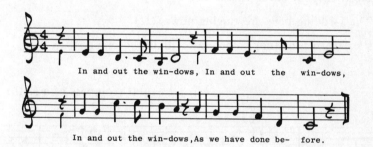

In and out the win-dows, In and out   the   win-dows,

In and out the win-dows, As we have done be- fore.

(*a*) In and out the windows,
In and out the windows,
In and out the windows,
As we have done before.

Stand and face your lover, (3)
As we have done before.

I'll go tell the bobby, (3)
As we have done before.

Sixty days in the tripe-shop, (3)
As we have done before.

(*b*)

aI/M (compass of a sixth)

Poor Ro-sie was a love-ly child, A love-ly child, a love-ly child,
Poor Ro-sie was a love-ly child, A   love-ly child.

Poor Rosie was a lovely child,
A lovely child, a lovely child,
Poor Rosie was a lovely child,
A lovely child.

An ancient castle was her home,
Was her home (etc)

A wicked fairy found her there, (etc)

She made poor Rosie go to sleep, (etc)

Poor Rosie slept a hundred years, (etc)

A handsome prince came riding by, (etc)

He took poor Rosie by the hand, (etc)

The wedding bells are ringing now, (etc)

(This last verse was sung rather faster than the others.)

(*c*)

aI (compass of a sixth)

CHORUS

Hul-la-ba-loo ba-loo,   Hul-la-ba-loo ba-light,
Hul-la-ba-loo ba-loo, Up-   on a Sat-ur-day night. HEUCH!

Hullabaloo baloo,
Hullabaloo balight,
Hullabaloo baloo,
Upon a Saturday night. HEUCH!

Put your right foot in,
Put your right foot out,
Shake it a little, a little,
And turn yourself about. HEUCH! (*Chorus*)

Put your left foot in,
Put your left foot out,
Shake it a little, a little,
And turn yourself about. HEUCH! (*Chorus*)

16   *Ball Games*

(*a*) Game game, ba' ba',
      Twenty lassies in a ra';
      No' a lad amang them a'
      Game game, ba' ba'.

(*b*) Mary Queen of Scots got her head chopped off
      For standin' at the bar,
      Smokin' a cigar,
      Ridin' on a gee-gee, HA HA HA.

interval of a minor third

Keep-ie clap-pie, Roll-ie back-ie, Un-der leg-gie, Through the moon-ie, dab-dab-dab.

(*c*) Keepie clappie,
      Rollie backie,
      Under leggie,
      Through the moonie,
      Dab – dab – dab.

17   *Skipping Games*

(*a*) All the girls in our town lead a happy life,
      Except Sheila Higgins, she wants to be a wife.
      A wife she shall be and a-courting she will go,
      A long way from Johnny because she loves him so.
      She cuddles him and kisses him, she sits upon his knee,
      She says, "My darling Johnny, when will you marry me?"
      Yes, no, yes, no, yes, no (etc, until the skipper misses step).

(b)

interval of a fourth

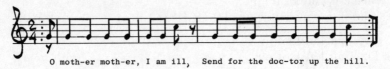

O moth-er moth-er, I am ill, Send for the doc-tor up the hill.

O, mother mother, I am ill
Send for the doctor up the hill.
Up the hill is far too far,
Send for a motor-car.
A motor-car is far too dear,
Send for a pint of beer.
A pint of beer is far too strong,
Send for a treacle-scone.
A treacle-scone is far too tough,
Send for a box of snuff.
A box of snuff will make you sneeze,
Send for a pound of cheese,
A pound of cheese will make you sick,
Send for the doctor, quick quick quick!

(c) Jelly on the table,
Jelly on the plate;
Wiggle-waggle, wiggle-waggle,
Jelly on the plate.

Ice-cream and jelly's
Good for your belly;
Wiggle-waggle, wiggle-waggle,
Ice-cream and jelly.

(d) I'm a little Brownie dressed in brown,
See my knickers hanging down;
Pull them up, pull them down,
I'm a little Brownie dressed in brown.

I'm a little Girl-Guide dressed in blue,
See how many actions I can do:
Stand at ease, bend your knees,
Salute to the king and bow to the queen
And throw a kiss to the good sailor boys,
ONE – TWO – THREE!

(*e*)   Used both as a skipping song and as an accompaniment to a ball-bouncing game, this popular children's chorus represents the most commonly reported Scots version of 'Seventeen Come Sunday' (Laws 0 17).

pI/M

O, whaur are ye gaun, my bon-nie wee lass?   Whaur are ye gaun, my
Whaur are ye gaun, my bon-nie wee lass?
dear-ie?
A mes-sage tae my mam-my.

O, whaur are ye gaun, my bonnie wee lass?
Whaur are ye gaun, my dearie?
Whaur are ye gaun, my bonnie wee lass?
A message tae my mammy.

Chorus: A ha-cha-cha-chee, an' a ha-cha-cha-chaw,
            A ha-cha-cha-chee an' a dandy;
            A ha-cha-cha-chee, an' a ha-cha-cha-chaw,
            A message tae my mammy.

O what is your name, my bonnie wee lass?
What is your name, my dearie?
What is your name, my bonnie wee lass?
My mammy ca's me Nancy. (*Chorus*)

O, can I get a kiss, my bonnie wee lass?
Can I get a kiss, my dearie?
Can I get a kiss, my bonnie wee lass?
I'll hae tae ask my mammy. (*Chorus*)

(*Note*: The chorus utilises the last line of each preceding verse.)

18 *An Impossible Task*

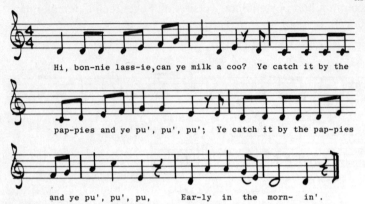

Hi, bonnie lassie, can ye milk a coo?
Ye catch it by the pappies and ye pu', pu', pu';
Ye catch it by the pappies and ye pu', pu', pu',
Early in the mornin'.

Hi, bonnie lassie, can ye milk a bull?
Ye catch it by the pappy and ye pu', pu', pu';
Ye catch it by the pappy and ye pu', pu', pu,
Early in the mornin'.

19 *A Matter of Choice*

aI/Ly (ending on VI)

O, mither, onybody, onybody, onybody,
O, mither, onybody but a creeshy weaver.
For I would rather lie my lane, lie my lane, lie my lane,
I would rather lie my lane than lie wi' a weaver.

20   *A drastic Remedy*

There may be more efficacious remedies for toothache than the one
suggested here, but there are few which can claim such ancient ancestry.
The doctors and resurrection men of the mumming and guising plays,
along with their distinguished colleagues of the *commedia dell arte* troupes,
have all in their time prescribed equally drastic remedies: "Cure for
toothache: take an apple, cut it into four parts, put one of the pieces into
your mouth and hold your head in the oven until the apple is baked."
(sixteenth-century MSS of the Harlequin, Guiseppe Domenico Biancolelli)

mI/Ly (ending on upper VIII)

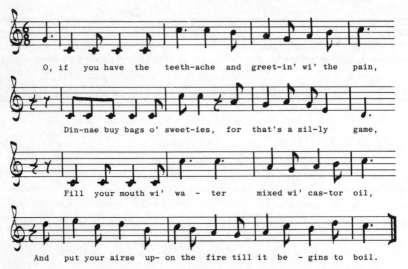

O, if you have the teethache and greetin' wi' the pain,
Dinnae buy bags o' sweeties, for that's a silly game,
Fill your mouth wi' water mixed wi' castor-oil,
And put your airse upon the fire till it begins to boil.

21 *The Provider*

pI/M

There was a wee hen in the mornin' went oot tae look for meat,
There was a wee lassie passin' by, she knocked it aff its feet;
The puir wee cratur was hungry, they wouldnae lea't alane,
Mony's the time it laid an egg for me and my wee wean.

22 *Town Rhyme*

pI

I cannae see the gaffer,
I cannae see the gaffer,
I cannae see the gaffer,
He's owre far awa'.

O, bring the bugger nearer, (3)
He's owre far awa'.

23 *Superman*

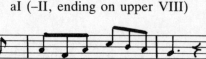

I'm Popeye the Eskimo,
I come from the land of the snow,
I lie on my belly and shiver like jelly,
I'm Popeye the Eskimo.

I'm Popeye the sailor man,
I come from the land of Japan,
I climb on the steeple and pee on the people,
I'm Popeye the sailor man (poop! poop!).

24 *Railway Art*

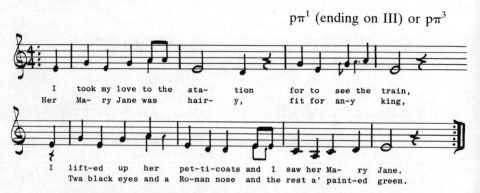

I took my love to the station for to see the train,
I lifted up her petticoats and I saw her Mary Jane;
Her Mary Jane was hairy, fit for any king,
Twa black eyes and a Roman nose and the rest a' painted green.

25   *Thin Man*

Man, man, you're awfu' thin,
Your bloody jaws is cavin'in;
Sic a man was never born,
As the shepherd o' the thorn.
He shot wee doggies just for fun
Wi' a double-barrelled gun.

MUSIC NOTE

I. The transcriptions

It was not difficult to notate the songs, as the Stewarts' sense of pitch and time is very accurate. The rhythms of the tune may alter from verse to verse depending on the words of the song, but such alterations are taken for granted and are rarely notated individually. Should either rhythmic or melodic decorations appear consistently throughout the song, we have given them (in the form of "an average tune") in the principle transcription of the melody.

The main form of decoration used by the Stewarts is what is informally termed *internal*, or *structural*, decoration. That is, the actual pitch structure of key notes or phrases has been altered. Where such changes have occurred, we have given the principle variations below the main notation, with a reference to the numbered bar in which the change takes place. Many of these structural alterations were permanently fixed or were tied to unusual phrasing in the words, or to sections of the verse in which the poetic footage was irregular.

The Stewarts' frequent, almost automatic use of *portamento* has not been notated other than in extreme cases. This habit of sliding from one note to another, especially in the case of larger intervals, gave a fluidity to the tune but at the same time tended to blur the sharpness of melodic line.

The texts on the whole, are very complete and coherent. Occasionally there are words which seem to make no sense at all. We have bracketed these in the body of the text and offer glosses in the margin.

Pace and spirit markings: Directives may be found in the upper left hand corner of each notation. These indicate the manner in which the song was sung. *Free* does not necessarily mean *slow* – it merely indicates that the song was sung with *pulse* rather than strict rhythm.

Metre: A number of the songs were sung free and unmeasured. It was difficult (but necessary) to cast them into a metre. In such cases, we used the text as a guide, speaking the words as poetry until the metre emerged.

Key: We have cast the songs neither into a standard key nor into the keys in which the songs were originally sung. We are hoping that the songs will continue to be sung, from this book, and have thus cast them within pitch ranges accessible to most singers, and into keys which are easily read. As is now common in folk-music collections, we mark sharps and flats in the signature only if they appear consistently throughout the song.

Mode and range: In the upper right-hand corner of each notation is to be found a combination of upper and lower case letters, occasionally followed by Roman numerals. These indicate the range and mode of the song.

The *range* covered by a melody is expressed by the lower-case letters *a, p* or *m*:

   a – authentic, in which the tune lies roughly between the tonic note and the octave above it. This interval is often extended to include the ninth.

   p – plagal, in which the tune lies roughly between the fifth above the tonic and the fourth below it. Again, a ninth is generally accepted.

   m – mixed, in which the tune has a range which exceeds a ninth in compass; which is a combination of those above; or which is a borderline case.

The *mode* in which the melody is cast is expressed by the upper-case letters *I, D, Ly, M* and *Ae*:

   I   – Ionian, a major-based mode (C-D-E-F-G-A-B-C)
   D   – Dorian, a minor-based mode (D-E-F-G-A-B-C-D)
   Ly – Lydian, a major-based mode (F-G-A-B-C-D-E-F)
   M   – Myxolydian, a major-based mode (G-A-B-C-D-E-F-G)
   Ae – Aeolian, a minor-based mode (A-B-C-D-E-F-G-A)

Mode-alternatives: a number of gapped, or hexatonic, scales – lacking an interval – could possibly be one of two modes and, where there is any doubt as to which mode is being employed, we use Bronson's system:

   I/M   – a tune containing the first six notes of a major-based scale but lacking the VII degree, could be either Ionian or Mixolydian.

   I/Ly   – a tune containing the first three and last three notes of a major-based scale but lacking the IV degree, could be either Ionian or Lydian.

   Ae/D – a tune containing the first and seventh notes of a minor-based scale but lacking the VI degree could be either Aeolian or Dorian.

   M/D – a tune possibly in Mixolydian or Dorian but lacking the III degree.

Pentatonic, or five-note scales are marked π followed by a small number to show which of the five possible inversions of the pentatonic series is applicable.

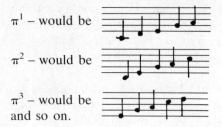

π^1 – would be

π^2 – would be

π^3 – would be
and so on.

There are, of course, borderline cases in which it is exceedingly difficult to decide which mode is being employed. A sense of tonality is built up through contact with a culture and through one's own experience and inclination. One listener might feel that, for instance, 'An Old Man He Courted Me' *ends* on the tonic, which would place the song in the *aM* category. Another might decide that the song ends on the lower V and mark the tune as *p I/M*. Where we felt there was some doubt, we indicated our preference first and placed the alternative afterwards.

Wherever the *range-mode* marking contains the word *inflected* this means that a certain interval may occasionally be raised or dropped by a half-tone, but that the mode is (for the most part) consistent. Missing intervals other than those automatically covered in a mode-alternative are marked thus: -III, -IV, and so on.

Layout: We have endeavoured to notate the music in such a manner as to best reveal its structure. Related lines and bars appear in vertical parallel so that parts of a tune – or tunes with a similar metre or poetic form – may be compared. When casting the music into its natural pattern, it is also possible to see the structure of the verse in relation to the structure of the tune. And, of course, the form of a song is easier to grasp at first sight if it is laid out symmetrically.

II.   The singers

The songs in this book are from three female singers, whose attitudes towards the music, whose repertoires and styles of singing reflect their family relationships. From a musical point of view, the family is matriarchal, for the men hardly sing at all. Belle herself knows practically every song in this book, but there are certain areas of song which have been apportioned out to the two girls, whose styles are derivative but · distinctive. For instance, Belle will not sing 'The Dawning of the Day', although she knows it. That song is Cathie's song. 'Tifty's Annie' is "Sheila's song" and 'The Twa Brithers' is "my mither's sang", and so on through the list. The three women appear to have divided the entire repertoire between them and their categorisation has been made with much the same kind of rigidity that characterises the older school of folklorists.

Belle is the guardian of the Child ballads, the big songs:

The old songs have the *cuinneog* [Gaelic for churn] ... They make you weep inside. Many's the time I've seen them singing the old songs and the tears just streaming down their cheeks.

Hers also are the bothy ballads, the difficult *canntaireachd*, the cant pieces, certain love songs, lowlife songs and fragments. Her voice matches this versatility in subject, being rich with just enough nasal tone, agile for 'The Overgate', full of concentration for 'The Bonnie Hoose o' Airlie' and light and gay for 'The Gaberlunzie Man'. She seems to sing for the content of the song, for the story, and her songs are longer than those of her daughters. Her longest song is fourteen verses and several pieces range from ten to fourteen stanzas, for Belle regards singing as a valid way of passing time. Even her incomplete songs give the impression of telling the full story, and the content of her songs is very important to her. She has a truly integrated approach. Her delivery is almost matter-of-fact and she rarely sings a song too slow or too fast, but is able to give each song its appropriate pace. She is quite audience-conscious and often she will catch the eye of a listener to establish contact at key points in the song, checking that he is getting as much as she is giving. She stands when she sings and moves her body slightly in rhythm with the song.

Roughly two-thirds of Belle's forty-eight songs are triple time and they are fairly evenly divided between authentic, plagal and mixed range. She has eleven pentatonic songs and about half her songs are in a major-orientated mode. Her tunes show more variety than those of Sheila and Cathie. Nine of the items do not end on the tonic, four contain inflected intervals and one an internal transition. She has two favoured poetic forms, AABB (the double couplet) and ABCB (the classic ballad quatrain form). Her preferred melodic structures are ABCD and ABAC.

Belle does not decorate heavily but limits herself to a tasteful porta-mento, occasional mordents and a delightful glottal flip which she uses frequently on fast or humorous songs. She also employs the *nya*, the nasal intonation characteristic of many Scots and Irish traditional singers. Belle called it "the richt auld way o' singin' things, the auld Tinkie-tone, the twangy kind o' singin'".

Cathie confesses that her first love is dancing, that she left the singing to the others. Her repertoire dovetails with Belle's in the field of rural Scots love songs, leaning heavily towards pieces of a sentimental and nostalgic nature. Her voice is unusual, having a low, almost throbbing timbre (often associated with crooning) combined with the high, nasal head-tones so common in her family. Where Belle emphasises content, Cathie seems to strive for atmosphere and the harking back to a romantic youth. Only two of her songs reach five verses and only four of her ten songs could be regarded as complete. She prefers unmeasured songs and her delivery is at times reminiscent of a certain type of pubsinger. She remains seated, reserved and the picture of concentration throughout her performance. Nine of her songs are in triple time, and she only slightly favours authentic over plagal and mixed range. The majority of her songs are in Ionian, and she has two pentatonic pieces. One of her songs contains inflected intervals and another ends on the non-tonic. Most of her songs are in the AABB verse form and she favours, if slightly, the ABCD tune-form.

Cathie's decorations appear to be built into her vocal style and not tied to particular songs. She employs heavy *portamento*, a small sob which seems to be an exaggeration of Belle's glottal flip, occasional passing tones, small mordents and anticipation. When she sings children's songs, of which she knows many, her manner and delivery are transformed into a charming innocence and agility.

Sheila gave us twenty-eight songs from her repertory, which crosses with Belle's in the areas of balladry and rural love songs. Her real *forte* is nineteenth-century Irish songs, because "I love the tunes". Sheila dwells on the parts of the tune which most appeal to her, and her voice has real edge, a nasal sharpness which is accentuated by the high, dramatic pitching of the songs. She leans towards grandeur and finer feelings, and prefers a stark, bare line to a cosy melody. Her longest song had fourteen stanzas, but the average length of her songs is five to seven verses. She is alone when she sings and radiates personal dignity. She sits with her hands clasped in her lap, leaning slightly forward in an attentive posture. Her face is up, her eyes focused unmoving on some distant object. Her mind is completely absorbed, her manner one of a person possessed. No expression passes over her countenance when she sings and her body sways slightly as if bending under the music. Although she is capable of singing up-tempo songs with good articulation and unerring pitch, she seems to prefer the slow, unmeasured songs. Nineteen of her songs are in triple time, spread out evenly in the range categories. Twelve of them are major-orientated and four are pentatonic. All of her songs end on the tonic and four of her tunes contain inflected intervals.

Eighteen of Sheila's songs are cast in the AABB verse structure. Eleven of these are carried by an ABBA musical structure, and eight of those eleven are nineteenth-century Irish pieces. Sheila's decorations are minimal, limited to *portamento*, a few mordents and a little internal structural variation of the tune. Her tonal variations are a modified version of Belle's, although her voice is richer than her mother's and more controlled.

All three women have the *nya* as a built-in vocal characteristic, and their singing voices are noticeably higher than their speaking voices. All three women are capable of smoothly covering a mistake, a forgotten line or verse, by passing without hesitation to the next word, line or verse. All three are capable of singing children's songs with the same approach and vitality as that used by children.

While the Stewart repertoire is democratic, it has its hierarchy, its aristocracy – the ballads – and its classes of songs, each with its time, place and function. On first glance, the songs seem to have been parcelled out according to who sings them best. On second glance, however, the division appears to have been based on preference and personality. As in many Travelling communities (and the Stewart family is a community in itself) the major Singer is surrounded by an audience, many of whom know the songs, and among whom are a number of apprentice singers. Undoubtedly, Sheila and Cathie played the apprentice role for years, and it seems to us that their repertoires crystallised when they were in their early twenties. As older women, they have now settled firmly into the non-Belle areas of the family tradition and seem to have learned very few new songs since we first recorded them. Indeed, Belle herself, who declared that she could remember a melody on one hearing and the words with two or three more hearings, appears to have added very few new songs to her stock in the last fifteen years.

Even as the respective repertoires have stabilised, so have the songs. Belle's 1975 rendition of 'The Overgate' was only one word different from her 1962 text. Sheila's 'Andrew Lammie' had one more verse in 1975 than it had in 1963. Similarly, the tunes vary little from year to year and, unlike a number of Traveller singers, the Stewarts have no trouble "getting into" a tune. The melody for the first verse is usually the same as that used in the rest of the song.

The Stewarts are all literate and know what the words mean, or can offer translations in borderline cases. There are few mistakes in pronunciation, almost no onomatopoeic substitutions. At points where their texts *do* depart from the norm, there is usually a logic behind the alteration (as in 'Fair Drummallochie').

Most of these inconsistent features seem to have come to stay. Irregular stanzas (such as verse two of 'The Overgate') stay irregular – yet seem fresh and unexpected with every rendition. There is never an attempt to add the lines back again. In many cases, the songs were handed down complete with charming melodic excisions and textual inaccuracies and it appears to be part of the duty of the traditional singer to hand them on in that condition to the next generation.

THE SONGS

1 The Fause Knight Upon the Road (Child 3)
2 The Twa Brothers (Child 49)
3 The Lowlands of Holland (Child 92, Appendix)
4 The Famous Flower of Serving-Men (Child 106)
5 Mary Hamilton (Child 173)
6 The Bonnie Hoose o Airlie (Child 199)
7 The Gypsy Laddie (Child 200)
8 The Baron of Brackley (Child 203)
9 The Braes o Yarrow (Child 214)
10 Lizie Lindsay (Child 226)
11 Andrew Lammie (Child 233)
12 The Gaberlunzie Man (Child 279, Appendix)
13 Here's a Health to All True Lovers
14 The Duke of Athol (Laws O 23)
15 The Rambling Irishman (Laws H 4)
16 Burns and His Highland Mary (Laws 0 34)
17 The Bonnie Irish Boy (Laws P 26)
18 Drummallochie
19 Queen Amang the Heather
20 Amang the Whinny Knowes
21 If I was a Blackbird
22 A Nobleman Lived in a Mansion
23 The Lovely Irish Maid
24 Busk Busk, Bonnie Lassie
25 Bonnie Lass, Come Owre the Burn
26 The Ball o' Kirriemuir
27 My Faither Was Hung for Sheep-Stealing
28 The Bonnie Lassie's Plaidie
29 Bonnie Bonnie Bessie Lee
30 John Peel
31 The Road to Dundee
32 Rosemary Lane (Laws K 43)
33 The Galway Shawl
34 The Bonnie Lass o' Fyvie

35   Madam, I Have Come to Court You
36   The Dawning of the Day (Laws P 16)
37   The Maid of Culmore
38   Green Bushes (Laws P 2)
39   Oxford City (Laws P 30)
40   The Nobleman's Wedding (Laws P 31)
41   The Banks of Red Roses
42   Hatton Woods
43   The Days Are Awa' That We Hae Seen
44   Bogie's Bonnie Belle
45   John Mitchel
46   The Lonely Banna Strand
47   Ballyjamesduff
48   The Country I'm Leaving Behind
49   Glen Swilly
50   Terence's Farewell
51   The Soor Mulk Cairt
52   Geordie Weir
53   The Cairn
54   Johnny My Man
55   The Real Old Mountain Dew
56   Blue Blazing Blind Drunk
57   The Hamilton Militiaman
58   An Old Man He Courted Me
59   The Overgate
60   The Bonnie Wee Lassie Fae Gourock
61   Betsy Bell
62   I'm No' Comin' Oot the Noo
63   Cod-Liver Oil
64   Twa Heids Are Better Than Ane
65   A Shilling or Twa
66   Twelve Bob and a Tanner
67   The Blarney Roses
68   Master McGrath
69   Kathleen Mavourneen
70   The Moss o' Burreldale
71   Hi, Bara Manishie

1 THE FAUSE KNIGHT ON THE ROAD
(*Child 3*)

Child gives only two versions of this old ballad and one of these is a mere
fragment. His note is rather perfunctory, certainly not as searching as
Barry's note in *The Bulletin*. He observes that "this ballad has failed of the
critical appraisal it deserves as a striking homiletic drama in two acts". In
order to appreciate Barry's analysis, a fuller text than ours would be
necessary.

In the older sets, the child is seven years old and consequently (according to Canon Law) is capable of making a moral decision. He is therefore
able to defend himself against the devil. The first of Barry's "acts",
therefore, is the basic temptation of a child by the devil. The second act
(which Barry calls "flyting") consists of a clash of wits, an exchange of
insults, a setting of tasks. Such a conflict had its reward (as in 'The Elfin
Knight,' Child 2) in the gaining of a reputation, or the gaining of a true
love. In 'The False Knight', and in early versions of Child 1 ('Riddles
Wisely Expounded'), the battle is far more serious, for the soul of a mortal
is at stake. The trump card of the interrogatee is to name the fiend, which
our child does by wishing his interlocutor in hell, or by pushing him into a
well before continuing his journey to school.

Mrs Stewart's text omits several motifs normally found in more complete
sets, but the story is nevertheless complete in her five stanzas. Although
the ballad is quite rare, remnants of it have been reported from Scotland,
Nova Scotia and the eastern and south-eastern states of North America.
Coffin mentions versions which are "Scotch-Irish" in background, but we
have not seen an Irish text and the only English text with which we are
familiar was probably learned from a Scot.

Barry observed that one of his New Brunswick informants said the piece
was "not a song but an old Galloway rhyme". Child, in his note, quotes
'Harpkin', possibly the rhyme in question.

'The False Knight on the Road', sung by Belle Stewart. Learned from Ruby Kelby's mother, Christina MacKenzie.

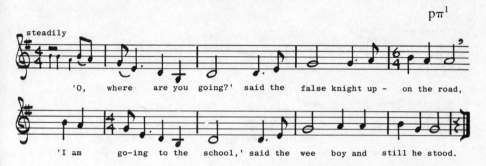

1   "O, where are you going?" said the false knight upon the road,
    "I am going to the school", said the wee boy and still he stood.

2   "What is that upon your back?" said the false knight upon the road,
    "That's my bannock and my book", said the wee boy and still he stood.

3   "O, will you give me share?" said the false knight upon the road,
    "No, I will not give you share", said the wee boy and still he stood.

4   "O, if I had you on the sea", said the false knight upon the road,
    "And a good ship under me", said the wee boy and still he stood.

5   "If I had you at the well", said the false knight upon the road,
    "And you were into Hell!" said the wee boy and still he stood.

2   THE TWA BROTHERS
(Child 49)

Six of the seven texts given by Child are from Scots sources. Bronson has forty-one versions in the main body of his collection, all from North America. In addition to eight more North American sets given in his Appendix, Bronson includes three complete versions and a fragment from Scotland.

Belle Stewart's text would appear to be unique in that it introduces a stepmother into the plot. Generally it is the father, mother or sister who is named as the instigator of the tragedy. In some of Child's texts, notably those that have crossed with 'Edward' (Child 13) the guilty brother is motivated by jealousy but, more often than not, he kills his sibling in a moment of spontaneous anger.

'The Twa Brothers', sung by Belle Stewart. Learned from her brother, Donald MacGregor.

pAe/D

O two pret-ty boys were gaun to the school And one eve-ning com-ing home,

Said Wil-liam to John, 'Can you throw a stone, Or can you play at ball, a ball,

Or can you play at ball?'

1   O, two pretty boys were gaun to the school
     And one evening coming home,
     Said William to John, "Can you throw a stone,
     Or can you play at ball, a ball,
     Or can you play at ball?"

2   O, says William to John, "I cannot throw a stone,
     Nor little can I play at a ball;
     But if you come down to yon merry green woods
     I'll play you a wrestling fall, fall,
     I'll play you a wrestling fall."

3   So when they came to yon merry green woods
     Beneath the spreading moon,
     The little penknife slipped out of William's pocket
     Which give John his deadly wound, wound,
     Which give John his deadly wound.

4   O, you'll take off your white Holland shirt
     And you'll tear it from gore to gore;
     And you shall bind my deadly wound,
     And they shall blood no more, no more,
     And they shall blood no more.

5   O, he took off his white Holland shirt,
     And he tore it from gore to gore;
     And he did bind his deadly wound,
     But they bled ten times more, and more,
     O, they bled ten times more.

6 O, what will I tell to your sister, dear,
This night when I go home?
You can tell her I'm away to a London school
And the good books I'll bring home, home,
And the good books I'll bring home.

7 And what will I tell to your father, dear,
This night when I go home?
You can tell him I'm away to a London school
And the good scholar I'll come home, home,
And the good scholar I'll come home.

8 And what will I tell to your sweetheart, dear,
This night when I go home?
You can tell her I am dead and in grave laid
And the grass is growing green, green,
And the grass is growing green.

9 And what will I tell to your stepmother, dear,
This night when I go home?
You can tell her I am dead and in grave laid,
For she prayed I might never come home, home,
For she prayed I might never come home.

3 THE LOWLANDS OF HOLLAND
(Child 92, Appendix)

The first printed version of this song appeared in Herd, in 1776. Child
mentions it in his short note to 'Bonny Bee Hom' (No. 92), a ballad with
which it shares a formula verse missing in our text.

'The Lowlands of Holland', sung by Sheila MacGregor. Learned from her aunt, Belle Higgins.

mI/Ly

1 The first night that I got married and lay on my marriage bed,
   There came a bold sea-captain and he stood at my bedside;
   Saying, "Arise, arise, my married man, and come along with me,
   To the low, lowlands of Holland and face your enemy."

2 Lie still, lie still, my bonnie bride, lie still and take your ease,
   For if I must go with these young men wherever that they please;
   For if I was at my liberty, as I have been before,
   I would stay with you all night, my love, and plough the seas no more.

3 My love he's built a mighty ship, a ship of noted fame,
   With four-and-twenty seamen bold to steer her o'er the main;
   But the night being dark and stormy and the seas begun to roar,
   Down went the ship with all her crew, at last to rise no more.

4 THE FAMOUS FLOWER OF SERVING-MEN
(*Child 106*)

The three examples of this ballad quoted by Child are from broadside sources and sorry specimens they are! The oral tradition has failed to produce improved varieties of 'The Famous Flower' and most of the recently collected versions known to us are either weak hybrids or stunted shoots bearing one or two imperfect blooms.

'When Dukes and Earls to A-Hunting Went', sung by Belle Stewart.

pπ[1]

1 O, when dukes and earls to a-hunting went,
   There was no one left but that silly old man;
   And when dukes and earls came home to dine
   They asked what news he had to tell.

2 "O, good news, good news I have", he said,
   "For your poor workman has become a maid."
   But never heard of nor seldom seen
   A poor working man to become a queen.

5 MARY HAMILTON
(*Child 173*)

Barry gives a version of 'Mary Hamilton' which is substantially the same as Mrs Stewart's. Commenting on Barry's text, Coffin writes: "Here is a lyric poem with but the merest suggestion of plot. Only the facts – that she was one of the Queen's favoured maidens and is now about to die – remain clear. Yet the emotional core – girlhood and its beauty snuffed out by law – is as clear as it was in Child A." A little further on he states: "The basic thing is that 'Mary Hamilton' as it is found today is almost always a lyric and that the tendency to preserve the core and not the plot of the song is typical."

'The Four Maries', sung by Belle Stewart. Learned from her brother, Donald MacGregor.

aI/Ly

1   Yestreen the Queen had four Maries,
    This nicht she'll hae but three;
    There was Mary Beaton and Mary Seaton
    And Mary Carmichael and me.

2   O, often hae I dressed my Queen
    And put gowd in her hair;
    But noo it's turned to dule and wae
    My hindmost hour's tae spare.

3   O, happy, happy is the maid
    That's born o' beauty free;
    It was my rosy dimple cheeks
    That brought this weird tae me.

4   They'll tie a napkin roond my e'en,
    And they'll no' let me see tae dee,
    And they'll no' let on to my folk at hame
    That I'm awa' owre the sea.

5 O, little did my mither ken
  When saft she cradled me,
  The land her bairn would traivel in
  And the death that she was to dee.

6 Yestreen the Queen had four Maries,
  This nicht she'll hae but three,
  There was Mary Beaton and Mary Seaton
  And Mary Carmichael and me.

6 THE BONNIE HOOSE O' AIRLIE
(*Child 199*)

Airlie Castle is located approximately nine miles northeast of Blairgowrie. Its destruction by the Earl of Argyll's covenanting forces occurred on July 7, 1640. For detailed historical references, see Ford, and Greig and Keith.

Child's A-text states correctly that the Earl of Airlie "is with King Charlie." In the other Child texts, events have moved forward a century and Airlie is now away with *Prince* Charlie. This historical time-transfer occurs also in our text.

The final transformation of the covenanting war into Jacobite rebellion is achieved in the final stanza of our text, when Cameron of Lochiel enters, ready for revenge. This element of retribution is a motif absent not only in all of the Child texts but in almost all of the versions recorded since.

'The Bonnie Hoose of Airlie', sung by Belle Stewart. Some verses learned at school, others from her brother, Donald MacGregor.

mI/Ly (ending on lower V)

It fell on a day, on a bon-nie sum-mer day, When the corn was ripe and yel-low, That there fell oot a great dis-pute Be - tween Ar-gyll and Air- lie.

1 It fell on a day, on a bonnie summer day,
  When the corn was ripe and yellow,
  That there fell oot a great dispute
  Between Argyll and Airlie.

2 Lady Margaret looked ower the high castle wa'
   And O, but she sighed sairly,
   When she saw Argyll and a' his men
   Come to plunder the bonnie hoose o' Airlie.

3 "Come doon, come doon, Lady Margaret", he said,
   "Come doon and kiss me fairly,
   Or gin the mornin's clear daylight
   I winnae leave a stannin' stane in Airlie."

4 I'll no' come doon, ye fause Argyll,
   Nor would I kiss thee fairly;
   I wadnae kiss the fause Argyll
   Though ye wadnae leave a stannin' stane in Airlie.

5 But if my guid lord had been at hame
   As he's awa' wi' Charlie,
   There wadnae come a Campbell frae Argyll
   Dare trod upon the bonnie green o' Airlie.

6 For I hae bore him seven bonnie sons,
   But the eighth yin has never seen his daddy,
   But if I had as mony owre again
   They wad a' be men for Charlie.

7 Argyle in a rage he kin'led sic a lowe
   That it rose to the lift sae red and clearly;
   And poor Lady Margaret' and a' her bairns
   Were smothered in the dark reek o' Airlie.

8 "Draw your dirks, draw your dirks!" cried the brave Lochiel;
   "Unsheathe your sword!" cried Charlie,
   "And we'll kin'le sic a lowe roond the fause Argyll
   And we'll licht it wi' a spark oot o' Airlie."

7 THE GYPSY LADDIE
(Child 200)

The Skene MSS (c. 1630) contains the earliest known text of this ballad. Its theme is one that lends itself to adaptation and relocation, a fact borne out by its many fine North American variants. An Irish version popularised on radio and television by a well-known singing group has tended to become the form of the ballad standard in Britain. During the last decade we have recorded five sets of the ballad from traditional singers, four of which agree in text and melody with the broadcast version.

A current parody circulating in British folk-clubs adds emphasis to the ballad's widespread popularity:

> Go fill up the tank of the 4-litre Jag,
> For the Mini is not so speedy-O;
> And I will drive till I find her alive
> Or dead with the hippies and the beatniks-O.
>
> What makes you leave your house and your car,
> The washing-machine and the telly-O?
> Your children three (not to mention me),
> To go with the hippies and the beatniks-O. (*NCS*)

'The Gypsy Laddie', sung by Belle Stewart. Learned from Nannie Donald-son, wife to her son Andy.

O, last night I lay on a fine feath-er bed, And O, but it was bon-nie, O; The night I will lie in a cold, cold barn Wi' the gyp-sies a' a-roond me, O.

1   O, last night I lay on a fine feather bed,
    And O, but it was bonnie, O;
    The night I will lie in a cold, cold barn
    Wi' the gypsies a' aroond me, O.

2   O, for some rode east and some rode west
    And some come through Strathbogie, O;
    But the bonniest wee lassie that ever I did see
    She's awa' with the gypsy laddies, O.

8   THE BARON OF BRACKLEY
(*Child 203*)

This brief fragment with its magnificent tune is all that Belle Stewart knew of 'The Baron of Brackley', a rare piece commemorating an affray which took place on September 16, 1666 between John Gordon of Brackley (a petty baron of the family of Aboyne, Aberdeenshire) and his neighbour, Farquharson of Inverey (a "renowned freebooter on Deeside", according to Jamieson).

The feud arose out of litigation concerning property rights. Livestock belonging to Inverey had strayed onto Gordon's land, whereupon Gordon is said to have claimed or seized them and ignored Inverey's request for restitution, thus giving Inverey cause to take them back by force. This he did, according to the ballad, by riding onto Gordon's land and driving the beasts out. Brackley's wife, Peggy (Katharine, Betsy), calls on her husband to defend his property but he points out that he is outnumbered a hundred to one. His wife then calls upon her maidens to bring their spinning rocks and reels in order to fight the battle that her husband has declined. The baron dresses for battle, goes out with four men and is slain. Alternative endings include (1) the baron's young son swearing to avenge the death of his father (2) the cursing of Peggy Gordon for her treachery and (3) the rejection of Peggy Gordon by Inverey, who returns to his wife and children after the battle.

The actual facts of the incident have been blurred by the passage of time and by the passionate attempts of each side to blacken the name of the other. The ballad which has emerged through the folk process is one which is usually sympathetic to the Gordon family.

The Glen Tannoch mentioned in the second stanza should, of course, be Glen Tanner, in southern Aberdeenshire.

'Arise, Betsy Gordon', sung by Belle Stewart. Learned from her uncle Henry MacGregor.

mAe/D

moderate, slightly free

2. So rise, Bet-sy Gor-don, and hand me my gun,

For I shall go out should I nev-er come in.

Through hed-ges and ditch-es ye can-nae be sure,

But the woods o' Glen Tan-noch I'll ride in one hour.

1 (2) Says the Baron of Brackley, O are ye within?
       There's sharp swords at your gate that will gar your blood spin.
       . . . .
       . . . .

2 (3) So rise, Betsy Gordon, and hand me my gun,
       For I shall go out should I never come in.
       Through hedges and ditches ye cannae be sure,
       But the woods o' Glen Tannoch I'll ride in one hour.

3 (1) As I came down by Brackley one morning so fair
       I espied a young lady a-dressing her hair.
       She was whistling and singing, all dancing with joy
       And she swore that one night with young Edward would lie.

9 THE BRAES O' YARROW
(Child 214)

First printed in Scott's *Minstrelsy* (1803), 'The Dowie Dens' is one of the most frequently reported Scots narratives. Almost all the recently recorded versions known to us have between ten and sixteen stanzas. Belle Stewart's eleventh verse, a standard motif in 'Bonny Barbara Allan' (Child 84) is a fairly common feature in Traveller versions.

'The Dowie Dens of Yarrow', sung by Belle Stewart. Learned from her cousin, Donald MacGregor.

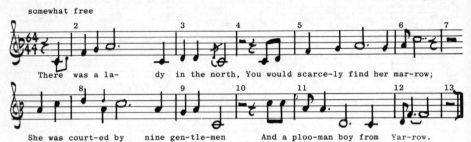

1   There was a lady in the north,
    You would scarcely find her marrow;
    She was courted by nine gentlemen
    And a plooman boy from Yarrow.

2   As he came owre yon high, high hill,
    And doon the glen so narrow,
    'Twas there he spied nine gentlemen
    Come to fight wi' him on Yarrow.

3   O, will you take the gun, the gun,
    Or will you take the arrow?
    Or will you take the gey broadsword
    And fight for me on Yarrow?

4   I will not take the gun, the gun,
    Nor will I take the arrow;
    But I will take the gey broadsword
    And fight for you on Yarrow.

5   Three he slew and three withdrew
    And three lay deadly wounded;
    Till false brother John stepped in behind,
    And pierced him through the bosom.

6   Go home, go home, you false young man,
    And tell your sister sorrow;
    That her true love, John, lies dead and gone
    On the dowie dens of Yarrow.

7   As she came ower yon high, high hill
    And down the glen so narrow,
    'Twas there she spied her brother, John,
    Returning home to Yarrow.

8   O, brother dear, I've dreamt a dream,
    I hope it won't prove sorrow,
    That my true love, John, lies dead and gone
    On the dowie dens of Yarrow.

9   O, sister dear, I read your dream,
    But I'm afraid it will prove sorrow,
    That your true love, John, lies dead and gone
    On the dowie dens of Yarrow.

10 Now, her hair it was three-quarters long
    And the colour of it was yellow;
    And she tied it roond her true love, John,
    And she carried him home to Yarrow.

11 O, mother dear, please make my bed,
    O, make it long and narrow;
    For if he has died for me last night
    I'll die for him tomorrow.

12 O, daughter dear, dry up your tears
    And greet nae mair in sorrow;
    For I'll wed you to a higher degree
    Than a plooman boy from Yarrow.

13 O, mother dear, you've seven sons,
    You can wed them all tomorrow;
    But a fairer flower there never grew
    Than my plooman boy from Yarrow.

14 And as I lie dying on my bed,
    I'll grieve nae more in sorrow;
    For I'll be with my plowman lad
    On the dowie dens of Yarrow.

Note: bars 2, 5, 8 and 11 are frequently altered to 5/4 meter thus: ♫ ♩. ♩
bars 3, 4, 7, 8, 9, 10 and 13–1 are often compressed into one 6/4 bar by
removing the minim rest.

10 **LIZIE LINDSAY**
(*Child 226*)

Five of Child's seven texts have twenty-three or more verses and tell a story far more complex than that found in most of the versions recently printed or collected in the field.

> A young man of good family disguises himself as a poor Highlander and, while in Edinburgh, courts Lizie Lindsay. He gives a fictitious description of his family, his home, and so on, and introduces himself, asking Lizie to go to the Highlands with him. She is loth to leave the town and the Lowlands to go with a stranger. Her serving-maid urges her to accept the offer and, finally, she does so. During the journey to the Highlands she begins to regret her decision. At the point where she is almost ready to turn back, they either arrive at his home or he takes her up a high hill to view the lands and property which she has gained through following him.

The ballad has been in print since 1787, when Johnson published, in the *Scots Musical Museum*, a one-stanza fragment contributed by Burns. According to Ford, "John Wilson, the famous vocalist, sang the piece into universal knowledge". There is a secondary form of the ballad, 'The Blaeberry Courtship', discussed by Laws (N 19), who calls it a 'modernisation of the story told in 'Lizie Lindsay'.

'Leezie Lindsay', sung by Belle Stewart. Learned from her cousin, Donald
MacGregor.

mI

1   Will ye gang to the Hielands, Leezie Lindsay,
    Will ye gang to the Hielands wi' me?
    Will ye gang to the Hielands, Leezie Lindsay,
    My bride and my darling to be?

2   Then I spoke to Leezie's auld mither
    And a canty auld body was she.
    Man, if I was as young as my dochter
    I wad gang tae the Hielands wi' thee.

3   Then I spoke to Leezie's own sister
    And a bonnie wee lassie was she.
    O, gin I was as auld as my sister
    I wad gang tae the Hielands wi' thee.

4   But to gang tae the Hielands wi' you, sir,
    I dinnae ken how that may be;
    For I ken no' the land that ye live in,
    Nor ken I the lad I'm gaun wi'.

5   O, Leezie, lass, ye maun ken little
    When you say that ye dinnae ken me;
    My name is Lord Ronald MacDonald,
    I'm the chief of a highland degree.

6   So she's kilted her coats o' green satin,
    And she's kilted them up tae her knee,
    And she's aff wi' Lord Ronald MacDonald,
    His bride and his darling to be.

11   ANDREW LAMMIE
(Child 233)

Peter Buchan declared that 'Andrew Lammie' was "one of the greatest
favourites of people in Aberdeenshire that I know". He had two texts in
his possession, the older one, closely related to Child's A and B-texts, and
the later one, which he professed to prefer and which he included in his
own *Gleanings*. He backed his preference by having thirty-thousand copies
printed and circulated throughout northeast Scotland. This "younger" text
of forty-nine stanzas presents the story more completely than does Mrs
MacGregor's set; though she had in her possession a forty-eight stanza
stall-copy (printed for a bookseller in Fintray), she preferred to sing her
own shortened version. The presence of such printed texts would appear to
have contributed greatly to the popularity of the ballad in northeast
Scotland.

   Annie's memory is kept alive by the people of Fyvie, who will point out
her grave in the Fyvie churchyard. Her name was Agnes Smith, probably
the daughter of one William Smith, a prosperous miller who lived at Mill o'
Tifty, Aberdeenshire. This mill, now a ruin, gave its name to the farm and
house which stood about half a mile north-east of the castle of Fyvie.
Buchan gives the date of her death as January 9, 1631, though a description
on the headstone reads January 19, 1673.

'Tifty's Annie', sung by Sheila MacGregor. Learned from Jock Whyte of
  Aberdeen.

pAe/D

Note: The fermatae are often held long enough to prolong the metre to 4/4.

1   At the mill o' Tifty's lived a man
    In the neighbourhood o' Fyvie,
    For he had a lovely daughter fair
    And they ca'd her bonnie Annie.

2   Her bloom was like the springin' floo'er
    That hails the rosy mornin',
    Her innocence and graceful mien
    Her beauteous face adornin'.

3   Noo, her hair was fair and her eyes were blue
    And her cheeks as red as roses,
    And her countenance was fair to view
    And they ca'd her Bonnie Annie.

4   Noo, Lord Fyvie he rode by the door
    Where lived Tifty's Annie;
    And his trumpeter rode him before
    Even this same Andra Lammie.

5   Noo, her mother cried her tae the door,
    Sayin', "Come here to me, my Annie.
    Did e'er ye see a prettier man
    Than the trumpeter o' Fyvie?"

6   And at nicht when all went tae their bed,
    A' slept fu' soond but Annie,
    Love so oppressed her tender breast
    And love will waste her body.

7   O, love comes in to my bedside
    And love will lie beyond me,
    Love so oppressed my tender breast
    And love will waste my body.

8   Noo, the first time me and my love met,
    It was in the woods o' Fyvie;
    For he ca'd me 'Mistress' but I said "No,
    I'm just Tifty's bonnie Annie."

9* Noo, wi' apples sweet he did me treat
    And wi' kisses saft and many,
    . . . .
    . . . .

10 Noo, I maun gang to Edinburgh toon
    And for a while maun leave thee;
    O, but I'll be deid afore ye come back
    In the green kirkyaird o' Fyvie.

11 Noo, her faither struck her wondrous sore
    And also did her mother;
    And her sisters also took their score
    But woe be to her brother.

12 Her brother struck her wondrous sore,
    Wi' cruel strokes and many;
    And he broke her back owre the temple stane,
    Ay, the temple stane o' Fyvie.

13 O mother dear, please make my bed
    And lay my face tae Fyvie;
    For I will lie and I will die
    For my dear Andra Lammie.

14* Noo, when Andra hame fae Edinburgh came
    Wi' muckle grief and sorrow;
    O, my love she died for me last night
    So I'll die for her tomorrow.

*Note: the starred stanzas were absent in the 1963 rendition but present in
       1975.

12 THE GABERLUNZIE MAN
(*Child 279, Appendix*)

Among Scots Travellers it is not unusual to find versions of this popular
ballad possessing occasional stanzas larded with cant words and phrases.
Belle Stewart's 'Gaberlunzie' has, unfortunately, been reduced to a mere
head and tail.

'The Auld Beggar Man', sung by Belle Stewart.

pI/M (ending on lower V)

O, a sprach-in' gad-gie bung owre yon lea, Sprach-in' a skip-per for cha-ri-ty;

Sprach-in' a skip-per for cha-ri-ty,Wad ye pad a sprach-in' gad- gie?

REFRAIN

Rad-lie,wi' my tow row ree.

1   O, a sprachin' gadgie bung owre yon lea,
    Sprachin' a skipper for charity;
    Sprachin' a skipper for charity,
    Wad ye pad a sprachin' gadgie?

Refrain: Radlie, wi' my tow row ree.

2   O, there's she's comin' oot owre yon lea,
    Wi' a black patch on her e'e;
    A baby on her back and anither in her lap
    And a third yin comin' hame (*refrain*)

Glossary
sprachin' – begging
gadgie   – man
skipper   – for kipper, sleeping place
pad   – lodge

13   HERE'S A HEALTH TO ALL TRUE LOVERS

Four stanzas of the following text can also be found in the revenant ballad, 'The Grey Cock' (Child 248). In that ballad, the cock is asked not to crow, for this would signal the coming of morn, by which time the supernatural visitor must away.

There are a number of songs which seem to derive from this ballad but which lack this vital supernatural element. The cock remains in many of them, but its crowing signifies the beginning of a work-day for the very alive lover who has spent the night in the arms of his beloved. This lover is usually a ploughman and one recently-collected version describes his work in detail:

> The day is dawin', the cocks are crawin'
> The bottom park I maun ploo this day;
> The factor's bell it will soon be ringing
> We are but servants and must obey.

The references given below are for the ballad *and* the related songs, as we have not attempted to extricate one from the others.

'Here's a Health to All True Lovers', sung by Belle Stewart. Learned from Alec's mother, Agnes Campbell.

mAe/D

free

Here's a health ——— to all true lov-ers

And here's to mine, where- ev- er she may be;

This ver- y night ——— I will go and see her,

Al-though she's man-y ——— a long mile from me.

1   Here's a health to all true lovers
    And here's to mine, wherever she may be;
    This very night I will go and see her,
    Although she's many a long mile from me.

2   Let the night be dark as the very dungeon,
Let not a star shine from above;
Still I will be guided, O safely guided
Into the arms of my own true love.

3   He then approached her bedroom window
His knee he placed on a cold, damp stone;
Through the panes of glass he then did call her,
My darling maid, do you sleep alone?

4   She raised her head from her soft white pillow,
Her hand she placed on her lily-white breast;
Through the panes of glass she gently whispered,
"Who's this disturbs my quiet night's rest?"

5   'Tis only I, my darlin' lover,
O open the door, love, and let me in;
For I am tired of this long night's journey,
And besides I am drenched to the very skin.

6   She opened the door with the greatest of pleasure,
She opened the door and he walked in;
They both embraced and they kissed each other,
Till the dawning of day it came creepin' in.

7   O, the cocks are crowing, love, I must be going,
The cocks are crowing, love, I must away;
The cocks are crowing, love, I must be going,
For we are but servants and I must obey.

14 THE DUKE OF ATHOL
(Laws O 23)

Child quotes Aytoun's statement that 'Richie Story' (Child 232) was recast
in a romantic form under the title 'Huntingtower', the alternative title for
'The Duke of Athol'. It quickly became a popular favourite and both
Christie and Kinloch reported it from tradition. It achieved its widest
popularity in the heyday of the Scots Choral Union when it became a set
piece for mixed-voice choirs.

'Huntingtower', sung by Belle Stewart. Learned "from a book".

aI

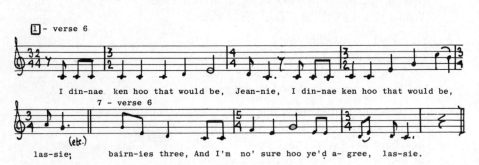

steadily, not too fast

When ye gang a-wa', Jim-mie, Far a-cross the sea, lad-die;

When ye gang tae Ger-man-y What will ye send to me, lad-die?

① - verse 6

I din-nae ken hoo that would be, Jean-nie, I din-nae ken hoo that would be,

7 - verse 6

(etc.)

las-sie; bairn-ies three, And I'm no' sure hoo ye'd a- gree, las-sie.

Note: Mrs Stewart sang to the accompaniment of the bagpipe chanter, and was obviously using the metre of the tune as normally played by that instrument. The shifting of metre was different for every verse.

1 When ye gang awa', Jimmie,
   Far across the sea, laddie;
   When ye gang tae Germany
   What will ye send to me, laddie?

2 I'll send ye a braw new goon, Jeannie,
   I'll send ye a braw new goon, lassie;
   And it shall be o' the silk and gold,
   Wi' flounces set aroond, Jeannie.

3 That's nae gift ava', Jimmie,
   That's nae gift ava', laddie;
   There's no' a goon in a' the toon
   I'd like when ye're awa', Jimmie.

4 When I come back again, Jeannie,
   When I come back again, lassie;
   I'll bring for ye a gallant gay
   To be your ain guidman, Jeannie.

5   Be my guidman yoursel', Jimmie,
     Be my guidman yoursel', laddie;
     And tak' me owre tae Germany
     Wi' you at hame to dwell, Jimmie.

6   I dinnae ken hoo that would be, Jeannie,
     I didnae ken hoo that would be, lassie;
     For I've a wife and bairnies three,
     And I'm no' sure hoo ye'd agree, lassie.

7   Ye should hae telt me that in time, Jimmie,
     Ye should hae telt me that in time, laddie;
     For had I kent o' your fause hairt,
     Ye'd ne'er hae gotten mine, Jimmie.

8   Dry that tearfu' e'e, Jeannie,
     My tale is a' a lee, lassie;
     I've neither wife nor bairnies three,
     And I'll wed nane but thee, Jeannie.

9   Think weel for fear ye rue, Jimmie,
     Think weel for fear ye rue, laddie;
     For I have neither gear nor land
     To be a match for you, Jimmie.

10   Blair in Athol's mine, Jeannie,
     Little Dunkel' is mine, lassie;
     St Johnson's Bower and Huntingtower,
     And a' that's mine is thine, Jeannie.

15 THE RAMBLING IRISHMAN
(Laws H 4)

The central character of the English versions of this song is not a rambling Irishman but a roving journeyman, whose trade is given as bricklaying or gardening. His travels take him to London or to Exeter, not to Philadelphia as in our text. In the United States the song has joined a large family of roving gamblers, 'guerilla boys', poor soldiers, and so on. In Canada and Australia, he remains 'the rambling Irishman'.

'The Rambling Irishman', sung by Sheila MacGregor. Learned from her
  father.

mM/D

with a swing

For I am   a ram-bl- ing I- rish- man, I tra-vel this coun- try o'er.

I formed a re- so- lu-   tion to try some oth- er shore;
I formed a re- so- lu-   tion and I think it's a ver-y good plan,

For to take a trip to A- mer- i- ca for to view that for- eign land.

1   For I am a rambling Irishman, I travel this country o'er.
    I formed a resolution to try some other shore;
    I formed a resolution and I think it's a very good plan,
    For to take a trip to America for to view that foreign land.

2   When I landed in Philadelphia, the girls all jumped with joy,
    Said one unto the other, "Here comes an Irish boy!"
    They invited me to dine with them, took me by thy right hand,*
    For there's friendship and good nature in the heart of an Irishman.

3   Now, I walked into a tavern, it was there to stay all night,
    And the landlady's daughter, in me she took delight;
    She never took her two eyes off me as I on the floor did stand,
    And she whispered to her mother dear, "I'm in love with that
        Irishman".

4   O daughter, my foolish daughter, what's this you are going to do?
    To fall in love with an Irishman, a man you never knew?
    To fall in love with an Irishman, I think it's a very good plan,
    For there's friendship and good nature in the heart of an Irishman.

5   So my rambles I mean to give over and settle down in life;
    And when I think I'm able, take this young girl for my wife;
    I'll work for her, I'll toil for her, I'll do the owld best I can,
    Then she ne'er can say that she rued the day that she wed with her
        Irishman.

* the sense would seem to be 'the' right hand, but the singer carefully pronounced
  'thy'.

16 BURNS AND HIS HIGHLAND MARY
(Laws O 34)

In May 1786, the poet Burns parted from Mary Campbell on the banks of the Ayr. Her destination was her home in the West Highlands, where she died shortly after. A number of Burns' poems were written either directly to Mary or had references to her. When Greig printed his text of this song, he commented that the Scots country people sing this song *about* Burns more than they sing songs *by* Burns. He wrote: "... the rustic, we admit, knows his Burns. He admires the poet's songs and likes on occasion to hear them rendered by those who can sing them. But they are hardly for him – as songs ... but he will sing about Burns and his songs, but it must be in lays that have got the folksong hallmark." Ord wrote: "... it is safe to say that no song touching upon the life of our national bard – not even one of his own – ever attained the same degree of popularity amongst country people as this one." Ford speaks of the popularity of the song as a broadsheet.

In a footnote to the song, Ord writes: "Mr. Walter Towers, Bonnybridge, Stirlingshire, informs me that the song was written about sixty years ago by a West of Scotland police constable named Thomson, who subsequently emigrated to Canada." Christie writes: "The editor found this air in an unfinished state among his father's papers. He often heard sets of it sung by itinerant ballad-singers on the major and minor scales. The set given here was arranged in 1850. It appears to be of Irish origin."

'Burns and Highland Mary', sung by Sheila MacGregor. Learned from her uncle, Donald.

aM

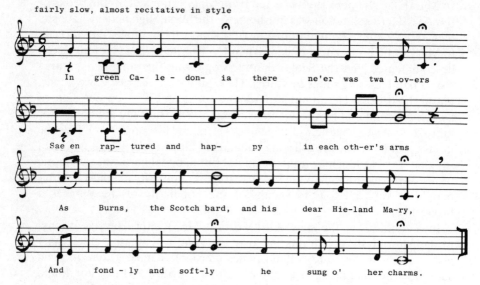

fairly slow, almost recitative in style

In green Ca-le-don-ia there ne'er was twa lov-ers

Sae en rap-tured and hap-py in each oth-er's arms

As Burns, the Scotch bard, and his dear Hie-land Ma-ry,

And fond-ly and soft-ly he sung o' her charms.

1   In green Caledonia there ne'er was twa lovers
    Sae enraptured and happy in each other's arms
    As Burns, the Scotch bard, and his dear Hieland Mary,
    And fondly and softly he sung o' her charms.

2   It was a May day and a' the floo'ers o' the summer
    Were all bloomin' in wildness, a' lovely and fair;
    When those twa lovers met in a grove o' green flowers
    That grew round the banks o' the clear winding Ayr.

3   But O, to them baith, it was a meeting fu' tender,
    And it was the last for a while they maun hae,
    For love's purest rapture they tasted thegither,
    When the red setting sun shone the close o' the day.

4   He kissed her red lips, they were sweeter than roses,
    And he pressed her lily-white breast to his heart,
    And tears fell like dewdrops sitting on his bosom,
    When he said, "My fond lover, alas, we maun part.

5   "Dinnae ye bide lang, my dear lass, in the Hielans;
    Dinnae ye bide lang, for I winna be there.
    For I love you sincerely, ay, far owre dearly
    To be happy sae far, my dear Mary, fae thee."

6   I winnae bide lang, my dear lad, in the Hielans,
    I winnae bide lang, for you winnae be there;
    For a'though I hae friends I like weel in the Hielans,
    The one I lo'e best's on the banks o' the Ayr.

7   "Noo, fareweel", said he, as he flew frae his Mary,
    "And fareweel", said Mary, for she could say nae mair.
    For little they kent they were pairting forever
    When they pairted that nicht on the banks o' the Ayr.

8   The green summer saw but a few sunny mornings,
    While she in the midst o' her beauty and pride,
    She was laid in her grave like a bonny young floo'er
    In the Greenock kirkyard on the banks o' the Clyde.

9   Noo, bring me the lilies and bring me the roses,
    And bring me the daisies that grow on yon vale,
    And bring me the sigh o' a midsummer's evening,
    And bring me the breath o' a sweet scented gale.

10 And bring me the sigh o' fond lover's bosom,
    And bring me the tear o' a fond lover's e'e.
    And I'll pour them a' doon on your grave, Hielan Mary,
    For the sake o' the Burns wha owre dearly loved thee.

11 Noo, Burns the Scotch bard, in his ain Caledonia
    Lamented his Mary on mony's the sad strain,
    And sair did he weep for his dear Hieland Mary
    And ne'er did his heart lo'e sae deeply again.

17 THE BONNIE IRISH BOY
(Laws P 26)

A more common ending of this song is for the heroine to die of a broken
heart after searching unsuccessfully for her lost lover. The happy ending of
Mrs MacGregor's version appears to be more popular with Scots Travellers.

'My Bonnie Wee Irish Boy', sung by Sheila MacGregor. Learned from her
mother.

aM (with inflected VII)

somewhat free

It was in Lon- don- der- ry that ci- ty of note and fame,

That first my bon-nie wee I- rish boy a- court- in' me he came;

He told me plea- sant sto- ries and said his bride I'd be,

But the face of my bon-nie wee I-rish boy I'm a- fraid I ne'er will see.

Note: the tune often goes into a 4/4 metre on the second and third lines of
the melody.

1 It was in Londonderry, that city of note and fame,
   That first my bonnie wee Irish boy a-courtin' me he came;
   He told me pleasant stories and said his bride I'd be,
   But the face of my bonnie wee Irish boy I'm afraid I ne'er will see.

2 I booked my passage to New York and in it there I have been,
   But the face of my bonnie wee Irish boy, he is nowhere to be seen;
   I've searched New York and Boston, I've searched them o'er and o'er,
   But the face of my bonnie wee Irish boy I'm afraid I will see no more.

3 Last night as I lay sleepin', sure, I dreamt I was his bride,
   And that we sat on a blue-bell hill, as we sat side by side,
   Gathering up primroses as we did in days of yore –
   But I woke, quite broken-hearted, in the city of Baltimore.

4   Quite early the next morning, sure, a knock came to my door,
    And I knew it was my own true love, the boy that I adore;
    So hastening up to let him in, my heart ne'er felt more joy,
    For I fell into the arms of my bonnie wee Irish boy.

5   So now that we are married, he is going no more to sea;
    I own I love him dearly and I know that he loves me –
    Our first wee son was called for him, our hearts' delight and joy,
    He's the picture o' his daddy, he's my bonnie wee Irish boy.

18   DRUMMALLOCHIE

This is one of that large group of songs in which a young man returns to his
sweetheart after a long absence and, unrecognised by her, tests her fidelity
by offering her marriage, riches and a more exalted social position. She
rejects this offer, whereupon he reveals his true identity and all is well. The
absence of the revelatory stanza in 'Drummallochie' has, to some extent,
transformed a "love-will-conquer-all" type of song into a melancholy
account of loyal but unrequited love.

Equally significant is the loss of the two Aberdeenshire place-names
which customarily round off each stanza thus: "But aye she sighed for
Sinnahard and for Drummallochie". Greig observed that the main charm
of the song lay in the happy combination of these two place-names.

'The Donside Lover', sung by Sheila MacGregor. Learned from Davie Stewart of Montrose.

aAe/D

fairly slow, rather free

'Twas on a cauld No- vem-ber nicht when fruits and flowers were gone,

One eve- ning as I wan-dered forth a- long the banks o' Don;

I o- ver-heard a fair maid, so sweet and low sang she,

My love is far frae Sun-ny Ha' and Fred-erick Mal-la-chree. —

1   'Twas on a cauld November nicht when fruits and flowers were gone,
    One evening as I wandered forth along the banks o' Don;
    I overheard a fair maid, so sweet and low sang she,
    My love is far frae Sunny Ha' and Frederick Mallachree.

2   Says I, "My pretty fair maid, why walk you here alone
    Lamenting for some absent one along the banks o' Don?
    Come tell the reason o' your grief, come tell it a' to me."
    But aye she sighed for Sunny Ha' and Frederick Mallachree.

3   Queen Mary on her Scottish throne was never half sae fair,
    And roond her broo hung many a curl and locks o' raven hair;
    Her cheeks were like the roses below her rollin' e'e,
    But aye she sighed for Sunny Ha' and Frederick Mallachree.

4   Young Peter was my true love's name, lived on the banks o' Don;
    He was as fair a young man as e'er the sun shone on –
    But the cruel wars o' Scotland has ta'en my love fae me,
    Nae mair we'll meet in Sunny Ha' nor Frederick Mallachree.

5   The cruel wars o' Scotland are sae cruel and severe;
    They cause mony's a fair maid to shed mony a sigh and tear,
    Tae tak' fae them their sweethearts as they have done to me –
    Nae mair we'll meet in Sunny Ha'nor Frederick Mallachree.

6   When Jacob saw his long-lost son he couldn't describe his love,
    He prayed to him a blessing to come from heaven above;
    And there before my maker's throne, I'll never bend my knee
    For him that's far frae Sunny Ha' and Frederick Mallachree.

7   Among some gentle hopes and fair, among companions gay
    That I may approach my true love and guard him night and day;
    And sometimes in yon merry braes I'll sob and sigh maybe
    For him that's far frae Sunny Ha' and Frederick Mallachree.

8   Says I, "My pretty fair maid, O gie to me your hand,
    For on the bonny banks o' Dee I hae but hoose and land;
    I'll freely gie them a' to thee if you will be my bride,
    And forsaken yon bonnie laddie that lives upon Donside."

9   "Young man," says she, "your offer's fair and what I must deny,
    For the sake of one young man I have to live and die;
    O seven long years since he left me, and seven I'll wait on thee,
    For him that's far frae Sunny Ha' and Frederick Mallachree."

10 I turned mysel' richt roond aboot, and made tae walk awa',
    And turnin' roond behind me, I heard her sob and say:
    "If my true love was here this nicht I'd a-swore that that was he
    But he is far fae Sunny Ha' and Frederick Mallachree."

19   QUEEN AMANG THE HEATHER

Tragedy arising out of social misalliance is as common a ballad theme as
the problems occasioned by that misalliance being resolved through the
power of love. 'Queen Amang the Heather' is a typical example of the
genre. It shares theme, landscape, characters and even some plot ingre-
dients with songs like 'The Lass of Glenshee', 'The Laird of Drum' and
'Glasgow Peggy'. With the last-mentioned ballad it can also claim a
melodic relationship.

'Queen Amang the Heather', sung by Belle Stewart. Learned from her brother, Donald MacGregor.

aM/D

Noo, as I roved out one sum-mer's morn
A-mang lof-ty hills and moor-land and moun-tain;
It was there I spied a love-ly maid
Whilst I, with oth-ers, was out a-hunt-ing.

1 Noo, as I roved out one summer's morn
   Amang lofty hills and moorland and mountain;
   It was there I spied a lovely maid
   Whilst I, with others, was out a-hunting.

2 No shoes, no stockings did she wear,
   Neither had she hat nor had she feather;
   But her golden locks aye in ringlets rare
   In the gentle breeze played on her shoulder.

3 O, I said, "Braw lassie, why roam your lane?
   Why roam your lane amang the heather?"
   And she says, "My faither's awa' frae hame,
   And I'm herdin' a' his ewes thegither."

4 Noo, I said, "Braw lassie, if you'll be mine,
   And care to lie on a bed o' feathers;
   In silks and satin it's you will shine
   And you'll be my queen amang the heather."

5 O, she says, "Kind sir, your offer is good
   But I'm afraid it was meant for laughter;
   For I know you are some rich squire's son,
   And I'm a poor lame shepherd's dochter.

6 "O, but had ye ha' been a shepherd loon
   A-herdin' ewes in yonder valley,
   Or had ye been a plooman's son,
   Wi' a' my heart I would hae lo'ed ye."

7 Noo, I hae been to balls and I hae been to halls
   I have been in London and Balquhidder;
   But the bonniest lassie that ever I did see
   She was herding ewes amang the heather.

8 Then we baith sat doon upon the plain
   We sat awhile and talked thegither;
   And we left the ewes for to stray their lane
   Till I wooed my queen amang the heather.

20 AMANG THE WHINNY KNOWES

All the sets of this piece known to us show considerable uniformity of text
and tune. Ford, writing in 1900, says: "It is quite evidently a modern
effusion, and the author may be living. I have met with it in various cheap
song sheets, but nowhere with any name attached." Greig described it as
"a pleasant lilt, and fairly popular. It is not, however, a true folksong, but
belongs to the class of what may be called 'composed' songs in the
construction of which a certain amount of literary skill and device is
exhibited."

   We have not heard of its being reported from places outside Scotland
and Northern Ireland.

'The Corncrake Among the Whinny Knowes', sung by Belle Stewart. Learned from her brother, Donald MacGregor.

mM/D

smoothly

O, the lass that I lo'ed best of all was hand- some, young and fair;

Wi' her I spent some hap-py nights up- on the banks o' Ayr.
Wi' her I spent some hap-py nights where yon wee burn- ie rows,

Whaur the ech- o mocks the corn- crake a- mang the whin-ny knowes.

1 O, the lass that I lo'ed best of all was handsome, young and fair;
   Wi' her I spent some merry nights upon the banks o' Ayr.
   Wi' her I spent some happy nights where yon wee burnie rows,
   Whaur the echo mocks the corncrake amang the whinny knowes.

2 O, we lo'ed each other dearly, disputes we seldom had,
   As constant as the pendulum, her heart beat always glad;
   We sought for joy and found it where yon wee burnie rows,
   Whaur the echo mocks the corncrake amang the whinny knowes.

3 O, ye maidens fair and pleasured dames drive to the banks o' Doon,
   You'll dearly pay for every scent to barbers for perfume;
   But rural joy is free to all where the scented clover grows,
   Whaur the echo mocks the corncrake amang the whinny knowes.

4 O, the corncrake is noo awa', the burnie's tae the brim;
   The whinny knowes are clad wi' snaw that haps the highest whin;
   When gloomy winter gangs awa' and the summer it clears the sky,
   O, we'll welcome back the corncrake, the bard of rural joy.

21 IF I WAS A BLACKBIRD

In our experience it is rare to hear this somewhat trite lovesong from the mouth of a Scots Traveller. Almost all our Traveller friends have heard the song at some time or another but none of them have been moved sufficiently by it to learn it. None, that is, except Belle Stewart. Among Irish and English Travellers, on the other hand, it is a perennial favourite.

'If I Was a Blackbird', sung by Belle Stewart. Learned from her brother, Donald MacGregor.

1 Noo, I am a young maiden, my story is sad,
   For years I've been courted by a brave sailor lad;
   He courted me truly by night and by day,
   Ah, but noo he has left me and gone far away.

2 And if I was a blackbird, could whistle and sing,
   I would follow the vessel my true love sails in,
   And on the top riggin' I would there build my nest,
   And I'd flutter my wings on his lily-white breast.

3 Noo, he promised to tak'me to Donnybrook Fair,
   For to buy me red ribbons to tie up my hair;
   And I know that some day he'll come back o'er the tide
   Ay, and surely he'll call me his own darling bride.

4 But if I was a scholar, could handle the pen,
   One secret love letter to my love I would send;
   I would tell him my sorrow, my grief and my pain
   Just since he's gaed and left me in yon flowery glen.

5* For if I could meet him, I would bow, I would kneel,
  O, if I could meet him, I would bow to his heel;
  ....
  Just since he's gaed and left me in yon flowery glen.

6 Noo, my parents they chide me and will not agree
   That me and my sailor boy married should be,
   But let them deride me or do what they will –
   While there's breath in my body he's the one I love still.

7 So, if I was a blackbird, could whistle and sing,
   I would follow the vessel my true love sails in (etc, as verse 2)

* These lines are sung, respectively, to lines 2, 3 and 4 of the music.

22 A NOBLEMAN LIVED IN A MANSION

Young women who are prepared to abandon all for love are common
enough characters in traditional song. Their sisters who insist that marriage
must precede the act are frequently depicted as resourceful young ladies,
adept at disguise and in possession of a whole armoury of stratagems. The
heroine of this song doesn't belong to either group – she is that "poor but
honest" (and boring) creature of the Victorian penny-novelette.

'A Nobleman Lived in a Mansion', sung by Belle Stewart. Learned from an old woman in Inverness, Sarah MacDonald.

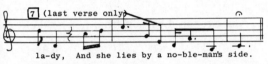

1   A nobleman lived in a mansion,
    He courted his own servant maid;
    'Twas neither for love nor for beauty,
    'Twas only to lead her astray.

2   One night as he entered her bedroom,
    As Mary was loosing her stays;
    O, many bright presents I'll give you
    One night for to lie by your side.

3   O, master, I wonder to hear you,
    A man of such honour and pride;
    To ask a poor innocent lassie
    One night for to lie by your side.

4   For if I were to fall with a baby,
    'Twould be the very first thing you'd deny;
    While me and my baby would perish
    And you in your mansion would lie.

5   But if you were to fall with a baby,
    'Twould be the very first thing I would do:
    I would write out a cheque for some money
    And build a fine cottage for you.

6   But he saw that he could not get round her,
    So he said he would make her his bride;
    So now she's a nobleman's lady
    And she lies by a nobleman's side.

23   THE LOVELY IRISH MAID

At first glance this song appears to bear some resemblance to 'Erin's Flowery Vale' (Laws 0 29), in which an observer overhears a conversation between a young girl and her lover, who is about to depart for America. The observer is still there in the final stanza to watch the denouement:

> She strove in vain him to detain, but while she did bewail,
> He bade adieu, and I withdrew from Dobbin's flowery vale.

A comparison of the two songs show that they are quite different pieces, though both of them deal with situations arising out of the Irishman's forced emigration. We take our title from the Newfoundland version which lacks our sixth stanza, ending with our fifth – a less effective conclusion in our opinion.

'Blackwaterside', sung by Sheila MacGregor. Learned from her mother.

mAe/D

1   As I roved out one evening so early as I strayed,
    'Twas in the merry month of June and the birds sang in the shade;
    And the sun it shone melodiously and decked all in her pride,
    With the primroses and daisies down by Blackwaterside.

2   I had not walked more than a mile when there a pair I spied,
    Two lovers walked as they did talk, down by Blackwaterside.
    He entwined his arms around her waist and this to her he said:
    "'Tis in America I'll prove true to my lovely Irish maid."

3   When you go to America and those Yankee maids you'll see,
    If they be fair and handsome there, you'll forget your love for me.
    You'll forget all your vows and your promises, just unto me you made –
    So stay at home and do not roam from your lovely Irish maid.

4   When I go to America, and those Yankee maids I'll see,
    If they be fair and handsome there, they'll remind me just on thee;
    For there's not a flower grows in yon bower, in yon mountain, valley or
        shade
    But will me remind on you, behind, my lovely Irish maid.

5   But many's the lad has left his home, bound for a foreign shore,
    They have left their wives and their own sweethearts their face to see no
        more;
    While sailing o'er the wide Atlantic, in sea their body was laid;
    So stay at home and do not roam from your lovely Irish maid.

6* Now to reflect that you are alone, I will never cross the tide,
    And if it be with your own consent, sure, I'll make you my bride;
    . . . .
    And we'll spend our days in happiness, down by Blackwaterside.

* *Note*: Mrs MacGregor sings directly from line 2 to line 4 as if accustomed to
    finishing the song off with a three-line stanza.

24   BUSK BUSK, BONNIE LASSIE

Over the years we have recorded this piece from several Scots Travellers
and in each case the air and text have been identical with those given here.
The interlocutory lines which form the first half of each of the two stanzas
are featured in 'Oh, No, No', a Scots song of the 'Lisbon' type (Laws N 8).
The melody given by Ord for this somewhat trite song appears to be a
simplified variant of the air associated with 'Busk Busk'.

'Bonnie Glenshee', sung by Cathie Higgins. Learned from her mother-in-law, Charlotte Higgins.

aI

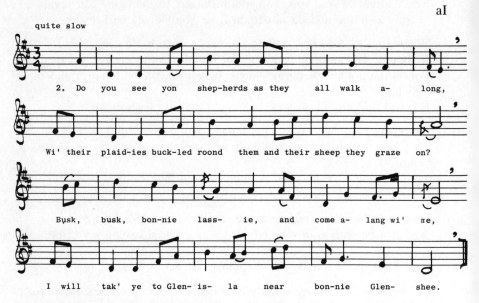

quite slow

2. Do you see yon shep-herds as they all walk a- long,

Wi' their plaid-ies buck-led roond them and their sheep they graze on?

Busk, busk, bon-nie lass- ie, and come a- lang wi' me,

I will tak' ye to Glen- is- la near bon-nie Glen- shee.

*1 Busk busk, bonnie lassie and come alang wi' me,
   I will tak' ye to Glenisla near bonnie Glenshee.

2 Do you see yon shepherds as they all walk along,
  Wi' their plaidies buckled roond them and their sheep they graze on?
  Busk busk, bonnie lassie, and come alang wi' me,
  I will tak' ye to Glenisla near bonnie Glenshee.

3 Do you see yon soldiers as they all march along,
  With their plaidies buckled roond them and their broadswords hung
     doon?
  Busk busk, bonnie lassie, and come alang wi' me,
  I will tak' you to Glenisla near bonnie Glenshee.

4 Do you see yon high hill a' covered wi' snaw,
  They have pairted mony a true love and they'll soon pairt we twa,
  Busk busk, bonnie lassie, and come alang wi' me,
  I will tak' ye to Glenisla near bonnie Glenshee.

* This couplet is sung, respectively, to lines 1 and 4 of the music.

25 BONNIE LASS, COME OWRE THE BURN

This song rarely exceeds two stanzas, but in spite of its brevity it is a great favourite among Scots Travellers.

'Bonnie Lass, Come Owre the Burn', sung by Belle Stewart. Learned from her uncle, Henry MacGregor.

mI/M

1   O, bonnie lass, come owre the burn,
    Dinnae stand there and mourn,
    For I'm the faither o' your get
    So what the devil ails ye?

26 THE BALL O' KIRRIEMUIR

The small Angus market-town of Kirriemuir seems, at first glance, to be an unlikely domicile for fantasy and its pale cousin, whimsy. And yet it was here that the author of Peter Pan and Mary Rose was born, scarcely a cock-stride, so to speak, from that scene of extraordinary sexual abandon celebrated in Scotland's most popular erotic song.

There is a legend to the effect that the events described in this ever-growing epic occurred at a Harvest Home held in the vicinity of Kirriemuir about 1885. Gershon Legman has pointed out that a full text of the song was printed ten years earlier in *Forbidden Fruit: A Collection of Tales, & c.*, c. 1875. He argues convincingly that 'Blyth Will and Bessie's Weddin', published almost a hundred years earlier in the *Merry Muses* is the direct ancestor of the modern 'Ball o' Kirriemuir'.

'The Ball o' Kirriemuir', sung by Belle Stewart. Learned from old Maggie
Kelby.

Chorus 1:   O, the ball, the ball,
            The ball o' Kirriemuir,
            O, the buckin' o' the sweetie-wife
            It was an awfae tear.

1   Some were in the barn
            And some among the kye,
            There was fowre-and-twenty weet things
            Hangin' oot to dry.

Chorus 2:   At the ball, the ball,
            The ball aneath the brig,
            O, siccan a carry-on there was
            It was an awfae rig.

2   Noo, some were in the barn
            And some among the stots,
            Ye couldnae see the kitchen flair
            For hips and hairy cocks.

Chorus 3:   At the ball, the ball,
              The ball aneath the brig,
              It's hi the ba' and ho the ba'
              The ball o' Kirriemuir.

3   The minister's dochter she was there
              And she was warst o' a',
              She cockit up her wooden leg
              And pished against the wa'. (chorus 3)

4   The hoosekeeper she was there
              And she was worst of a',
              She gaed and telt the minister
              What they did against the wa'. (chorus 3)

5   Noo, here's to auld Kirriemuir
              And here's to the ba',
              I cannae sing anither verse
              My thrapple's owre sma'. (chorus 2)

27 MY FAITHER WAS HUNG FOR SHEEP-STEALING

Among Scots Travellers this bawdy lyric must rank as a strong challenger
to 'The Ball of Kirriemuir' in the popularity stakes. For detailed discus-
sions of it, see Cray, and MacColl and Seeger.

'When I Was a Hedger and Ditcher', sung by Belle Stewart. Learned from
  Willie Kelby.

aAe

1 When I was a hedger and ditcher
   And up to me arse in the snow;
   And the deil took a-haud o' my pintle
   And he swore he would never let go.

Chorus: With my ring to my doo to my daddie
   My ring to my doo to my day,
   And the deil took a-haud o' my pintle
   And he swore he would never let go.*

2 O, my faither was hanged for sheep-stealing
   My mother was burned for a witch;
   And me and my bawdy hoosekeeper
   Man, she was a son of a bitch. (chorus)

3 When I was a hedger and ditcher
   An' up to me arse among muck;
   I earned five bob every morning
   For learning young ladies to buck. (chorus)

* Each chorus finishes with the last two lines of the preceding verse.

28 THE BONNIE LASSIE'S PLAIDIE

Robert Ford described this favourite song as having "the true marrow of
the Scottish lyre in it. Humourous, and although a little high kilted, it is by
no means rudely indelicate." Mr Ford goes on to say: "My friend, Mr D.
Kippen of Crieff, has it that the song was composed by an Irishman who

lived in Crieff, near to the Cross, in the early years of the present century, and was known familiarly by the name of 'Blind Bob'."

In some of the versions collected since that footnote was written, the kilt appears to be in some danger of disappearing altogether.

'Fleshy Robbie', sung by Belle Stewart. Learned from her grandmother, Mary Reid.

mI (ending on III)

moderate, slightly free

O, Flesh- y Rob- bie lived in-to Crieff,
And doon came a bon-nie lass to buy some beef;
And he whupped her in his air-ms and doon the road he ran,
And the wear-y, wear-y wind blew her plaid- ie a-wa'.

1   O, Fleshy Robbie lived into Crieff.
    And doon come a bonnie lass to buy some beef;
    And he whupped her in his airms and doon the road he ran,
    And the weary, weary wind blew her plaidie awa'.

29 BONNIE BONNIE BESSIE LEE

Robert Nicoll of Tulliebeltane (1814–37) was the author of the song whose title inspired the following quatrain. In its time, Nicoll's song was tremendously popular, though scarcely anyone remembers it today and those who lilt this amorous jingle are usually unaware of its respectable parentage.

'Bonnie Bonnie Bessie Lee', sung by Belle Stewart. Learned from her brother, Donald MacGregor.

jauny

Bon-nie   bon-nie   Bess- ie Lee,   Come to bed and   cud- dle me;

Draw the blan- kets   owre your knee   To keep your puss-y war - m.

1   Bonnie bonnie Bessie Lee,
    Come to bed and cuddle me;
    Draw the blankets owre your knee
    To keep your pussy warm.

30   JOHN PEEL

It is doubtful whether any other song in the English repertory has exercised the talents of bawdy parodists to the extent that 'John Peel' has. Here is a typical example of the genre.

'John Peel', sung by Belle Stewart. Learned "at school".

Do ye ken John Peel? Ay, I ken him awfae weel,
He sleeps wi' his wife, but he cannae get a feel;
He sleeps on his side and he cannae get a ride
And he rises wi' a horn in the mornin'.

31   THE ROAD TO DUNDEE

This popular Scots song appears to have first found its way into print in
Gavin Greig's weekly folksong column in *The Buchan Observer*, 1908. The
fact that it has not, to our knowledge, been previously published in any of
the Scots collections or miscellanies would seem to point to a comparatively recent date of composition. Greig commented on the uniformity of
the texts "until they come to deal with the parting of the somewhat strange
couple". By way of illustration he gives the following stanza:

> Here's twenty bright guineas, a Scotch Duke's my father,
> He's bound to support me, so let it go free;
> Call in by yon tavern and tak' a wee drappie,
> For a body that's travellin' it will help him a wee.

This alternative ending is not commonly found in Scotland but occurs in an
Ontario version:

Here is twenty bright guineas, my father's a Scotch Duke;
He's bound to support me, a lady gone free;
Call in to Victoria and have a wee droppie,
As we gang along on the road to Dundee.

An Irish version of the song, shorter and with altered place-names, is
attributed to the Antrim poet, MacKay.

'The Road and the Miles to Dundee', sung by Belle Stewart, to the same
tune as 'Johnny, My Man'. Learned from her brother, Donald Mac-
Gregor.

aAe/D

not too fast, slightly free

Cauld win-ter was howl-ing owre moor and owre moun-tain,
One morn-in' at day-break I met a wee lass-ie

And bleak was the surge o' the dark roll-ing sea;

Wha asked me the road and the miles to Dun-dee.

1 Cauld winter was howling owre moor and owre mountain,
   And break was the surge o' the dark rolling sea;
   One mornin' at daybreak I met a wee lassie
   Wha asked me the road and the miles to Dundee.

2 "O", says I, "my wee lassie, I cannae weel tell ye –
   The road and the distance I cannae weel gie;
   But if you'll permit me to gang a wee bittie,
   I'll show you the road that leads on to Dundee."

3 The lassie consented and she gied me her airm,
   No' a word did I speir wha the creature might be;
   She appeared like an angel in feature and form
   As she walked by my side on the road to Dundee.

4 Noo, at length wi' the hill o' Strathmartin behind us,
   And the spires o' the toon in full view we could see;
   She says, "My kind sir, I will never forget ye
   For showin' me sae far on the road to Dundee.

5 "So, this ring and this purse take to show I am grateful,
   And some simple token I trust ye'll gie me;
   And in time to come I'll remember the laddie
   That showed me the road and the miles to Dundee."

6 So I took a gold pin frae the scarf on my bosom
   And I said, "Tak' you this in remembrance o' me."
   And fondly I kissed the sweet lips o' the lassie
   As I pairted wi' her on the road to Dundee.

7 Noo, I'll gang into Victorum's and I'll tak' a wee drappie
   Oh the road gettin' hame it will help me a wee;
   And fondly I'll think on that bonnie wee lassie,
   The lassie I left on the road to Dundee.

8 Noo, here's to that lassie, I will never forget her,
   And every young laddie that's listenin' to me:
   O, never be sweir to convoy a wee lassie
   If it's only to show her the road to Dundee.

32 ROSEMARY LANE
(Laws K 43)

Rosemary Lane, according to F. H. Habben's *London Street Names* (1896)
"was so named from its prolific production of the odoriferous herb". By
the eighteenth-century doss-houses, rag-yards and numerous grog-shops
had banished "the wafts of pure fresh air laden with this and kindred
sweet-smelling herbs" and, like the nearby Ratcliff Highway, it had
become a place "offensive to eye and nose alike". Today it is a rather
desolate thoroughfare of warehouses and council-house blocks. The old
name has gone too: it is now called Royal Mint Street.

'Bell-Bottom Trousers', sung by Belle Stewart.

pI

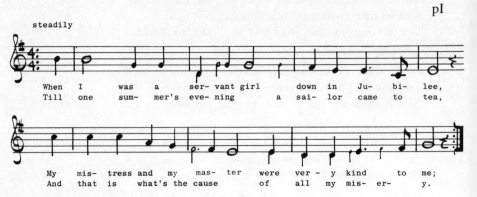

steadily

When I was a ser-vant girl down in Ju-bi-lee,
Till one sum-mer's eve-ning a sai-lor came to tea,

My mis-tress and my mas-ter were ver-y kind to me;
And that is what's the cause of all my mis-er-y.

1   When I was a servant girl down in Jubilee,
     My mistress and my master were very kind to me;
     Till one summer's evening a sailor came to tea,
     And that is what's the cause of all my misery.

2   He asked for a candle to light him into bed,
     He asked for a hankie to tie around his head;
     Me being a foolish girl and thinking it no harm,
     I jumped into bed to keep the sailor warm.

3   Early next morning when the sailor woke,
     He took from his pocket a five-pound note;
     Saying, "Take this, my darling, for the damage I have done
     I'm leaving you in charge of a daughter or a son.

4   "If it is a girl you may nurse it on your knee,
     But if it is a boy, send the bastard out to sea;
     Bell-bottom trousers and suit of navy-blue,
     And make him climb the rigging as the old man climbed up you."

33   THE GALWAY SHAWL

Frank Harte of Dublin writes: " 'The Galway Shawl' is not a very serious song and has always been sung at a kind of popular level and of late was adopted by the showband crowd. The town in the first verse should read *Oranmore*. The song is sung to a variant of an old Irish air called 'Eochaill' (Youghal in English)."

Recently the air has been used to carry new words for songs in the plays *Red Roses for Me* (Sean O'Casey) and *The Quare Fellow* (Brendan Behan).

'The Galway Shawl', sung by Sheila MacGregor. Learned from Greta
   Stewart of Banff.

pI/Ly

very freely

In   Ar - n - more in the   County Gal- way
I   spied a col- leen, she was tall and hand- some

One   sum- mer's eve- nin'   in the   month of   May;

And   she has sto- len —— my   heart a- way.

1   In Arnmore in the County Galway
    One summer's evenin' in the month of May;
    I spied a colleen, she was tall and handsome
    And she has stolen my heart away.

2   For she wore no jewels nor no costly diamonds,
    No paint, no powder, no, none at all;
    But she wore a bonnet with a shamrock on it
    And around her shoulders a Galway shawl.

3   Now, we went on walking and we went on talkin'
    Till her father's cabin it came into view;
    And she asked me in to meet her father
    And to play him the owld 'Foggy Dew'.

4   Now, she took me into her humble fireside
    Just to meet her father who was six feet tall;
    And her mother she had the kettle boiling
    Still my eyes remained on her Galway shawl.

5   Now I played to him the owld 'Stacks of Barley'
    But the owld man's glory was 'The Foggy Dew';
    And she sang each note like an Irish linnet
    Till the tears rolled down from her eyes of blue.

6   Now, very early the next mornin'
    As I held the road back to Donegal;
    And she said goodbye as we kissed and parted –
    Still my heart remains on her Galway shawl.

34   THE BONNIE LASS O' FYVIE

Like 'The Road to Dundee', this is one of those songs which has come to
be regarded as something of a regional anthem and, as is common with
anthems, both its text and its air appear to have been standardised into a
solitary version. Almost seventy years ago, Gavin Greig published two
substantially different versions of the song in *The Buchan Observer* in
order to illustrate "how words may vary ... in two versions of a well
known local ballad ... even when these were picked up in the same
parish".

Since scarcely any of the many recently collected sets of the song show
other than the most minimal word changes, it would seem that the
standardisation of the text has taken place in the course of the last seventy
years. Of the tune, Greig said: "I have noted it from a number of different
singers, and find that the versions do not vary much". During the last forty
years, the tune has become increasingly popular and is now a standard
piece with brass and pipe bands, and a hard favourite with Scots street
musicians.

'The Bonnie Lass of Fyvie', sung by Sheila MacGregor. Learned from her mother.

pI

steadily

There was a troop of I- rish dra- goons

Come march- in' doon through Fy- vie, O,

The cap-tain fell in love wi' a ver- y pret-ty maid,

Her name it was Pret-ty Peg- gy, O.

1 There was a troop of Irish dragoons
   Come marchin' doon through Fyvie, O,
   The captain fell in love wi' a very pretty maid
   Her name it was pretty Peggy, O.

2 Come doon the stair, pretty Peggy, he said,
   Come doon the stair, pretty Peggy, O.
   Come doon the stair, tie up your yellow hair
   And say your last fareweels tae your daddie, O.

3 As they come doon by auld Meldrum toon,
   The captain they had to carry, O.
   When they come to auld Aberdeen,
   The captain they had to bury, O.

4 There's many a bonnie lass fae the Howe of Auchterless,
   Many a bonnie lass in the Gairvie, O.
   Many a bonnie Jean in the toon o' Aberdeen,
   But the floo'er o' them a' lies in Fvvie, O.

35 MADAM, I HAVE COME TO COURT YOU

This courtship dialogue, which is closely related to 'The Paper of Pins', 'No Sir, No', and 'The Keys of Canterbury', has rarely been reported from Scotland. Versions similar to ours have been recorded in England, Northern Ireland and North America. The piece is also found as a children's game-song.

'Owre Yon Hills There Lives a Lassie', sung by Sheila MacGregor. Learned from her mother.

aM

1   Owre yon hills, sure, there lives a lassie,
    But her name I do not know;
    But this night I will go and see her,
    Whether she be high or low.

2   Lassie, I hae come to see thee
    But perhaps it is in vain;
    But if you'll kindly entertain me,
    Maybe I'll call back again.

3   Lassie, I have got gold and silver,
    Lassie, I have got diamond stones;
    And lassie, I have got ships in the ocean
    And they'll be yours, love, if you'll be mine.

4   O, what care I for your gold and silver?
    O, what care I for your diamond stones?
    And what care I for your ships in the ocean?
    Sure, all I want is a good young man.

36 THE DAWNING OF THE DAY
(*Laws P 16*)

MacKenzie has pointed out "the resemblance between this song and the stall ballad of 'The Shannon Side'". It is more than probable that both of them have a common parent in the Irish song 'Fainne Geal An Lae' (The Dawning of the Day) which Dr Joyce published in his *Ancient Irish Music* along with a literal translation of the Gaelic text.

In its complete form, the song tells the following story:

> A man meets a young girl at the dawning of the day. He seduces her and then deserts her. When they meet several months later, the girl asks the young man to marry her but he tells her he has just married a rich wife. The song ends with a warning against false deceivers.

A shorter version, of which our set is a good example, has the lovers reunited in the final (generally the third) stanza.

'The Dawning of the Day', sung by Cathie Higgins. Learned from her mother.

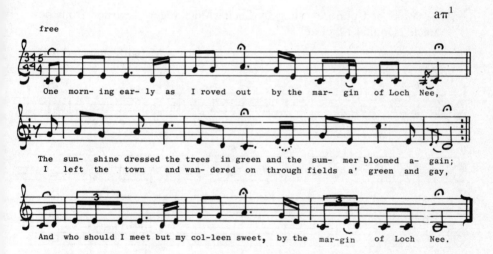

1 One morning early as I roved out by the margin of Loch Nee,
   The sunshine dressed the trees in green and the summer bloomed again;
   I left the town and wandered on through fields a' green and gay,
   And who should I meet but my colleen sweet, by the margin of Loch Nee.

2   No cap nor cloak did this maiden wear, her neck and her feet were
        bare;
    Down to the grass her ringlets fell, her glossy golden hair;
    Her milking pail was in her hand, she was lovely, young and gay,
    And she bore the part of a Venus bright by the dawning of the day.

3   On the mossy bank, sure I sat me down with this fair maiden by my
        side,
    With gentle words I courted her and I asked her to be my bride;
    She said, "Young man, don't bring me blame, but let me go away,
    For the morning's light it is shining bright by the dawning of the day."

37   THE MAID OF CULMORE

The village of Culmore lies some five miles north of Londonderry, at the
southern end of Loch Foyle. The song given here does not seem to have
travelled far – or often – from that region.

'The Maid of Culmore', sung by Sheila MacGregor. Learned from her
    uncle, Donald MacGregor.

mM (with inflected VII)

1   From sweet Londonderry to fair London town,
    There's no better harbour on earth can be found;
    Where the children each evening do play around the shore,
    And the joy-bells were ringing for the maid of Culmore.

2 Noo, the first time I met her, O she passed me by –
   And the next time I met her she bid me goodbye;
   But the last time I met her she grieved my heart sore,
   Saying, "Adieu, Londonderry, and away from Culmore."

3 Noo, if I had the power a storm I'd rise,
   For the wind to blow high and to darken the sky,
   For the wind to blow high and the salt seas for to roar
   On the day that my love sailed away from Culmore.

4 To the north of America, my love, I'll go to see;
   'Tis there I know no-one, nor no-one knows me;
   And if I do not find her, I'll return home no more,
   Like an eagle I'll wander for the maid of Culmore.

38 GREEN BUSHES
(*Laws P 2*)

The use of the word *dancer* for damsel in the first stanza of our text evokes
a rather startling picture but one not entirely lacking in charm. Most of the
published versions of the song are from English sources, though a footnote
to the chapbook version published in Ord states that the song is Irish.

'Green Bushes', sung by Cathie Higgins. Learned from her uncle, Donald
    MacGregor.

1   For as I was a-walking one morning in May,
    To hear the birds whistle and hear danskins play;
    I spied a young dancer, so sweetly sang she
    Down by the green bushes where she chanced to meet me.

2   O, why are you loitering here, pretty maid?
    "I wait for my true love, now", softly she said;
    Shall I be your true love, and will you agree
    Down by the green bushes where you chanced to meet me?

3   I will give you fine beavers and fine silken gowns,
    I will give you flounced petticoats flounced to the ground,
    I will give you fine jewels and live but for thee
    If you leave your own true love and marry with me.

4   I want none of your beavers or fine silken clothes,
    For I'm not so poor as to marry for clothes.
    But if you'll be constant and true unto me,
    I shall leave my own true love and marry with thee.

5   For when he came there and found she was gone,
    He looked very foolish and cried quite forlorn:
    "She's gone with the lord and forsaken me,
    Down by the green bushes where she vowed to meet me."

39 OXFORD CITY
(*Laws P 30*)

Oral transmission would appear to have produced only the most minimal changes in this widespread song. Occasionally the jealous lover is a sailor or a ploughman but more frequently he is a house-servant who gains the love of the daughter of the house only to lose it. The average length of the text is seven to ten stanzas, though broadsides have been reported which have eleven stanzas. It is not unusual to find verses from 'Oxford City' combined with those from 'Down in the Groves', a song with a similar theme.

'The Jealous Lover', sung by Sheila MacGregor. Learned from Bella Higgins.

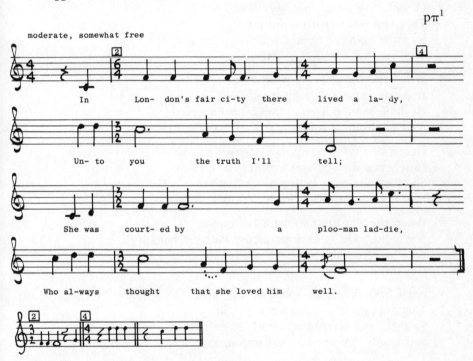

1 In London's fair city there lived a lady,
   Unto you the truth I'll tell;
   She was courted by a plooman laddie,
   Who always thought that she loved him well.

2 She loved him too, but at a distance,
   Till she became not quite so fond;
   He said, "My dear, why do you slight me,
   I'm afraid you love some other one.

3 "For if you do, why don't you marry
   And put an ending to my strife?
   For I would work both late and early
   If you would become my be-wedded wife."

4 For I'm too young, too young to marry,
   Too young to claim those marriage vows;
   For when you're married your pleasure's over,
   And all your joyful time is gone.

5 O, not long after – not very long after –
   To a ball this fair maid did go;
   She was followed by her jealous young man
   Who meant to be her overthrow.

6 While she was dancing with another,
   Jealousy arose within his mind;
   He took some poison between his fingers
   And he dropped it into a glass of wine.

7 Here's one for you, my fairest jewel,
   Here's one for you and another for me.
   She took the glass between her fingers
   And drunk it up with her heart's delight.

8 When she was finishing with her liquor
   She cried, "Dear, O dear, please take me home!
   For I'm afraid this wine we've drunken
   Has put an end to my joyful time."

9 For I have drunk the same as you, love,
   That I may die just the same as you.
   So they both clasped into each other's arms,
   Fair maids, beware of cruel jealous men!

40 THE NOBLEMAN'S WEDDING
(Laws P 31)

Generally, in this song, the unfortunate heroine chooses to spend her last
night with her mother and not – as in our version – with her new husband.

The change is not a crucial one, and the main line of the plot remains unaffected.

'The Nobleman's Wedding', sung by Cathie Higgins. Learned from her
  mother.

mI

quite free

O, late last night I was asked to a wed-ding,

The wed-ding of a fair maid who proved to be un- kind;

As she looked in the eyes of her new in-ten-ded lov-er,

Thoughts of her old love run still through her mind.

1   O, late last night I was asked to a wedding,
    The wedding of a fair maid who proved to be unkind;
    As she looked in the eyes of her new intended lover,
    Thoughts of her old love run still through her mind.

2   Supper was over and all things was ended,
    Every young man had to sing the bride a song;
    Till it came to the turn of her old intended lover,
    Thoughts of her old love run still through her mind.

3   O, how can you sit at another man's table,
    How can you drink of another man's wine?
    And how can you lie in the arms of another
    When oft-times, dear, oft-times you have lain in mine?

4   Sobbing and sighing, she went to her bedroom;
    Sobbing and sighing, she went to her bed;
    And early next morning, her bridegroom awakened,
    And turning around, he found his bride was dead.

5   O Annie, dear Annie, I knew you never loved me,
    Your love and my love would never agree;
    For I ken fine I've ta'en ye frae a better
    Ta'en ye frae a better than ever I could be.

41   THE BANKS OF RED ROSES

In its eighteenth-century broadside form, this popular song is represented as a somewhat slight collection of innocent and inconsequential floater verses. Since then, it has changed radically. In Ireland, a young man's violin – or tuning fork – robs the broadside's "pretty brown girl" of her virginity; in Scotland, she loses her life. The transformation of this simple pastoral piece into a murder ballad is, we suggest, of a comparatively recent date. In its murder form, the song does not appear – to our knowledge – in any Scots collection printed before 1970.

'The Banks Amang Red Roses', sung by Belle Stewart. Learned from Ruby Kelby.

$m\pi^1$

fluid, slightly free

Noo, when I was a young thing and eas- y led a- stray,
A- fore that I would work I would rath- er sport and play;
And a- fore that I would work, I would rath-er sport and play
With my John-ny on the banks a- mang red ro ——— ses.

1   Noo, when I was a young thing and easy led astray,
    Afore that I would work, I would rather sport and play;
    And afore that I would work, I would rather sport and play
    With my Johnny on the banks amang red roses.

2   On the banks of red roses, my love and I sat doon,
    He took oot his charm box for to play his love a tune.
    In the middle o' the tune, his love sat doon and cried,
    "O my Johnny, O my Johnny, dinnae leave me!"

3   He took oot his pocket knife and it being long and sharp,
    And he pierced it through and through his ain bonnie lassie's heart;
    And he pierced it through and through his ain bonnie lassie's heart;
    And he left her lying low amang red roses.

42 HATTON WOODS

This appears to be a strictly local song in Aberdeenshire, which has two places by the name of Hatton, one a small village halfway between Aberdeen and Fraserburgh and the other – Hatton Fintray – situated by the river Don about ten miles northwest of Aberdeen. The only printed version of the song that we have found is in Ord, a six-stanza piece similar to ours except for the place names in the fourth stanza: "There's Castem, and there's Cadem Mills and Leather Mills likewise".

'Hatton Woods', sung by Sheila MacGregor and Cathie Higgins.

pπ[1]

fairly slow, quite free

O, ye com-rades and com-pan-i-ons___ and all ye fe-males dear,

To my sad la-men-ta-tions I pray ye lend an ear;

For once I lo'ed a bon-nie lass but to me she proved un-true,

And she left me doon by Hat-ton Woods my fol-ly for to rue.

1   O, ye comrades and companions and all ye females dear,
    To my sad lamentations I pray ye lend an ear;
    For once I lo'ed a bonnie lass but to me she proved untrue,
    And she left me doon by Hatton Woods my folly for to rue.

2   Noo, I courted wi' yon bonnie lass a twelvemonth and a day,
    Sometimes amang the green grass, sometimes amang the hay;
    I courted her the lee lang nicht, till the dark o' the next day,
    Till she said, "My ain dear Sandy, lad, it's time ye were away."

3   O, says I, "My ain dear Molly, lass, when shall we set a time
    When you and I'll get married and hands together join?
    (We'll) sit in your ain cottage then and either spin or sew   [You'll?]
    Whilst your ain dear-hearted Sandy lad goes whistlin' at the ploo."

4   Noo, there's Cadem and there's Cadem Mills and Lowthrie Mills
        likewise;
    There are woods and waters many unseen unto your eyes;
    But the bonnie woods o' Hatton they aye grow green in May,
    And 'twas there the bonnie lassie lived that stole my heart away.

5 Noo, my blessings on you, bonnie lass, wherever she may be,
   I wish no evil unto her although she slighted me;
   I only hope that she might say sometime before she'll dee:
   "O, I wish I'd wed yon plooman lad that sang sae sweet to me."

43 THE DAYS ARE AWA' THAT WE HAE SEEN

The opening couplet of this fragment is often found in Scots sets of 'Lang a-
Growing' and in 'Rap at the Door.' The concluding couplet, however,
establishes beyond question that it is to 'The Days are Awa' That I Hae
Seen' that our fragment rightfully belongs.

'The Days Are Awa' That We Hae Seen', sung by Sheila MacGregor.
   Learned from her cousin, Martha Stewart.

1 O, the trees are growing heich, my lad, the grass is growing green,
   The days are past and gone, my laddie, you and I have seen;
   But there'll be a welcome where I should have been,
   So begone, laddie, wha cares for ye?

44 BOGIE'S BONNIE BELLE

As far as we know, none of the major collections of Scots songs printed
before 1960 include this tremendously popular bothy ballad. In spite of

this, or perhaps because of it, almost every Scots singer from whom we have recorded songs has been able to supply us with a version of it. In each case, to our surprise, the narrative has been complete.

'Bogie's Bonnie Belle', sung by Belle Stewart. Learned from Frank Kelby.

pI/M (ending on lower V)

steady, moderate

Ae Whit-sun's day at Hunt-ly Toon, it was there I did a- gree

Wi' auld Bo- gie- side, a fairm- er, a six- month for to fee.

1   Ae Whitsun's day at Huntly Toon it was there I did agree
    Wi' auld Bogieside, a fairmer, a six-month for to fee.

2   Noo, Bogie was a greedy man and I did know that well,
    But he also had a dochter, her name was Isabel.

3   Noo, Belle she was the bonniest lass in a' the countryside,
    And very soon I lost my hairt to Belle o' Bogieside.

4   For often on a simmer's nicht I would wander wi' my dear,
    For to watch the trooties lowpin' in Bogie's water clear.

5   I slipped my airms aroond her waist and the feet fae her did slide
    And it was there I ta'en my will o' her at Bogie's bonnie side.

6   For nine lang months were past and gone and she brocht forth a son
    And aul' Bogie he did send for me to see whit could be done.

7   Noo, I said that I would marry her but O no, that wadnae dae,
    For I'm nae match for Bogie's Belle, and she's nae match for me.

8   O, noo she's married tae a tinkler chap and she bides in Huntly Toon
    And wi' Tilly pans and ladles she scours the country roond.

45 JOHN MITCHEL

John Mitchel was born in Dungiven, County Derry, Ireland, in 1815 and was a founding member of the Young Ireland Party, whose aim was to unite the Catholics and Protestants of Ireland in a final attempt to sever the union with England. After the rising of 1848, the leaders of the party (among whom were Thomas Davis, Gavan Duffy, John Mitchel, John Dillon and William Smith O'Brien) were transported for treason felony to Van Diemen's Land. Mitchel's sentence was for fourteen years but he escaped to America where he fought on the side of the South in the Civil War. While in the United States he published a number of pro-slavery newspapers, all of them short-lived, which lost him any American support for the Irish cause that he had had. He returned to Ireland in 1875, was elected MP for Tipperary, but died at Newry later the same year.

The song has had some circulation on broadsheets but does not appear to have become very popular. Sheila MacGregor's text substitutes the "standard of revolt" for the "standard of repeal". Her fifth stanza is one found often in songs about Van Dieman's Land.

'John Mitchel', sung by Sheila MacGregor. Learned from her mother.

mAe/D

1   I am a true-born Irishman, John Mitchel is my name,
    And for to join my countrymen from Newry town I came;
    I struggled hard both day and night to free my native land,
    From which I was transported unto Van Dieman's Land.

2   When first I joined my countryman it was in 'forty-two,
    And what did follow after I will now explain to you;
    For I raised the standard of revolt and I gloried in the deed
    And I vowed to heaven I ne'er would rest till old Ireland would be
       freed.

3 So, while here in (present) close confine, await my trial
     day,   [prison?]
   My loving wife, she came to me and this to me did say:
   "O, John, my dear, keep up heart, (undaunted) never be!
                                                           [and daunted?]
   For 'tis better to die for Ireland's rights than to live in slavery."

4 O, when I received my sentence, in irons I was bound;
   When hundreds of my countrymen were rallied all around.
   I was offered then my liberty if I'd forsake the cause,
   But I'd rather die a thousand deaths than to bow to English laws.

5 So, last night as I lay sleeping, sure, I dreamt a very strange dream:
   I dreamt I was in old Ireland, down by a bubbling stream,
   With a pretty girl beside me and her to my command,
   But when I awoke my poor heart broke, I was in Van Dieman's Land.

6 So farewell, my wife and children, in heaven I'll wait for you;
   Farewell, all true-born Irishmen, farewell, my country too.
   There's one request I'll ask of you when liberty you'll gain,
   Just think of poor John Mitchel who now wears a convict's chain.

46 THE LONELY BANNA STRAND

This somewhat incoherent fragment is part of an eight-verse ballad dealing
with Sir Roger Casement's ill-fated attempt to obtain arms from Germany
in preparation for the Easter Rising (1916). The German ship with its cargo
of arms was intercepted by the British and the car sent to meet Casement
crashed over a cliff. Casement was captured, charged with treason, and
hanged.

'The Lonely Banna Strand', sung by Sheila MacGregor. Learned from her
uncle, John Stewart.

aM/D

1 O, it was on a Friday morning all in the month of May,
   When a German ship lay anchored away out in the bay;
   With fifty-thousand rifles and them to my command,
   But I couldn't give a warning to the lonely Banna Strand.

2 Now a motorcar came flying through the early mornin' gloom
   When young Roger (howsha Hogan) was bent into his doom;
   When a (thunderdash) came over him and it did not take them long
   To pull out young Sean Hogan at the station of (Noch Long).

3 ....
   ....
   Now, he's buried in an English tomb where no man speaks his name,
   May the wild wild waves roll over him on the lonely Banna Strand.

47 BALLYJAMESDUFF

Percy French, who wrote this song, is perhaps better known as the author
of 'Abdul, the Bulbul Ameer', a song which Carl Sandburg described as
"a familiar of robustuous and grandiloquent men in both metropolitan

centres of urban activity and in wilderness outposts of the Northwest Mounted, so to speak." Ballyjamesduff is in County Cavan.

'Ballyjamesduff', sung by Sheila MacGregor. Learned from her mother.

pI/M (with inflected IV)

1   O, the Garden of Eden has vanished, they say,
    But I know the lie of it still;
    You turn to the left near the Bridge of Finae
    And you stop when halfway to Coothill.
            'Tis there you will find it, I know sure enough,
            When Fortune has come to my call;
            For the grass it is greener on Ballyjamesduff,
            And the blue sky is over it all.

2 My mother once told me that when I was born
    The day that I first saw the light,
    I looked down that street on that very first morn
    And I gave a great cry of delight.
        Now, most newborn babies appear in a huff
        And start with a terrible squall,
        But I knew I was born on Ballyjamesduff
        And that's why I smiled on them all.

3 ....
    ....
    ....
    ....
        That baby's a man now, he's toilworn and tough
        And whispers come over the sea:
        O, come back, Paddy Riley, to Ballyjamesduff,
        Come home, Paddy Riley, to me.

4 Sure, I love the young women of every land –
    Och, that always came easy to me;
    Just barring the belles o' the blackamoor brand
    And the chocolate (shapes) of Fiji.   [shades?]
        Now their sighs of love was just moonshine and stuff
        And it never did trouble my brain;
        But the bells will be ringin' in Ballyjamesduff
        For me and my Rosie Coleraine.

48 THE COUNTRY I'M LEAVING BEHIND

Frank Harte reports a version of this song "from Ulster ... around
Donegal and Derry. The air has no greater merit than the words sung to
it." He observes that Irish Country and Western musicians are currently
recording many songs of this type.

'My Barge Leaves the Harbour Tomorrow', sung by Cathie Higgins.
Learned from her mother.

pI (with inflected II)

1   My barge leaves the harbour tomorrow,
    Across the wide ocean to go;
    And Katie, my burden of sorrow
    It's more than I wish you to know.

2   There's a dreary dark cloud hangin' o'er me,
    And a mighty big load on my mind,
    As I think on the prospects before me
    And the country I'm leavin' behind.

3   Farewell to the green hills of Erin
    And the darling so faithful and kind;
    But where'er I may be, my true love I'll see
    And the country I'm leavin' behind.

49   GLEN SWILLY

The river Swilly runs through North Donegal and empties into the long, narrow sea lough, Lough Swilly. Mrs MacGregor's alteration of the place-name's central vowel is a minor change compared with Sam Henry's version, in which Glen Swilly has become Glen O'Lee.

'Glen Swallee', sung by Sheila MacGregor. Learned from a record.

pπ[1]

steadily

At- ten- tion pay, my coun- try- men, and hear my maid- en news –

Al- though my tale is sor- row- ful I hope you'll me ex -cuse;
I left my na- tive coun- ter- ee a for- eign land to see,

And I bid fare- well to Don-e - gal, like- wise to Glen Swal- lee.

1   Attention pay, my countrymen, and hear my maiden news –
Although my tale is sorrowful I hope you'll me excuse;
I left my native counteree a foreign land to see,
And I bid farewell to Donegal, likewise to Glen Swallee.

2   'Twas on a summer's morning at the dawning of the day
I left my peaceful happy home to wander far away;
And as I viewed the grand old glen perhaps no more to see
For I thought my heart would surely die in leavin' Glen Swallee.

3   No more among the sycamore I'll hear the blackbird sing
No more I'll hear the blithe cuckoo to welcome back the spring;
No more I'll plow those far-off fields, sa cushla gal machree[*]
On a foreign soil I'm doomed to toil far away from Glen Swallee.

[*] *a cuisle geal mo croide* – bright pulse of my heart

50 TERENCE'S FAREWELL

The Dublin collector, Frank Harte, writes: "This song was written by Lady Dufferin who wrote another song in the same vein called 'The Emigrant's Farewell', better known as 'I'm Sitting on the Stile, Mary'. Both of these were great tearjerkers and very popular as party pieces dealing as they do with the curse of emigration. 'Terence's Farewell' was made popular by the singing of the late John McCormack."

'Oh, My Kathleen, You're Going to Leave Me', sung by Cathie Higgins. Learned from Andy MacGregor.

mAe

slow, rather free

O, my Kath-leen, you're go-ing to leave me, all a- lone by my-self in this place;

And I'm sure that you'll nev-er de-ceive me, al- though there is truth in thy face.

Though Eng-land's a beau-ti-ful coun-try full of el-e-gant boys, O what then?

(He'll) be speak-in' such beau-ti-ful English, sure, I won't know my Kath-leen a- gain.

1   O, my Kathleen, you're going to leave me, all alone by myself in this place;
    And I'm sure that you'll never deceive me, although there is truth in thy face.
    Though England's a beautiful country full of elegant boys, O what then?
    (He'll) be speakin' such beautiful English, sure, I won't know my Kathleen again.   [You'll?]

51 THE SOOR MULK CAIRT

The author of this excellent song was Thomas Johnstone of Eaglesham, Renfrewshire. Norman Buchan, M.P., writes: "About twenty years ago I met either the daughter or the grand-daughter or Thomas Johnstone of Eaglesham. He was a music-hall entertainer, presumably a singer-comic. I also met an old man at that time who described him having impromptu ceilidhs on the platform of the Central Station on a Saturday night when the farmworkers returned to the villages. He knew the song ('The Soor Mulk Cairt') from that village also. I would place it around the 1880's to 1890's."

The song appears to have achieved instant and widespread popularity. Over the years, textual and melodic changes have produced some interesting versions, including one sung from the woman's point of view:

O, I like the way he glances wi' his e'en sae blue,
I like the way he follows up the harrow wi' the ploo;
He's ta'en awa' my fancy and stole awa' my hairt,
Through ridin' a' through Glesca in a soor mulk cairt.

'The Soor Mulk Cairt', sung by Belle Stewart. Learned from a broadsheet.

aD

brisk
for verses 1, 2, 3, 5 & 6

I am a coun- try chap- pie and I'm serv- ing at Pol — noon,

A farm near Ea- gle- sham, that fine old- fash- ioned toon

Whaur, wi' the milk each morn- in', a lit- tle af- ter three,

We tak' the road richt mer- ri- ly, my auld black horse and me.

for verses 4 & 7

O, wi' cheeks as red as ro- ses and e'en sae bon- nie blue,

Danc- in' and glanc- in', she pierced me through and through;

She fair- ly won my fan- cy and she stole a- wa' my heart,

Ay, driv- in' in - to Gles- ca in my soor- mulk cairt.

1 I am a country chappie and I'm serving at Polnoon,
A farm near Eaglesham, that fine old-fashioned toon
Whaur, wi' the milk each mornin', a little after three,
We tak' the road richt merrily, my auld black horse and me.

2 And the other morning early as The Borlin I did pass,
I chanced there to foregather wi' a winsome country lass;
O, says I, "My winsome lassie, if you are going that airt
I'll drive ye into Glesca in my soor-mulk cairt."

3 Noo, I raised her up beside me and we soon got on to crack,
And I slipped my airm aroond her waist as by my side she sat;
I tell't the auld, auld story as the woods around me rang
Wi' the singin' o' the mavis and the blackbird's cheery sang.
    * And gaun hameward in the gloamin' I wad press her tae my
        heart,
    And remind her o' her promise in the soor-mulk cairt.

4 O, wi' cheeks as red as roses and e'en sae bonnie blue,
Dancin' and glancin', she pierced me through and through;
She fairly won my fancy and she stole awa' my heart,
Ay, driving into Glesca in my soor-mulk cairt.

5 ....
....
Noo we're ettled to get married just aboot next August Fair,
When a' oor auld acquaintances I hope to see them there.

6 She's never had a hurl inside a carriage a' her days.
So when that I proposed to hae a coach and pair o' greys,
"Na na", says she, "oor money's scarce, ye ken we cannae spare't,
I'd raither hae the joltin' o' the soor-mulk cairt."

7 Cheeks as red as roses (etc., as in verse 4)

* *Note*: Lines five and six of verse 3 are sung to the same music as lines three and
      four.

52 GEORDIE WEIR

The countryman's adventures in the big town was a popular broadside
ballad theme in Shakespeare's day. The chapbooks extended its popularity
and later it became a staple item in early 19-century songsters, garlands
and miscellanies. The early music-hall, particularly in the provinces, gave
the genre another lease of life. Glasgow, Aberdeen and Dundee were
among the large urban centres where music-hall made use of locally
recruited comedians, singers and songwriters. On occasion, the music-hall
writers were not averse to refurbishing popular bothy ballads for the stage.
More common was the practice of writing songs which imitated the form
and idiom of the bothy ballads but which replaced their specific satire with
low comedy situations and ideas drawn from a variety of sources.

The traffic in forms and ideas was a two-way one and many a music-hall song fashioned on a bothy ballad found its way back into the bothies where it was, in its turn, adapted, changed and sometimes absorbed into the bothy repertory. At the same time, the creators of the bothy ballads were themselves being influenced by music-hall songs and were producing lyrics in which the locale of the "fairmtoon" and the feeing market was being abandoned in favour of the industrial town with its gin palaces, lodging houses, whores and wide-boys on the make.

Whether 'Geordie Weir' was born in a bothy or a music-hall, or whether he is of mixed percentage, he and his like turn up frequently in the repertories of Scots traditional singers.

'Geordie Weir', sung by Belle Stewart. Learned from her brother, Donald MacGregor.

mM/D

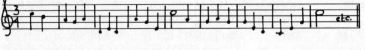

1   Noo, I'm a saft country chiel and my name's Geordie Weir,
    I suppose you all wonder what I'm doin' here;
    But it's just on a visit to Glesca I've come
    For to see a lot of folk I hannae seen for a lang.

2 Noo, I met a braw lassie but O, she was shy,
  Wi' a smile on her lips and a tear in her eye;
  We'd a few drams together till the drink took my head
  And she stole all my money, bad scran to her breed!

3 So, I wish I was back in Smarendale Rye,
  You'd ne'er see my face till the day that I die;
  If only I could manage the price o' my train
  You would ne'er see my face back in Glesca again.

4 Whaur to sleep the first nicht was a mystery to me,
  For I hadnae as much as a crooked bawbee;
  Till I met an acquaintance and he didnae grudge
  For to pay for my bed in a big model-lodge.

5 And when I got my tea, get oot for a stroll,
  I went to a windey to view a wax doll;
  And I lee it to yourself, is it no' a hard egg
  When a dog comes and makes a lamp-post o' your leg?

6 So I wish I was back in Smarendale Rye (etc.)

7 When I got under cover, fegs! yon was a fricht!
  I must say that my friends had a gey lively nicht.
  It was just like a battlefield on the bed-claes,
  For the Zulus were runnin' afore the Scotch Greys.

8 So I wish I was back in Smarendale Rye (etc.)

53 THE CAIRN

This song is published in *Buchan Bothy Ballads* under the title of 'The Buchan Plooman', written and composed by G. S. Morris. A popular north-east entertainer, Morris began writing songs in 1930. All his songs are written in Aberdeenshire dialect and almost all of them are humourous and lean heavily on the Scots music-hall tradition and occasionally on the bothy song tradition. There is no doubt that Morris was a songwriter of considerable talent; unfortunately one cannot always be certain that songs attributed to him are indeed his. He is credited as author and composer of all the thirty-one songs printed in the two slim volumes published by Kerr, but at least five of those songs had appeared in print before Morris was ten years old and another three or four of them are of doubtful origin. 'The Cairn' belongs in this latter category.

'The Cairn', sung by Belle Stewart.

mI (with inflected IV ending on upper VIII)

1   O, I bothied for a sax-month at a place they ca' The Cairn,
When I gaed hame the bothy lads, they took me for a bairn;
Wi' horny hands they ate boiled spuds, the bothy flair they happit,
Wi' my sharney buits I trampit them doon, and I says, "I like mine chappit!"

Chorus: HEUCH!
　　　　Lilta faloora lido, tooral ooral ay,
　　　　I'll ca' your horse, I'll sort your nowt, or big a ruck o' strae,
　　　　I'm as happy's a lark fae dawn tae dark and singin' a' the day,
　　　　HEUCH!
　　　　Lilta faloora lido, tooral ooral ay.

2　　　The nicht I married Mary Anne I got most awfu' fu',
　　　　When the minister started to tie the knot there was a how-do-ye-
　　　　　do;
　　　　He says, "What is your name, my man, and have you got the
　　　　　ring?"
　　　　But you shoulda seen the mannie's face when I began to sing,
　　　　　(chorus)

54 JOHNNY MY MAN

Scotland has produced some of the most joyful convivial songs in praise of
drink. The opposite side of the coin is inevitable, though – unlike many
temperance songs – 'Johnny My Man' is neither maudlin nor stridently
militant. It probably started life in the latter half of the nineteenth-century,
a period of massive temperance reform and has been something of a
favourite ever since. Greig, Ford and Ord have all commented on its
popularity as a street-song and on the multiplicity of penny-sheets containing its text. Our text corresponds almost word for word with the
printed sets.

'Johnny My Man', sung by Belle Stewart. Learned from her brother,
Donald MacGregor.

aAe/D

moderate, slightly free

O, John- ny my man, do you no' think o' ris- ing?

The day's far spent and the nicht's com-in' on;

Your sil-ler's a' done and the stoups stand be- fore ye,

O rise up, my John-ny, and come a-wa' hame.

1   O, Johnny my man, do you no' think o' rising?
    The day's far spent and the nicht's coming on;
    Your siller's a' done and the stoups stand before ye,
    O rise up, my Johnny, and come awa' hame.

2   Noo, wha is't that I hear speakin' sae kindly?
    It's surely the voice o' my ain wifie, Jean.
    O, come in bye, my dearie, and sit doon beside me,
    For it's time enough yet to be gaun awa' hame.

3   O but, Johnny my man, oor wee bairnies are greetin'
    There's nae meal in the barrel to fill their wee wames;
    When you sit here a-drinkin' you leave me lamenting,
    So rise up, my Johnny, and come awa' hame.

4* O, Jeannie my lass, when we first fell a-courtin',
    There was naething but love then to trouble our mind;
    And we spent a' wor time 'mang the sweet-scented roses,
    And we ne'er thocht it lang to be gaun awa' hame.

5   I remember richt weel, John, the time that you speak o',
    And weel I remember that sweet flowery glen,
    But they days are past and will never return, love,
    So sit doon beside me, no' think o' gaun hame.

6 Ah, but Johnny he rose and he banged the door open,
Saying, "Cursed be the tavern that e'er let me in!
And cursed be the whisky that mak's me sae frisky,
So rise up, my Jeannie, we'll haud awa' hame."

7 Noo, Johnny gangs oot ilka fine summer's evenin',
Wi' his wife and his bairnies sae trig and sae bien,
When a wee while sinsyne, sure, in rags they were running,
As Johnny sat fu' in the ale-hoose at e'en.

8 Contented and crouse he sits by his ain fireside,
And Jeannie a happier wife there is nane;
For nae mair tae the ale-hoose at nicht does he wander
But is happy wi' Jean and his bairnies at hame.

* *Notes*: In the light of the following verse, perhaps this first line should be:
"O, Johnny my man, when we first fell a-courtin',"

55 THE REAL OLD MOUNTAIN DEW

Colm O'Lochlainn, in a note on this popular piece, writes: "I first heard this song at a meeting of newly released political prisoners in December, 1916. I am told it was written by Phil O'Neill of Kinsale." During the last twenty years or so it has become a stock item in the repertoires of popular singing-groups.

'A Bucket of the Mountain Dew', sung by Sheila MacGregor. Learned
from her mother.

pπ[1]

enthusiastically

O, up- on yon hill there stands a still

With the smoke reach- ing up to the sky;

Wi' the smoke and the smell you can ver- y eas- y tell

That there's pot- een there close by.

CHORUS

For it fills the air wi' a per- fume rare

And it lies be-tween me and you;

So it's home we will roam and we'll have a- noth-er bowl

Or a buck-et of the moun- tain dew.

1   O, upon you hill there stands a still
         With the smoke reaching up to the sky;
         Wi' the smoke and the smell you can very easy tell
         That there's poteen there close by.

Chorus: For it fills the air wi' a perfume rare
            And it lies between me and you;
            So it's home we will roam and we'll have another bowl
            Or a bucket of the mountain dew.

2   O, the Free State soldiers are dressed in green
            And the civvie guards in blue;
            For it's their whole delight to be out at night
            In search of the mountain dew. (*Chorus*)

3   O, to hell wi' the peelers of Donegal,
            Likewise the gaugers too,
            They may roast in hell, for they'll never get a smell
            Nor a bucket of the mountain dew. (*Chorus*)

4   So to hell with the pills that cure all ills
            If you take a touch of the flu;
            For I will give you a cure that is safe and sure,
            Get paralytic on the mountain dew. (*Chorus*)

56   BLUE BLAZING BLIND DRUNK

As a commentary on the vicious circle of drunkenness–wife–beating–drunkenness, the following three verses could scarcely be bettered. Perhaps their excellence is due to the fact that they lack the pious moralising tone which is the distinguishing mark of so many temperance songs.

'Blue Blazing Blind Drunk', sung by Sheila MacGregor. Learned from her mother.

aAe

1   O, for whisky I ne'er was a lover
    But what can a poor woman do?
    I'll go and I'll drown all me sorrows –
    But I wish I could drown Mickey too.

2   So when Mickey gets home I'll get battered,
    He'll batter me all black and blue;
    And if I say a word I'll get scattered
    From the kitchen right ben to the room.

3   So I'll go and I'll get blue blazing blind drunk
    Just to give Mickey a warnin' –
    And just for spite, I will stay out all night
    And come rollin' home drunk in the mornin'.

57 THE HAMILTON MILITIAMAN

A good deal of Glasgow humour possesses the sardonic quality which illuminates this brilliant urban parody of 'The Dying Soldier'. We have heard it described as a music hall song but its length (ten stanzas) makes that seem unlikely and, surely, its general tone would be considered too wry for a stage song. All that can be said with any certainty is that its author was a Glaswegian, for no-one else could handle with such sureness the nuances of the Glesca tongue.

'The Hamilton Militiaman', sung by Belle Stewart. Learned from a broadsheet.

mI

1 A Hamilton militiaman ae nicht got roarin' fu',
   And want o' a woman's tender hand to haud his burnin' broo;
   His comrade stood beside him as he saw him turnin' seik,
   And he held his hand up to his lug to hear his crony speak.

2 ....
   ....
   Tak' my tourie as a token tae the land I left wi' pride,
   For I was born in Glesca, dear auld Glesca on the Clyde.

3 Tell my mither that her other sons will comfort her the same,
   For I was aye a prodigal and I never cared for hame;
   My faither was a sodger and I often heard him tell
   Hoo mony kinds o' punishment he brought upon himsel'.

4* But when he kicked the bucket and he gaed beyond the storm
   I let them stick to a' he had, but I kept his uniform;
   And when I put them on, I wished I had a horse to ride,
   Alang the streets o' Glesca, dear auld Glesca on the Clyde.

5   Tell my sister no' to greet for me, nor let her spirits doon,
   If she sees a poor fellow lying drunk aboot the toon;
   But look upon him proudly and tenderly reflect
   Her brother, like the rest of them, could always tak' his whack.

6* And if some fellow asks her hand, just tell her for my sake
   To tak' that poor fella, though he hasnae got a make.
   And open up my faither's grave and lay (them) side by side,   [us?]
   As an honour tae auld Glesca, dear auld Glesca on the Clyde.

7   But there's anither, no' a sister, when I gaed awa' she cried;
   "Poor lad", said she, as true as steel, though often she's been tried.
   And though betimes she made a haul and dodged the Dees awhile,
   Gey often she's been grippit, ay, and landed in the jail.

8   So tell her afore I see her or even send a line
   That I may be imprisoned withoot the option o' a fine;
   But we'll hae a spree thegither yet though she should pawn her plaid,
   When I get back to Glesca, dear auld Glesca on the Clyde.

9   Noo, the drunken sodger staggered and his tongue wagged to and fro,
   His e'en put on a sleepy look and tried, but couldnae throw,
   His comrade tried to lift him, but when he felt the load,
   He let him doon and spread hissel' beside him on the road.

10 The golden moonbeams flickered owre their faces wi' a smile,
   When twa bobbies cam' and marched our gallant heroes aff to jail;
   And as their funds were doon their throat, their fines were never paid,
   So they bid farewell to Glesca, auld Glesca on the Clyde.

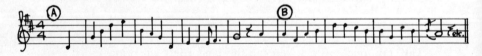

* Melodically, this tune fits into the ABBA category, but verses 4 and 6 use a
  BABA format.

58   AN OLD MAN HE COURTED ME

Herd's collection has a five-stanza song entitled 'Scant of Love, Want of
Love', in which the following two verses are found:

(1) The auld man he corted me,
       Scant of love, want of love;
     The auld man he corted me,
       Thoughtless as I am.
     And I for the sake of pelf,
       Yielded to give myself
     To the cauld arms of
       The silly auld man.

(3) The auld man and I went to bed,
       Scant of love, want to love,
     The auld man and I went to bed,
       Handsome as I am;
     The auld man and I went to bed
       But he neither did nor said,
     What brides expect, when laid
       By a gudeman.

The song goes on to describe the old man falling asleep while his young wife rises and spends the night with a younger man:

      So should all young wives treat
      Fumbling old men.

The numerous versions reported during the last fifty years from Scotland, England, Ireland and North America indicate that an evolutionary process has changed and simplified the basic form of the song. It would appear likely that the first major change was the transformation of the last line of the opening stanza into a refrain. At another stage of development one of the stanzas (our fifth) was adopted as a chorus. The ultimate regularisation of the stanzaic pattern is best demonstrated by a text from Utah, all four stanzas of which are in the following form:

(2) When it struck nine o'clock, aye down O down;
     When it struck nine o'clock, aye derry down;
     When it struck nine o'clock, all the doors he did lock.
     Girls, for my sake never wed an old man. (Hubbard)

This simple structure with its repetitions and recurrent refrains facilitates improvisation and probably accounts for the fact that many of the later printed versions are substantially longer than Herd's text.

Gershon Legman has advanced the theory that 'An Old Man He Courted Me' is connected with 'The Carle Cam' Ower the Croft', a song with a similar theme and with which it shares certain metrical features.

'Never Wed an Auld Man', sung by Belle Stewart. Learned from Big
Willie White.

pI/M (ending on lower V) *or* aM/D

1   An auld man came a-courtin' me,
             Hi doo a darrity,
         An auld man came a-courtin' me,
             Hi doo a day;
         An auld man came a-courtin' me,
             Hi doo a darrity,

Refrain: Maids, when you're young, never wed an auld man.

2   For when we went to the church,
             Hi doo a darrity,
         When we went to the church,
             Me being young;
         When we went to the church,
             I left him in the lurch. (*Refrain*)

3   And when we went to our tea,
        He started teasing me,
    When we went to our tea,
        Me being young;
    When we went to our tea,
        He started squeezing me. (*Refrain*)

4   And when we went to our bed,
        He lay as he was dead,
    When we went to our bed,
        Me being young;
    When we went to our bed,
        He lay as he was dead. (*Refrain*)

5   For he had no tooral,
        No right fal the dooral, O,
    He had no tooral,
        No, Devil the one!
    He had no tooral
        To fill my falooral, So (*Refrain*)

6   But when he fell fast asleep,
        Out of bed I did creep,
    When he fell fast asleep,
        Me being young;
    When he fell fast asleep,
        Out of bed I did creep
        Into the arms of a handsome young man.

7   For he had a tooral, aye,
        Right fal de dooral, O –
    He had a tooral,
        A helluva one!
    He had a tooral
        That filled my falooral, So (*Refrain*)

8   And there we played pitch-and-toss,
        High doo a darrity,
    There we played pitch-and-toss,
        All the night long;
    There we played pitch-and-toss,
        My maidenheid I lost. (*Refrain*)

59 THE OVERGATE

This popular cautionary tale is found in two forms. One of them chronicles the misadventures of an unidentified narrator, the other adds a tailpiece to the chronicle and identifies the narrator as a farm-servant.

'The Overgate', sung by Belle Stewart. Learned from her brother, Donald MacGregor.

aM/D

O, as I gaed up the O-ver-gate I met a bon-nie wee lass;

She winked to me wi' the tail o' her e'e as I was a-walk-in' past.

REFRAIN

Wi' my too-ri-na,   lilt fa lad-die,   Lilt   fa lad-die   too-ri-nee.

[1] - for verse 2 only

Noo, I asked her if she'd tak' a glass, Says I, 'I'm owre fae Auch-ter-much-ty,

REFRAIN

Tae the mar-ket   wi' some swine.' Wi' my too-ri-na (etc.)

1   O, as I gaed up the Overgate
        I met a bonnie wee lass;
        She winked to me wi' the tail o' her e'e
        As I was a-walkin' past.

Refrain: Wi' my toorina, lilt fa laddie,
        Lilt fa laddie toorinee.

2   Noo, I asked her if she'd tak' a glass,
        Says I, "I'm owre fae Auchtermuchty
        Tae the market wi' some swine." (*Refrain*)

3   I took her tae a sittin'-room
A wee bit doon the burn,
It's true what Robbie Burns said,
A man was made to mourn. (*Refrain*)

4   For hot pies and porter
She ate them by galore;
She ate and drank as much as serve
An elephant for a year. (*Refrain*)

5   Noo, then we baith gaed up the stair
To hae a contented sleep;
When an awfu' knock cam' tae the door
At the breakin' o' daylight.* (*Refrain*)

6   It was a big fat bobbie,
He got me by the tap o' the hair;
And he gied me the whirlyjig
Richt doon to the fit o' the stair. (*Refrain*)

7   Noo, I gaed up the stair again,
Ay, seekin' oot my claes;
"Ye'll better get oot o' this, young man,
Or I'll gie ye sixty days." (*Refrain*)

8   But I says, "I've lost my waistcoat,
My watch-chain and my purse!"
Says she, "I've lost my maidenheid
And that's a damn sicht worse!" (*Refrain*)

9   Noo, there is a maid upon oor farm,
She is a dainty dame;
She milks the kye at early morn,
Gin dinnertime it's cream. (*Refrain*)

10   There is a cattleman on the farm,
Will Garthill is his name;
And he'll tak' ilka pint you'll gie 'm,
But he will pay for nane. (*Refrain*)

11   There is a man upon the farm
He has a wooden leg;
And he dolts aboot fae barn tae byre
Suckin' ilka egg. (*Refrain*)

12   Noo, I'll go back to Auchtermuchty,
          Contented I will be,
          Wi' the breakin' o' the five-pound note
          Wi' the lassie in Dundee. (*Refrain*)

* In 1962, Belle sang *daylight* almost as *delight*. In 1975, she pronounced *delight* quite clearly.

60   THE BONNIE WEE LASSIE FAE GOUROCK

This small Renfrewshire seaside resort on the southern shore of the Firth of Clyde was once one of the famous holiday centres for Glasgow's working-class population. During the week of Glasgow Fair, the traditional holiday period, it still attracts a fair number of Glaswegians but it is not what it was. An increasingly sophisticated working-class now travels further afield for its pleasures and a "booze-up" in Rothesay or the nice smell of a first-class hotel in Gourock is not the stuff of dreams for folk who have become familiar with a fortnight in the Canary Islands or the Costa Brava. In the 1920s, however, Gourock and its neighbours, Rothesay and Dunoon, provided music-hall comedians and singers with the raw material for innumerable jokes and songs.

'The Bonnie Wee Lassie Fae Gourock', sung by Belle Stewart. Learned off a broadsheet.

mI (with inflected VII)

briskly

1. O, I'm Pip- er Mac- Far- lane and I'm on the beer,
CHORUS: O, for she is a bon- nie wee beau- ti- ful thing,

But still I'm in love wi' a bon- nie wee dear;
I popped her the ques- tion and bought her the ring;

You would love her your- sel' if ye on- ly could see 'er,
And we're gaun to get mar- ried some time in the spring -

DC al fine

Her faith- er's a gro- cer in Gou- rock.
But I din- nae like ask- in' her faith- er.

And the first time I met her I'll nev- er for- get,

The rain it was rain- ing, the weath- er was wet;

I kissed her and told her that she was a pet,

To CHORUS

Ay, the bon- nie wee lass - ie fae Gou- rock.

1   O, I'm Piper MacFarlane and I'm on the beer,
But still I'm in love wi' a bonnie wee dear;
You would love her yoursel' if ye only could see 'er,
Her faither's a grocer in Gourock.
     And the first time I met her I'll never forget,
     The rain it was raining, the weather was wet;
     I kissed her and told her that she was a pet,
     Ay, the bonnie wee lassie fae Gourock.

Chorus: O, for she is a bonnie wee beautiful thing,
I popped her the question and bought her the ring;
And we're gaun to get married some time in the spring –
But I dinnae like asking her faither.

2   Noo, I took my wee sweetheart, I did bye the bye,
To spend a few days wi' my auld friend, MacKay;
And says Mac, "Who's the lass?" "Do you no' ken?" says I,
"That's the bonnie wee lassie fae Gourock."
     Mac started to tickle her under the chin,
     When who but his wife, Mistress Mac, should come in.
     She shifted his whiskers and half o' his chin
     Owre the bonnie wee lassie fae Gourock. (*Chorus*)

3   Noo, I borrowed twa pound frae me auld friend, MacKay,
And I took my wee sweetheart to dine at The Cry,
When a masher he started a-winkin' his eye
At my bonnie wee lassie fae Gourock.
     Her temper it rose and she fair played the deuce
     She walloped his neck wi' the leg o' a goose,
     She hunted the masher all over the hoose,
     'Twas a glorious victory for Gourock! (*Chorus*)

4   Noo, I bought my wee lassie a nice bit o' lace,
A hat and some powder to puff on her face,
And we caused a sensation all over the place,
Me and my lassie fae Gourock.
     I treated her handsomely, just like a swell,
     Took her roond to the back o' a first-class hotel,
     Stuck her nose through the window to get the nice smell
     For she ne'er got a smell like 't in Gourock. (*Chorus*)

61 BETSY BELL

Songs which combine the couthy sentimentality of the kailyard with a standardised comic dialect were the stock-in-trade of Scots music-hall performers right up until the late 1930s. Aspiring songwriters, stimulated by the commercial success of singing comedians like Harry Lauder and Will Fyffe, kept the sheet-music presses busy even during the economic crisis of the late twenties and early thirties. 'Betsy Bell' would appear to be a typical product of that period.

'Betsy Bell', sung by Belle Stewart. Learned off a broadsheet.

pI (with inflected VI)

1   Noo, my name is Betsy Bell, in the Overgate I dwell,
    Nae doot ye'll wonder what I'm daein' here;
    But if ye wait a wee, sure my tale I'll tell to thee,
    It's a tale nae doot ye'll think is very queer.

2   For I'm lookin' for a lad and he may be guid or bad,
    For I'm gaun to tak' the first yin that I see;
    He may be young or auld, or grey-heided, friends, or bald –
    It's onything that wears the breeks for me.

3   O, but for lads I've had my share, sure I've ha'en a score or mair,
    But hoo they threw me up I dinnae ken;
    For I'm neither prood nor shy that the lads should pass me by,
    O, I wonder what's a-dae wi' a' the men.

4   Noo, as I gaed oot last nicht, I met wi' Sandy Richt
    And he hauled me in as I was passin' by;
    He asked me if I'd wed, so this is what I said,
    "Man, if you are quite agreeable, so am I."

(verse 2 is occasionally repeated here)

62   I'M NO' COMIN' OOT THE NOO

The figure of half-a-crown as a weekly instalment, given in the second
stanza, suggests that this song belongs to the early 1930s. By that time, the
music-hall comic song tradition had become the stock-in-trade of the
"variety theatre" comic and the semi-professional public-house singer. The
fleas of our third stanza and the bugs in 'Geordie Weir' ("those permanent
and unwelcome lodgers of the urban poor") are a common feature in songs
of the period.

'I'm No' Comin' Oot The Noo', sung by Belle Stewart. Learned from Tommy Bonthron, a ploughman.

mI (ending on upper VIII)

cheerfully

O, a nice wee lass, a bon-nie wee lass, is bon-nie wee Jean-nie Mac- Kay,
I said that I wad take her tae a mu- sic hall, you see.

A ni- cer lass than Jean- nie you could nev-er ev-er spy;
So dressed up nice and trick- y she come danc- in' roond for me;

somewhat free

And when I heard her at the door – I was sor-ry I had to roar:

CHORUS (in rhythm)

I'm no' com- in' oot the noo, the noo, I'm no' com- in' oot the noo,

I'm aw- fae sor- ry, Jean-nie, for dis - ap- point- ing you;

My mith-er's ta'en my claes to the pawn to raise a bob or two,

And I've on-ly a muff- ler roond my neck and I'm no' com-in' oot the noo.

1   O, a nice wee lass, a bonnie wee lass, is bonnie wee Jeannie
        MacKay,
      A nicer lass than Jeannie you could never ever spy;
      I said that I wad take her tae a music-hall, you see,
      So dressed up nice and tricky she come dancin' roond for me;
        And when I heard her at the door –
      I was sorry I had to roar:

Chorus: I'm no' comin' oot the noo, the noo, I'm no' comin' oot the noo,
         I'm awfae sorry, Jeannie, for disappointin' you;
         My mither's ta'en my claes to the pawn to raise a bob or two,
         And I've only a muffler roond my neck and I'm no' comin' oot
            the noo.

2   O, I bought a nice new raincoat from a Jew ca'd Mr Sleek;
         I said that I wad pay him at a half-a-croon a week;
         He got the first instalment, that is all he got, you see,
         So yesterday he sent a lawyer's letter roond to me:
              Come roon' an' pay me for my coat –
              And in reply to him I wrote:

Chorus: I'm no' comin' oot the noo, the noo, I'm no' comin' oot the noo,
         I'm awfae sorry, Mr. Sleek, for disappointin' you;
         I forged the cheque and I got the nick, so tooral-ooral-oo,
         In ten years' time I may get oot but I'm no' comin' oot the noo.

3   In a grand hotel where I reside the service is a treat,
         For a' the fleas come rinnin' out when I'm belaw the sheet;
         I cannae get a wink o' sleep, I think it is a shame,
         So I bought some Keating's Powder just to spoil their little
            game.
              Last night when I went into bed –
              A million little voices said:

Chorus: O, we're no' comin' oot the noo, the noo, we're no' comin' oot
            the noo,
         You put some Keating's Powder on the bed-clothes, that is true.
         And if we come oot we'll all be killed, and that wad never do,
         We'll hae revenge some ither nicht, but we're no' comin' oot the
            noo!

63   COD-LIVER OIL

"Dr De Jongh's celebrated Cod-Liver Oil" was the subject of an intensive
advertising campaign in the 1880s. That campaign inspired the popular
stage song which can still be heard from singers in Ireland, Scotland and
North America.

'Cod-Liver Oil', sung by Sheila MacGregor. Learned from her mother.

mAe/D

moderate

I'm a young mar- ried man and I'm ti - red of life,

For years I've been wed to a sick-ly young wife;

She does noth-ing all day now but sit down and cry,

And wish-ing to God eve- ry day she would die.

1 I'm a young married man and I'm tired of life,
   For years I've been wed to a sickly young wife;
   She does nothing all day now but sit down and cry,
   And wishing to God every day she would die.

2 So a friend of me own came to see me one day,
   And he said that my wife she was pining away;
   But if you get a bottle from dear Doctor John,
   'Tis ten unto one that your wife will get strong.

3 So a bottle, a bottle I bought for to try,
   And the way that she drunk it you'd swear she was dry;
   And another and another she vanished the same,
   You would swear she had cod-liver oil on the brain.

4 O doctor, O doctor, O dear Doctor John,
   Your cod-liver oil is so pure and so strong,
   I'm afraid of me life I'll go down in the soil
   If my wife don't stop drinkin' your cod-liver oil.

5 Now, my house it resembles a big chemist shop,
   It's covered with bottles from bottom to top,
   And in the morning when the kettle does boil,
   You would swear it was singing for cod-liver oil.

6 So doctor, O doctor, O dear Doctor John,
   Your cod-liver oil is so pure and so strong,
   I'm afraid of me life I'll go down in the soil
   If my wife don't stop drinking your cod-liver oil.

64   TWA HEIDS ARE BETTER THAN ANE

Each stanza of the following text is an exact parallel of stanzas written by
G. S. Morris for a song which shares the same title. Compare, for example,
Morris's third stanza with our second:

> Things had gane fairly weel, I wis noo a gey chiel,
> O' the term it jist wintet [wanted] near three weeks,
> Tired o' my single life, I had chosen a wife,
> Tae patch up bit nae tae wear my breeks.
> So ae nicht, bold as brass, I gaed owre tae my lass
> An' says, "Will ye mairry me, Jean?"
> She answered, the limmer, "Though ane o' them's timmer,
> Weel! Twa heids are better than ane!"

Subject matter, metre and arrangement of lines are pretty much the same
in both texts; indeed, their similarity suggests that one is a completely
rewritten copy of the other.

'Twa Heids Are Aye Better Than Ane', sung by Cathie Higgins. Learned from her mother.

aI

1   O, richt weel dae I mind on the days o' lang syne
    When I was a laddie sae wee;
    O, whenever I'd gang, ay, and dae something wrang
    My mither wad lecture to me.
            She wad cry oot, "My bairns, keep awa' fae a' hairm
            Or ye'll rue whit events ye begin."
            And I'd never think twice for to tak' her advice
            For twa heids are aye better than ane.

2   It's when a young chiel intends to dae weel
    Of coorse he looks oot for a wife;
    A bonnie wee tairt wi' a true lovin' hairt
    To sew on his buttons for life.
          He ca's her his plum, ay, his yummy-yum-yum,
          And he tickles her under the chin;
          And he whispers, "My dear, let's get married next year
          For twa heids are aye better than ane."

3   Noo, last Saturday nicht, man, I got sic a fricht
    That I nearly drapped aff my pins;
    For the wife, I declare, just as sure as ye're there
    She made me the present o' twins.
          I cried oot, "O Jean! What the hell d' ye mean?
          That's an awfu'-like thing that ye've done."
          And she cried oot alood, "Man, ye ought to be prood,
          For twa heids are aye better than ane."

4   . . . .
    . . . .
    . . . .
    . . . .
          Noo, never be first to shake hands wi' yersel'
          Or talk aboot whit ye hae done;
          And never think twice for to tak' an advice
          For twa heids are aye better than ane.

65   A SHILLING OR TWA

The six-stanza version of this song published by John Ord in 1930 was
"printed in an old broadside published in Glasgow many years ago."
Previously he had appealed to the readers of a weekly newspaper for a
traditional version but, "was only successful in recovering a couple of
verses of it from an old lady in Kilmarnock". Gavin Greig made a similar
appeal to the readers of *The Buchan Observer* but this too only produced a
solitary fragment. The editors of this collection have fared no better and it
would seem that 'A Shilling or Twa' has never become firmly established in
the traditional repertoire.

'A Shilling or Twa', sung by Cathie Higgins. Learned from Andy Mac-
Gregor.

aAe *or* pI (ending on lower VI)

Chorus: O, what a grand thing is a shilling or twa,
            (O,) what a grand thing is a shilling or twa;
            It's poor o' the hand, ever wanting the land*,
            The steady command o' a shilling or twa.

1   A penniless pocket's a pitifu' case,
            It soon maks an auld friend put on a new face;
            Sour looks and sour faces will a' wear awa'
            If you can but show them a shilling or twa. (*Chorus*)

* The more common rendition of this line is "May the poor of the land never want
  in their hand".

66   TWELVE BOB AND A TANNER

On 19 April 1920, the price of a bottle of whisky rose from ten shillings and sixpence to twelve and six. On 27 September 1939, the price rose again, this time to fourteen shillings and threepence. The song was obviously made during that period.

'Twelve Bob and a Tanner', sung by Belle Stewart, who learned it "from a record".

aI (with inflected IV)

1   O, noo I used to meet wi' some auld friends o' mine,
         When whisky was cheap and it gaed doon like wine;
         Noo, I never meet them I'm sorry to tell –
         I dodge roond the corner and drink my mysel', Since it's

Chorus: Twelve and a tanner a bottle, ay, that's what it's costin' the day!
Twelve and a tanner a bottle, man, it tak's all your pleasures
away.
Afore ye can get a wee drappie ye have to spend a' that ye've
got;
So hoo can a fella be happy when happiness costs such a lot?

2   Noo, there's taxes on this and there's taxes on that,
While we're gettin' lean the officials gets fat;
I must admit it's a bit underhand
Puttin' the tax on the fat o' the land, For it's (*Chorus*)

67   THE BLARNEY ROSES

Frank Harte informs us that this song "was sung mainly for the crack and
the chorus that everybody could join in on. There was a parody written to
the same air, and much the same words, during the troubles here when the
IRA captured General Lucas and were holding him as ransom for some
republican prisoners. One of the lines went 'Can anybody tell me where
did General Lucas go?' "

'The Blarney Roses', sung by Sheila MacGregor. Learned from her father.

mI/Ly

1   O, it's over in dear old Ireland near the town of Cushendall,
'Twas there I met a young damsel there, the fairest of them all;
'Twas with me young affections and me money she did go,
And she said that she belonged to where the Blarney roses grow.

2 Can anybody tell me where the Blarney roses grow?
'Tis maybe down in Limerick Town, or over in Mayo;
'Tis somewhere in the Emerald Isle and this I'd like to know,
Can anybody tell me where the Blarney roses grow?

68 MASTER MCGRATH

Ballads celebrating the prowess of prize-fighters, racehorses and other sporting champions were a common feature of the nineteenth-century scene, particularly in Ireland. Of the three or four that have survived the passage of time, none is more popular than 'The Ballad of Master McGrath'.

'Master McGrath', sung by Sheila MacGregor. Learned from her mother.

aI

1 On the twelfth of November that day of renown,
Sportsmen and keepers they left Lurgan Town,
And a gale on the Channel it soon swept them o'er
On the thirteenth they landed on fair England's shore.

2 O, but when they arrived in that great London Town
Sportsmen and keepers they all gathered round;
And one of the gentlemen gave a "Ha ha!
Is that the great dog ye call Master McGrath?"

3   Now, Lord Lurgan stepped forward and said, "Gentlemen,
    Is there any among you got money to spend?
    You great nobles of England, I don't care a straw,
    There's five-thousand-to-one on ye, Master McGrath."

4   Now, the hare she led off now, as swift as the wind,
    It was sometimes in front, ay, and sometimes behind,
    But Rose took the first turn, accordin' to law,
    The next one was given by Master McGrath.

69   KATHLEEN MAVOURNEEN

Mrs MacGregor heard this piece sung by an Irish Traveller during the
berry-picking at Blairgowrie. It is a parody of the opening lines of 'The Old
Bog Hole', an Irish-American stage-song.

'Kathleen Mavourneen', sung by Sheila MacGregor.

aD

O, Kathleen Mavourneen, a cushla machree,
Would you fancy the bouncing young Barney McGee?
The pig is in the byre and the cow is on the grass,
I'm a decent married woman, tak' your hands off me arse!

70 THE MOSS O' BURRELDALE

Two distinctly different songs share this title. One of them, written by G. S. Morris in the 1930s, has been published in various collections; the other rarely finds its way into print, though most Scots Travellers are familiar with it and often preface their rendering of it with "this is the auld and true way of it". There is, however, far less unanimity when it comes to giving the exact location of "The Moss". A Banffshire Traveller told us that Kinkell Brig (Perthshire) was the true location; her daughter, on the other hand, believed that The Moss was in the Aberdeenshire parish of Keithall and Kinkell; others have sited Burreldale in the vicinity of Clatt (West Aberdeenshire) and in the Aberdeenshire parish of Rayne. An Argyllshire Traveller's version of the song opens with the line: "It was on the night of old St Cyrs". This obviously refers to the annual fair of St Serf's held originally at St Sair's, or St Serf's Hill, Aberdeenshire, and later at nearby Kirkton-of-Culsalmond.

'The Moss o' Burreldale', sung by Belle Stewart. Learned from Alec's
mother.

aD

brisk

O, there were Stew-arts, Mac-Ken-zies and Mac-Phees,

So   neat- ly   as   they   plet their knees—

They   wal-loped the tin just   at their ease,

Up-   on   the Moss   o'   Bur-rel- dale.

etc.

1   O, there were Stewarts, MacKenzies and MacPhees,
    So neatly as they plet their knees –
    They walloped the tin just at their ease,
    Upon the Moss o' Burreldale.

2   Now, the women they fought wi' jug and pail
    So neatly as they faced the gale
    To see which o' them wad get best sale
    Aroond the Moss o' Burreldale.

3   And it bein' the market o' auld Kinkell,
    The men had horses for to sell;
    They filled their bellies full o' ale
    And trampit back to Burreldale.

71 HI, BARA MANISHIE

We have collected this fragment of a cant song several times, always with
but one stanza. We have also heard it sung by Travellers who claim to have
heard other stanzas. Translated, it reads:

> Hi, bonnie lassie, will ye go with me?
> Hi, bonnie laddie, I dinnae ken your face.
> Will ye come, will ye hurry, will ye come to the camp?
> If you don't get food, you'll get some drink.

'Hi, Bara Manishie', sung by Cathie Higgins. Learned from her mother-in-
law, Charlotte Higgins.

pI

Hi, bara manishie, will ye bing wi me?
Hi, bara gadgie, I dinnae jan your fee;
Will ye bing, will ye ja, will ye bing tae the wattle?
If ye dinnae get habben, ye'll get some peeve.

MAK'-YE-UPS

Sandy's Legs
A Poem (untitled)
Song for Donald and Andy
Song for Donald
The Stewarts of Berrybank
Down by the Shielin'
Whistlin' at the Ploo
Loch Duich

Pattie and Chrissie
The Nicht o' Cathie's Weddin', O
Brochie and the Highland Chief
The Stewart Faim'ly
Glenisla
The Berryfields o' Blair
Scotland's Aye Your Hame

Note

Belle Stewart didn't begin writing songs and verses until her children were grown up and married. Since then, she has composed a number of noteworthy pieces, all of them to traditional melodies. The best known of these is 'The Berryfields of Blair'.

Many of her songs are so intensely personal in feeling that one cannot imagine anyone but Belle singing them. Indeed, commenting on the verses which lament the deaths of her two brothers, she writes: "It still hurts me to read them, nevermind to sing them." It is, like many of the sets of verses written about her family, a private soliloquy which, notwithstanding its AABB rhyming system, its iambic heptameters and its tune, is not really designed for singing. One gets the impression that the act of writing such a piece was an end in itself, a therapeutic exercise to assuage private grief.

Songs like 'Glenisla' and 'Scotland's Aye Your Hame', with their specific references to members of the Stewart family, appear to have been composed for singing in the immediate family circle and nowhere else. Like most of Belle's "serious" songs, they convey strong feelings of nostalgia and melancholy.

'The Stewart Faim'ly' is a typical example of the "throwaway" songs which Belle writes and sends to friends as letters of thanks. Often they will run to twenty or more verses.

It is in her convivial songs that Belle really comes into her own as a songwriter, for it is then that she abandons completely the nineteenth-century "kailyard" influences and becomes part of that older, rip-roaring tradition that produced 'The Tretis of the Tua Mariit Wemen and the Wedo' and 'The Ball o' Kirriemuir'. Her epithalamium on the wedding of her daughter Cathie falls naturally into that large group of poems and songs which describe scenes of communal revelry and which are common to both the Scots literary and folksong traditions.

And how 'Brochie and the Highland Chief' would have delighted that ither makar, him that followed the ploo in Ayrshire a while back ...

SANDY'S LEGS

Sandy's legs was bandy,
His knees was fu' o' hair.
And every time he lifted his kilt,
He gave three cheers for Blair.

A POEM
(*untitled*)

It happened at the berry-time when the travellers came to Blair;
They pitched their tents on the berryfields without a worry or care.
But they hadn't been long settled there when some heid yins cam' frae
    Perth
And told them they must go at once and get off the face o' the earth.

These folk, of course, were worried, for of law they had no sense;
They only came to the berryfields to earn a few honest pence;
But it was hard to make them stay there when the policemen said to go,
So they just packed up and took the road – to where, I do not know.

It's a hard life being a traveller, but I've proved it to be true,
I've tried in every possible way to live with times that's new.
But we're always hit below the belt, no matter what we do –
But when it comes to the Judgment Day we'll be just the same as you.

SONG FOR DONALD AND ANDY

aπ⁵

'Twas on a cauld De-cem-ber nicht when fruits and flooérs were gone,

My brith-er An-dy left me tae be wi' his brith-er Dan;
The sor-row they hae left be-hind is more than tongue can tell,

For I am their on-ly sis-ter and I dear-ly loved them well.

1   'Twas on a cauld December nicht when fruits and flooérs were gone,
    My brither Andy left me tae be wi' his brither Dan;
    The sorrow they have left behind is more than tongue can tell,
    For I am their only sister and I dearly loved them well.

2   When I sit and think on days gone by, it mak's my heart so sair,
    When I think aboot the happy days the three o' us spent in Blair;
    O, I ken I have my bairns, and I have my man and a',
    But never in this wide, wide world were there brithers like my twa.

3   O Donal', dear, I miss ye, for ye were sae dear to me.
    We loved each other dearly and we always did agree,
    But me and Andy aye fell oot, we were an awfu' twa,
    O, please forgive me, Donal' dear, I miss him maist o' a'.

4   Noo, Jeannie has a gey sair hairt, and so has Mary too,
    When they sit and think aboot the things the baith o' you did say;
    And of course, there is their bairns, it's hard on them and a',
    But me, my life is empty since I parted fae you twa.

5   But I hope that God will ease the pain as weeks and months go by,
    For whenever I am by mysel' my e'en are never dry.
    O, I ken I'm no' the only yin, for you a' feel it tae,
    But it's grand to ken we'll meet again on our Good Lord's Judgment
       Day.

SONG FOR DONALD

pI/M

smoothly

O, Don- ald, I'll tell   ye   a   sto- ry that's true,

O' things that hae hap-   pened   tae   me and tae   you –

When   ye were   a   lad-   die   and   free frae all care,

Ye   bade   wi' your mith-er   and   set- tled in   Blair.

1 O, Donald, I'll tell ye a story that's true,
   O' things that hae happened to me and to you –
   When you were a laddie and free frae all care,
   Ye bade wi' your mither and settled in Blair.

2 O, the times they are changed and they're no' just the same,
   It's a gey lot o' years since ye ca'd me your wean;
   I used to torment you when we were at hame,
   But I aye got the best o't, for you took the blame.

3 Do ye mind o' the time when you bocht me the pram?
   Ye were in the sodgers, a strappin' young man.
   Ye bocht it in Perth and ye ta'en it to Blair,
   And ye didnae worry, though your pockets were bare.

4 Although I'm no' wi' ye, I ken hoo ye feel,
   Ye've had mony a thocht since ye lay doon no' weel;
   O' the good times and bad times ye've had, you and me,
   O' the things ye've done for me, and I aye let you flee.

5 No, I cannae leave Jean oot, that wadnae be fair,
   For you ken her and me are a helluva pair;
   When we get thegither, oor tongues never tire,
   Do you mind when she swept up your last pound in the fire?

6   At least you have Sheila no' far frae ye noo,
    And the love ye have for her has always been true;
    I suppose she'll nip in for a wee cup o' tea,
    It's a while since she said, "I'll bide wi' ye for three".

7   It will nae be lang till the auld year fa's,
    And I wonder what you'll get fae Auld Santa Claus;
    If ye hang up your stockin', ye never can tell:
    Ye may get a visit fae auld Granny Belle.

THE STEWARTS OF BERRYBANK

(To the tune of 'The Ball o' Kirriemuir', No. 26)

1   O, Frank and Ruby cam' fae Banff
            Their bairns wi' them tae,
            They come to Belle and Alec
            For to have their Hogmanay.

Chorus 1: At the Stewarts, the Stewarts,
            The Stewarts o' Berrybank,
            O, sic a carry-on we had
            That nicht wi' Ruby and Frank.

2   Noo, first they got a cuppa tea
            And syne they got a dram,
            And Frank took oot his walloper
            And put it in Ruby's hand, (Chorus 1)

3   O, Ruby says, "I'm flamin' sick,
            I've gien ye a' I can!
            And I'm shamed to deith wherever I gang
            Wi' that dirty wee red-heided man." (Chorus 1)

4   Noo, Andy he come ben the hoose
            He wasnae fit to stand;
            He says, "Will the Lord take care of us
            If ye see whit's in Nanny's hand."

Chorus 2: Ben the room, the room,
            The room at Berrybank;
            And Nanny took it in her hand,
            It fairly made her gant.

5 Noo, Cathie she come up the road
  Her bairns in a pram;
  And she says, "I'm feelin' awfae dry,
  Can ye no' gie me a dram?" (Chorus 1)

6 Noo, Alec he was sittin' there,
  A tune gaed through his mind;
  He lifted up his bagpipes
  And played 'For Auld Lang Syne'. (Chorus 1)

7 And Belle MacGregor she was there
  And she was warst of a',
  Her hair it used to be awfu' black
  But noo it's as white as sna'. (Chorus 1)

8 Noo, Frank's gaed doon to Andy's
  'The Shielin' is his hame,
  He fell and broke his four ribs
  And he'll never come back again,

Chorus 3: Tae the Stewarts, the Stewarts,
  The Stewarts o' Berrybank,
  But we'll never forget the happy day
  We had wi' Ruby and Frank.

DOWN BY THE SHIELIN'

aAe/D

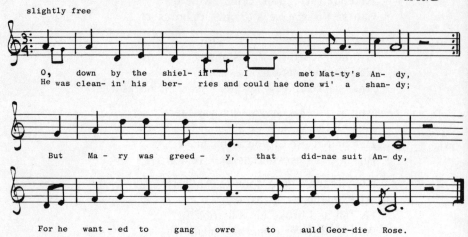

slightly free

O, down by the shiel- in' I met Mat-ty's An- dy,
He was clean- in' his ber- ries and could hae done wi' a shan- dy;

But Ma- ry was greed - y, that did-nae suit An- dy,

For he want - ed to gang owre to auld Geor-die Rose.

1   O, down by the shielin' I met Matty's Andy,
    He was cleanin' his berries and could hae done wi' a shandy;
    But Mary was greedy, that didnae suit Andy
    For he wanted to gang owre to auld Geordie Rose.

2   But the time it wore on and the snaw it was fa'in',
    Though Mary got her way, but still she was thrawn;
    But there'll be drink in The Shielin' though Mary starts squealin'
    For it winnae be long till the auld year fa's.

3   Now if a' stories are true I'll soon loss my lassie
    Gin another year's time there'll be a wonk in her chassis;
    For she's gaun to be wed to Haud-Oot-o'-My-Road-Lassie
    But when that day comes roon, she can just please hersel'.

4   Noo, I have a brother and his name it is Donal'
    He's often no' weel, ay, and that mak's him grummel;
    But when he argues wi' Jean he can mak' the hoose rummel,
    But to try and misca' him, that wadnae be fair.

WHISTLIN' AT THE PLOO

(To the tune of 'Hatton Woods', No. 42)

1. O, I'm just a common plooman lad that whistles at the ploo,
   The story I'm aboot to tell will seem gey queer to you;
   For I'm no' keen on skiffle groups nor onything that's new,
   But I am quite contented just gaun whistlin' at the ploo.

2. Noo, I'm workin' wi' a farmer and he bides no' far frae Crieff;
   But if he'd hired a teddy-boy, I'm sure he'd come to grief;
   Wi' this newfangled rock-and-roll and ither things that's new,
   Na, he wadnae be contented just gaun whistlin' at the ploo.

3. Now, just tak' a common plooman lad that warks amang the neeps;
   I'm sure he wadnae feel at ease in a pair o' yon ticht breeks;
   Nor wi' his hair grown owre lang and hingin' owre his broo,
   Na, he wadnae be contented just gaun whistlin' at the ploo.

4. But we canna blame the teddy-boys, that's just their way o' life,
   So I think that I will settle doon and tak' mysel' a wife;
   We'll bide in yon wee cotter-hoose and she'll ne'er hae cause to rue
   O' the day she wed her plooman lad that whistles at the ploo.

5. Noo, I think my story's ended, but I'm sure that you'll agree,
   There's nae life like a plooman's life as far as I can see;
   We rise content in the mornin' and we wark the hale day through
   And we never seem to worry when we're whistlin' at the ploo.

LOCH DUICH

aπ¹

slow, steadily

As I was walk-ing with my lov-er Down a glen that was so fair;

There I heard a pi- per play-ing And his mu- sic filled the air.

1   As I was walking with my lover
     Down a glen that was so fair;
     There I heard a piper playing
     And his music filled the air.

2   And I listened to the music
     As it sounded loud and clear;
     I sat doon among the bracken
     Wi' the lass that I love dear.

3   The tune he played it was 'Loch Duich',
     That's a grand old Scottish air,
     There I wooed and won my lassie
     Amang the heather blooming fair.

PATTY AND CHRISSY

a𝜋[1]

energetically

O, now Pat-tie dear, and did you hear   The   news that's come to Blair?

That   you were stand-ing grib-bing your chaet At the fit o' your ain   stair.

1   O, now Pattie dear, and did you hear
    The news that's come to Blair?
    That you were standing gribbing your chaet
    At the fit o' your ain stair.

2   O, and Chrissie she came fae the shop
    With a basket in her hand;
    Says she, "Will the Lord take care of us!
    What's that in my man's hand?

3   "Noo, I've heard of German sausages
    And red polony too;
    But it's awfu' like a carrot
    And the point of it is blue.

4   "O bairns dear, come owre here
    And go and shut the door –
    If the hantle see what's in his hand
    We're jailed forevermore."

5   Now, Chrissie was dumbfoundered,
    And she sat doon on a chair;
    Says she, "You've never been the same
    Since you've come back from Blair.

6   "For it must have been yon lassies
    That come to Alec's shop
    That made ye take the notion
    For to rub your candy rock."

7   But the berry-time will come again
    And I hope we'll a' be spared
    For to hae another carry-on
    At the berryfields o' Blair.

THE NICHT O' CATHIE'S WEDDIN'

aM (-VI, compass of a sixth)

slightly free

Noo, friends, if ye have time to spare, Just come ye in and draw up a chair,

And I'll tell ye o' a hell-u-va tear, The nicht o' Cath-ie's wed-din', O.

REFRAIN (in tempo)

O, a dir-rum a doo and a doo and a day, A dir-rum a doo and a dad-dy, O,

O, a dir-rum a doo and a doo and a day, The nicht o' Cath-ie's wed-din', O.

1 Noo, friends, if ye have time to spare,
   Just come ye in and draw up a chair,
   And I'll tell ye' o' a helluva tear,
   The nicht o' Cathie's weddin', O.

Refrain: O, a dirrum a doo and a doo and a day,
   A dirrum a doo and a daddy, O,
   O, a dirrum a doo and a doo and a day
   The nicht o' Cathie's weddin', O.

2 Noo, Jean MacGregor she was there,
   Wi' her golden locks and her great lang hair,
   And Donald was dancin' like a huggin' bear
   The nicht o' Cathie's weddin', O.

3 There was Mary Kelly and Andy Mack,
   They baith come in to gie us their crack,
   For they never speak ahin' naebody's back,
   At least, that's what they're sayin', O. (*Refrain*)

4 Then come John and Mary Anne
   Wi' a thing in her belly like a chapin can,
   Says John, "I've gien ye a' I can
   The nicht afore the weddin', O."

5   There was Jimmy Higgins and wee black Kate,
           They were standin' at the gairden gate;
           Says he, "I think I'll gie ye the bait
           And never mind the weddin', O." (*Refrain*)

6   And Alec he was there himsel',
           And of course his wife was Granny Belle,
           But his happiest days were in Dunkeld
           Afore he met the lasses, O.

7   But noo he's turnin' auld and grey
           And of course, like me, he's had his day,
           For he could make his chanter play
           When he was wi' the lasses, O. (*Refrain*)

8   Noo, Sheila and Andy come up from Blair
           And Sheila she sat doon on a chair;
           Says she, "There'll be a helluva tear
           The nicht o' Cathie's weddin', O."

9   Noo, I think I've made it clear and plain
           I've spoke aboot naebody but my ain;
           And I'll maybe come by this way again
           To remind ye o' the weddin', O.

BROCHIE AND THE HIGHLAND CHIEF

This is about Brochie and the Highland Chief. Brochie – her own name is
Martha Burke. I don't know how they call her Brochie, there's nothing in
the world to look at her to call her Brochie, her name's Martha, and her
husband's name is James Stewart, but he prefers to be called "The Highland Chief." His father and mother, as far as I know, died when he was
very, very young. He was taken to this borstal and reared up there, and
he's a fairly religious person. On Sunday, when they're very, very much
down and out, he prefers to sing hymns.

So one day, Jimmy took it in his head that he would go and sing this
small village and sing a hymn. He took Brochie with him. Brochie was at
the one side of the street and Jimmy was at the other, and they were
singing this hymn and begging, naturally. So a gentleman passed, and he
had given Brochie something, and Jimmy was at the opposite side of the
street . . . and he was very, very curious to see what Brochie had got from
the gentleman. So they were singing the hymn of 'Nearer, My God, to
Thee'. He wanted to know what Brochie had got, so he sang it in the
Romani cant. And this is what he sang:

O, what did the gadgie feek to thee?
　　Nearer, my God, to Thee.
O, the gadgie bung me one cordee.
　　Nearer, my God, to Thee.
Would you tell the gadgie to bing it in his jeer!
　　Nearer, my God, to Thee.

Well, one day my husband and I were down to the River Tay having a picnic on a Sunday afternoon, and it was sweltering heat, it was terrific heat. So we left the River Tay and we come up to the main road where our car was, and when we came there we noticed this James Stewart and his wife, Martha Burke. He had an enormous big barrow, you know, one of these barrows that you hurl stuff from the railway stations in Scotland, which are very, very heavy iron wheels; and the heat was terrific. He was sitting beside the barrow, and O, he was terribly tired, the sweat was just pouring off him. Well, I felt sorry for Jimmy, but I laughed as a matter of fact, and on the way home to Blairgowrie, I made up this song about Brochie and the Highland Chief.

1　Noo, there was a lady in the North,
　　You would scarcely find her marrow;
　　She was courted by the Hieland Chief
　　And he had a twa-wheeled barrow.

2　Now, he went up by Ballinluig,
　　And roond by Aberfeldy;
　　Says he, "I am the Hieland Chief"
　　Says she, "You never telt me".

3　So he went in tae the bar one day
　　And he bocht wine in a bottle,
　　Says he, "I'll hae a drink o' this
　　Then I'll gie you the dottle".

4　O, they went ahin a wee whin bush
　　And the sun was shinin' bonnie;
　　Said he, "You'll hae to grib my chaet
　　For I'm botherit wi' my Johnnie".

5　Noo, the lady she has left the Chief
　　And she's gone back to Yarrow;
　　But mony's the time she sits and thinks
　　On the Chief and his wee barrow.

6　Now, Brochie she searched high and low,
　　Through all the lands of Yarrow;
　　Until she found her Hieland Chief
　　And his wee twa-wheeled barrow.

7 Now, his carrie was twelve inches long,
   And the colour of it was yellow;
   And he bung it in tae Brochie's chaet
   At the back o' his wee barrow.

8 O Jimmy, that's an awfu' thing,
   I have never seen its marrow;
   And gin another nine months' time
   I'll be bigger than your barrow.

9 So the time wore on and she got sick
   Ower the heids o' Jimmy's carrie;
   So noo she has a braw young son
   For to hurl his father's barrow.

(To the tune of 'The Braes o Yarrow', No. 9)

THE STEWART FAIM'LY

mI

steadily

'Twas   on a Sat-ur-day af- ter - noon, A wee be-fore the   sun- gaed doon

That   Ew-an cam' fae Lon- don Toon To   meet the Stew-art   faim- ly.

1 'Twas on a Saturday afternoon,
   A wee before the sun gaed doon,
   That Ewan cam' fae London Toon
   To meet the Stewart faim'ly.

2 When he come in we were gey shy,
   But we got acquaint as time gaed by –
   And afore he left you could hear him cry
   "You are a helluva faim'ly!"

3 Noo, to me his wife was awfae nice,
   For she gied me some good advice:
   To never dae the same thing twice
   For it might upset the faim'ly.

4   So noo we ken them awfae weel,
    And Ewan is an honest chiel;
    We've telt him tales that would scare the deil
    That terrible Stewart faim'ly.

5   Noo, we've had mony a happy nicht
    And whiles my e'en's been awfae ticht
    And Betsy sees that we're a' richt
    By feedin' the Stewart faim'ly.

6   Then as we a' gaed ben the room,
    And we a' got sittin' doon,
    We had a dram to keep us in tune
    Me and the Stewart faim'ly.

7   Noo, I think I've havered long enough –
    For Ewan and Peggy maun be tough
    To put up wi' that awfae stuff
    That they got fae the Stewart faim'ly.

GLENISLA

O, keen blaws the wind roond the neuks o' the shiel-in,

And auld Mal-lin-prom- is is cov-ered wi' snaw;

Hoo changed frae the time since he went up Glen- is- la

Look- in' for rags and a wee taste o' bla.

1 O, keen blaws the wind roond the neuks o' the shielin'
  And auld Mallinpromis is covered wi' snaw;
  Hoo changed frae the time since we went up Glenisla
  Lookin' for rags and a wee taste o' bla.

2 O, we went by Forter or mebbe the Linns
  Lookin' for rags and a wee puckle skins;
  But naebody kenned what we had tae bear
  With the hardships and cauld till we got back to Blair.

3 Ay, but me and my mither we aye trauchled through
  And we aye got the price o' a wee taste o' brew;
  And Donal' and Jimmy they aye did their share
  And that was the reason we never left Blair.

4 But the times they are changed and we cannae help that
  But mony's the nicht when we sit doon to crack;
  We think on wor mither wha noo is awa'
  But it's grand to hae memories that we can reca'.

Note: Mallinpromis is the name of a type of raspberry.

THE BERRYFIELDS O' BLAIR

aM

moderate

When ber- ry time comes roond each year,Blair's pop- u- la- tion's swel-lin',

There's eve- ry kind o' pick-er there and eve- ry kind o' dwel-lin;

There's tents and huts and car - a- vans, there's both-ies and there's biv-vies,

Ay, and shel- ters made wi' tat-tie bags and dug- outs made wi' div-vies.

1   When berry-time comes roond each year, Blair's population's swellin',
    There's every kind o' picker there and every kind o' dwellin';
    There's tents and huts and caravans, there's bothies and there's
        bivvies,
    Ay, and shelters made wi' tattie-bags and dugouts made wi' divvies.

2   There's traivellers fae the Western Isles, fae Arran, Mull and Skye,
    Fae Harris, Lewis and Kyles o' Bute they come their luck to try;
    Fae Inverness and Aberdeen, fae Stornaway and Wick,
    A' flock to Blair at the berry-time, the straws and rasps to pick.

3   Noo, there's corner-boys fae Glesca, kettle-boilers fae Lochee,
    And miners fae the pits o' Fife, mill-workers fae Dundee;
    And fisherfolk fae Peterheid, and tramps fae everywhere,
    A' lookin' for a livin' aff the berryfields o' Blair.

4   Noo, there's some wha earn a pound or twa, some cannae earn their
        keep,
    And some would pick fae morn to nicht, and some would rather sleep;
    There's some wha has to pick or starve and some wha dinnae care,
    There's some wha bless and some wha curse the berryfields o' Blair.

5   Noo, there's families pickin' for one purse and some wha pick alane,
    And there's men wha share and share alike wi' wives that's no' their
      ain;
    There's gladness and there's sadness tae, there's happy hairts and sair,
    For there's comedy and tragedy played on the fields o' Blair.

6   But afore I've put my pen awa', it's this I would like to say:
    You'll traivel far afore you'll meet a kinder lot than they;
    For I've mixed wi' them in field and pub, and while I've breath to spare,
    I'll bless the hand that led me to the berryfields o' Blair.

SCOTLANDS AYE YOUR HAME

(To the tune of 'The Hamilton Militiaman', No. 57)

1   It happened in the month of March to folk that I know well,
    That they made up their minds to go in a foreign land to dwell;
    Their boat came in at Greenock and the gangway was let doon,
    And Andra played them all aboard wi' a guid auld Scottish tune.

2   I saw them as they stood on deck and the tear bedimmed their e'e,
    As they waved goodbye to their ain dear land tae sail across the sea;
    They've been oot there a guid while noo and they've had their ups and
      doons,
    But Andra will aye work awa' as lang as he plays his tunes.

3   There's 'John MacDonald of Glencoe', a tune that I know well;
    What the bagpipes means to a real true Scot is more than tongue can
      tell,
    For they bring that wee lump tae your throat nae matter what's your
      name,
    And the tears will fa' when your pipes will blaw when ye're awa fae
      hame.

4   In foreign lands, their ways are strange and things are no' the same,
    And nae matter hoo they treat ye there auld Scotland's aye your hame.

(Verse 4 is sung to the second half of the melody)

GLOSSARY

aebody   everybody

agley   obliquely; off in a wrong direction

ahint   behind

ain (adj.)   own

airt   direction; point of the compass

ay   yes

aye   always

bachies   from bauchles: old, out-of-shape shoes, slippers

bairn   a child

bannock   a sort of cake toasted in the embers

bara   alternative pronunciation of the cant word barrie: good, gentle

barra   wheelbarrow

been   the Stewarts regard this as a cant word, meaning good, kind, etc. It is, of course, the same word as the Scots bien, the Latin *bene*

ben   the interior of a house

besom   a broom for sweeping

bien   good, well

big (v.)   to build

bing   from cant: to go, to make

bivvies   abbreviation for bivouac tents

bla   from cant: meal, corn

borstal   name of a town in Kent, now generally applied to a system adopted there for reforming 'juvenile adult' offenders

bothy   a place where male farm-servants are lodged

bothy songs   songs composed by, or from the repertory of, farm-servants

bow-tent   a tent improvised by throwing a tarpaulin over two bent saplings

brae   the side of a hill, an acclivity

braw   brave, handsome, agreeable

bree (n.)   brow, eyebrow; also brew

breeks   trousers, breeches

broo (n.)   the unemployment bureau; also brow

buck   a Gorgio man who marries a Traveller woman

buits   (pronounced bits) boots

bumbee   bumblebee

burn(ie)   stream(let)

busk   1.   to dress, attire oneself or make ready
          2.   to perform in the street

canntaireachd   (pronounced kăn · tŭ raχ) the vocal notation traditionally used in pibroch in which the melody is represented by vowels and the grace notes by consonants

canty   cheerful

carrie   from cant: penis

cauldrife   very sensible to cold

ceilidh   (pronounced kā· lē) a community gathering at which singing and dancing may take place

chaet   from cant: thing, object

chap (v.)   to mash, knock

chapin can   a quart can

cheroot   a small cigar

chiel   a fellow

claes   clothes

coo   cow

cooer   cower, snuggle

cotter-hoose   a tied cottage

couthy   warm, snug, comfortable

crack (n. and v.)   gossip, talk

creeshy   greasy, dirty

crouse   brisk, lively, bold

cuddy   donkey

c' wa'   come away

dae   do
Dees   abbreviation for Detectives
deil   the devil
didekai   a person of mixed Gypsy and Gorgio parentage
divvies   from divots, divets: thin, flat turfs used for roofing cottages
dochter   daughter
dolt aboot   to walk in an uncoordinated fashion
dottle   1.   a small particle
            2.   a stopper, cork or bung
dover awa'   to fall into a slight, unsettled sleep
dram   a small quantity of liquor, usually whisky
dule   grief
dursnae   dare not

ettle   to propose, intend

fae   from
fag (-end)   cigarette (end)
feek   from cant: to make, find
fly, to be   to be cunning, to have one's wits about one
forbye   as well as
frae   from
freedyeuch   from cant: smallest possible thing

gadgie   from cant: man
gaed   went
gant   to yawn
gar   to make
gauger   exciseman
gee-gee   horse
gey   moderately, fairly
get (n.)   a contemptuous designation for a child
gie, gied, gien   give, gave, given
gin   if; by
girnin'   weeping, crying
gouldritch   melancholy
gowd   gold
greet   to weep
gribbin' (his chaet)   from cant: doing (his thing)
grieve (n.)   an overseer

hae   to have
hantle   from cant: folk, people

hap   to cover, dress, clothe
haud   to hold
haver   to talk foolishly
Hogmanay   strictly speaking, the last day of the year, but now generally applied to New Year's Eve
hoose   house
horner   one who makes horn spoons
howk   to dig
hurl (n. and v.)   ride

ilka   every

jeer (n.)   from cant: the buttocks

kailyard   a kitchen garden; also applied to those Scots writers who relegated the Scots language to sentimental and generally puerile themes
keek   to look
ken   to know
kinnel   to kindle
knowe   a small hill
kyards   Aberdeenshire word for Travelling people
kye   cattle

lave   the rest, the remaining ones
limmer   woman
lo'e   to love
loon   boy, youth
lowe   a blaze
lowse   to loose
lug   ear
lum   chimney
lum-hat   tall hat

makar   a poet
make (n.)   an equal
mapamound   the world
marrow   a match, an equal
mavis   the thrush
midge   to move slightly
model-lodge   a cheap lodging-house
moich   soft in the head
mowdit   probably a form of moidert: stupid, dull
mutch   a cap, headress for a woman

needies   Travellers
neeps   turnips

neuk the corner
nicht night
nowt (sort your) cattle (attend to)
owre over
oxter the armpit

pintle the penis
pishmol an ant
plet to clench, a term used by
  blacksmiths
polis the police
poteen liquor distilled from potatoes
potters the name given to Travellers in
  Scottish border regions
preen (n.) a pin
puckle a small quantity
puddock a frog

quean a young woman

richt right

scran from cant: food
sharney bedaubed with cow-dung
shaw (as of turnips) to remove the
  foliage
sheen shoes
shielin' a hut
sib related by blood
sic, siccan such
sinsyne since
skyowt twisted, distorted
sneck to latch
sned to cut, prune
snottem a stick on which a kettle is
  hung for boiling

speir to ask
stottin' staggering, lurching
stoup a pitcher or vessel for carrying
  water
strae straw
sweir reluctant
syne afterwards, since

tatties potatoes
thon, thonder yon, yonder
thrapple the windpipe, also the throat
thrawn awkward, distorted,
  cross-grained
ticht tight
Tilly pans a brand name for kerosene
  lamps
timmer timber
toffs gentlefolk
tourie Glengarry bonnet
trauchle to trudge
trig neat, trim
turlies sheep-dung

wae woe
wame stomach
wean child
weird (n.) fate, destiny
whaup the curlew
whin the common furze or gorse
wi' with
wonk a swelling
wyss wise, prudent

yestreen yesterday
yin one

BIBLIOGRAPHICAL REFERENCES

The Childrens Material

1 *For a Child at the Breast* Rymour, Vol. I, p. 53.

2 *The Body Route* Chambers (1), pp. 16–21; Ford (1), pp. 10–20; Gullen, pp. 8–10; Opie (3), p. 103 & pp. 198–9; Ritchie (1), pp. 4–6; *Rymour*, Vol. I, pp. 50, 54, 210, 233; also Vol. II, p. 98.

3 *Fingers or Toes* Chambers (1), p. 20; Ford (1), p. 10; Gullen, pp. 8–9; Halliwell (2), p. 93; Northall, pp. 416–17; *Rymour*, Vol. I, p. 93.

5 *Hand Clapping* Fraser, pp. 13–14; Halliwell (1), p. 133; Ritchie (1), p. 5.

6 *To a Snail* Gullen, p. 61; Halliwell (2), p. 165; Northall, pp. 328–9; *Rymour*, Vol. II, p. 112.

7 *Dandling Rhyme* Montgomerie, p. 86; Ritchie (2), p. 54; *Rymour*, Vol. I, p. 223 and 239.

11 *Dandling song* Allan (Tyneside), pp. 210–11; Chambers (1), p. 18; Ford (1), p. 129; Fraser, p. 6; Halliwell (1), p. 158; Mason, p. 38; Montgomerie, pp. 89–90; *Rymour*, Vol. III, p. 179; Stokoe and Reay, pp. 76–7.

12 *Spider Tale* Fraser, pp. 28–9; Opie (2), p. 38; Ritchie (1), p. 6; Seeger, p. 126.

13 *Nursing Rhyme* Ford (1), p. 133; Opie (3), pp. 186–7; *Rymour*, Vol. I, p. 89; also Vol. III, p. 105.

14 *Counting-out Rhymes* (a) Fraser, p. 26; Gullen, p. 32; Opie (1), p. 54; Ritchie (1), p. 41. (b) Bolton, p. 24; Ritchie (1), pp. 135 and 139; *Rymour*, Vol. I, p. 87. (c) Gullen, p. 17; Opie (1), p. 37; Holbrook, p. 57.

15 *Ring Games* (a) Chase, pp. 14–15; Fraser, p. 111; Gomme, Vol. II, pp. 123–43; Jones and Hawes, pp. 76–7. (b) *Henry Collection*, No. 599; Newell, pp. 223–5. (c) Chambers (1), pp. 137–9; Chase, pp. 6–9; Ford (1), p. 60; Fraser, p. 199; Gomme, Vol. I, pp. 352–61; Halliwell (1), pp. 143–4; Halliwell (2), pp. 117–18; Mason, p. 12; Newell, p. 131; Ritchie (1), pp. 160–1.

16 *Ball Games* (a) Gullen, p. 20; Ritchie (1), p. 87. (b) Ritchie (1), pp. 29–30. (c) Ritchie (1), p. 83.

17 *Skipping Games* (a) Gomme, Vol. I, pp. 2–6; Holbrook, pp. 94–5. (b) *JAF*, Vol. 53 (1940), p. 165; Opie (2), p. 34; Ritchie (1), p. 88; Ritchie (2), p. 31. (c) Ritchie (1), p. 133; Rutherford, p. 58. (d) Ritchie (1), pp. 132–3. (e) Baring-Gould and Sheppard, pp. 150–1; Botkin (Playparty), pp. 69–70; Butterworth, pp. 16–17; Dick, No. 187; Ford (3), Vol. I, pp. 102–5; *Gardiner MSS*, Nos. H-1203 and H-1351; *Henry Collection*, Nos. 152 and 793; *JFSS*, Vol. I, pp. 92–3; also Vol. II, pp. 9–10 and 269–71; also Vol. IV, pp. 291–3; also Vol VI, p. 7; Kidson and Moffat, pp. 2–3; MacColl and Seeger, pp. 168–9; *Museum*, No. 288; Purslow (3), p. 104; Reeves (1), pp. 238–239; Seeger and MacColl, p. 7; Sharp, Vol. I, pp. 104–6; Sharp and Karpeles (2), Vol. I, pp. 422–9.

18 *An Impossible Task*   Opie (2), p. 27; Reeves (2), pp. 220–1; Thompson (Stith), Motif No. H1024.1.
19 *A Matter of Choice*   Hecht, p. 185; *Rymour*, Vol. II, p. 27.
20 *A Drastic Remedy*   Duchartre, p. 141.
21 *The Provider*   Gullen, p. 78.
22 *Town Rhyme*   Ritchie (2), pp. 94–5.
23 *Superman*   Opie (2), p. 112; Ritchie (1), p. 90; Ritchie (2), p. 35; Rutherford, p. 123.

The songs

1 *The Fause Knight upon the Road* (Child 3)
Bronson (also Appendix) and Coffin.
British: Chambers (1), p. 66; *JEFDSS*, Vol. VIII, p. 169; also Vol. IX, pp. 156–7; *Scottish Studies*, Vol. IX, pp. 9–14.
N. American: Bulletin, No. 11, pp. 8–9; Flanders, Vol. I, pp. 80–1; Moore, pp. 11–12.
General: Wimberley (under Riddlecraft and Devil).

2 *The Twa Brothers* (Child 49)
Bronson (also Appendix) and Coffin.
British: *JEFDSS*, Vol. VIII, pp. 112–13.
N. American: *Dusenbury MSS*, No. 24 6b; Moore, pp. 38–41; Peacock, Vol. III, pp. 827–30.

3 *The Lowlands of Holland* (Child 92, Appendix)
Bronson and Coffin.
British: Ashton, p. 59; Chambers (2), pp. 412–13; *Gardiner MSS*, No. H–1040; Greig, Nos. 83 and 135; *Henry Collection*, No. 180; *JEFDSS*, Vol. VII, pp. 242–3; *JFSS*, Vol. III, pp. 307–9; Logan, pp. 22–5; MacColl and Seeger, pp. 78–81; O'Lochlainn (2) p. 223; Ord, pp. 328–32; Purslow (2), p. 54; Reeves (1), pp. 180–2; Reeves (2), pp. 151–2, Sharp (2), Vol. II, pp. 16–17; Sharp and Karpeles (2), Vol. I, pp. 108–13.
N. American: Flanders and Olney, pp. 113–14 and 118–19; Randolph, Vol. I, pp. 339–40; Sharp and Karpeles (1), Vol. I, p. 200.

4 *The Famous Flower of Serving Men* (Child 106)
Bronson (also Appendix) and Coffin.
British: Bell, pp. 192–3; *Gardiner MSS*, No. HP–1322; Greig, No. 118; MacColl and Seeger, pp. 81–6; Purslow (1), pp. 34–5.
N. American: Moore, pp. 81–4.

5 *Mary Hamilton* (Child 173)
Bronson (also Appendix) and Coffin.
N. American: Creighton (1), pp. 10–11; Moore, pp. 93–4.

6 *The Bonnie House o' Airlie* (Child 199)
Bronson and Coffin.
British: Blackie, pp. 185–7; Christie, Vol. II, pp. 276–7; Ford (3), Vol. II, pp. 167–9; Greig, No. 58; Greig and Keith, pp. 123–5; MacColl and Seeger, pp. 89–91; Ord, p. 470.
N. American: Barry, Eckstorm and Smyth, pp. 258–64; Moore, pp. 95–7.

7 *The Gypsy Laddie* (Child 200)
   Bronson (also Appendix) and Coffin.
   British: Baring-Gould and Sheppard, pp. 102–3; Gillington (2), pp.
                       12–13; Greig, No. 110; *Henry Collection*, No. 124; *JEFDSS*,
                       Vol. V, pp. 14–15; *New City Songster*, Vol. 4/5, p. 20; Smith,
                       pp. 161–4; Sharp, Vol. I, pp. 13–16; Sharp and Karpeles (2),
                       Vol. I, pp. 160–70; Williams, pp. 120–2.
   N. American: Combs and Wilgus, pp. 205–6; Creighton (1), pp. 12–13;
                       Dusenbury MSS, No. 39 10b; Fowke, pp. 18–19; Hubbard,
                       pp. 26–7; Karpeles, pp. 313–14; Moore, pp. 97–100; Pea-
                       cock, Vol. I, pp. 194–7.

8 *The Baron of Brackley* (Child 203)
   Bronson (also Appendix).
   British: Buchan (Peter), pp. 68–73; Christie, Vol. I, pp. 20–21;
                       Jamieson, Vol. I, p. 102; Ree, pp. 88–92 (with an excellent
                       historical note); *Scottish Studies*, Vol. XVIII, pp. 16–17.

9 *The Braes o' Yarrow* (Child 214)
   Bronson (also Appendix) and Coffin.
   British: Greig, No. 57; Herd, Vol. I, p. 68; *JEFDSS*, Vol. V, p. 77;
                       JFSS, Vol. V, pp. 110–16; Kidson, pp. 21–4; MacColl, pp.
                       14–15; Ord, pp. 426–7; *Rymour*, Vol. I, pp. 44–5; *Scottish
                       Studies*, Vol. VII, pp. 115–17; also Vol. XVIII, pp. 15–16;
                       Thomson, Vol. II, pp. 34–9.
   Broadsides: MacNie of Stirling (1824).
   N. American: Fowke, pp. 62–3; Karpeles, pp. 95–6; Moore, pp. 104–6.
   General: Cazden, Norman: an article entitled 'Story of a Catskill
                       Ballad', printed in *The New York Folklore Quarterly*, winter
                       1952, pp. 245–66.

10 *Lizie Lindsay* (Child 226)
   Bronson (also Appendix) and Coffin.
   British: Ford (3), Vol. II, pp. 205–7; Glen, No. 434; *Museum*, No.
                       434.
   N. American: Moore, pp. 110–11.

11 *Andrew Lammie* (Child 233)
   Bronson (also Appendix) and Coffin.
   British: Christie, Vol. I, pp. 48–9; Greig, Nos. 16 and 34.

12 *The Gaberlunzie Man* (Child 279, Appendix)
   Bronson and Coffin.
   British: Christie, Vol. II, pp. 104–7; Farmer, Vol. I, pp. 1–4; Ford
                       (3), Vol. I, pp. 241–3; Glen, No. 226; Greig, Nos. 30 and 38;
                       Greig and Keith, pp. 223–6; *Henry Collection*, No. 810; Herd,
                       Vol. II, pp. 49–51; MacColl and Seeger, pp. 104–5; *Museum*,
                       No. 226; Ord, pp. 375–7; *Rymour*, Vol. I, p. 183.
   N. American: Moore, pp. 128–31.

13 *Here's a Health to All True Lovers*
   Child (No. 248), Bronson and Coffin.
   British: Chambers (2), pp. 285–7; Chappell, Vol. II, p. 731; *JEFDSS*,
                       Vol. VII, pp. 97–8; Hughes, Vol. II, pp. 64–9; MacColl, p.
                       24.

N. American: Creighton and Senior, pp. 31–3; Fowke, p. 105; Karpeles, pp. 100–2; Sharp and Karpeles (1), Vol. I, p. 259.
General: See also Child No. 77, 'Sweet William's Ghost'.

14   *The Duke of Athol* (Laws O 23)
Child (No. 232).
British: Christie, Vol. I, pp. 166–7; Ford (2), pp. 121–3; Kinloch, pp. 170–3; Rogers, pp. 62–3.

15   *The Rambling Irishman* (Laws H 4)
British: Baring-Gould and Sheppard, pp. 16–17; Reeves (2), p. 186.
Broadside: *British Museum*, LR 271 a 2, Vol. II, p. 239; also 1871 f. 13.
N. American: Creighton (1), p. 43; Fowke, pp. 92–3.
Alt. titles: The Roving Journeyman (Gambler, Soldier); Roving Jack; The Gambling Man; The Guerilla Boy.

16   *Burns and his Highland Mary* (Laws O 34)
British: Christie, Vol. I, pp. 62–3; Ford (3), Vol. I, pp. 124–6; Greig, No. 76; Ord, pp. 354–5.
Broadsides: *Madden Collection*: M 16–135–136 (W. and T. Fordyce at Newcastle); also M 16–472 (John Ross, Newcastle; also M 18–782 (Harkness).
N. American: Barry, pp. 88–9; Creighton (1), pp. 125–6; Creighton (2), pp. 88–9; Peacock, Vol. II. pp. 427–9.
Alt. titles: The Parting of Burns and (His) Highland Mary; The Banks of the Ayr.

17   *The Bonnie Irish Boy* (Laws P 26)
British: Greig, No. 48; *Henry Collection*, No. 168; *JFSS* Vol. I, p. 17; Kidson, pp. 152–3; Ord, pp. 162–3.
Broadsides: *Madden Collection*: M 18–619 (John Harkness of Preston); also M 24–218 (Haly of Cork).
N. American: *Fowke MSS*; Hubbard, p. 136; Peacock, Vol. II, pp. 560–3.
Alt. titles: Bonnie Young (Wee) Irish Boy.

18   *Drummallochie*
British: *FMJ*, Vol. I, pp. 82–4; Greig, No. 22; Ord, pp. 34–7.

19   *Queen Among the Heather*
British: Blackie, pp. 54–5; Greig, No. 44; *Henry Collection*, No. 177; Kennedy, p. 318; Ord, p. 433; *Scottish Studies*, Vol. XVI, pp. 153–4.

20   *Amang the Whinny Knowes*
British: Ford (3), Vol. II, pp. 244–6; Greig, No. 175; *Henry Collection*, No. 18.

21   *If I was a Blackbird*
British: *Gardiner MSS*, Nos. H–355 and H–356; Hamer, p. 52; *Henry Collection*, No. 79; MacColl and Seeger, pp. 139–41; O'Lochlainn (1), p. 92; Purslow (3), p. 57; Reeves (1), p. 163; Sharp and Karpeles (2), Vol. I, pp. 493–4.
Alt. titles: The Blackbird; My Love.

22   *A Nobleman Lived in a Mansion* – no references.

23   *The Lovely Irish Maid*
N. American: Peacock, Vol. II, pp. 551–2.

24 *Busk Busk, Bonnie Lassie*
    British: Buchan and Hall, p. 111; Greig, Nos. 107 and 141; MacColl
                      and Seeger, pp. 143–4; Ord, pp. 136–7.

25 *Bonnie Lass, Come Owre the Burn*
    British: Buchan and Hall, p. 7.

26 *The Ball o' Kirriemuir*
    British: Kerr (2), pp. 40–1; *Merry Muses*, pp. 23–4.
    N. American: Cray, pp. 34–5 and 155; Legman, pp. 172–3, 227–8, 231, 377,
                      and 423–4.

27 *My Faither was Hung for Sheep-stealing*
    British: Bell, p. 398 ; Chappell (2), Vol. II, pp. 450–1; Dick, pp.
                      414–15 (note only); Dixon and Bell, p. 175; Ford (3), Vol. I,
                      pp. 229–30; Greig, No. 18; *Henry Collection*, No. 551; Herd,
                      Vol. II, pp. 81–3; Kennedy, p. 502; MacColl and Seeger, pp.
                      162–5; Ritchie (2), pp. 103–4; Sharp (Cuthbert); Sola Pinto
                      and Rodway, pp. 438–9; Thomson, Vol. I, pp. 69–70; *The
                      Thrush*, pp. 145–6; Williams, pp. 226–7.
    N. American: Brown, Vol. II, pp. 456–7; Cray, pp. 23–4 and 222–6;
                      Flanders, Ballard, Brown and Barry, pp. 223–4; Flanders and
                      Olney, pp. 176–7; Gardner and Chickering, pp. 435–6;
                      Lomax, pp. 134–5; Randolph, Vol. I, pp. 385–6; Sandburg,
                      p. 381.
    Alt. titles: My Father's a Lawyer in England; My Sister She Works in a
                      Laundry; (My God), How the Money Rolls In; Nobody
                      Comes to Marry Me.

28 *The Bonnie Lassie's Plaidie*
    British: Ford (3), Vol. I, pp. 74–5; Ord, pp. 96–7; Seeger and
                      MacColl, p. 100.
    Alt. titles: The Wind Blew the Bonnie Lassie's Plaidie Awa'.

29 *Bonnie Bonnie Bessie Lee* – no references.

30 *John Peel* – no references.

31 *The Road to Dundee*
    British: Buchan (Norman), pp. 66–7; Greig, No. 51; Kerr (2), pp.
                      68–9; O'Lochlainn (1), p. 188; Ord, pp. 151–3.
    N. American: Fowke, pp. 132–3.
    Alt. titles: Sweet Carnloch Bay.

32 *Rosemary Lane* (Laws K 43)
    British: Buchan and Hall, p. 83; *Hammond MSS*, Nos. D-153 and D-
                      154; Hugill, pp. 498–501; *JEFDSS*, Vol. VI, p. 18; *JFSS*, Vol.
                      VI, pp. 1–3; MacColl and Seeger, pp. 166–7; Purslow (2), p.
                      42; Purslow (3), p. 99; Reeves (1), p. 223; Reeves (2), pp.
                      181–3; *Rymour*, Vol. II, p. 188; Sharp and Karpeles (2), Vol.
                      I, pp. 671–9.
    Broadsides: *British Museum*, No. 1876 e 2, p. 66 (Jackson of Birmingham).
    N. American: Cray, pp. 32–3 and 160–2; *Fowke MSS*.
    Alt. titles: Home, Dearest, Home; When First I Went to Service; He
                      Called for a Candle; The Sailor Boy; Never Trust a Sailor;
                      Servant of Rosemary Lane.

33 *The Galway Shawl*
    British: *Henry Collection*, No. 652; Joyce (2), No. 680.

34 *The Bonnie Lass o' Fyvie*
    British: Christie, Vol. I, pp. 276–7; Ford (3), Vol. I, pp. 133–5;
                        Greig, No. 15; Kerr (2), pp. 8–9; Ord, pp. 304–5.

35 *Madam, I Have Come to Court You*
    British: Broadwood and Maitland, pp. 90–1; Butterworth, pp. 2–3;
                        Gardiner MSS, Nos 62 and 491; Gomme, Vol. I, pp. 320–3;
                        Halliwell (1), pp. 188–9; *Hammond MSS*, No. 892; *Henry
                        Collection*, No. 532; *JEFDSS*, Vol. I. pp. 133–4; *JFSS*, Vol
                        III, pp. 267–8; also Vol. IV, pp. 297–300; Northall, p. 376.
    N. American: Belden, pp. 506–7; Botkin (2), pp. 784–5; Botkin (Play-
                        party), pp. 356–7; Brown, Vol. III, pp. 23–4; Cox, pp.
                        465–6; Creighton (2), p. 121; Eddy, pp. 222–3; Flanders and
                        Brown, pp. 154–5; Gardner and Chickering, pp. 418–19;
                        Huntington, pp. 194–5; Lomax, p. 314; Moore, pp. 217–18;
                        Newell, pp. 55–6; Sharp and Karpeles (1), Vol. II, pp.
                        279–80.
    Alt. titles: Lady on a Mountain; There Stands a Lady on a Mountain;
                        Yonder Stands a Lovely Creature; The Spanish Lady (Mai-
                        den); The Scottish Merchant's Daughter; Tarry Trousers;
                        Eighteen-Eighteen; Uh-Uh, No.

36 *The Dawning of the Day* (Laws P 16)
    British: Gillington (1), pp. 10–11; Joyce (1), p. 8; Joyce (2), No. 774;
                        Ord, p. 163; Rooney, p. 22; Sharp and Karpeles (2), Vol. I.
                        pp. 651–5; Thompson (Harold), p. 384.
    Broadsides: *British Museum*: LR 271 a 2, Vol. VI, p. 107 (no imprint); also
                        LR 271 a 2, Vol. VII, p. 9 (Jaques of Manchester); also LR
                        271 a 2, Vol. VII, p. 39 (Bebbington of Manchester); also 1871
                        f. 13 (no imprint).
                        Madden Collection: John Pitts, M 8–189 and 904; E. Hodges,
                        M 11–35; W. & T. Fordyce, M 16–357; J. Swindells, Man-
                        chester, M 18–119; J. Wheeler, Manchester, M 18–475;
                        Harkness, Preston, M 18–587; Wm. Pratt, Birmingham, M
                        21–111.
    N. American: Fowke, pp. 72–3; Thompson (Harold), pp. 384–6.

37 *The Maid of Culmore*
    British: *Henry Collection*, No. 687.

38 *Green Bushes* (Laws P 2)
    British: Baring-Gould and Sheppard, pp. 86–7; Broadwood and Mait-
                        land, pp. 70–1; Gillington (2), pp. 4–5; Hamer, pp. 42–3;
                        Hammond MSS, Nos. D–202 and D–559; *Henry Collection*,
                        Nos. 119 and 143; *JFSS*, Vol. V, pp. 177–8; also Vol. VIII, p.
                        209 and pp. 112–13; Joyce (2), pp. 24–5; Kennedy, p. 356;
                        Kidson, pp. 47–8; Kidson and Moffat, pp. 40–1; MacColl and
                        Seeger, pp. 221–4; Ord, p. 147; O'Shaunessy, pp. 39–40;
                        Petrie, Nos. 222, 223, 368, 369, 370, 603, 674 and 771; Purslow
                        (2), p. 38; Reeves (1), p. 133; Sharp, Vol. I, p. 58; Sharp and
                        Karpeles (2), Vol. I, pp. 593–6;

Broadsides: British Museum LR 271 a 2, Vol. II, p. 194 (Hodges and Pitts); also Vol. VI, p. 144 (Such).
N. American: Creighton and Senior, pp. 20–1; Karpeles, p. 244.
Alt. titles: Down By Those Green Bushes.

39 Oxford City (Laws P 30)
British: Gardiner MSS, Nos. Hp–340 and Hp 353; Greig, No. 137; Hamer, p. 36; JEFDSS, Vol. IX, pp. 194–5; JFSS, Vol. II, p. 37, pp. 157–8 and p. 200; also Vol. VII, pp. 41–3; Kennedy, p. 715; MacColl and Seeger, pp. 240–1; Purslow (1), pp. 46–7; Sharp and Karpeles (2), Vol. I, pp. 310–12.
Broadsides: British Museum, LR 271 a 2, Vol. I, p. 85 (Pitts); also Vol. IV, p. 392 (Catnach); also Vol. V, p. 26 (Such); also Vol. VII, p. 158 (Livesey of Manchester).
N. American: Creighton (2), pp. 121–2.
Alt. titles: In Oxford Town; In Midfordshire; Newport Street; The Poisoned Cup; Poison in a Glass of Wine; Jealousy.

40 The Nobleman's Wedding (Laws P 31)
British: Graves, pp. 146–7; Greig, No. 24; Hammond MSS, No. 429; Henry Collection, No. 60; JFSS, Vol. VIII, pp. 4–5 and 202–5; Joyce (2), pp. 224–5; Kennedy, p. 364; Ord, pp. 132–3; Petrie, Nos. 491–5; Purslow (2), pp. 61–2; Sharp and Karpeles (2), Vol. I, p. 267.
N. American: Hubbard, pp. 47–8; Karpeles, pp. 124–5; Peacock, Vol. III, pp. 691–2.
Alt. titles: The Awful Wedding; The Faultless Bride; The Unconstant Lover; The Love Token; Down in MyGarden; The Orange and the Blue; All Round My Hat.

41 The Banks of Red Roses
British: Buchan and Hall, p. 52; Cunningham, Vol. II, p. 316; Glen, No. 7; JFSS, Vol. II, p. 254; Joyce (2), No. 128; MacColl and Seeger, pp. 235–7; Museum, No. 7; O'Lochlainn (1), p. 158; Reeves (2), p. 115.
Broadsides: MacNie of Stirling, 1825; Madden Collection, M 4–85 and M 4–86 (c. 1790).
N. American: Doerflinger, pp. 315–16; Greenleaf and Mansfield, pp. 210–11; Peacock, Vol. II, pp. 497–8.
Alt. titles: The Banks of the Dizzy; The German Flute; or any combination of words involving 'banks' and 'roses'.

42 Hatton Woods
British: Ord, p. 185.
Alt. titles: The Bonnie Woods o' Hatton.

43 The Days are Awa' That We Hae Seen
British: JEFDSS, Vol. IV, pp. 183–4; Ord, p. 179.
General: Greig, No. 139; Logan, pp. 363–4.

44 Bogie's Bonnie Belle
British: Kennedy, p. 766; Kerr (1), Book I, pp. 16–17; MacColl and Seeger, pp. 261–2.

45 John Mitchel
British: Galvin, p. 45; Henry Collection, No. 179; O'Lochlainn (2), pp. 54–5; Zimmerman, pp. 239–40.

Broadsides: *British Museum*, LR 271 a 2, Vol. V, p. 8 (Such).

46   *The Lonely Banna Strand*
     British: Galvin, pp. 57–8.

47   *Ballyjamesduff* – no references.

48   *The Country I'm Leaving Behind* – no references.

49   *Glen Swilly*
     British: Henry Collection, No. 672.
     Alt. titles: Glen o' Lee.

50   *Terence's Farewell* – no references.

51   *The Soor Mulk Cairt*
     British: Buchan (Norman), pp. 92–3; MacColl, p. 41.

52   *Geordie Weir* – no references.

53   *The Cairn*
     British: Kerr (1), Book I, pp. 18–19.
     Alt. titles: The Buchan Plooman.

54   *Johnny, My Man*
     British: Ford (3), Vol. II, pp. 254–6; Greig, No. 5; *Henry Collection*,
                           No. 807; Ord, pp. 367–8.
     Broadside: *British Museum*, 1871 f. 13.
     Alt. titles: Donald, My Man.

55   *The Real Old Mountain Dew*
     British: O'Lochlainn (1), pp. 128–9.
     N. American: Botkin (3), pp. 736–7.
     Alt. titles: Good Old Mountain Dew.

56   *Blue Blazing Blind Drunk* – no references.

57   *The Hamilton Militiaman* – no references.

58   *An Old Man He Courted Me*
     British: *Gardiner MSS*, No. Hn–1015; Herd, Vol. II, pp. 63–4
                           (Appendix); *JFSS*, Vol. II, p. 273; Joyce (2), No. 228; Kidson,
                           p. 92; Kennedy, p. 464; Petrie, No. 531; Purslow (2), p. 66;
                           Seeger and MacColl, p. 34; Sharp and Karpeles (2), Vol. II, p.
                           30; *Scottish Studies*, Vol. XVI, pp. 147–8.
     N. American: Fowke, pp. 32–3; Hubbard, p. 156.
     General: Herd, Vol. II, pp. 33–4 ('The Carle Cam' Ower the Croft').
     Alt. titles: Ne'er Wed (Marry) an Auld Man; Maids, When You're
                           Young; Maids, While You Live, Never Wed an Auld Man.

59   *The Overgate*
     British: *FMJ*, Vol. III, pp. 60–1; Kennedy, p. 418; MacColl and
                           Seeger, pp. 175–7.

60   *The Bonnie Wee Lassie fae Gourock* – no references.

61   *Betsy Bell* – no references.

62   *I'm no' Comin' oot the Noo* – no references.

63   *Cod-Liver Oil*
     British: O'Lochlainn (2), pp. 60–1.

N. American: Greenleaf and Mansfield, p. 316; Lomax and Seeger, pp. 116–7; Peacock, Vol. I, pp. 48–9.

64   *Twa Heids are Better than Ane*
British: Kerr (1), Book II, pp. 42–3.

65   *A Shilling or Twa*
British: Greig, No. 140; Kerr (2), pp. 22–3; Ord, pp. 388–9.

66   *Twelve Bob and a Tanner* – no references

67   *The Blarney Roses* – no references.

68   *Master McGrath*
British: O'Lochlainn (1), pp. 66–7.

69   *Kathleen Mavourneen* – no references.

70   *The Moss o' Burreldale*
British: Buchan and Hall, pp. 106–7; Kennedy, pp. 779–80; Kerr (1), Book I, pp. 32–3; MacColl and Seeger, pp. 355–7.

71   *Hi, Bara Manishie*
British: MacColl and Seeger, p. 363.

GENERAL BIBLIOGRAPHY

In order to avoid duplication, we have omitted those bibliographical references given in Child, Bronson and Coffin.

Folklore and folksong

Aarne and Thompson   Antti Aarne and Stith Thompson, *The Types of the Folktale* (Helsinki, 1961).
Allan   David Allan, *Songs of the Lowlands of Scotland* (Edinburgh, 1799).
Allan (Tyneside)   Thomas and George Allan, *Allan's Illustrated Edition of Tyneside Songs and Readings* (London, 1921).
Ashton   John Ashton, *Real Sailor Songs* (London, 1891).
Aytoun   W. E. Aytoun, *The Ballads of Scotland* (Edinburgh, 1858).

Baring-Gould and Sheppard   Sabine Baring-Gould and H. Fleetwood Sheppard, *Songs of the West* (London, 1905).
Barry   Phillips Barry, *The Maine Woods Songster* (Cambridge, Massachusetts, 1939).
Barry, Eckstorm and Smyth   Phillips Barry, Fanny Hardie Eckstorm and Mary Winslow Smyth, *British Ballads from Maine* (New Haven, Connecticut, 1939).
Belden   H. M. Belden, *Ballads and Songs* (Columbia, Missouri, 1940).
Bell   Robert Bell, *Early Ballads* (London, 1877).
Blackie   John Stuart Blackie, *Scottish Song* (Edinburgh, 1899).
Bolton   Henry Carrington Bolton, *Counting-Out Rhymes of Children* (New York, 1888; reprint 1969).
Botkin (1)   Benjamin A. Botkin, *A Treasury of New England Folklore* (New York, 1947).
Botkin (2)   Benjamin A. Botkin, *A Treasury of Western Folklore* (New York, 1951).
Botkin (3)   Benjamin A. Botkin, *A Treasury of Southern Folklore* (New York, 1949).
Botkin (Play-party)   Benjamin A. Botkin, *The American Play-Party Song* (Lincoln, Nebraska, 1937).
British Museum   LR 271 a 2: a collection of ballads, chiefly Catnach and Pitt, 1800–70. Ten volumes. 1871, f. 13: a collection of ballads printed on single sheets, 1750–1840.
Broadwood and Maitland   Lucy E. Broadwood and J. A. Fuller Maitland, *English County Songs* (London, 1893).
Bronson   Bertrand Harris Bronson, *The Traditional Tunes of the Child Ballads* (Princeton, New Jersey, 1959–72, 4 vols).
Brown   *The Frank C. Brown Collection of North Carolina Folklore* (Durham, North Carolina, 1952, 7 vols).

Buchan and Hall   Norman Buchan and Peter Hall, *The Scottish Folksinger* (London, 1973).

Buchan (Norman)   Norman Buchan, *101 Scottish Songs* (Glasgow and London, 1962).

Buchan (Peter)   Peter Buchan, *Ancient Ballads and Songs of the North of Scotland* (Edinburgh, 1875, 2 vols).

Bulletin   Bulletin of the Folksong Society of the Northeast (Cambridge, Massachusetts, 1930–7).

Butterworth   George S. K. Butterworth, *Folk Songs from Sussex* (London, 1913).

Chambers (1)   Robert Chambers, *Popular Rhymes of Scotland* (Edinburgh, 1841).

Chambers (2)   Robert Chambers, *The Songs of Scotland Prior to Burns* (Edinburgh, 1862).

Chappell   William Chappell, *Popular Music of the Olden Time* (London, 1850–9, 2 vols).

Chase   Richard Chase, *Hullabaloo and Other Singing Folk Games* (Cambridge, Massachusetts, 1949).

Child   Francis J. Child, *The English and Scottish Popular Ballads* (Cambridge, Massachusetts, 1882–98, 5 vols).

Christie   William Christie, *Traditional Ballad Airs* (Edinburgh, 1876–81, 2 vols).

Coffin   Tristram P. Coffin, *The British Traditional Ballad in North America* (Philadelphia, 1950).

Combs and Wilgus   Josiah H. Combs (ed. D. K. Wilgus), *Folk-Songs of the Southern United States* (Austin, Texas, 1967).

Cox   John Harrington Cox, *Folk-Songs of the South* (Cambridge, Massachusetts, 1925).

Cray   Edward Cray, *The Erotic Muse* (New York, 1969).

Creighton (1)   Helen Creighton, *Folksongs from Southern New Brunswick* (Ottawa, 1971).

Creighton (2)   Helen Creighton, *Maritime Folk Songs* (Toronto, 1962).

Creighton and Senior   Helen Creighton and Doreen H. Senior, *Twelve Folk Songs from Nova Scotia* (London, 1953).

Cunningham   Allan Cunningham, *Songs of Scotland* (London, 1825, 4 vols).

Dick   James C. Dick, *The Songs of Robert Burns* (London, 1903).

Dixon and Bell   James Henry Dixon and Robert Bell, *Ballads and Songs of the Peasantry of England* (London, 1857).

Doerflinger   William M. Doerflinger, *Shantymen and Shantyboys* (New York, 1951).

Duchartre   Pierre Louis Duchartre, *The Italian Comedy* (New York, 1966).

Dusenbury MSS   The Dusenbury Songs (transcribed and notated by Laurence Powell), from the singing of Mrs Emma Dusenbury of Menas, Arkansas, between August 1933 and August 1936. Manuscript copy in the possession of the authors of this book.

Eckstorm and Smyth   Fannie H. Eckstorm and Mary Winslow Smyth, *Minstrelsy of Maine* (Boston, 1927).

Eddy   Mary O. Eddy, *Ballads and Songs from Ohio* (New York, 1939).

Farmer   John S. Farmer, *Merry Songs and Ballads* (1897, 5 vols).

Flanders   Helen Hartness Flanders, *Ancient Ballads Traditionally Sung in New England* (Philadelphia, 1960–5, 4 vols).

Flanders and Brown   Helen Hartness Flanders and George Brown, *Vermont Folksongs and Ballads* (Brattleboro, Vermont, 1931).

Flanders and Olney   Helen Hartness Flanders and Marguerite Olney, *Ballads Migrant in New England* (New York, 1953).

Flanders, Ballard, Brown and Barry   Helen Hartness Flanders, Elizabeth F. Ballard, George Brown and Phillips Barry, *The New Green Mountain Songster* (New Haven, Connecticut, 1939).

FMJ   Folk Music Journal, of the English Folk Dance and Song Society (London, 1965 –   ).

Folklore Fellows Folklore Fellows Communications (Helsinki, Suomalainen Tiedeakatemia, Academia Scientiarum Fennica).

Ford (1)   Robert Ford, *Children's Rhymes* (Paisley, 1903).

Ford (2)   Robert Ford, *The Harp of Perthshire* (Paisley, 1893).

Ford (3)   Robert Ford, *Vagabond Songs and Ballads of Scotland* (Paisley, 1899–1901, 2 vols).

Fowke   Edith Fowke, *Traditional Singers and Songs from Ontario* (Hatboro, Pennsylvania, 1965).

Fowke MSS   Edith Fowke manuscripts of unpublished collected material. Sections of this manuscript, in carbon, in the library of the authors of this book.

Fraser   Amy Stewart Fraser, *Dae Ye Min' Langsyne?* (London, 1975).

Galvin   Patrick Galvin, *Irish Songs of Resistance* (New York, 1962).

Gardiner MSS   George B. Gardiner Manuscripts (undertaken chiefly in Hampshire and Dorset, 1905–9). At present located in the Cecil Sharp House, London.

Gardner and Chickering   Emelyn E. Gardner and Geraldine Chickering, *Ballads and Songs of Southern Michigan* (Ann Arbor, Michigan, 1939).

Gillington (1)   Alice E. Gillington, *Eight Hampshire Folksongs* (London, n.d. [1907]).

Gillington (2)   Alice E. Gillington, *Songs of the Open Road* (London, 1911).

Glen   John Glen, *Early Scottish Melodies* (Edinburgh, 1900).

Gomme   Alice Bertha Gomme, *The Traditional Games of England, Scotland and Ireland* (reprint, New York, 1964, 2 vols).

Graves   Alfred Perceval Graves, *The Irish Song Book* (London, 1895).

Greenleaf and Mansfield   Elizabeth B. Greenleaf and Grace Y. Mansfield, *Ballads and Sea Songs of Newfoundland* (Cambridge, Massachusetts, 1933).

Greig   Gavin Greig, *Folksongs of the Northeast* (reprint, Hatboro, Pennsylvania, 1963).

Greig and Keith   Gavin Greig and Alexander Keith, *Last Leaves of Traditional Ballads and Ballad Airs* (Aberdeen, 1925).

Gullen   F. Doreen Gullen, *Traditional Number Rhymes and Games* (London, 1950).

Halliwell (1)   James Orchard Halliwell, *The Nursery Rhymes of England* (London, 1842; reprint, London, 1970).

Halliwell (2)   James Orchard Halliwell, *Popular Rhymes and Nursery Tales of England* (London, 1949; reprint, London, 1970).

Hamer   Fred Hamer, *Garners Gay* (London, 1970).

Hammond MSS   The manuscripts of Henry and Robert Hammond, (undertaken chiefly in Hampshire and Dorset, 1905–10). At present located in the Cecil Sharp House, London.

Hecht   Hans Hecht, *Songs from David Herd's Manuscripts* (London, 1904).

Henry Collection   Sam Henry Collection, Central Library, Belfast, Northern Ireland.

Herd   David Herd, *Ancient and Modern Scottish Songs* (Edinburgh, 1776, 2 vols).

Holbrook   David Holbrook, *Children's Games* (Bedford, 1957).

Hubbard   Lester A. Hubbard, *Ballads and Songs from Utah* (Salt Lake City, 1961).

Hughes   Herbert Hughes, *Irish Country Songs* (London, 1914, 2 vols).

Hugill   Stan Hugill, *Shanties from the Seven Seas* (London, 1961).

Huntington   Gale Huntington, *Songs the Whalemen Sang* (Barre, Massachusetts, 1964).

JAF   Journal of American Folklore (Philadelphia, 1888–   ).

Jamieson   Robert Jamieson, *Popular Ballads and Songs* (Edinburgh, 1806, 2 vols).

JEFDSS   Journal of the English Folk Dance and Song Society (London, 1932–64).

JFSS   Journal of the Folk Song Society (London, 1899–1931).

Jones and Hawes   Bessie Jones and Bess Lomax Hawes, *Step it Down* (New York, 1972).

Joyce (1)   Patrick Weston Joyce, *Ancient Irish Music* (Dublin, 1873; reprint Dublin, 1912).

Joyce (2)   Patrick Weston Joyce, *Old Irish Folk Music and Song* (Dublin, 1909).

Karpeles   Maud Karpeles, *Folksongs from Newfoundland* (London, 1971).

Kennedy   Peter Kennedy, *Folksongs of Britain and Ireland* (London, 1975).

Kerr (1)   James S. Kerr, *Buchan Bothy Ballads* (Glasgow, n. d.).

Kerr (2)   James S. Kerr, *Cornkisters* (Glasgow, 1950).

Kidson   Frank Kidson, *Traditional Tunes* (Oxford, 1891).

Kidson and Moffat   Frank Kidson and Alfred Moffat, *A Garland of English Folksongs* (London, 1926).

Kinloch   George R. Kinloch, *Ancient Scottish Ballads* (London, 1827).

Laws   G. Malcolm Laws, Jr., *American Balladry from British Broadsides* (Philadelphia, 1957).

Legman   Gershon Legman, *The Horn Book* (New York, 1964).

Linscott   Eloise Hubbard Linscott, *Folk Songs of Old New England* (New York, 1939).

Logan   W. H. Logan, *A Pedlar's Pack of Ballads and Songs* (Edinburgh, 1869).

Lomax   Alan Lomax, *Folksongs of North America* (London, 1960).

Lomax and Seeger   Alan Lomax (Ruth Crawford Seeger, music ed.), *Our Singing Country* (New York, 1949).

MacColl   Ewan MacColl, *Scotland Sings* (London, 1953).

MacColl and Seeger   Ewan MacColl and Peggy Seeger, *Travellers' Songs from England and Scotland* (London, 1977).

MacNie   (printer, W. MacNie), *Nineteenth-Century Scottish Broadside Ballads* (Stirling, 1825).

MacKenzie   W. Roy Mackenzie, *Ballads and Sea Songs from Nova Scotia* (Cambridge, Massachusetts, 1928).

Madden Collection   The Madden Collection of Broadsides and Slip-songs (Cambridge University Library, Cambridge).

Mason   M. H. Mason, *Nursery Rhymes and Country Songs* (London, 1878).
Merry Muses   The Merry Muses of Caledonia, ed. James Barke and Sydney Goodsir Smith (Edinburgh, 1969).
Montgomerie   Norah and William Montgomerie, *Scottish Nursery Rhymes* (London, 1946).
Moore   Ethel and Chauncey O. Moore, *Ballads and Folk Songs of the Southwest* (University of Oklahoma Press, 1964).
Museum   The Scots Musical Museum, ed. James Johnson (Edinburgh, 1787, 6 vols).

New City Songster   New City Songster, a yearly issue of contemporary songs (London, 1967–1985).
Newell   William Wells Newell, *Games and Songs of American Children* (New York, 1883).
Northall   G. F. Northall, *English Folk-Rhymes* (London, 1892).

O'Lochlainn (1)   Colm O'Lochlainn, *Irish Street Ballads* (Dublin, 1939).
O'Lochlainn (2)   Colm O'Lochlainn, *More Irish Street Ballads* (Dublin, 1965).
Opie (1)   Iona and Peter Opie, *Childrens Games in Street and Playground* (Oxford, 1969).
Opie (2)   Iona and Peter Opie, *Lore and Language of School-children* (Oxford, 1959).
Opie (3)   Iona and Peter Opie, *The Oxford Dictionary of Nursery Rhymes* (London, 1951).
Ord   John Ord, *The Bothy Songs and Ballads of Aberdeen, Banff and Moray, Angus and the Mearns* (Paisley, 1930).
O'Shaunessy   Patrick O'Shaunessy, *Yellowbelly Ballads* (Lincoln, 1975).

Peacock   Kenneth Peacock, *Songs of the Newfoundland Outports* (Ottawa, 1965, 3 vols).
Petrie   George Petrie, *The Complete Petrie Collection of Irish Music*, ed. Charles Villiers Stanford (New York, 1902–5).
Purslow (1)   Frank Purslow, *The Constant Lovers* (London, 1972).
Purslow (2)   Frank Purslow, *Marrowbones* (London, 1965).
Purslow (3)   Frank Purslow, *The Wanton Seed* (London, 1968).
Randolph   Vance Randolph, *Ozark Folksongs* (Columbia, Missouri, 1946, 4 vols).
Ree   The Reverend Stephen Ree, *Gordon Ballads* (The New Spalding Club, Aberdeen, n.d.).
Reeves (1)   James Reeves, *The Everlasting Circle* (London, 1960).
Reeves (2)   James Reeves, *The Idiom of the People* (London, 1958).
Ritchie (1)   James T. R. Ritchie, *Golden City* (Edinburgh, 1965).
Ritchie (2)   James T. R. Ritchie, *The Singing Street* (Edinburgh, 1964).
Ritson   Joseph Ritson, *Scotish Song* (revised edition, Glasgow, 1869, 2 vols).
Rogers   Charles Rogers, *The Scottish Minstrel* (Edinburgh, 1870).
Rooney   Hubert E. Rooney, *The Well-Known Songs of Ireland* (Dublin, n.d.).
Rutherford   Frank Rutherford, *All the Way to Pennywell* (Durham, 1971).
Rymour   Rymour Club Miscellanea (Edinburgh, 1911–28, 3 vols).

Sandburg   Carl Sandburg, *The American Songbag* (New York, 1927).
Scott   Sir Walter Scott, *Minstrelsy of the Scottish Border* (Edinburgh, 1932 reprint, 4 vols).
Scottish Studies   Scottish Studies, Journal of the School of Scottish Studies

(University of Edinburgh, 1957–   ).

Seeger   Ruth Crawford Seeger, *American Folksongs for Children* (New York, 1948).

Seeger and MacColl   Peggy Seeger and Ewan MacColl, *The Singing Island* (London, 1960).

Seeger MSS   Ruth Crawford Seeger Manuscripts, a portion of which are in the possesion of the authors.

Sharp   Cecil J. Sharp, *English Folksongs* (London, 1920, 2 vols; reprinted in one book, London, 1959).

Sharp and Karpeles (1)   Cecil J. Sharp and Maud Karpeles, *English Folk Songs from the Southern Appalachians* (London, 1932, 2 vols).

Sharp and Karpeles (2)   Cecil J. Sharp, *Cecil Sharp's Collection of English Folk Songs*, edited by Maud Karpeles (London, 1974, 2 vols).

Sharp   Cuthbert Sharp, *The Bishoprick Garland* (Newcastle upon Tyne, 1834; reprint, 1969). Unpaginated.

Smith   Laura Alexandrine Smith, *Through Romany Songland* (London, 1889).

Sola Pinto and Rodway   Vivian de Sola Pinto and Allan E. Rodway, *The Common Muse* (New York, 1957).

Stokoe and Reay   John Stokoe and Samuel Reay, *Songs and Ballads of Northern England* (Newcastle upon Tyne, 1892).

Thompson (Harold)   Harold W. Thompson, *Body, Boots and Britches* (New York, 1962).

Thompson (Stith)   Stith Thompson, *Motif-Index of Folk Literature* (Helsinki, 1932–6, 6 vols).

Thomson   William Thomson, *Orpheus Caledonius* (London, 1725, 2 vols; facsimile of 1733 edition reprinted in Hatboro, Pennsylvania, 1962).

Thrush   The Thrush: A Choice Selection of the Most Admired Popular Songs (London, n.d.).

Williams   Alfred Williams, *Folk-Songs of the Upper Thames* (London, 1923).

Wimberly   Lowry C. Wimberly, *Folklore in the English and Scottish Ballads* (Chicago, 1928; reprint, New York, 1965).

Zimmerman   George Denis Zimmerman, *Songs of the Irish Rebellion* (Pennsylvania, 1967).

Works dealing specifically with Travellers

Acton   Thomas Acton, *Gypsy Politics and Social Change* (London, 1974).

Adams, Okely, Morgan and Smith   Barbara Adams, Judith Okely, David Morgan and David Smith, *Gypsies and Government Policy in England* (London, 1975).

Barrère and Leland   A. Barrère and C. G. Leland, *A Dictionary of Slang, Jargon and Cant* (London, 1897).

Black   George F. Black, *A Gypsy Bibliography* (Edinburgh, 1909).

Boswell   S. G. Boswell, *The Book of Boswell* (London, 1970).

Brockie   William Brockie, *The Gypsies of Yetholm* (Kelso, 1884).

Clébert   Jean-Paul Clébert, *The Gypsies* (London, 1963).

Crabb   James Crabb, *The Gipsies' Advocate* (Edinburgh, 1831).

Fairley   John A. Fairley, *Bailie Smith of Kelso's Account of the Gypsies of Kirk Yetholm in 1815* (Hawick, 1907).

Gillington   Alice E. Gillington, *Gypsies of the Heath* (London, 1916).
Gmelch and Langan   Sharon Gmelch and Pat Langan, *Tinkers and Travellers* (Dublin, 1975).
Groome   Francis H. Groome, *In Gypsy Tents* (Edinburgh, 1880).

Hoyland   John Hoyland, *The Gypsies* (York, 1816).
_____ *Journal of the Gypsy Lore Society* (1st series, 1888–92; 2nd series, 1907–16; 3rd series, 1922–   ).

Leland   Charles G. Leland, *The English Gypsies and Their Language* (London, 1873).

McCormick   Andrew McCormick, *The Tinkler-Gypsies* (London, 1907).
MacRitchie   David MacRitchie, *Scottish Gypsies Under the Stewarts* (Edinburgh, 1894).
Morwood   Vernon S. Morwood, *Our Gypsies in City, Tent and Van* (London, 1885).

Rehfisch   Farnham Rehfisch, *Gypsies, Tinkers and Other Travellers* (London, 1975).

Sampson   John Sampson, 'English Gypsy Songs and Rhymes' (pub. in *Journal of the Gypsy Lore Society*, Vol. 2, Edinburgh, 1891).
Simson   Walter Simson, *A History of the Gypsies* (London, 1865).
Smart and Crofton   B. C. Smart and H. D. Crofton, *The Dialect of the English Gypsies* (London, 1875).
Sutherland   Anne Sutherland, *Gypsies: The Hidden Americans* (London, 1975).

Ward-Jackson and Harvey   C. H. Ward-Jackson and Denis E. Harvey, *The English Gypsy Caravan* (Newton Abbot, England, 1972).
Wood   Manfri Frederick Wood, *In the Life of a Romany Gypsy* (London, 1973).

INDEX OF TITLES
AND FIRST LINES

TITLES are given in upper-case type.
THE STEWARTS' TITLES, where they differ radically from the definitive title or
   first line, are given in upper-case italics.
The first lines are given in lower-case type.